Practical HRM for Global Professionals
English ‹›› Japanese

英語de人事
エイゴデジンジ

日英対訳による実践的人事

白木 三秀／ブライアン・シャーマン 著
Shiraki Mitsuhide / Bryan Sherman

文眞堂

Read, Think and Act!

Thank you very much for picking up this book!
With this book, you can take the next step towards building up your global HRM (Human Resource Management) success competencies.

この本を手にとっていただき，感謝いたします！
本書により，グローバル人的資源管理（Human Resource Management：HRM）で成功するコンピテンシーを形成するために，次の一歩を踏み出してください。

Message From the Authors

What makes this book unique?

Throughout this book which is written in an easy-to-understand format in both English and Japanese, readers can gain a better understanding of how global HRM theories and concepts are put into practice in companies that operate globally. In this way, you can attain both an understanding of HRM and practical skills to communicate in English about HRM.

Section I of this book focuses on the basic theories and concepts in global HRM, and includes case study examples derived from the actual experience of Japanese managers who have been expatriated overseas.

Section II presents sample conversations from a fictional company. The sample conversations represent realistic conversations which may be carried out in English within global companies. Each sample conversation corresponds to the theme from each of the chapters of Section I. At the end of each chapter, some of *the Key Phrases and Expressions* are taken up and examined in depth.

We hope that the enjoyment of reading through the case studies and sample conversations will help you understand the basic theories and concepts of global HRM more deeply.

Who is this book for?

This book is useful of course for HR professionals who plan global HRM initiatives and develop HR systems. However, as global HRM is carried out by line managers who manage subordinates within various business units, this

著者からのメッセージ

どういう点でこの本がユニークなのか？

　分かりやすい英語と日本語双方で書かれた本書を通じて，読者は，グローバル展開をする企業においてグローバル HRM の理論及び概念がどのように実践されているのかについての理解を深めることができます。こうして，HRM についての理解と HRM について英語でコミュニケーションをとる実践的なスキルの双方を同時に習得することができます。

　Section I は，グローバル HRM の基本的な理論と概念に焦点を当てており，さらに，日本人海外派遣者の方々が実際に経験した事例を含めています。

　Section II は，架空の会社でのサンプル・カンバセーションを取り上げています。サンプル・カンバセーションは，グローバル企業内で英語を用いて行われるリアリスティックな会話を描写しています。各サンプル・カンバセーションは，Section I の各章のテーマに対応しています。各章の最後には「重要表現」をいくつか取り上げ，より深く吟味します。

　事例およびサンプル・カンバセーションを楽しく読み進むことで，読者はグローバル HRM の基本的理論や概念をより深く理解することができると思います。

どういう人のための本なのか

　グローバル HRM を企画し，その制度を策定する人事担当者の方に本書を読んでいただきたいと思っています。しかし，グローバル HRM を具体的状況において実施するのは，人事担当者ではなく，事業部門において実際に部下を持

book is useful for any business manager. It is no exaggeration to say that about 80% of the content of this book deals with global HRM issues that arise in business units other than the HR Department.

Specifically, this book is intended for the following people:

- Business people, students or anyone who wants to acquire basic knowledge about global HRM
- Line managers abroad who carry out global HRM initiatives while using English
- Business people who will soon be expatriated overseas
- Professionals in charge of corporate headquarters functions who are tasked with planning and executing global HRM policies and systems
- HR professionals who need to arrange HR meetings in a global setting

Please make meaningful use of this book!

Additionally, if you would like to study more about HRM, please join us in the 「英語 de 人事®」 On-line Learning Lounge. (See next page.)

つライン・マネジャーであります。本書が取り扱う内容の8割くらいは人事部門以外の事業部門で生じるグローバル HRM の諸問題を取り扱っているといっても過言ではありません。

　具体的には，本書は次のよう方々を対象としています。

- ・グローバル HRM に関する基本的知識を身に付けたいビジネス・パーソン，学生など
- ・英語でグローバル HRM の実践を迫られている海外赴任中のライン・マネジャー
- ・これから海外赴任をする予定のビジネス・パーソン
- ・グローバル HRM の政策，制度を企画・策定しなくてはならないコーポレート本社の人事担当者
- ・グローバルな場面で HR の会議を持つ必要のある人事担当者

本書をぜひとも有意義に活用してください！

　さらに HRM についてより勉強したい人は「英語 de 人事®」オンラインラーニングラウンジにご参加ください（次頁参照）。

Introduction of 「英語 de 人事®」 On-line Learning Lounge

By joining the 「英語 de 人事®」 On-line Learning Lounge, you will be able to:

- Listen to the text of this book in English
- Test your understanding of concepts
- Watch related videos
- Share your opinions
- Meet other people
- Enjoy HRM!

「英語 de 人事®」 On-line Learning Lounge

Visit http://www.eigodejinji.com/ for more information.

英語 de 人事® オンライン・ラーニング・ラウンジのご紹介

「英語 de 人事®」オンライン・ラーニング・ラウンジに参加すると以下のことがより可能になります。

・この本のテキストを英語で聞く
・概念の理解度をテストする
・関連動画を見る
・意見を共有する
・他の人に会う
・HRM を楽しめる！

「英語 de 人事®」オンライン・ラーニング・ラウンジ

http://www.eigodejinji.com/ にアクセスしてください。

Our Vision for This Book

There are a multitude of books written on the topic of Human Resource Management (HRM). Why have we decided to add another book to this vast library?

This uniquely bilingual book contains 10 chapters regarding relevant and important theories and concepts in global HRM, 17 case studies which are derived from the real-world experience of Japanese managers working overseas (See note below.), and a series of sample conversations that take place in a fictional, yet close to real-life global Japanese company. Our vision is for this book to become recognized as an all-in-one entertaining English and Japanese reference for anything HRM-related.

Readers such as current HR professionals, current or future overseas expatriates, any other business people who have related interests, and students who want to work in global companies can accomplish the following two learning objectives:

1) To learn about global HRM theories and concepts as expressed in both Japanese and English. In this way, readers can increase their knowledge about the ideas presented, and then compare how the ideas are expressed in both languages to further deepen their understanding.

2) To understand how to naturally communicate in English about the HRM theories and concepts presented in this book.

本書の構想

　人的資源管理（Human Resource Management：HRM）に関しては，数多くの書籍がこれまでに書かれている。では何故，これまでの文献の山に加えて，我々がもう一冊を書くことにしたのか？

　ユニークなバイリンガルで書かれた本書は，グローバル HRM に関連する重要な理論及び概念に関する 10 の章，17 のケース・スタディを含み，それらの事例（注）は海外で働く日本人マネジャーの実世界での経験の記録である。また，サンプル・カンバセーションは，架空の，しかし現実に近い日本のグローバル・カンパニーで行われる一連の会話から導き出されたものである。我々の構想は，本書が HRM に関連するあらゆる事項を含むオールインワンの英語と日本語で書かれた楽しい文献となることである。

　本書の読者，すなわち現職の HR マネジャー，現在あるいは将来の海外派遣者，本テーマに関心を有する他の全てのビジネス・パーソン，さらには将来グローバル企業で働きたい学生は，次の2つの学習目的を達成することが可能となる。

　第1に，グローバルな舞台における HRM の理論及び概念を日本語と英語の両言語で学ぶことができる。これにより，読者はこれらの考え方に関する知識を増やし，また，それらの考え方が日英両言語でどのように表現されるかを比較する中で，その理解を深めることができる。

　第2に，本書で提示されている HRM の理論及び概念について，自然に英語でコミュニケーションをとる方法を，楽しみながら理解してもらう。

In this book, you will find inspiration for thinking and communicating about some of the following topics of interest:

- The value of the HR Department in a company (Chapter 1)
- The importance of employer branding (Chapter 2)
- A simple and effective process for giving feedback (Chapter 3)
- Globally acceptable compensation practices (Chapter 4)
- Career trajectories and people development initiatives (Chapter 5)
- The importance of succession planning in talent management (Chapter 6)
- The risks of discrimination and harassment (Chapter 7)
- How to establish and maintain the employment relationship between companies and employees (Chapter 8)
- Selecting the right people to become expatriates (Chapter 9)
- How to develop an effective and respectable HR Department in the global headquarters (Chapter 10), and
- How to communicate appropriately to make good relations between the global headquarters and counterparts in the overseas subsidiaries (Chapter 10 supplement)

We hope that readers will be able to utilize the learning from this book for increasing their ability and confidence to express ideas in both English and Japanese regarding important HRM topics.

Note: Please note the authors have received express permission from the Japan Overseas Enterprises Association (JOEA) to adapt and modify case studies from the organization's publication, "The Expatriate's Handbook" as had been published on a country-specific basis over various years.

　本書では，次の興味深いトピックのいくつかについて考え，コミュニケーションするためのインスピレーションを見つけることができる。

・企業の人事部の価値（第1章）
・エンプロイヤー（雇用主）ブランディングの重要性（第2章）
・フィードバックを提供するためのシンプルで効果的なプロセス（第3章）
・グローバルに受け入れられる報酬慣行（第4章）
・キャリアの経路パターンと人材育成の取り組み（第5章）
・人材管理における後継者計画の重要性（第6章）
・差別と嫌がらせのリスク（第7章）
・企業と従業員の雇用関係を確立および維持する方法（第8章）

・駐在員になるための適切な人々を選抜する（第9章）
・グローバル本社で効果的で立派な人事部を開発する方法（第10章）

・グローバル本社と海外子会社のカウンターパートとの良好な関係を築くための適切なコミュニケーション方法（第10章補足）

　読者が，本書から学んだことを活用し，重要なHRM関連事象に関して自分の考えを英語ならびに日本語で表現するという能力を高め，自信を深めてくれることを希望する。

注：一般社団法人日本在外企業協会の許可を得て，同協会『海外派遣者ハンドブック』（各国別，各年版）の事例を若干，モディファイして活用させていただいた。

Acknowledgments

This book was originally conceived by the authors in 2017 as a project of the virtual research facility within Waseda University called the Institute for Transnational Human Resource Management.

The authors are indebted to the support and contributions of others including the following individuals and organizations.

Professor Konishi Kazuhisa, Waseda University, initially proposed the project and provided invaluable advice and support in the initial development of this book.

Additionally, Shimizu Aya provided administrative support that was invaluable to the project.

Irene Zamora, PhD candidate at the Graduate School of Economics, Waseda University, provided helpful comments on the English language text and research of additional reading resources.

Additional ideas and support were provided by the dedicated staff of Gramercy Engagement Group.

We are thankful to the Japan Overseas Enterprises Association (JOEA) for allowing us to use the organization's publication, "The Expatriate's Handbook" in order to introduce concrete examples into this book.

謝　辞

　本書は，もともと著者らが属するバーチャルな研究所である早稲田大学トランスナショナル HRM 研究所の独自プロジェクトとして 2017 年から構想されたものである。

　著者らは，以下の個人や組織の支援と貢献に感謝している。

　早稲田大学の小西和久教授は，最初にこのプロジェクトを提案し，この本の最初の開発に貴重な助言とサポートを提供して下さった。

　さらに，清水綾さんは，このプロジェクトにとって貴重な管理サポートを提供してくれた。

　早稲田大学大学院経済学研究科博士課程のイレネ・サモラさんは，英語の文章への有益なコメントと追加的参考文献の検索という貢献をしてくれた。

　追加のアイデアおよび支援は，グラマシーエンゲージメントグループの献身的スタッフによって提供された。

　一般社団法人日本在外企業協会からは，『海外派遣者ハンドブック』に書かれている多くの事例の利用を認めていただき，本書をより具体的なものにすることができたと感謝する。

Of course, we would like to provide our appreciation to our publisher, Bunshindo, especially President Maeno Takashi, Maeno Kota and Yamazaki Katsunori.

In order to bring the publishing of this book to fruition, we have relied upon the contributions of other individuals and organizations as well. We express our sincere appreciation to all.

Tokyo, Japan
March 2020

Shiraki Mitsuhide
Bryan Sherman

　もちろん，出版に際しては，文眞堂の前野隆社長と前野弘太氏，山崎勝徳氏にご尽力をいただいた。記して深謝する。

　この本を出版できたのは，上記以外の多くの方々や組織の貢献にも依存している。それらの方々にも謝意を表する。

東京にて
2020 年 3 月吉日

白木 三秀
ブライアン・シャーマン

Contents

SECTION 1

Theories, Concepts & Case Studies

CHAPTER 1
Introduction to Human Resource Management

CHAPTER 2
Hiring Employees

CHAPTER 3
Performance Management

目　次

SECTION 1

理論および概念＆ケース・スタディー

CHAPTER 1
人的資源管理入門

CHAPTER 2
社員の採用

CASE STUDY 2.1

CASE STUDY 2.2

CHAPTER 3
パフォーマンス・マネジメント

CASE STUDY 3.1

SECTION II
サンプル・カンバセーション

Theories, Concepts & Case Studies

理論および概念&ケース・スタディー

Introduction to Human Resource Management

What Is Human Resource Management (HRM)?

Human Resource Management (HRM) refers to all of the efforts that a company makes to employ, develop and utilize people for carrying out its business strategy while providing employees with a suitable environment for conducting work that is valuable for society.

Among the typically described managerial resources of *people, materials and money*, HRM activities encompass all of the various company-wide, people-related issues. Since the corporation accomplishes nothing without people, HRM is, in essence, the very management of the corporation itself.

Origin of Modern HRM

Back at the end of the eighteenth century, the **industrial revolution** changed the nature of work. Businesses were no longer small organizations that could be managed by a single owner. As a result, many support functions were

人的資源管理入門

人的資源管理（HRM）とは？

人的資源管理（HRM）とは，企業が事業戦略を遂行するために従業員を雇用し，育成し，活用するために行う全ての努力を指し，同時に，社会に役立つ仕事を行うための適切な環境を従業員に提供することも指している。

HRM は経営資源である「ヒト，モノ，カネ」のなかで HRM の対象領域は，企業内の人々にかかわる様々な課題を包摂する。企業は，人の存在なくして何事も達成できないので，HRM は本質的には企業経営そのものである。

現代 HRM の起源

18 世紀後半，**産業革命**は仕事の性格を一変させた。企業はもはや一人の所有者が管理しうる小さな組織ではなくなった。その結果，様々な支援機能が特定分野に特化する個々の構成員に委譲されるのである。こうした機能のひとつ

delegated to individuals who began to specialize in specific areas. One of these functions became known as **Personnel Management**. The usage of the term **Personnel** had come to be associated primarily with the administrative affairs of hiring and employing people in the organization.

The term Personnel gave way to what we refer to today as **Human Resource Management (HRM)** in order to more fully encompass consideration of how employees impact the results of the organization from strategy planning to execution.

More recently, the term **Human Capital Management (HCM)** is increasingly being used. The term emphasizes the recognition of employees as capital assets in the organization. This is because employees have intrinsic value with their competencies and experiences that can be applied to increasingly challenging tasks for the production of economic and social gain. Most of the discourse about people as assets in an organization supports the notion that people are not simply *resources* to be used up and depleted.

However, the term HRM is still often used to represent the function in companies that handles all people-related issues. In the usage of this term, the concept of a *resource* is akin to that of an *asset* or *the very source* from which various types of value can be produced. While the term HRM may continue to be used, it should be understood that the notion of people as capital assets is more apt than the notion of people as simply being finite resources of the company.

The Mission of the Human Resources (HR) Department in an Organization

The **C-suite executives** (CEO, COO, CFO, etc.) of the organization are

が**人に関わる管理**（パーソネル・マネジメント）である。**パーソネル**という用語は，組織が人を採用・雇用する管理的な業務を主として意味するようになった。

　パーソネルという概念を，従業員がどのように戦略立案から実施まで組織に影響を与えるかという点にまで拡大するために，パーソネル・マネジメントという用語は今日，**人的資源管理**（Human Resource Management：HRM）に代替されるようになった。

　最近では，**人的資本管理**（Human Capital Management：HCM）という用語も使われ始めている。この用語は，従業員を組織の資本資産として認識すべきであることを強調する。HCM という用語が使われる背景には，組織を構成する人々が行動特性および経験という本質的な価値を備えており，ますます困難となる課題に対応し，より大きな経済的，社会的成果を生み出すために必要となるという認識がある。組織の構成員を重視する議論の多くは，人は企業にとっての資本財であり，単に消耗する「資源」ではないことを示している。

　しかし，企業の人事関連事項を取り扱う機能を表す用語として HRM が今なお盛んに用いられている。この用語においては，「resource」という概念は，「材料」という意味ではなく，いろいろな価値を生み出す「資産」や「源泉」という意味を含んでおり，実質的に HCM を含んでいると考えられる。HRMは今後とも用いられるであろうが，その際，企業にとって人は使えばなくなるような単なる材料ではなく，資産であるとの認識がより適切であるということを理解すべきである。

人事部の組織内での役割

　C××という経営幹部（最高経営責任者，最高執行責任者，最高財務責任者

concerned with all aspects of the business—from setting the business direction, to developing products and services, to making financial plans, and then to considering people-related issues. The top mission of the HR Department, in service to the executive management, is to deal with all aspects of people-related issues. The HR Department endeavors to ensure that the company employs, develops, and retains people that are necessary to work in accordance with the company's corporate philosophy, directives, and business plan(s) in the present time as well as into the future. In this way, HR work is both present and future oriented.

The Roles of an HR Department

In order to carry out the aforementioned mission, the HR Department should carry out various roles.

On a practical day-to-day level, the HR Department should *create efficient processes for organizational effectiveness* in areas such as the hiring of new graduates and mid-career employees, performance management, compensation and benefits, training and development and more. Once employees are accepted into the organization, the HR Department provides the basic foundation for employee satisfaction through the on-time payment of salary and provision of various benefits such as medical insurance, paid or unpaid time off, pension plans and other fringe benefits as elected by the company.

While in recent years, the administration of such tasks may be outsourced or pooled into a **shared services center (SSC)**, it should be understood that process efficiency in HR administration is vital for the foundation of HR activities that support organizational effectiveness.

It is sometimes said that the *customers* of the HR Department are the

など）が組織内で遂行する経営管理は，事業のあらゆる局面に関係しており，事業の方針設定から，製品・サービスの開発，財務計画，人事政策までを含む。人事部の最も重要な職務は経営幹部をサポートするために，従業員に関連する全ての事柄を管掌することである。人事部は，現在並びに将来にわたる企業の理念，方針，および事業計画の実現のために必要な人材を採用し，育成し，確保できるように努力をすることである。したがって，人事部は現在と将来の双方を見据えなければならない。

人事部の役割

　前述のような人事関連の職務を遂行するために，人事部は様々な役割を果たすべきである。

　人事部は日常業務として，新規学卒者，中途採用者の双方を含む新入社員の採用，パフォーマンス・マネジメント，報酬・福利厚生，研修・能力開発などの領域で「効果的な組織のために効率的なプロセスを確立」しなければならない。新入社員を採用後，彼らが満足を得られるよう，人事部は定期的な給与と付加給付という基本的な土台を提供する。付加給付には，医療保険，有給・無給の休暇，年金，及びそれぞれの企業が選択するその他の付加給付などが含まれる。

　一方，近年これらの業務をアウトソーシングしたり，**シェアード・サービス・センター（SSC）**に集約されたりするかもしれないが，人事管理におけるプロセス効率は人事活動の基盤に不可欠であり，それが効果的組織を支えていることを理解する必要がある。

　人事部のいわゆる「顧客」は会社の従業員であると言われることがある。し

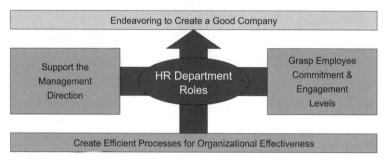

Figure 1.1   HR Department Roles

employees in the company. However, such a notion does not account for the additional role of the HR Department to *support the management direction* by conveying important information to employees that comes from the executive management. Sometimes, the executive management looks to the HR Department to affect changes in employee thinking and behavior to align with new business goals. (Refer to Figure 1.1.)

Likewise, the HR Department needs to understand whether the employee workforce is capable of carrying out work with a high sense of belonging to the organization (commitment) and engagement (positive attitude towards the work itself). In this way, the HR Department needs *to grasp employee commitment and engagement levels.*

When these roles are effectively balanced, the HR Department is positioned as an intermediary between the executive managers of the organization and the employees in the organization.

Lastly, the HR Department should remain committed in the endeavor to continually ensure that the company is a good company: good for creating economic value, good for employees, and good for society. In carrying out this role of *endeavoring to create a good company*, the HR Department

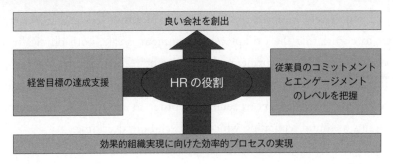

図 1.1　人事部の役割

かし，こうした考え方は，経営幹部から従業員に対する重要なメッセージを伝達することによって「経営方針を支援する」という人事部門が担うもうひとつの役割を考慮に入れていない。経営幹部は時には，新たな事業目標に沿うよう従業員の思考や行動に変化を加えることを人事部門に期待する（図 1.1 参照）。

　同時に，人事部は，従業員が高いレベルの企業へのコミットメント（帰属意識）とエンゲージメント（仕事への主体的取り組み）とをもって仕事を遂行する能力があるかどうかを理解する必要がある。つまり，人事部は，仕事に対する「従業員のコミットメントとエンゲージメントのレベルを把握する」必要がある。

　これらの役割が効果的にバランスされた時に，人事部は経営幹部と従業員の間の仲介者として機能することが可能となる。

　最後に，自社が経済価値の創出においても，また従業員と社会にとっても良い会社であり続けるよう，人事部はその努力を惜しんではならない。「良い会社を作り出すための努力をする」という役割を果たす上で，人事部は従業員と経営者間の関係を客観的に観察し，物理的にも心理的にも安全な職場環境

should objectively monitor the interactions of employees and managers in order to ensure that the workplace environment is safe, both physically and psychologically. HR Departments should also be ready to receive and respond to any concerns, complaints or grievances from employees, management or even external stakeholders in society in order to ensure that the company maintains its sound reputation which has been built over time.

HR Value Creation

The abovementioned roles are key roles that the HR Department carries out on a day-to-day basis. Additionally, in order to create long-term value, the HR Department develops and executes the **HR strategy** for the future in accordance with the **business strategy** that the company executives have formulated. (Refer to Figure 1.2.)

Any HR professional who is responsible for developing the HR strategy should firstly be well aware of the business strategy of the company. The business strategy can be defined as the plan which the executive management declares for desired business results to be attained from the business activities to be pursued in the medium-to-long-term.

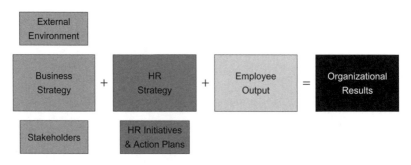

Figure 1.2 HR Value Creation Process

を確保しなければならない。人事部は，会社がこれまで培ってきた評判を維持するために，従業員，経営管理職，さらには社外の利害関係者（ステークホルダー）が持つ会社に関する懸念，不満，苦情の窓口となり，対応する必要もある。

人事の価値創出

　上述の役割は人事部が日常的に遂行する主要な役割である。さらに，人事部は長期的な価値を生み出すため，企業の経営幹部が策定する**事業戦略**に呼応した将来の**人事戦略**を策定し実行する（図1.2参照）。

　人事戦略策定の責任を負う人事担当者は，先ず企業の事業戦略を熟知していなければならない。事業戦略とは経営幹部が目標とする事業成果を上げるために提示する計画のことであり，事業成果は中・長期に遂行すべき事業活動から得られるものである。

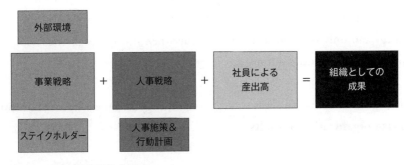

図 1.2　人事の価値創出プロセス

The business strategy is informed by the **external environment**. The external environment refers to any external factor that may have a positive or negative impact on the company's operations within the political, economic, social, technological, legal and natural environmental landscape. The business strategy is also formed in response to the needs and wants of various **stakeholders** which include not only stockholders, but also society at large.

Once this business strategy is made clear, the HR professional should engage in dialogue with the business managers and gather information to understand how the HR Department can support such a business strategy and related priorities from the *people perspective*. To determine how well the current organization is aligned with and capable of supporting this business strategy, the HR professional should question the sufficiency of the current headcount (quantity of employees) and/or whether employees are capable and willing to carry out the strategy (quality of employees). Then the HR strategy can be formulated around a plan to increase or decrease headcount, shift employees to different business areas or otherwise train or retrain employees to handle a variety of assignments. This HR strategy will direct the formulation of specific **HR initiatives & action plans** to be undertaken and provide clarity on the right goals to be set in the short-term.

Because nothing gets achieved in the company without an understanding of the corporate direction and the concerted efforts of employees, the HR strategy can only be deemed to create value when it impacts the behaviors of employees that produce outputs.

The alignment of the business strategy, HR strategy and the **employee output** leads to **organizational results**.

　事業戦略は**外部環境**の影響を受ける。外部環境は，政治的，経済的，社会的，技術的，法律的な状況，ならびに自然環境を意味する包括的用語であり，企業のビジネスにプラスやマイナスの影響を与える可能性がある全ての外的要因を意味する。事業戦略はまた，株主のみならず社会一般を含む様々な**ステークホルダー**の要望・要求に対応して策定される。

　この事業戦略が明確になると，人事部は事業責任者と意思疎通を図り，人事部として事業戦略と関連優先事項を「人の観点」からいかに支援すべきかを検討する。現在の組織がこの事業計画にどの程度適合しているか，どの程度支援可能かを判断するために，人事部は，現在の人員数（従業員の量）が十分か，及び／あるいは当該の戦略を遂行するために能力や積極性（従業員の質）に問題はないかといった角度から検討しなければならない。その上で，人員の増減や配置転換，あるいは様々な業務を遂行するために従業員の訓練や再訓練を行うといった計画を実施するために人事戦略が策定される。この戦略に沿って具体的な**人事施策ならびに行動計画**が策定され，その結果，設定すべき短期目標が明確となる。

　会社は企業の方向性の理解と従業員の努力なくして，達成し得ることはない。成果を生むのは従業員の行動であり，これにインパクトを与えうる時，初めて人事戦略は価値を発揮することができる。

　一貫した事業戦略，人事戦略，それに**従業員の仕事成果**が**組織成果**を生み出すことになる。

Qualifications for HR Professionals

In a world where the pace of globalization and technological innovation is gathering speed, the need has emerged for a clear indication about how HR professionals should dynamically respond to the increasing complexities of HR work. In response to this need, one reputed authority, **Society for Human Resource Management (SHRM)**, has created such a standard for HR professionals. SHRM has developed a competency model consisting of nine (9) core competencies as follows: 1. Human Resource Expertise, 2. Relationship Management, 3. Consultation, 4. Leadership and Navigation, 5. Communication, 6. Global and Cultural Effectiveness, 7. Ethical Practice, 8. Critical Evaluation and 9. Business Acumen.

As we can see from these selected competencies, an HR professional needs to have **knowledge** about HR practices specifically and business in general. HR professionals also need to have the **skill** to be analytical, to build relationships, to communicate and to lead across cultures effectively. At the same time, they must possess the **qualities** of ethical behavior and leadership to be respectable.

HRM by Line Managers

How does the mission, role and work of the HR managers who work within the HR Department differ from that of line managers who are managing and directing the work of employees in other departments throughout the company? Generally, the HR Department and the line management should take on complementary roles.

HR専門家の要件

　グローバリゼーションと技術革新が急速に進む世界において，複雑化する人事関連の仕事にダイナミックに対応できる人事専門家に求められる要件を明確にする必要性が高まった。こうした必要性に対応し，権威ある機関である**全米人材マネジメント協会（Society for Human Resource Management：SHRM）** は，人事専門家のために必要な基準を作成した。SHRMは，次の9つの行動特性（コンピテンシー）で構成されるモデルを提示した：①人事業務での執行能力（HR Expertise），②人間関係と調整能力（Relationship Management），③コンサルテーション（Consultation），④リーダーシップと方向性の提示（Leadership & Navigation），⑤効果的コミュニケーション（Effective Communication），⑥グローバル・文化的な効果性（Global and Cultural effectiveness），⑦倫理観（Ethical Practice），⑧評価力（Critical Evaluation），⑨ビジネス洞察力（Business Acumen）

　上記に挙げられているコンピテンシーが示すように，HR専門家は特にHR実務の専門知識とビジネス全般に関する**知識**を持つ必要がある。また，HR専門家は，分析能力，人間関係構築能力，コミュニケーション能力，それに異文化への効果的な対応能力という**スキル**も要求される。同時に，倫理的に行動し，リーダーシップ力を発揮し，尊敬に値するこれらの**資質**を併せ持つ必要がある。

ライン・マネジャーによるHRM

　人事部で働くHR管理職の任務・役割・仕事は，社内の人事部以外の部門で従業員を管理・指揮するライン・マネジャー（現場の部下あり管理職）の役割・仕事とどのように異なるのだろうか？　概して言えば，両者は補完的な役割を果たすべきである。

Similarly, both the line managers and the HR Department management should make efforts to equally understand the specific knowledge, skills and career intentions of employees in the company.

The HR Department occasionally stands above the line managers by developing, determining and implementing processes for performance management and talent management; the line managers should carry out these processes to produce desired results through the people whom they are responsible for managing. At other times, the HR Department may conduct *organizational health-checks* to make investigations in response to complaints or grievances against line managers from their subordinate employees.

On the other hand, the HR Department provides service to the line managers in response to their need for a skilled, capable and motivated workforce by supporting the hiring and development of employees.

Conclusion

The HR function within modern business practices is a professional area as much as other functions such as accounting or marketing; that is to say that it is imperative to have the knowledge and experience for accurately developing and carrying out HR initiatives.

Furthermore, because nothing in business gets accomplished without the drive and efforts of people, we can say that the HR professional who impacts the work of the employees is thereby impacting the results of the business itself.

　また，ライン・マネジャーと人事部の HR 専門家は共に，社内の従業員が持つ専門知識，技能，ならびにキャリア意識を理解するよう努めるべきである。

　人事部は時には，ライン・マネジャーの上に立って，パフォーマンス・マネジメントやタレント・マネジメントのプロセスを策定し，決定し，導入する場合がある。一方，ライン・マネジャーはこれらのプロセスを実施し，管理責任下の部下を通じて期待される成果を生み出す必要がある。また，人事部はライン・マネジャーに対する部下からの不満や苦情を受けて，「組織診断」のための調査を行うこともある。

　他方，技能レベルが高く，有能で，モチベーションの高い人員に対するライン・マネジャーのニーズに応えて，人事部は，従業員の採用並びに育成に協力するというサービスを提供する。

結　　論

　人事機能が今日果たす役割は，経理やマーケティングと同様に専門知識が要求される分野であるが，同時に，的確な人事施策を策定・実施するには知識や経験も求められる。

　さらに，人のやる気や努力なしにはビジネスでは何も達成されない。したがって，従業員の仕事に影響を与える HR 専門家は事業そのものの成果にも影響を与えていると言えよう。

References & Suggestions for Additional Reading

Sharma, R. C. and N. Sharma (2018), "Human Resource Management in Retrospect and Prospect", *Human Resource Management: Theory and Practice*, Sage, Chapter 1.

Bratton, J. and J. Gold (2017), "Corporate Strategy and Strategic HRM", *Human Resource Management: Theory and Practice*, 6th Edition Palgrave, Chapter 2.

Storey, J., P. M. Wright and D. Ulrich (2019), "HR Competences and the HR functions", *Strategic Human Resource Management: A Research Overview*, Routledge Focus, pp. 43-57, Chapter 4.

Huselid, M. A. (1995), "The Impact of Human Resource Management Practices on Turnover Productivity and Corporate Financial Performance", *Academy of Management Journal*, 38 (2), pp. 635-672.

Ulrich, D., J. Younger, W. Brockbank and M. Ulrich (2012), *HR from the Outside In: Six Competencies for the Future of Human Resources*, New York: McGraw-Hill.

さらに学びたい人のための参考文献

Sharma, R. C. and N. Sharma (2018), "Human Resource Management in Retrospect and Prospect", *Human Resource Management: Theory and Practice*, Sage, Chapter 1.

Bratton, J. and J. Gold (2017), "Corporate Strategy and Strategic HRM", *Human Resource Management: Theory and Practice*, 6th Edition Palgrave, Chapter 2.

Storey, J., P. M. Wright and D. Ulrich (2019), "HR Competences and the HR functions", *Strategic Human Resource Management: A Research Overview*, Routledge Focus, pp. 43–57, Chapter 4.

Huselid, M. A. (1995), "The Impact of Human Resource Management Practices on Turnover Productivity and Corporate Financial Performance", *Academy of Management Journal*, 38 (2), pp. 635–672.

Ulrich, D., J. Younger, W. Brockbank and M. Ulrich (2012), *HR from the Outside In: Six Competencies for the Future of Human Resources*, New York: McGraw-Hill.

Hiring Employees

How Are People Hired by a Company?

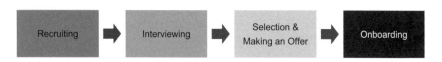

Figure 2.1   Hiring Process

Every company wants to attract, hire and employ a skilled workforce of employees that will actively contribute to the company's mission. After all, it has been said time and time again by many companies that their greatest asset is the people that make up the organization.

Therefore, the process for hiring new employees by recruiting, interviewing, selecting and making an offer, along with onboarding is crucial. (See Figure 2.1.)

Recruiting: Employer Branding as a First Step

Recruiting starts with attracting candidates to the company. As consumers

社員の採用

企業はどのように人を採用するのか？

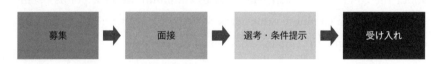

図 2.1　採用プロセス

　企業は自社が掲げる使命に積極的に貢献しうる技能を有する人材を引き付け，採用し，雇用することを目指している。結局のところ，これまで繰り返し指摘されてきたように，多くの企業にとっての最大の資産は，組織を構成する人だからである。

　したがって，求人，面接，選考・条件提示，及び受け入れにより新入社員を採用するプロセスは非常に重要である（図 2.1 参照）。

募集：エンプロイヤー・ブランディングこそが第一歩

　募集は求職者を自社に引き付けることから始まる。消費者が魅力的な商品を

purchase products that have strong appeal, people also seek out employment within organizations that have a strong appeal.

The appeal of a company is conveyed by the brand of the company; the brand molds the image of the company for both current and future employees. Therefore, **employer branding** is crucial for attracting and retaining employees.

Employer branding includes all the efforts to make the company a desirable place to work. While not everyone will be motivated by the same factors, a desirable place to work usually includes some of the following elements: a clear vision and mission, challenging assignments, a positive work atmosphere and future growth opportunities.

To develop an **employer branding strategy** is to define a few core points about the company's attractiveness and to communicate such points openly and widely. Such communication starts during the recruitment phase and also continues well after the employee has joined the company.

To develop an employer branding strategy, it is important to think of the **employee value proposition (EVP)**. According to a survey by McKinsey & Co. (Mckinsey Global Survey, *The War for Talent 2000*), the EVP is the answer to the question, "Why would a talented person want to work here?" There are four elements to an EVP as follows:

A. Great company:

In a great company, employees genuinely care for each other because there is trust and open communication. Additionally, the company's mission is motivating, and employees feel inspired by the mission of the company.

購入するように，求職者も魅力的な企業への就職を希望する。

企業の魅力はそのブランドから伝わる。そしてブランドは，現在と将来の社員にとっての企業イメージを醸成する。こうして，**エンプロイヤー・ブランディング**は従業員を引き付け，定着させるためには極めて重要なこととなる。

エンプロイヤー・ブランディングには，その会社をより望ましい職場にするためのあらゆる努力が含まれる。動機付けとなる要因は必ずしも全ての従業員に共通するものではないが，望ましい職場には明確なビジョンと使命，やりがいのある仕事，良好な職場の雰囲気，将来的な成長の可能性などが含まれる。

エンプロイヤー・ブランディング戦略の構築は，企業が持つ幾つかの中核的な魅力を明確にし，広く公表することにある。このような魅力の共有は求人と募集の段階から開始され，採用後も長期にわたり継続される。

こうしたエンプロイヤー・ブランディング戦略の構築には，**従業員のための価値提案（EVP）**という概念を考慮することが重要である。マッキンゼー・アンド・カンパニーの調査（Mckinsey Global Survey, *The War for Talent 2000*）によると，EVP は「なぜ有能な人材がここで働きたいのか？」という問いへの答えとなる。EVP は次の４つの要素から構成されている。

A．卓越企業
卓越企業には信頼感と活発なコミュニケーションが存在するので，社員の間には真に配慮し合う関係が見られる。また，その企業が掲げる使命は社員のやる気を高め，社員はその使命に鼓舞される。

B. Great leaders:

Great leaders really do treat people with trust and respect, and honor the intelligence of all who contribute to the institution. They endeavor to find the balance between giving people independence to accomplish great things and providing the guidance to help them do it. Great leaders build organizational capacity to achieve results by unleashing the latent talent of others.

C. Great job:

A great job is demanding and challenging, and full of content that each employee finds interesting and important. At the same time, a great job provides people with a sense of satisfaction because of the contributions made through one's efforts.

D. Attractive compensation:

Money is provided to employees to pay their bills. However, money is also paid as a means for providing recognition of contributions and fair treatment of employees. As a sign of respect, talented individuals expect that their companies provide compensation which is commensurate with their efforts and the results they produce.

Recruiting: Tools & Methods

Years ago, companies used to place job advertisements in newspapers. Candidates would read such advertisements in the *want-ads* and if interested in applying, they would have to send their resume and explanatory cover letter to the hiring company via postal mail. An HR representative of the hiring company would then open the letter, review the resume and make a decision: (1) to contact the candidate and start the interview process or (2) to file the resume away for future reference or (3) to discard the resume.

B．優れたリーダー

優れたリーダーというものは例外なく，信頼感と敬意を持って人と接し，組織に貢献する全ての人の知性を尊重する。また，彼らは，人が大きな業績をあげられるよう，自主性を認める一方で，助言を与えることにより，両者間の調和を取るように努力する。優れたリーダーは人の潜在能力を引き出すことで組織の成果が生まれるように働きかけをする。

C．やりがいのある仕事

やりがいのある仕事は，要求度が高く，挑戦的で，各従業員が興味を持ち，重要と考える内容を持つ。同様に，やりがいのある仕事は，自らの努力を通じて生み出した貢献であるため，人々に満足を与える。

D．魅力的な報酬

金銭は従業員に生活費として支払われる。しかし，金銭はまた，従業員の貢献度の認知と公平な処遇を示す尺度でもある。優秀な人は，自分への尊敬の証として，彼らの努力と生み出された成果に応じた報酬を会社が提供することを期待する。

募集：手段と方法

かつて，企業は求人広告を新聞に載せた。求職者は「案内広告」の求人欄を読み，応募に興味がある場合に履歴書とカバーレターを封書で求人募集をする企業に送付した。人事担当はそれを開封し，レターを読み，履歴書に目を通し，(1)求職者に連絡を取り，面接を開始するか，あるいは，(2)履歴書を将来の候補者としてファイルしておく，(3)履歴書を廃棄する，といった決定をしていた。

Then, the process was further modernized when candidates would opt to send resumes via email along with an introductory letter. Or, candidates may have applied to the company via an online portal recruitment site on which companies may post open job advertisements.

Until recently, if a candidate had become interested in a company, the candidate may have viewed the corporate website for gathering primary information. While the corporate website still remains an important *entrance point* into the company with information about the company's products, services and corporate data, **social networking sites (SNS)** and **company (employer) review sites** have become the next generation for information dissemination and gathering. On such sites, potential employees can read information posted by current or former employees. Also, such sites allow for HR staff as well as other hiring managers to directly interact with potential candidates.

Interviewing: Two-Way Communication

Regardless of how a potential employee comes into contact with the hiring company, it remains customary for representatives of the hiring company to meet with the candidate to conduct an interview. During the interview, the hiring company wants to assess whether the candidate has the skills and mindset to perform adequately within the company. Likewise, during the interview, the candidate is also assessing whether the company would be a good place to pursue a career. In this way, an interview is a *two-way* assessment. Therefore, an interviewer needs to have the following skills and mindset in order to conduct an adequate interview:

- Ability to create an environment for comfortable discussion
- Ability to determine appropriate questions to assess the candidate's skills,

その後，こうしたプロセスは，より近代化され，求職者は履歴書をカバーレターと共に電子メールに添付して送付するようになった。あるいは，企業が求職者を公募することが可能な求人ポータルサイトを通じて応募する場合もある。

最近までは，志願者が企業に興味を持つと，主な情報収集手段として企業のサイトにアクセスしたであろう。企業のサイトは製品・サービス情報，企業データ，採用情報が掲載されており，未だにその企業への重要な「エントリーポイント」である。他方で，**ソーシャル・ネットワーキング・サイト（SNS）**や**企業（雇用主）レビュー・サイト**が今や情報の発信と収集の次世代型サイトとなっている。これらのサイトでは，就職志願者は現社員や元社員からの情報に接することが出きる。また，人事部スタッフやその他の部署の採用担当者も志願者と直接コンタクトを取ることができる。

面接：双方向のコミュニケーション

志願者と求人企業の最初のコンタクトがどのようなものであろうとも，その企業の社員が志願者と面接することが通例となっている。面接時に，企業側は志願者が採用された場合に社内で必要とされる技能や考え方（マインドセット）を保有しているかどうかの評価を目指している。同様に，面接を通じて，志願者も経歴を積むために望ましい会社かどうかの評価をしている。このように，面接は「双方向」の評価プロセスであり，したがって面接者は，適切な面接を実施するために次のような技能や心構えが必要である。

- リラックスして議論ができる雰囲気を作り出す能力
- 求職者の技能，経験，労働観を見極めるための適切な質問を設定する能力

experiences and work ethics

• Ability to listen effectively and know when to ask appropriate follow-up questions to fully understand the candidate's intentions

• Mindset to act as a fair representative of the company throughout the entire interview by, for example, showing up on time for the interview, reviewing the candidate's resume in advance, and answering questions from the candidate when possible

Selection & Making an Offer: Setting the Appropriate Conditions for People to Join the Company

Once a company determines that it would like to hire a candidate, an offer of employment needs to be made.

Generally, an **employment offer letter** includes such information as the following: work location, work hours, job position, starting salary and notable benefits. As well, mention may be made of a variable bonus if there is any.

In some countries, it may be typical for a company to make an offer of employment to new graduates without mention of the specific job content for which the candidate is being hired. This is because the employee's job content is expected to change over time through various position rotations. In other countries, an offer of employment is directly tied to a specific position so the offer letter would always include mention of the work content.

There may be differences in the approach that companies take to the offer process. In some cases, it is understood that the offer process is a negotiation. Under such circumstances, the hiring company may make an initial salary offer with the expectation that the candidate may counter-offer. A candidate may cite personal skills or past accomplishments to make an appeal for a higher

- 求職者の発言を正確に聴取し，意図を充分に理解するために，適切な追加質問をする能力
- 面接の開始時間を守る，志願者の履歴書に事前に目を通す，志願者からの質問にできるだけ答えるなど，面接全般を通じて，会社の代表として適切に行動する心構え

選考と条件提示：入社のための適切な雇用条件の設定

会社側が求職者の採用を決定したい場合，雇用条件を提示しなければならない。

一般的には，**雇用提示のレター**には勤務地，勤務時間，役職，初任給，付加給付金，ならびに変動賞与がある場合には，これも含まれる。

いくつかの国では，新卒志願者に対して具体的な仕事内容を明記せずに雇用が提示されることが通常である。その理由は従業員の仕事内容は人事異動により時の経過とともに変化するためである。他の国では，雇用の提示は特定の職位と直接結びついており，雇用提示書には仕事内容が記載されている。

雇用の提示プロセスは会社によって異なる場合がある。時には，提示プロセスは交渉を通じて行われるものと考えられている。このような状況では，会社は，求職者がカウンターオファーを提示するとの予測のもと，先ず，給与条件を提示する。求職者は自らの技能や過去の成果をあげて条件の改善を目指す。あるいは，求職者が複数の企業から雇用条件の提示を受けている場合には，そ

salary offer. Or when the candidate has received multiple offers from different companies, the candidate may try to leverage this position to negotiate a higher salary offer from the first-choice company.

However, there are times when the company is not accustomed to negotiating offers and the first offer is the final offer.

Onboarding: Induction Into the Company

Upon starting work at the company, the **new hire** may feel a combination of nervousness, excitement and motivation. It is important to help the new hire quickly acclimate to the new company environment and be able to start working productively. To do this, the initial induction process into the company is key. The induction process normally includes a combination of the following: handling of administrative procedures, appropriation of work tools, introduction to the work environment, and an explanation of initial expectations and work tasks. If a new hire reports to work on the designated first day and the company has not prepared adequately for inducting the new employee, the new hire may feel frustration and be dismayed.

Firstly, the HR Department should have a packet of documents prepared for the new hire. Such documents may include any of the following: an employment contract for both the employee and company to sign, registration form for automatic salary payment, application form for select benefits, and a copy of the company rules and regulations.

After such initial administrative procedures, the new hire may be provided with an ID card, set up with a new email address, and provided a personal computer along with other tools for conducting work.

の立場を利用して，第一志望の会社からの給与条件の改善を試みるであろう。

　しかし，雇用条件の交渉が習慣となっていない場合，会社が最初に提示した条件が最終条件となる場合もある。

受け入れ：入社

　入社時の**新入社員**は通常，緊張と興奮とやる気が入り混じった状態にある。新入社員が新たな企業環境に早期に順応し，生産的な仕事を開始できるよう，サポートすることが重要である。そのためには，受け入れ過程が重要となる。受け入れ過程には通常，以下の一連のことが含まれる。すなわち，事務的手続きの処理，仕事用具の貸与，職場環境への導入，当座の会社側の期待と仕事上の任務の説明などである。新入社員が初出勤した際に会社が受け入れ体制を十分整備していないとすれば，その新入社員は不満や落胆を感じるであろう。

　先ず，人事部は新入社員用の書類一式を準備する必要がある。例えば，次のような種類が含まれる：会社と社員双方がサインする雇用契約書，給与自動振込申請書，各種の福利厚生申請書，そして就業規則集。

　上記のような事務手続きが終了後，新入社員には社員証が渡され，電子メール・アドレスが設定され，そして仕事のための各種道具とともにパソコンが提供される。

On the first day of employment, it is also crucial that the new employee be introduced to others in the department or team and for everyone to be informed about why the new employee has been hired. Then, the direct supervisor and the new hire should have a discussion about initial expectations and immediate work to be undertaken.

When the induction process is conducted smoothly with clear information exchanged, both the company and the new hire can begin the working relationship with mutual understanding and satisfaction.

Onboarding: The First Three to Six Months of Employment

The first three to six months of employment in a company remain important for assessing the appropriateness of the decision to hire the new employee. Such a period of time may be referred to as the **Introductory Period** or **Probation Period**.

Companies may evaluate the employee's initial performance during this period. In the case that the company is not satisfied with the employee's performance or attitude, a decision may be made to terminate the employment of the new hire before any more time passes.

In the case that the company is satisfied with the employee's performance during the Introductory Period, it is normally advisable for the HR Department representative to have a brief discussion with the new hire to understand how satisfied the new employee is with the working conditions, relations with others in the working group and the overall comfort within the company. When the new hire is experiencing difficulties within this Introductory Period, there may be a need to make modifications in the employee's assignment to retain the employee for the longer term.

　また，最初の出勤日に新入社員を所属部門やチームの同僚に紹介し，この新入社員がなぜ採用されたかを説明することも重要である。その後，直属の上司は新入社員とミーティングを持ち，会社側の期待内容と新入社員の取り組むべき最初の仕事について話し合わなければならない。

　受け入れ過程で明確な情報が交換され，受け入れ過程がスムーズに行われるならば，会社と新入社員双方は相互理解と満足を伴う仕事関係を開始することができる。

受け入れ：採用後の最初の3〜6か月

　新入社員が採用された後の3〜6カ月間は，その採用判断の適正さを評価する上で重要な期間となる。この期間は一般的には**導入期間**または**試用期間**と呼ばれる。

　企業は新入社員の採用直後の仕事ぶりをこの期間に評価することができる。もし企業が新入社員の仕事ぶりまたは勤務態度に満足が得られない場合には，早いうちに，この新入社員の雇用を終了することができる。

　企業側が導入期間中の新入社員の仕事ぶりに満足している場合，人事担当者が新入社員と短時間の面談を持ち，色々な仕事環境，他の社員との関係，会社に対する全般的な快適性に関して新入社員がどの程度満足しているかを聴取することは通常，望ましいことである。新入社員が試用期間中に困難な状況に遭遇している場合には，より長期の雇用を可能にするために，仕事の内容に調整を加える必要があるかもしれない。

Commentary: Induction practices in Japan vs. overseas

Understanding that new graduates have little to no practical work experience prior to joining a company, Japanese companies have followed a long-held practice of hiring new graduates for their latent potential and providing practical training within the initial onboarding period. As part of the induction process, the new graduate typically undergoes extensive training in order to develop the mindset and skills that the company deems to be important for success within the company. The knowledge and skills that the new graduate had acquired during university days is not weighted heavily by the hiring company.

Conversely, in other countries, it is generally expected that the previous study of the new graduate should be indicative of the skills and proclivities of the individual for a specific line of work at the time of entering the company. In such cases the company may make an offer of employment for a specific job position.

In Japan however, an initial offer of employment to a new graduate typically does not specify the job position for which the person is being hired. The offer is to join the company with the implicit understanding that the actual work assignment will be changed multiple times over the course of the individual's working career.

In Japanese, it is often quipped that when looking for employment, Japanese are not *job seekers*, but are rather *company seekers*.

解説：新入社員受け入れの日本と外国の比較

　日本企業は，これまで長きにわたり，新卒者は入社前には殆ど，あるいは全く実務経験を有していないとの前提に立ち，彼らの潜在的な可能性を見て採用し，入社直後の受け入れ過程を通じて実務訓練を実施してきた。受け入れ過程の一環として，社内で成功するのに会社が重要と考えるマインドセットとスキルを身に着けるため広範な訓練を新卒者は一般的に受けることになる。新卒者が大学時代に獲得した知識やスキルは，採用する会社にそれ程重視されていない。

　これに対し，他の国では，大学時代の専攻が新入社員の入社時に特定の仕事分野に適した技能や傾向を示す場合が多いと一般的に期待されている。このような場合，企業は特定の担当職務を明記して採用通知を出すことになる。

　一方日本では，新卒者に対する採用通知には彼が従事するであろう特定の担当職務は明記されていない。そのような新入社員の採用通知が出されるのは，実際の業務は在職中に何度か変更されるとの暗黙の了解に基づいている。

　日本語で就職活動とは，皮肉にも，本来の「就職」を求めての行動ではなく，「就社」を求めての行動を意味することが多い。

References & Suggestions for Additional Reading

Ployhart, R. E., J. A. Weekley, and J. Dalzell (2018), "Recruiting Talent Globally", *Talent Without Borders: Global Talent Acquisition for Competitive Advantage*, Oxford University Press, Chapter 4.

Klein, H. J., B. Polin and K. L. Sutton, (2015), "Specific Onboarding Practices for the Socialization of New Employees", *International journal of selection and assessment*, Vol. 23 (3), p. 263-283 (ISSN: 0965-075X, 1468-2389; DOI: 10.1111/ijsa.12113).

Ploum, L., V. Blok and T. Lans (2017), "Toward a Validated Competence Framework for Sustainable Entrepreneurship," *Organization & Environment*, Volume: 31, issue: 2, pp. 113-132 (https://doi.org/10.1177/1086026617697039).

Cascio, W. F. and H. Aguinis (2019), "Recruitment", *Applied Psychology in Talent Management*, 8th Edition, SAGE, pp. 256-275, Chapter 11.

Lievens, F. and D. Chapman (2019), "Recruitment and Selection", in Wilkinson, A., N. Bacon, S. Snell and D. Lepak (eds), *The SAGE Handbook of Human Resource Management*, Second Edition, Sage, pp. 123-150, Chapter 8.

Mosley, R. (2014), *Employer Brand Management: Practical Lessons from the World's Leading Employers*, Wiley.

さらに学びたい人のための参考文献

Ployhart, R. E., J. A. Weekley, and J. Dalzell (2018), "Recruiting Talent Globally", *Talent Without Borders, Global Talent Acquisition for Competitive Advantage*, Oxford University Press, Chapter 4.

Klein, H. J., B. Polin and K. L. Sutton, (2015), "Specific Onboarding Practices for the Socialization of New Employees", *International journal of selection and assessment*, Vol. 23 (3), p. 263-283 (ISSN: 0965-075X, 1468-2389; DOI: 10.1111/ijsa.12113).

Ploum, L., V. Blok and T. Lans (2017), "Toward a Validated Competence Framework for Sustainable Entrepreneurship", *Organization & Environment*, Volume: 31, issue: 2, pp. 113-132 (https://doi.org/10.1177/1086026617697039).

Cascio, W. F. and H. Aguinis (2019), "Recruitment", *Applied Psychology in Talent Management*, 8th Edition, SAGE, pp. 256-275, Chapter 11.

Lievens, F. and D. Chapman (2019), "Recruitment and Selection", in Wilkinson, A., N. Bacon, S. Snell and D. Lepak (eds), *The SAGE Handbook of Human Resource Management*, Second Edition, Sage, pp. 123-150, Chapter 8.

Mosley, R. (2014), *Employer Brand Management: Practical Lessons from the World's Leading Employers*, Wiley.

CASE STUDY 2.1

Finding an Adequate Replacement for a Vacant Position

Question for consideration

When an overseas subsidiary of a Japanese company suffers a sudden resignation of a valued employee, there may be a frantic search for a replacement candidate in order to fill the vacancy. **In such a case, is it better to promote someone early from within or seek fully qualified candidates from outside the company?**

Case study detail

Overseas Subsidiary: **Meihan Electronics USA, Inc.**
Shindo Takao, President
Scott Morris, HR Manager

Meihan Electronics USA, Inc. has been experiencing steady growth recently. **President Shindo Takao** is pleased with the results, but recently operations have been negatively impacted by the sudden resignation of certain employees. Last week, one of the assistant managers in the Manufacturing Technology Department left the company, and a difference of opinion arose between President Shindo and **Scott Morris, HR Manager** about how to fill the vacancy. The following conversation ensued:

Shindo: How shall we fill the vacant assistant manager position in the

CASE STUDY 2.1

空席ポジションの適任者の見つけ方

本事例の着目点

　日本企業の海外子会社が，重要な従業員の突然の離職により困る場合には，その空席を埋めるために必死になって補充人員を探すことになるだろう。このような事態において，内部の人材をやや早めに登用するか，あるいは社外から十分な資格要件を有する候補者を採用するか，どちらが望ましいのだろうか？

事例の詳細

海外子会社：名阪エレクトロニクス USA Inc.

社長：進藤孝雄氏

人事マネジャー：スコット・モリス氏

　製造業の名阪エレクトロニクス USA は，業績を順調に伸ばしてきている。**社長の進藤孝雄氏**は，それを嬉しく思っている。しかし，最近，ある従業員の突然の退職により業務への悪影響が出てきている。先週，製造技術部門のアシスタント・マネジャーが退職し，その空席をどのように埋めるかで，進藤社長と**人事マネジャーのスコット・モリス氏**との間で意見の相違が生まれた。次のような会話が交わされた。

進藤：製造技術部門のアシスタント・マネジャーの後任をどうしようか。外部

Manufacturing Technology Department? Is it possible to recruit a competent individual from outside the company?

Morris: Well, I'm not sure about that. But we may be able to promote from within rather than having to hire from outside. Come to think of it, the up-and-coming ones in the department think that they're on the road to becoming assistant managers.

Shindo: Really? But I don't think that any of the staff are old enough . . . I mean, have enough experience yet.

Morris: Well, let's see. How about we post the job opening internally and see who wants to apply to the open position?

Shindo: If we posted this job internally, how many people do you think would apply for it?

Morris: I think there may be more than a handful of interested applicants from both within the department and outside as well.

Shindo: What? From other departments as well?

Morris: That's right. Although managers of those departments would hate to see any of their competent staff transferring to other departments.

Shindo: That would create chaos.

Morris: Well, we do talk about creating opportunities for our employees to grow and develop. This seems like one of those chances, no?

から良い人材をスカウトする方法はありますか？

モリス：そうですね。うーん。それはどうですかね…。他方で，外部から採用するよりも内部から昇進させるという手もありますね。実は考えてみますと，あの部門の有望な若手は，みんな自分がアシスタント・マネジャーになれると思っていますよ。

進藤：えー，本当に？　しかし，あの部門のスタッフはまだ若すぎ…，いや，経験がまだ浅すぎるんじゃあない？

モリス：さあ，それはどうでしょうかね。社内で募集をかけてみて，その空席にだれが応募するか見てみましょうか？

進藤：もし，内部で後任を募集するとしたら，どれくらいの人数が応募してくると思う？

モリス：そのようになれば，製造技術部門だけでなく他の部門からの応募も見込まれますので，数人どころか，かなりの数になるでしょうね。

進藤：えー，他の部門からも？

モリス：ええ，そうですよ。ただ，そのような場合，そこの部門長は，有能な部下が他の部門に移っていくことを嫌がるでしょうね。

進藤：それは無茶苦茶になるね。

モリス：ええ，でも，わが社では，自社の社員が成長し，伸びていくためのチャンスを作ることをよく話していますよね。これは，まさに，そのようなチャンスそのものではないでしょうか？　違いますか？

Shindo: Hmm, but if we put people into positions for which they are not yet qualified nor experienced, operations may suffer. In Japan, we normally make promotion decisions only after the individual demonstrates the skills for the next level position.

After some further consideration, President Shindo authorized an internal job posting policy to provide current employees with the opportunity to apply for open positions before the company seeks external candidates.

As a result, three internal employees had expressed interest in the open assistant management position. However, ultimately, an external candidate who had sufficient technical and managerial experience was hired. While the process took some time, in the end, the three internal employees came to recognize their personal developmental issues and the company benefitted from hiring new talent from the external market.

Learning points

An internal job posting policy provides for a method of seeking candidates from within the company when a position becomes vacant. It can be considered to be a tool for identifying potential candidates from within the organization that were not initially recognized. However, as we can see in this case, the decision to hire from outside the organization may ultimately be made if the best possible candidate cannot be found within.

In this case, the decision was made to hire an external candidate rather than to promote from within. We can assume that the external candidate already had some proven experience that would be relevant to the open position, whereas the internal candidates did not have such proven experience. Such a hiring decision would be consistent with a directive to

進藤：うーん。しかし，まだ経験も資格も足りないような人をそのようなポジションに就けると，業務が滞るかもしれないね。日本では，その個人が次の上位ポジションに必要なスキルを示した場合に初めて昇格決定がなされるものですよ。

　進藤社長はその後の熟慮の末，会社が社外の候補者を募集する前に，現従業員が空席のポジションに応募するチャンスを与えるため，社内募集の実施を承認した。

　その結果，3名の従業員が，アシスタント・マネジャーのポジションに興味を示した。しかし，結局のところ，技術的にも管理職経験においても十分な資格を有する外部の候補者が採用された。この採用プロセスには時間がかかったが，最終的にはその3名の応募者は自分の成長課題を認識し，また，会社は外部市場から新たな優秀人材を採用できるというメリットを得た。

学習ポイント
　社内の人材募集方針では，空席ポジションが出た場合には社内から候補者を探すという方針が示されている。当初は認識されていなかった，組織内の潜在的な候補者を識別するためのツールと見なすことができる。ただし，この事例でわかるように，組織外から採用するという決定は，最善の候補者が社内で見つからない場合に最終的になされるものかもしれない。

　この事例では，内部から昇進させるのではなく，外部の候補者を採用することになった。外部の候補者は空席ポジションに関連するであろう経験をすでに持っていたが，内部の候補者はそうではなかったと仮定することができる。そのような採用の決定は，従業員が自分の現在のポジションに居ながら新しい仕事を実行するために必要な能力を発揮したと見なされた

determine promotions to new positions (or higher grades) only after the employee is deemed to have demonstrated the necessary capability to perform at that level while in one's current position. However, in environments that experience rapid growth and high turnover, such a standard for promotion may not always be practical. Rather, if people are to be promoted from within, it may be necessary to promote based upon a judgment of latent potential rather than actual demonstrated achievement.

後にのみ，新しいポジション（またはより高いグレード）への昇格を決定する一般的方向性と一致する。しかし，急成長と高離職率とを経験している環境下では，そのような昇進の基準は現実的ではないかもしれない。むしろ，人々を社内から昇進させるのであれば，実際に示された成果ではなく，潜在的可能性の判断に基づいて昇進させる必要があるかもしれない。

CASE STUDY 2.2

The Key to Successfully Hiring Local Talent to Start Up the Overseas Subsidiary of a Japanese Company

Question for consideration

The quality of the top management that is initially hired when a company is in the start-up phase will have a large impact on the development of the business. **What factors should influence the initial hiring decisions of management at the overseas subsidiaries of Japanese companies?**

Case study detail

Japanese HQ: Kokusai Buhin Co., Ltd.

(US-based subsidiary: Kokusai Buhin USA, Inc.)

Endo Takeshi, President

James Smith, EVP of Operations candidate

Endo Takeshi, currently the Global Procurement Manager of Kokusai Buhin Co., Ltd. will shortly be expatriated to the USA as the **President** of the newly established subsidiary. Kokusai Buhin is a tier one supplier to major automotive manufacturers.

Endo is now visiting the USA again on a business trip for the second time in the past three months. On the past trip, he spent the week busily registering the US subsidiary and meeting with potential partner companies.

He has returned this time to interview some candidates for the position of

CASE STUDY 2.2

現地の優秀人材を採用するための鍵：
日本企業が海外子会社を立ち上げる場合

本事例の着目点

現地法人がスタートアップの段階において最初に採用する現地人トップ・マネジメントの質が，その後の現地法人の経営に大きな影響を持つであろう。日本企業の海外現地法人においては，どのような要素がマネジャーの初採用の決定に影響を与えるのだろうか？

事例の詳細

日本本社：国際部品株式会社

（アメリカ現地法人：国際部品 USA）

アメリカ現地法人社長：遠藤武氏

アメリカ現地法人副社長の候補者：ジェイムズ・スミス氏

国際部品株式会社の部品調達部長である**遠藤武氏**は，新たに設立されたアメリカ現地法人に近々**社長**として派遣されることになっている。国際部品株式会社は，主要自動車メーカーへのティア・ワンのサプライヤーである。

遠藤氏は，過去3カ月のうちで2回目のアメリカ出張を現在行っている。前回は，アメリカ現地法人を登記し，将来のパートナー企業の人たちと打ち合わせをするために忙しい1週間を過ごした。

今回彼は，複数の現地法人の副社長候補者と面接をするために戻ってきた。

EVP of Operations. As the incumbent in this position will work directly under Endo, he is particularly interested in finding the right candidate to hire.

Previously, Endo had received a valuable piece of advice from the local branch manager of a Japanese bank with which his company conducts business in Japan. He recommended a headhunting firm that has experience in working for Japanese companies in the USA.

Endo contacted the headhunting firm and requested resumes of candidates with experience in business development within the automotive supplier industry. He strongly insisted that the smooth operations of the subsidiary would be predicated upon the successful hire of a person with relevant experience as well as strength of character (i.e., mental toughness, reliability, leadership, etc.).

While the initial batch of candidates he interviewed seemed to have the necessary qualifications, he did not feel that he had found the person to whom he would like to extend an offer of employment. Some critical factor was missing, but he could not yet put his finger on it.

Then, one day, Endo interviewed **James Smith**. Endo ultimately decided to extend an offer of employment to Smith who was currently the General Manager of business development at a tier two automotive supplier. Smith was a candidate who stood out from the others. Not only did he have a wealth of knowledge about, and track record in, the automotive industry, he was particularly familiar with Japanese business practices as he had previously studied in Japan during his college days. Such a combination of knowledge and experience proved to be rare among candidates.

While Endo initially knew that US-based industry experience and a strong

このポジションに就任する人は直属の部下となるため，遠藤氏は，良い候補者を見つけることにとりわけ強い関心を持っている。

　米国法人の設立準備について，以前，日本で取引のある銀行の現地支店長から貴重なアドバイスをもらった。彼は，アメリカに進出している日本企業と取引き経験のあるヘッド・ハンティング会社を紹介してくれた。

　遠藤氏は，そのヘッド・ハンティング会社に連絡を取り，自動車部品業界での事業開発経験のある候補者の履歴書を求めた。彼は，子会社の円滑な運営は，優れた資質（例えば精神的強靭性，信頼性，リーダーシップなどを含むような資質のこと）を持ち，また関連分野の経験を有する人材の採用の成否にかかっているということを強く主張した。

　彼が面接をした最初の候補者数人は必要な資格要件を備えているようであった。しかし，彼は，採用を決めたいと思えるような人を見つけたという確信をまだ得られなかった。何か重要なものが欠けているようであったが，彼にはそのカギとなる要素がまだ見極められていなかった。

　その後のある日，遠藤氏は**ジェームズ・スミス氏**の面接を行った。遠藤氏はついに，ティア・ツーの自動車サプライヤーの現職の事業開発部長であるスミス氏に対し，採用の意思表示をすることにした。スミス氏は他の候補者から抜きん出る候補者であった。彼は，自動車業界における豊富な経験と知識を有しているのみならず，学生時代に日本留学を経験し，日本のビジネス慣行を特によく知っていた。このような知識と経験の組み合わせは，数多くの候補者の中で際立っていた。

　遠藤氏は当初，アメリカでの業界経験と強い意志の保有が候補者の資格要件

character were necessary requirements of candidates, he came to recognize that the inclination to work effectively with members of management from Japan would be the special key to success.

Furthermore, Endo was now excited to learn about American society, culture, and ways of thinking from Smith—an important learning element that would contribute to the sound growth of Kokusai Buhin's operations in the USA.

Learning points

When a Japanese company establishes a presence in a new market in a foreign country, Japanese-affiliated firms already conducting business locally, including banks, are a useful source of information on local business conditions.

It goes without saying that a crucial element for successfully launching a new foreign entity is to hire local talent. To that end, it is recommendable to engage a reliable local headhunting firm to assist your search for competent candidates to fill the important positions of the local entity.

While it will be prudent to employ competent individuals that possess deep knowledge of the local market for products your company specializes in, it is advisable to seek out those individuals who can also act as *bridge people*. Not only can *bridge people* carry out their own assigned work, they can also assist the expatriate management in *translating* the expectations of the Japanese headquarters to other locally hired employees. Moreover, if the headquarters aims to promote a globally unified corporate philosophy of values and ways of working among the global subsidiaries, such *bridge people* will serve a vital role in promoting the desired corporate culture.

として重要であると理解していたが，他方で，日本からの経営管理層と効果的に仕事を進めるという性質も成功のための重要な鍵であると認識するようになっていった。

　さらに遠藤氏は，米国の社会や文化，米国人の考え方についてスミス氏から学ぶことができることに興奮を覚えている。そのような学びは，国際部品 USA の順調な成長に貢献する重要な要素となっている。

学習ポイント

　日本企業が海外の新マーケットに進出する際には，すでに現地で事業を行っている銀行を含む日系企業は，現地事情に関する有用な情報源となりうる。

　現地会社を新たに創業する場合，現地の優秀人材の採用が成功のための大きな鍵となることは言うまでもない。そのためには，この事例のように，現地の信頼できるヘッド・ハンティング会社を使い，重要ポジションに就く有能な候補者を探すことも考えられる。

　現地の業界に精通した優秀人材を採用することは賢明なことであるが，同時に，「ブリッジ人材」としても活躍できる人材を見つけ出すことにも考慮する必要があろう。「ブリッジ人材」は，自分自身に与えられた仕事を遂行するのみならず，同時に，日本本社が現地採用の人材に期待することを「理解し適切に伝える」ことにより，海外派遣者のマネジメントを補佐することもできる。さらに，もし本社が世界を繋ぐ経営理念や仕事の作法をグローバルに分散する子会社間に浸透させようとする場合，このような「ブリッジ人材」は本社が望む企業文化を浸透させるに際し，大変重要な役割を果たすことになろう。

Performance Management

What Is Performance Management?

Performance Management is a key HR process for holding everyone in a company accountable for producing expected results. Performance management is characterized by on-going communication between management and employees.

This communication includes discussions about the following elements:

A) Company mission, strategy and objectives
B) Expectations for department, team and individual work
C) Actual short-term goals for achievement and competencies for development
D) On-going review and feedback
E) Evaluation

The **Performance Management Process (PMP)** is a two-way cycle of

CHAPTER 3

パフォーマンス・マネジメント

パフォーマンス・マネジメントとは？

　パフォーマンス・マネジメントは全ての社員に対し，責任を持って期待された成果を出させる重要な人事プロセスである。パフォーマンス・マネジメントの特徴はマネジメントと社員の間のコミュニケーションが継続的に行われることにある。

　このコミュニケーションでは次のような要素についてのやり取りが行われる。

A）企業の理念，戦略，中期目標
B）部・課，チーム，社員各自の仕事に対して期待されること
C）具体的な短期的目標，および開発すべき行動特性（コンピテンシー）
D）継続的なレビュー（観察）とフィードバック
E）評価

　パフォーマンス・マネジメントのプロセス（PMP）は，双方向の循環的な

communication. On the one hand, company management needs to ensure that employees understand the company strategy and objectives so that they can contribute effectively through their work. On the other hand, the employees need to raise concerns and opinions about how to get their work accomplished.

Additionally, employees must be active in seeking to develop their own skills and abilities in order to conduct satisfactory work.

Now, we will look at each element of this process.

A) Company Mission, Strategy and Objectives

In every fiscal year, it is common for the executive management to clarify the corporate direction by espousing the relevant strategy to meet certain targets.

Such targets may be quantitative such as revenue, profit, or cost reduction targets. The targets may also be qualitative such as targets for new service/ product development or new market entry. The key point to understand is that companies must be responsive to changing conditions and set targets to remain competitive in their areas of pursuit. Likewise, the executive leadership must take steps to ensure that the employees within the organization clearly understand this direction. To ensure such understanding, it is common for the management to provide employees with written internal memoranda, and to conduct company-wide meetings or use other methods of communication.

B) Expectations for Department, Team and Individual Work

Once the corporate direction for the fiscal year (half-year or quarter) is communicated throughout the organization, the communication process may

コミュニケーションである。先ず，経営管理職は社員に対し，それぞれの業務を通じて効果的に貢献ができるよう経営戦略や中期目標を理解させることが重要である。一方で，社員は業務をどのように達成するかに関して懸念事項や見解を示す必要がある。

　さらに，社員は職務を十分に遂行するために，自らの職務能力を積極的に高めなければならない。

　では，このプロセスの各要素についてみてみよう。

A) 企業の理念，戦略，中期目標

　経営幹部は通常，年度毎に，特定の目標を達成するために適切な戦略を宣言することにより，会社が進むべき方向性を明確にする。

　こうした目標は売上高，利益，コスト削減などの定量的な場合もあれば，新サービス・新製品の開発や新たな市場への参入などの定性的な場合もある。重要なポイントは，企業は変化するビジネス環境に応じて，それぞれの専門分野で競争力を維持するための目標を設定しなければならないということである。そして，管理職は自社の社員がこの方向性を明確に理解するように，社内メモを配布し，全社規模で会議を開催し，あるいはその他の意思疎通の手段を講じなければならない。

B) 部・課，チーム，社員各自の仕事に対して期待されること

　年度（あるいは半期や四半期）毎の経営の方向性が組織内で伝達されると，部・課やチーム・レベル別の段階でさらなる意思疎通が図られ，全社的戦略や

continue at the department or team level whereby each part of the company considers how it can best contribute to the corporate strategy and objectives.

For example, if a corporate objective for the first half-year is to determine whether the company should actually set up operations in a new market within the following fiscal year, there may be discussion at the department level about how this objective can be supported. Then, within the HR Department, during this half-year, it may be necessary to research current labor conditions in the new market area, to understand how to set up HR processes therein, and to otherwise consider how to support business start-up operations in order to minimize any inherent risks of conducting business within the new market.

To carry out such work effectively, accountability for tasks needs to be assigned to each professional in the team.

C) Determining Actual Goals for Achievement and Understanding Competencies for Development

Once the accountabilities are clarified, it is necessary to develop an action plan. The action plan is normally defined through the development of multiple goals. This is sometimes referred to as **annual goals setting** or **Management by Objectives (MBO)**. Ideally, supervisors and employees should write down about three to five **SMART goals**. SMART goals are Specific, Measurable, Achievable, Related and Time-bound. In other words, the goals should be clear enough so that anyone can read and understand the required targets. Goals may be team-based, but it is common for goals to be assigned to individuals.

As time goes by, the goals should be periodically reviewed and revised as necessary to reflect changes in the business conditions.

目標にどのように貢献すべきかが検討される。

　例えば，企業の上期における目標が，次年度に新市場でビジネスを展開するかどうかの決定をすることであれば，部・課レベルでこの目標にどのよう対応できるのかを議論することになろう。それに伴い，この上期中に人事部では，新市場地域における現行の労働条件を調査し，そこでの人事プロセスをどのように設定するかを検討し，さらには新市場でビジネスを遂行することに伴うリスクを最小化するためにビジネスの立ち上げをどのように支援するか，対応策を練ることが必要となるだろう。

　一連の作業を効果的に行うために，チームの中の各専門担当者に当該業務を割り当てる必要がある。

C）具体的な短期的目標，および 開発すべき行動特性（コンピテンシー）

　当該業務が割り当てられた後，行動計画を作成する必要がある。行動計画は通常，複数の目標を設定する過程で明確になる。これは**年度目標の設定**，あるいは，**MBO（目標管理制度）**と呼ばれる。理想的には，上司と部下は3〜5項目の**SMART ゴール**を書き出す。SMART とは Specific（具体的），Measurable（測定可能），Achievable（達成可能），Related（経営目標に関連する），Time-bound（時間的制約がある）の頭文字をとったもので，言い換えれば，目標はだれが読んでも理解できるように明確に記述されていなければならない。目標はチーム全体で設定される場合もあるが，たいてい目標は個人ごとに割り当てられる。

　時間の経過と共に，これらの目標は再検討され，ビジネス環境が変化する場合には必要に応じて定期的に改訂されなくてはならない。

In addition to setting work goals for achievement, companies that have developed a **competency framework** may hold employees accountable for increasing their capacity in accordance with such specifically selected competencies.

Examples of competencies are as follows: Teamwork (Cooperation), Continuous Learning, Organizational Management, Communication, or Initiative. In a competency framework, the competency areas may be consistent throughout all levels in the organization. However, the definition for the standard level of acceptable behavior may differ among hierarchical levels in the organization.

At the beginning of the fiscal year, it is important for both the manager and employee to mutually confirm understanding about the definitions of the competencies. As well, they should discuss and agree on what behaviors the employee should demonstrate during the fiscal year to be evaluated favorably in accordance with the competency definitions.

D) On-Going Review and Feedback

Managers should regularly observe the work of the employees in their department, compare the current status to the pre-determined goals and competency standards and then provide feedback as necessary to their subordinates.

When the work of the subordinates is not leading towards expected achievement levels, the manager should provide some type of critical feedback to the subordinate. In this case, critical feedback is not meant to scold or discipline an employee. Rather, critical feedback is a conversation that contains elements of a coaching-style dialogue that pursues improvement. In such a

　達成すべき業務目標の設定に加えて，**行動特性要件（コンピテンシー・フ
レームワーク）** を明らかに示した企業は，従業員がその定義された行動特性要
件に従って自らの能力を向上させていくことが求められる。

　こうした行動特性要件の例：チームワーク（協調性），継続的学習，組織管
理能力，コミュニケーション能力，あるいは率先力。行動特性要件の項目は組
織内の全ての職層に共通するであろう。しかし，各要件の行動レベルの定義
は，組織内の職層間で異なる可能性がある。

　年度初めにおいて，上司と部下がコンピテンシーの定義についての理解を相
互に確認することは重要である。そしてコンピテンシーの定義に従って高く評
価されるために，年度内にどのような行動を示すべきかについて議論し，合意
を得ることが必要である。

D）継続的なレビュー（観察）とフィードバック

　管理者は日常的に，部下の業務を観察し，それぞれの時点における成果をあ
らかじめ設定された目標やコンピテンシーの基準と比較し，必要なフィード
バックを部下に与えなければならない。

　部下の業務が期待された達成水準を満たしていない場合には，管理者は何ら
かの建設的なフィードバックをしなければならない。この場合のフィードバッ
クは，叱責や懲罰を意味するものではない。むしろこのフィードバックは，改
善を求めるために行うコーチング（気付きを与えること）の要素を含む対話を
意味する。こうした対話では，管理者は先ず部下の業務に対する懸念や観察さ

dialogue, the manager should first clearly state their concerns or describe the perceived problem. Next, by comparing the current situation to the expected standard, the manager can objectively and fairly raise issues for discussion. Thereafter, the manager should have a dialogue with the employee to discuss a plan for improvement. A simple question about what the employee can do to improve the situation may be sufficient to get the subordinate to think more deeply about their goals and work towards improvement. Or, the conversation may reveal deficiencies in the subordinate's way of thinking and approach to the given tasks. When critical feedback discussions occur timely and periodically, the manager can guide the subordinate to successful achievement of pre-determined goals.

Even if the subordinate is on target to achieve goals or is even on track to exceed expectations, it is advisable for the manager to provide positive feedback in the form of **praise and recognition** to the employee. Praise and recognition discussions require just a short amount of time. In such discussions, the manager should clearly identify what has been done well by the employee and then explain the positive effects that such performance has had on the organization or related stakeholders such as customers. Finally, such a conversation may be closed with an expression of appreciation for the efforts of the individual. When feedback is effectively conveyed by the manager, such an exchange can naturally lead the employee to feel positive about his/her work accomplishments. Additionally, such feedback can lead to the continuation of the current performance or inspire even higher levels of performance. The lack of such praise and recognition can lead the subordinate to erroneously believe that his/her efforts are neither necessary nor appreciated; if this were to happen, the highly performing employee may step down their efforts, or worse, may even begin to seek employment elsewhere.

Therefore, it is recommended to make time for feedback as a part of on-going

れる問題点を明確に伝えなければならない。次に，現状と期待値を比較することによって，管理者は議論すべき問題点を客観的かつ公平に指摘できる。そして，管理者は部下と，必要とされる改善を図るための計画を話し合わねばならない。現状を改善するために何をすべきか，という単純な問いかけを部下にすることで，達成すべき目標を認識させ，改善に向けた行動を取らせることが可能となる場合がある。あるいは，このような話し合いにより，特定の職務に関する不十分な認識や取り組みが明らかになる場合がある。こうした建設的なフィードバックを適時，定期的に行うことで，管理者は部下が所定の目標を達成するよう指導することができる。

　部下が期待通り目標に到達できそうか，または期待以上の場合には，上司は**称賛と認知**という形でフィードバックを与えることは望ましい。部下の努力を容認し，讃えるために要するフィードバックの時間は僅かなものである。そのフィードバックにおいて上司は部下の功績が何であるかを明らかにし，また，組織あるいは顧客などの利害関係者が享受した利益を説明する必要がある。最後に，部下の努力に対する管理者としての感謝の言葉を述べることでそのフィードバックは完了する。マネジャーによりフィードバックが効果的に伝達されれば，部下自らが仕事の成果を肯定的に捉えることになる。さらには，効果的なフィードバックは，こうした現状の努力水準を維持し，より高いパフォーマンスも生み出す。一方，このような賞賛と評価のフィードバックが欠如する場合には，部下は自らの努力が不必要であるとか，認められていないという間違った認識を持つ可能性もある。このような事態が起こると，生産性の高い部下のやる気が削がれるかもしれないし，さらに最悪の場合には彼らは離職を考えはじめる可能性もある。

　したがって，週単位で実施される定例のチーム・ミーティングや必要に応

communication during weekly team meetings or *touch-base* status update meetings as needed. The investment of 30 minutes to 1 hour each week for managers and employees to celebrate their progress towards the achievement of goals and/or to raise any concerns that they have is a great way to uncover problems and align the work of the individual members.

As well, this space for communication provides all employees the chance to express opinions and needs for additional resources, assistance, or training in order to carry out the required work. Healthy work environments allow for employees and managers to speak frankly and openly about such issues.

E) Evaluation

The final step of the performance management process is to conduct an evaluation of results. Evaluation is characterized by reflection upon the work that had been carried out and the ascertainment of the achievement level of previously determined goals. If results are not reviewed, analyzed and evaluated, it is very difficult for companies to learn from successes and failures. Evaluation meetings enable managers and employees to discuss and determine the effectiveness of efforts towards the production of desired outcomes and to consider how, if at all, changes in approach should be made for future pursuits.

Secondly, the results of work accomplishments are also normally considered in making human resource-related decisions regarding promotions/demotions, compensation, training, and even employment termination.

In the next section, we will discuss these human resource-related concerns.

じて実施される進捗確認ミーティング（「タッチベース」ミーティングともいう）において，日常的コミュニケーションの一環としてフィードバックの時間を持つことが望ましい。マネジャーと部下がかける週に 30 分から 1 時間の投資は，管理者と部下がゴール達成への過程を認め，そして／または，当面の課題を示すことは，未然に問題を発見し，社員間の業務の足並みを揃える上で極めて効果的である。

　上記に加え，こうしたコミュニケーションの場は，全従業員が意見を表明し，また期待される職務を遂行するために必要な経営資源，支援，研修などの必要性を表明する良い機会となる。健全な職場環境は，こうした問題点を管理者と従業員が自由かつ率直に話し合うことを可能にする。

E）評価

　パフォーマンス・マネジメント・プロセスの最終ステップは，結果に対する評価を実施することである。評価は，実施された業務を振り返ることであり，また，以前設定された目標に対する達成水準を把握することである。結果を振り返り，分析し，評価するプロセスがなければ，企業が成功や失敗から学ぶことは極めて困難となる。評価面談を通じて，管理者と社員は期待された成果の創出に向かっての努力が効果的になされたかどうかを議論し，そして将来の達成目標に向かって取り組みの変化が必要か否かを検討することができる。

　次に，仕事成果の結果は通常，昇進・降格，報酬，研修，さらには解雇のような人的資源に関連する意思決定の際にも用いられる。

　次項では，こうした人的資源関連の事項を検討していく。

Considering Performance Evaluations

In its purest form, evaluation is the last step of a healthy performance management process.

However, performance evaluations become controversial in cases whereby the mandates of the HR Department are divorced from a healthy performance management process and viewed by employees and management solely as a bureaucratic and administrative exercise in filling out forms. As a result, HR mandated performance evaluations have been stopped in some companies that have not seen the value in the evaluation process.

In most countries, performance evaluations are not legally required. However, when carried out, performance evaluations must be legally defensible. That is to say that the elements of the performance evaluation must be relevant to the business and be non-discriminatory.

To ensure that the performance evaluation process is appropriate, the HR Department must implement a process that has the following elements: (a) clear criteria, (b) established review cycle times, and (c) fair methods.

Performance Evaluation Process Elements: (a) Clear Criteria

The most important element of the performance evaluation is the determination of what should be evaluated. The formal performance evaluation sheet may include different sections that require evaluation of the following criteria:

• Work-related goals/Management by Objectives (MBO)

業績評価の検討

　本質的に，業績評価は健全な業績管理プロセスの最終段階に該当する。

　しかし，業績評価が問題となるのは，人事部の指示が業績管理のあるべき姿から乖離し，従業員ならびに管理職によって単にお役所的あるいは事務的に評価表を埋める作業に過ぎないと解釈された場合である。その結果，人事部の指示による業績評価プロセスに価値を見出さない企業では，業績評価を取りやめる場合もある。

　ほとんどの国では，業績評価の実施は法定されていない。しかし，実施される場合には，業績評価は法的拘束力の範囲になければならない。つまり，業績評価の要素はその事業に関連するもので，差別的なものであってはならない。

　業績評価プロセスを適切に構築するためには，人事部は以下の諸要素を含むプロセスを導入しなければならない。つまり，(a)明確な評価基準，(b)明示された評価時期の循環，(c)公正な評価方法。

業績評価プロセスの諸要素：(a)明確な評価基準

　業績評価を実施する上で最も重要なことは，何が評価されるべきかを決めることである。正式な業績評価表には次のようないくつかのセクションが含まれる場合がある。各セクションは次のような基準に基づく評価を求める。

・仕事関連の目標／目標による管理（MBO）

- Competency development level
- Adherence to company rules and regulations (attendance record, ethics, etc.)

An employee's **career development plan (CDP)** may be included as the last section of the performance evaluation form, albeit such a section is not evaluated quantitatively.

Secondly, it is also critical to consider the comparative weighting of the abovementioned evaluation criteria within the performance evaluation form. A high weighting on the achievement of work-related goals emphasizes actual contributions made within the 12-month performance evaluation period (short-term). On the other hand, a high weighting on competency development emphasizes human growth over the medium-to-long-term. A focus on adherence to company rules and regulations would emphasize compliance. The determination of the comparative weighting of criteria is normally influenced by factors such as corporate culture or the position of the evaluated individual within the organizational hierarchy.

Additionally, the nature of the work that is conducted should be taken into consideration as well when determining the weighting of criteria. For creative work that requires employees to proceed by a trial-and-error approach, it may be difficult to evaluate employees upon the outcome of pre-determined goals. Rather, the work process followed by the employees as indicated by the competencies for the employee, may be given more weight in the final evaluation. Conversely, for some work such as sales or project management, the expected level of achievement may be *all or nothing* so an evaluation of the short-term outcome is given more importance than the medium-to-long-term growth of the employee.

- コンピテンシーの到達レベル
- 社内規則の遵守（出勤態度，倫理観など）

　従業員の**キャリア開発プラン（CDP）**は，業績評価表の最後の欄に記載されているかもしれない。しかし，その欄は定量的な評価対象ではない。

　次に，業績評価表の中ですでに述べたような評価の基準の相対的な重みづけを考慮することもまた重要である。仕事関連の目標の達成度に大きな重み付けを行うのは，12カ月間の業績評価期間内（短期）に行われた現実の貢献を重視しているためである。他方，コンピテンシーの到達レベルに大きな重みづけを行うのは，中・長期の人間の成長を重視しているためである。社内規則の遵守に焦点を合わせるのは，コンプライアンスを強調しているが故である。基準間の相対的な重みづけの決定は通常，企業文化や被評価者の組織内の階層レベルなどの要因によって影響を受ける。

　さらに，基準間の重みづけを決定する際には，業務の性質も考慮に入れる必要がある。創造的な業務においては，試行錯誤的なアプローチが従業員に要求され，前もって決定された目標が達成されたか否かで評価をすることは困難な場合がある。むしろ，従業員のコンピテンシーの発揮度合によって示された業務プロセスへの最終評価に，より大きな比重を置くことがある。逆に，販売やプロジェクト管理といった業務は達成の期待レベルは「全部かゼロかの世界」であり，中長期の従業員の成長よりも短期的結果に対する評価に比重が置かれることになる。

Performance Evaluation Process Elements: (b) Established Review Cycle Times

As explained previously, in an effective performance management process, discussions should be carried out as often as necessary between employees and management to deal with any emerging issues so that employees can receive timely feedback (coaching) and support to optimize their work results.

When the performance management process is managed under an HR mandate, minimum review cycle times are established to formalize evaluation results. Normally, the HR Department selects one of the two generally recognized standard times in the year when performance evaluation results may be formalized: a) on the anniversary of the employee's date of hire or b) at the end/beginning of the fiscal year.

In companies that choose to conduct individual performance evaluations throughout the year on the anniversary date of employment, the advantage is that there are fewer reviews to conduct at one time. The disadvantage is that it is difficult to align results with the annual decision period regarding promotions/demotions and salary adjustments.

When all employee evaluations are conducted at the same time of the fiscal year, managers, as well as the HR Department, may find it difficult to complete performance evaluations on time if there are many to conduct. In this way however, the review cycle can be aligned so that it is relevant to the fiscal year business cycle. Furthermore, promotions/demotions and salary adjustments can be considered all together based upon review of evaluation results.

業績評価プロセスの諸要素：(b)明示された評価時期の循環

上述の通り，効果的な業績管理プロセスにおいては，当面の課題に対応するために，管理者と従業員の間で必要な頻度で対話が行われなければならない。これにより，業績を最適化するために従業員は適時のフィードバック（コーチング）と支援を受けることができる。

業績管理プロセスが人事部の指示で管理される場合には，評価結果を確定するために，最低限の循環的な評価時期が決められている。通常，業績評価結果を正式に決定するに際して，人事部は，年内に一般的に認められている2回の標準的な時期のうちのどちらかを選択する：a) それぞれの従業員の入社記念日，あるいは，b) 期末または期初。

年間を通じて，従業員それぞれの入社記念日に業績評価を行うことを決めた企業では，評価業務が分散化されるという利点がある。不利な点は，評価結果を昇格・降格や給与改定の年次の決定時期に一致させることが困難なことである。

全ての従業員の評価が年度の同時期に行われる場合には，管理者ならびに人事部は評価の数が多い時には期限内に評価を完了することが困難となるかもしれない。しかし，この場合には業績評価時期と事業年度を一致させられるという利点がある。さらに，昇格・降格と給与改定を業績評価に基づき，同時に行うことが可能となる。

Performance Evaluation Process Elements: (c) Fair Methods

Evaluation methods are classified into three categories: 1) comparison methods, 2) rating methods, and 3) narrative methods.

Comparison methods compare employees to each other. One type of comparison method is *ranking* whereby managers list up all employees from the highest-level performer to the lowest. Another type of comparison method is a *paired comparison* whereby each employee in a group is individually compared to the other employees to determine the relative strengths and weaknesses of all employees in the group. In companies that use the comparison method appraisal, employees may tend to be competitive and teamwork tends to be weak.

Rating methods evaluate the performance of individuals separately and do not make comparisons among employees. A type of rating method used is the *rating scale*. In this method, ratings of *5, 4, 3, 2, 1* or *S, A, B, C, D* differentiate levels of performance. Each level is associated with a descriptive phrase.

Here is a **sample rating scale**.
(5) Results significantly exceed expectations
(4) Results exceed expectations
(3) Results meet expectations
(2) Results below expectation
(1) Results extremely below expectation or no results produced

Another rating method is the *checklist*. In a checklist method, managers select a rating from a descriptive list that most closely indicates the evaluation level for the employee.

業績評価プロセスの諸要素：(c)公正な評価方法

　業績評価は次の３つの範疇に分類される：1) 比較による評価，2) 格付け法
による評価，3) 記述式評価。

　比較による評価では従業員が相互に比較される。ひとつの比較による評価の
タイプは「順位法」であり，その場合に管理者は従業員を最高位のパフォーマ
ンス発揮者から最下位のパフォーマンス発揮者までに順序付けする。もうひと
つの比較による評価のタイプは「一対比較法」であり，グループの中の相対的
な強みと弱みを明らかにするため，各従業員は，グループの中の別の従業員全
員と１対１で比較される。比較による評価方法を用いる会社では，従業員は相
互に競争的であり，チームワークは弱い傾向にある。

　格付け法による評価は，個人の業績を個別に評価し，従業員間の比較は行わ
ない。格付け法による評価のひとつは「格付け尺度」である。この評価では
「5, 4, 3, 2, 1」や「S, A, B, C, D」などという評価尺度を用いて業績レベル間
で差をつける。それぞれのレベルには記述的文章が付される。

　次に**格付け尺度の例**を示す。
5　業績が期待を大幅に上回る
4　業績が期待を上回る
3　業績が期待通り
2　業績が期待を下回る
1　業績が期待を大幅に下回る，または業績なし

　もうひとつの格付けによる評価法は「チェックリスト法」である。この方法
においては，管理者は，記述的文章のリストから従業員の評価レベルを最も近
い点数を選択する。

Here is a **sample checklist**.

- [ ] Is always reliable and gets work done on time
- [ ] Is generally reliable, but is sometimes late
- [ ] Requires reminders and does not adequately manage own work
- [ ] Is not reliable and cannot manage own work appropriately

A third method is the *narrative method*. In this method, the manager writes up a detailed description of the evaluated individual's performance.

During the review period, the manager observes the work behavior of the subordinate and takes note of particularly positive and negative performance examples. At the end of the performance review period, the manager then presents an evaluation of performance to the subordinate in a written narrative based upon the observation notes.

The determination of the most appropriate evaluation method may be based upon the evaluation criteria. When evaluating the achievement of goals, the rating scale method is appropriate. When evaluating the demonstration of competencies, the checklist or narrative method is suitable. The comparison method is suitable for both goal achievement evaluation and competency development evaluation, albeit it is a rather time-consuming method.

Note: Performance Review, Performance Appraisal or Performance Evaluation: which term is best? The terms are identical in meaning. All of these terms refer to *Evaluation* which is the final step of the Performance Management process as described above. Generally, a company should select one term and use it consistently.

次のような**チェックリストの例**がある。

■　常に信頼でき，仕事を時間内に終わらせる

■　概ね信頼できるが，仕事が時に遅延

■　催促が必要で，自分の仕事の管理能力が不十分

■　信頼性がなく，自分の仕事の管理能力がない

3番目は「記述式評価」で，管理者が被評価者の業績を詳しく書き込む。

　評価対象期間に管理者は部下の業務上の行動を観察し，特にその中で成功事例と失敗事例をその都度記録する。評価期間の最後に管理者は，部下に対して上記の観察記録に基づいた記述の形で業績評価を示す。

　最も適切な評価方法であるかどうかは，評価基準に依存する。目標の達成度を評価する場合には，格付け法による評価が適切である。コンピテンシーの発揮度合を評価する場合には，チェックリスト法または記述式が目的に合致する。比較による評価は，目標達成評価ならびにコンピテンシー開発評価の双方に対して適切であるが，それはかなり時間のかかる方法である。

注：performance review, performance appraisal, performance evaluation のいずれの用語が最適なのか？　どちらでも意味は同じある。何れも上記に述べてきたように，パフォーマンス・マネジメントのプロセスにおける最後の段階である「評価」を意味する。一般的には，各企業はいずれかひとつを選択し，一貫して同一表現を使用すべきである。

Commentary by the author (Bryan Sherman): Is it true that the performance management practices within Japanese companies are different from the practices of companies that originate from other countries?

I have found that performance management practices, whether in Japanese companies or elsewhere, have converged around similar processes and standards as described in this chapter.

In Japan, as in other countries, it is recognized that outcomes and results derive from the efforts of individual employees working within the collective organization.

That being said, there are comparative differences among companies in the degree to which employees are held personally accountable for achieving goals and for the consequences of unsatisfactory performance.

For example, I understand that in some Japanese companies a lack of achievement of predetermined goals may lead to the decision to demote the non-performing employee to a lower position. However, when I worked as a consultant in the United States and Japanese clients had indicated that they would like to demote an employee due to performance issues, the American consultants would advise against such an action. Rather, the advice was to provide the non-performing employee with a clear evaluation and a performance improvement mandate along with the warning that the lack of improvement may lead to employment termination.

I understand that these differences in the consequences of poor performance are due to different implicit assumptions held about the very

著者（ブライアン・シャーマン）による解説：日本企業におけるパフォーマンス・マネジメントの実践は，他国の企業の実践と異なるというのは本当だろうか？

　日本企業においても他の国の企業においても，パフォーマンス・マネジメントの実践は，本章で述べてきたように，似たようなプロセスと基準に収斂してきている。

　他の国におけると同様に日本でも，成果と結果は組織で働く従業員個々人の努力から生まれるということは認識されている。

　とはいえ，従業員が自らの目標達成に責任を持ち，不満足な成果に対する帰結への責任の在り方には，その程度においてかなりの違いがみられる。

　例えば，何社かの日本企業では，事前に決められた目標が達成できない場合，その成果の芳しくない従業員を降格させるという決定がなされるであろう。しかしながら，私が米国において人事コンサルタントとして勤務していた時の顧客である日本からの駐在員は，業績の問題を抱える従業員を降格させたいという意思を示したが，米人コンサルタント側はそのような対応をしないようにアドバイスをした。むしろ，そのアドバイスは，業績の低い従業員に対して明確な低い評価と業績改善の要求をしっかりと伝えるとともに，その後の改善が見られない場合には解雇につながることがありうることを示すというものであった。

　業績の未達成の帰結におけるこのような違いは，社内における雇用の本質そのものに関わる暗黙の理解に根付くものであると考えられる。日本で

nature of employment within a company. In Japan, there is an enduring implicit assumption that employment is for the long-term. So, a demotion is a way to re-assign an employee to a role whereby he/she can more effectively perform and reinforce learning at the current time in order to once again be promoted in the future over the course of a long-working career at the company.

In the United States, there is an assumption that employment is conditionally based upon the evidence that the assigned work can be completed. Therefore, the advice not to demote an employee is based upon the idea that the demoted employee would become so de-motivated and develop an ill-feeling towards the company that he/she would not be able to complete any other assigned work. Rather, a decision to terminate employment due to poor performance may, in the end, assist the employee to find work elsewhere that is more suitable for the employee's skill set.

In my work as an HR manager and consultant, I have come to understand that concepts of performance management have become somewhat standardized globally. However, underlying assumptions about the significance of performance issues within employment lead to consequences that are not so uniform the world over.

は，雇用は長期的なものであるという長きにわたる暗黙の想定が今も存在する。したがって，降格というものは，同一企業における長いキャリアの中で，将来，再度昇進するために現在，より効率的に成果を出し，学びを強化できる役割に再配置することの一環となっている。

　米国では，雇用というものは与えられた仕事を完全にこなせるという証拠に基づくものであるという想定が存在する。このため，従業員を降格させてはいけないというアドバイスは，降格された従業員はモチベーションが大きく下がり，会社に反感を持ち，他に与えられた仕事をこなせられないという考えに基づいている。むしろ，業績未達成による解雇という決定は，最終的には，その従業員の技能によりふさわしい仕事をその従業員が他で見つけるのを助けることになるであろう。

　人事マネジャーとしてまた人事コンサルタントとしての仕事を通じて，パフォーマンス・マネジメントの考え方は世界中である程度まで標準化されてきたが，他方で，雇用中のパフォーマンスの重要性に対する暗黙の想定とその帰結は世界中でそれほど一様ではない，ということを私は理解するに至った。

References & Suggestions for Additional Reading

Brown, M. (2019), "Understanding Performance Appraisal: Supervisory and Employee Perspectives", in Wilkinson, A., N. Bacon, S. Snell and D. Lepak (eds.), *The SAGE Handbook of Human Resource Management*, Second Edition, Sage, pp. 195-209, Chapter 12.

Cappelli, P. and A. Tavis (2016), "The Performance Management Revolution", *Harvard Business Review* (https://hbr.org/2016/10/the-performance-management-revolution).

Morishima, M. (2008), "Performance Management in Japan", in Varma, A., P. S. Budhwar and A. DeNisi, *Performance Management Systems: A Global Perspective*, Ney York, N.Y.: Routledge, pp. 222-238.

Tse, A. (2016), "Performance and Talent: Essentials of Development Discussions and Plans", in Zeuch, M. (ed.), *Handbook of Human Resources Management*, Springer-Verlag Berlin Heidelberg, pp. 457-482.

さらに学びたい人のための参考文献

CASE STUDY 3.1

Setting Goals for the Fiscal Year With Locally Hired Managers

Question for consideration

Setting goals for the fiscal year cooperatively between managers and employees is an important step within the performance management process. **What should a manager do when he wants the subordinate to work towards achieving even more challenging goals in the coming year?**

Case study detail

Company: Tokyo Electronics, USA
Sano Takeshi, President
Paul Rodriguez, Vice President of Sales
Tom Beck, General Manager of Sales

Tokyo Electronics, USA was established about 15 years ago for selling electrical components in the market in the USA. The company is now headed by **President Sano Takeshi**, along with a limited number of Japanese expatriates who supervise administrative and R&D activities. **Vice President Paul Rodriguez** oversees all sales-related activities for North America.

The company has established an organization to empower locally hired employees who have extensive knowledge of the local market. However, Sano focuses a lot of energy on expressing his vision for how the Sales Department

CASE STUDY 3.1

現地採用管理者とともに年度目標の設定を行う

本事例の着目点

　管理職と従業員の間で協調して年度の目標を設定することは，パフォーマンス・マネジメント・プロセスの重要なステップのひとつである。**次年度，さらに高い目標を達成すべき頑張りを部下に望む場合，管理職は何をすべきだろうか？**

事例の詳細

会社：東京エレクトロニクス・アメリカ社

社長：佐野毅氏

営業担当副社長：ポール・ロドリゲス氏

営業部長：トム・ベック氏

　東京エレクトロニクス・アメリカ社は，米国市場における電気部品の販売会社として約15年前に設立された。同社は現在，**佐野毅社長をトップ**として，管理部門および研究開発の活動を担当するために派遣されている数名の日本人駐在員がいる。**ポール・ロドリゲス副社長**は，北米の全ての営業関連活動を統括している。

　同社は，設立以来，現地市場についての豊富な知識を持つ現地採用の従業員に権限を委譲する組織となっている。しかし，佐野氏は，売上と利益をさらに伸ばすために，営業部門をどのように運営すべきかに関する自分のビジョンを

should be managed in order to drive revenue and profit.

At the beginning of the new fiscal year, Sano endeavors to have goals mutually agreed upon between managers and subordinates. He has also kept in mind that Rodriguez was not satisfied with the former president of the company, who tended to impose goals on his subordinates unilaterally.

Before the start of each fiscal year, Sano holds a budget planning meeting with Rodriguez where he lays out five major target areas for achievement: sales growth, market share, headcount, productivity (measured by sales per employee), and SG&A (Selling, General and Administrative expenses: for example, sales expenses as measured by percentage of sales).

In setting qualitative and quantitative measurements for the targets, the two will have lengthy and detailed discussions. In a recent meeting, for example, they had the following discussion about the targets for the next fiscal year:

Sano: Let's talk about sales growth. Our sales grew only by 1% last fiscal year, so I would like to see 5% growth next fiscal year.

Rodriguez: Amid current dull economic forecasts, a sales growth target of 5% is higher than those of our rivals. Unless our goal is more realistic, we would likely fall short of the target. How about a 2% growth target instead?

Sano: 2% seems too low. Why not set the target at 3%?

Rodriguez: That's still quite a challenge, but I'll do my best to achieve the target by motivating my staff to achieve it as a Department goal.

示すことに心血を注いでいる。

　新年度の初めに，佐野氏は上司と部下の間で相互に合意された目標を持つべく努めている。彼はまた，ロドリゲス氏が，一方的に部下に目標を課す傾向があった前の社長に不満を持っていたことは心にとめている。

　そのため佐野氏は，新しい年度が始まる前に，ロドリゲス氏との予算計画会議を持ち，そこで売上の伸び，市場シェア，人員数，生産性（従業員1人当たりの売上高で算定），および販売管理費（SG&A：例えば，売上高の何パーセントかで算定される売上のための費用）など達成すべき5つの主たる目標領域を詳しく説明する。

　ターゲットの定性的および定量的算定値を設定する際には，この2人は時間をかけて詳細な議論を行うであろう。例えば彼らは，最近のミーティングで次年度の目標について以下のように話し合った。

佐野：売上高の伸びについて話し合おう。昨年度の売上高は1％増だったので，来年度は5％の成長を見たいね。

ロドリゲス：現在の鈍い経済予測の中で，5％の売り上げ成長目標は，私たちのライバル企業の目標数値よりも高いですよ。私たちの目標がより現実的でないと，私たちは目標値を下回ることになりますよ。むしろ，2％の成長目標ではいかがですか？

佐野：2％では低すぎるね。目標を3％に設定してはどうかな？

ロドリゲス：それはまだかなり難しいレベルです。しかし，その目標を達成するために私は最善を尽くします。部局の目標としてそれを達成できるようスタッフに発破をかけます。

Thereafter, Rodriguez held a meeting with **Tom Beck, General Manager of Sales**.

Rodriguez: In my meeting with President Sano, we have agreed to a sales growth target of 3% for the next fiscal year. I would appreciate it if you would coordinate with your staff in order to have detailed plans set up to achieve this goal.

Beck: That's not an easy goal. But I'll ask the manager of each product line to thoroughly review their product portfolio and sales prospects to work towards achieving this ambitious target.

Rodriguez: I know it'll be a challenge. I appreciate all of your efforts.

Learning points

Setting goals through mutual discussion between managers and employees is a crucial element of an effective performance management process. While the employees may feel stress from the high expectations of their superiors, it is acceptable to set high targets for the growth of the company and the individuals as well.

In this case, the push back from the locally hired managers was minimal because we can assume that President Sano and Vice-President Rodriguez have developed a relationship of mutual trust.

Therefore, we can conclude that not only does a company need to have a clear process of performance management in place, it needs to continually reinforce this process through trust, open communication and

　その後，ロドリゲスは，**営業部長のトム・ベック氏**とミーティングを行った。

ロドリゲス：佐野社長との私の会議では，来年度の売上高成長目標3%に合意しました。この目標を達成するために詳細な計画を立てるようスタッフと調整してもらえれば有り難い。

ベック：それは簡単な目標ではありませんね。しかし，私は，この野心的な目標を達成するために，製品ポートフォリオと販売見通しを徹底的に見直すように各製品ラインのマネジャーに依頼します。

ロドリゲス：それが難しいことだということは私も分かっています。あなたの頑張りに感謝します。

学習ポイント

　上司と従業員の間の相互の議論を通じて目標を設定することは，効果的なパフォーマンス・マネジメント・プロセスの重要な要素である。従業員は上司からの高い期待からストレスを感じるかもしれないが，会社と個人双方の成長のために，高い目標を設定することは容認されるであろう。

　今回の事例では，佐野社長とロドリゲス副社長とが信頼関係を築いてきたと考えることができるため，現地採用マネジャーからの反作用は最小限となった。

　したがって，会社はパフォーマンス・マネジメントの明確なプロセスを整備する必要があるだけでなく，信頼，オープンなコミュニケーション，および継続的により高いレベルの目標を達成しようという動因を通じて，

the drive to continually achieve higher level goals.

このプロセスを継続的に強化する必要がある。

CASE STUDY 3.2

Good Results Do Not Always Lead to a Satisfactory Performance Evaluation

Question for consideration

A performance evaluation may include both an assessment of the results of an employee's work as well as the manner in which the work is accomplished. **What should be done to ensure that locally hired managers at the overseas subsidiary of Japanese companies fully understand the basis for the evaluation score?**

Case study detail

Company: Overseas subsidiary of a Japanese company
Yonemura Yoshiro, President
Lou Nicholson, Sales Manager

President Yonemura Yoshiro is in his third year of an expatriate assignment at the overseas subsidiary of his company. The time of year to conduct evaluations of the locally hired managers has come. He is especially troubled over the evaluation of a **Sales Manager, Lou Nicholson.** This is because Nicholson expresses strong likes and dislikes toward certain people, and he has increasingly become distrusted by some of his subordinates. As well, from time to time, he speaks towards expatriates in a manner that is rather aggressive.

Given these circumstances, Yonemura has decided to provide Nicholson with

CASE STUDY 3.2

結果が良かったというだけでは
満足のいくパフォーマンス評価にはならない

本事例の着目点

　業績評価には，従業員の仕事の結果への評価と仕事遂行上の態度への評価の双方が含まれる。**日本企業の海外子会社の現地採用管理職に評価スコアの基本を十分に理解してもらうためには，何をなすべきだろうか？**

事例の詳細
会社：日本企業の海外子会社
社長：米村芳郎氏
セールス・マネジャー：ルー・ニコルソン氏

　米村芳郎社長は，自社の海外子会社に駐在して３年目になる。現地採用の管理職の評価を実施する時期が来た。彼は**セールス・マネジャーであるルー・ニコルソン氏**の評価で特に悩んでいる。これは，ニコルソン氏が特定の人々に対して好悪の感情を強く出すため，彼に対し部下の何人かがますます不信感を募らせているためである。また，時々，彼はかなり攻撃的な態度で駐在員に向かって話すこともある。

　このような状況のもと，米村氏はニコルソン氏を前年より低く評価すること

an evaluation that is lower than the previous year.

Yonemura: As compared to the previous year, your evaluation has gone down from *3: Meets Expectations* to *2: Needs Improvement*. I would like for you to sign this form to acknowledge my evaluation.

Nicholson: Why has my evaluation gone down so much? Please explain the rationale. I can't accept this as an accurate evaluation.

In response, Yonemura explained the abovementioned points regarding Nicholson's demeanor. Nicholson was still not satisfied with Yonemura's explanation and continued to plead his case for a higher evaluation.

Nicholson: I am satisfactorily carrying out my work. My department's performance results have improved since the previous year. Despite this, I cannot understand why my evaluation can be reduced so drastically. I implore you to explain in more clear detail what the actual problem is.

Yonemura: Without a doubt, the results of your department have indeed improved. However, I think that it is equally important to strive to be trusted by your subordinates and to work well with other managers and expatriates from Japan. Accordingly, it is natural to consider these points as important elements at the time of evaluation.

Nicholson: I really can't understand your way of thinking. I can understand that good working relations are important. But, if performance results do not increase, then all is for naught. Therefore, getting results is priority one. Trust and collaborative relations are secondary. If you say that I am not trusted by my subordinates and that I am not working collaboratively with other managers and Japanese expatriates, you should clearly explain the negative

に決定した。

米村：昨年と比較して君の評価は「3：期待通り」から「2：改善を要する」に
下がりました。私の評価を承認して，この書類に署名してもらえますか。

ニコルソン：なぜ私の評価がそんなに下がるんですか？　その根拠を説明して
ください。これを正しい評価として受け入れることはできません。

　これを受けて，米村氏はニコルソン氏の態度に関する上記の点について言及
した。ニコルソン氏は米村氏の説明に満足せず，引き続きより高い評価を要求
し続けた。

ニコルソン：私は自分の仕事を十分に遂行しています。私の部門の業績は前年
より改善しています。それにもかかわらず，私の評価がなぜそれほど劇的に下
げられるのか理解できません。実際の問題が何であるかを，より明確，かつ詳
細に説明してください。

米村：確かに，君の部門の実績は目に見えて向上している。しかし，部下から
信頼され，他の管理職や日本からの海外駐在員と上手く働くことも同様に重要
だと思いますよ。したがって，評価時にこれらの点を重要な要素と見なすのは
当然ですよ。

ニコルソン：私はあなたの考え方がどうしても理解できません。職場の良い人
間関係が重要であることは理解できます。ただ，そうであっても，パフォーマ
ンスの結果が向上しない場合は，全て無意味ではないですか。したがって，結
果を出すことが最優先されるべきです。信頼関係や協力関係は二次的なもので
す。私が部下から信頼されておらず，他の管理職や日本人駐在員と協調的に働
いていないと言うのであれば，それが私の職務の執行に対しどのように悪影響

impact upon the execution of my duties. If indeed there was such a negative impact, then I could be satisfied with this evaluation.

Yonemura found himself in a difficult position given this refutation from Nicholson. Yonemura did not actually take notes of actual facts. Ultimately, he simply explained about two to three points from memory. To this, Nicholson responded.

Nicholson: I don't recall these events. Please tell me in what month, on what day and at what time there was such an occurrence. Tell me also what type of actual impact there was on my work. If you can't do so, I cannot accept this evaluation.

Yonemura: Not writing down notes of these events was my error. However, I am sure that there was a negative impact upon your work . . . .

To bring this discussion to a close, he explained that being trusted by one's subordinates and developing the skills of subordinates is an important element of the work of a manager at this company. However, there was some lingering uneasiness in the relations between President Yonemura and Nicholson for some time thereafter.

Learning points

The conversation between Yonemura and Nicholson illustrates the problems that can occur in performance evaluation discussions.

On the one hand, the evaluator does have the responsibility for clearly explaining the factual basis of an evaluation. President Yonemura's lack of

が及んだのか，明確に説明してください。本当にそのような悪影響があったなら，私はこの評価に納得できます。

　米村氏は，ニコルソン氏からの反論を受けて，困難な立場に立たされた。米村氏は実際には実態を記録していなかった。最終的に彼は，記憶から2〜3の点だけ説明した。これに対して，ニコルソン氏は反論した。

ニコルソン：私はこれらの出来事を思い出せません。何月，何日，何時にそのようなことが起こったのか教えてください。また，私の仕事に対して実際にどのような影響があったのか教えてください。それができなければ，私はこの評価を受け入れることができません。

米村：これらの出来事についてメモを書き留めていなかったのは私のミスです。しかし，私は，これらの点が君の仕事に悪影響を及ぼしていると確信していますよ…。

　この話し合いを締めくくるために，米村氏は，部下から信頼され，部下のスキルを伸ばすことが，同社マネジャーの仕事の重要な要素であると説明した。しかし，その後，米村社長とニコルソンの間では，ぎくしゃくとした関係がしばらく続いた。

学習ポイント

　米村氏とニコルソン氏の会話は，パフォーマンス評価の議論で発生しがちな問題を提示している。

　他方で，評価者は評価の根拠を事実に基づき明確に説明する責任がある。米村社長の具体的な証拠の欠如は彼の評価の説得力を低下させた。

detailed evidence diminished the impact of his evaluation.

However, Nicholson's reaction and continual obstinate attitude towards Yonemura is also evidence of this locally hired manager's lack of interpersonal skills.

We can say that Yonemura's evaluation was problematic not because his judgment was wrong, but because of a deficiency in the evaluation system. In this evaluation system, there is no differentiation being made between performance results (MBO) and the skills and methods followed to pursue such results (competencies). If the company implemented a competency framework, the President could cite an employee's failure to demonstrate the required behaviors in areas such as Staff Development, Trustworthiness and/or Collaboration. With such a competency framework as the basis for evaluation, even when the performance goals are achieved, a critical evaluation of specific competencies can elucidate areas for improvement.

Additionally, when a manager is not satisfied with a subordinate's performance and/or behavior, it is advisable to have more frequent communication with the subordinate in order to express the perceived problems and to seek out improvement before the performance evaluation period begins. Given the nature of the conversation in this case study, we can assume that Yonemura also failed to express his concerns early on to Nicholson. The seemingly sudden nature of Yonemura's critical evaluation may have also triggered Nicholson's defensive posture.

With an improved evaluation structure, more note taking on the actual critical incidents that affect the evaluation and more frequent

　しかし，ニコルソン氏の米村氏に対する反発，および，変わらぬ頑なさもまた，この現地採用マネジャーの対人スキルの欠如を示す証拠である。

　米村氏の評価には，彼の判断が間違っていたためではなく，評価システムの不備に問題があった。この評価システムでは，パフォーマンスの結果（MBO）と，そのような結果を追求するために必要なスキルならびに方法（コンピテンシー）との間に区別は行われていない。もし会社がコンピテンシー・フレームワークを導入していたならば，社長は，人材育成，信頼性，および／または協力関係などにおいて必要とされる諸行動を示すことによって，その従業員の失敗を指摘することができたであろう。このようなコンピテンシー・フレームワークを評価の基礎として使用することによって，パフォーマンス目標が達成された場合でも，特定のコンピテンシーを批判的に評価することで改善の余地がある部分を明らかにすることができる。

　さらに，マネジャーが部下のパフォーマンスや行動に満足していない場合は，パフォーマンス評価期間が始まる前に，気づいた問題点を示し，改善の努力をさせるために，部下とより頻繁にコミュニケーションをとることが求められる。このケース・スタディの会話の内容を考えると，米村氏もニコルソン氏に早くから懸念を表明していなかったものとみられる。米村氏の厳しい評価が一見突然行われたように見えたこともまた，ニコルソン氏の防衛的態度を引き起こすことになったのかもしれない。

　評価制度が改善され，評価に影響を与える実際の重大な出来事が記録され，さらに部下とのより頻繁なコミュニケーションが行われることで，米

communication with one's subordinates, the type of conversation that ensued between Yonemura and Nicholson can be avoided.

In addition, it is advisable to recall that having good interpersonal relations within the workplace is one of the *hygiene factors* referred to within Herzberg's two-factor theory of motivation; good communication is a basic element for improving human relationships.

村氏とニコルソン氏の間で交わされたような種類の議論を回避することができるであろう。

なお，ハーズバーグのモチベーションの2要因論のうちの「衛生要因」（hygiene factor）には，人間関係の良好性が含まれており，人間関係が良くなるための基本的要素として良好なコミュニケーションがあることを理解しておきたい。

Compensation & Benefits

Compensation & Benefits (C&B)

In exchange for labor, companies provide employees with **compensation and benefits (C&B)**. The compensation and benefits package that a company provides to employees is a major factor in the hiring and retention of employees. Developing and handling a compensation and benefits program is a key responsibility of HR managers.

Compensation and benefits are forms of monetary and non-monetary rewards respectively. The term **total compensation (or total rewards)** is used to refer to the combined value of all monetary (salary and bonuses) and non-monetary (benefits) compensation that are provided to employees. (Refer to Figure 4.1.)

Compensation Philosophy

The minimum level of compensation and benefits that companies need to provide is normally stipulated by various labor laws. However, beyond such

CHAPTER 4

報酬と福利厚生

報酬と福利厚生（C&B）

　労働に対して，企業は従業員に**報酬と福利厚生（C&B）**を支給する。報酬と福利厚生の組み合わせは従業員を採用・定着させるために重要な要素である。報酬と福利厚生の制度の構築と運用はHRマネジャーの重要な職務である。

　報酬・福利厚生は金銭的対価と非金銭的対価から構成される。**トータル・コンペンセーション**（または**トータル・リワーズ**）という用語は，従業員に支給される全ての金銭的報酬（給与及びボーナス）と非金銭的報酬（福利厚生）の包括的な価値を指している（図4.1 参照）。

コンペンセーション・フィロソフィー

　会社が従業員に支給しなければならない最低限の報酬と福利厚生は通常，各種の労働法で規定されている。しかし，最低限の法的要求を超える部分の報酬

Total Compensation				
Cash Compensation			Benefits	
Fixed Salary	Allowances	Variable Pay	Standard benefits	Fringe benefits
Company-elected (other than minimum wage which needs to set per minimum wage laws)			Legally required	Company-elected	Company-elected

Figure 4.1   Components of Total Compensation

minimum legal requirements, the determination of compensation and benefits programs is partly analytical and rational and partly creative.

The first step is to consider a **compensation philosophy** to attract, motivate and retain the best employees. This is a high-level statement that guides the development and implementation of the compensation and benefits programs. In essence, the compensation philosophy is a guide to understand how much cost the company is willing to bear to retain its people.

A compensation philosophy may be a written encapsulation of the result of years of actual practice. Or, in the case of new organizations, it may be made deliberately in coordination with executive management. For example, a compensation philosophy may indicate the importance of variable pay versus base pay. In comparison to other companies in the same industry or geographic area, the compensation philosophy may state whether the company wants to provide monetary and non-monetary rewards that are above external market standards, at the market standard or even below external market standards. In the case that the offered salary is below market, the company should be able to make up for the lack of salary with something else of value that would be attractive to employees such as extraordinary learning and development opportunities that cannot be experienced at other companies so easily or benefits not offered elsewhere.

トータル・コンペンセーション				
金銭対価			福利厚生	
固定給	諸手当	変動給	標準的福利厚生	フリンジ ベネフィット
所定 （最低賃金法で決められる最低額を上回る部分）			法定	所定	所定

図4.1　トータル・コンペンセーションの構成要素

と福利厚生制度の決定は，ある程度までは分析的かつ論理的であるが，ある程度までは創造的でなくてはならない。

　先ず，検討すべきは優秀な人材を引きつけ，動機づけし，保持するために必要な**コンペンセーション・フィロソフィー**である。これは，報酬・福利厚生制度を設計し，実施するに際しての高次の表明となる。要するに，コンペンセーション・フィロソフィーは，人材を確保するためにどれだけの費用を負担する意志があるのかを理解するための指針となる。

　コンペンセーション・フィロソフィーは，長年の実践の積み重ねの文書的表現かもしれない。あるいは，設立後間もない企業においては，経営幹部の意向を汲みながら慎重に設計される場合もある。例えば，コンペンセーション・フィロソフィーは，固定給と比較して変動給にどれくらいの重さを置くかを示している場合もある。コンペンセーション・フィロソフィーは，同業あるいは同地域内の他社と比較して，自社の金銭的・非金銭的報酬を外部市場水準より高く設定するか，同レベルに設定するか，あるいはより低めに設定するかを示している場合がある。給与を市場水準より低めに設定する場合には，その給与の不足分は従業員にとって魅力があり価値のある何か，例えば他社では簡単には経験できないような特別な教育訓練機会や他では得られない福利厚生などで補うべきである。

Compensation philosophies differ from company to company due to factors such as, but not limited to, the corporate culture and the values thereof. In companies that focus primarily upon current performance, compensation is closely tied to the results that the individual produces. Such a way of thinking may be referred to as **performance-based compensation.**

In other companies that emphasize loyalty and longevity, compensation may be tied more closely to factors of seniority, rather than the individual results that are produced. In this case, such a way of thinking may be referred to as **entitlement-based compensation.**

Even if a company has a clearly established compensation philosophy, exceptional measures should be taken to account for changing market conditions. Such external market conditions include the current economic climate, changes in the labor market, industry trends and competition for talent.

Components of Monetary Compensation

The monetary compensation that is provided to employees is usually divided into three categories: fixed salary, allowances and variable pay. Let's understand the details of each of these categories.

A. Fixed salary

Fixed salary is provided to employees on regularly scheduled pay days. Fixed salary, also referred to as base pay, is a guaranteed amount of salary that the employee expects to be paid unconditionally. Such fixed salary may be referred to on an annualized, monthly or hourly basis. In some countries, it is customary to discuss fixed salary as an annualized amount (yearly) even though the salary will actually be paid in 12 equal monthly installments. If,

　コンペンセーション・フィロソフィーは多くの場合，企業文化やその中の価値観などを中心とする要因によって企業間で異なる。現行の業績に主眼を置く企業では，報酬は各従業員が生み出す成果と密接に関係している。このような考え方は，**業績連動型報酬**と呼ばれる場合がある。

　従業員の忠誠心や長期勤続を重視する企業では，報酬は各従業員が生み出す成果よりも年功序列要素により強く結びついている場合がある。このような場合，そのような考え方はいわゆる**権利連動型報酬**ということができる。

　しかし，企業が明確なコンペンセーション・フィロソフィーを確立している場合でも，変動する外部市場環境に合わせるべく例外的措置をとることも必要である。そのような外部市場環境には，現下の経済情勢，労働市場の変化，業界の趨勢，それにタレント人材の争奪戦などが含まれる。

金銭的報酬の構成要素

　従業員に支払われる金銭的報酬は通常，3つのカテゴリー（範疇）に分類される。すなわち，固定給，諸手当，それに変動給である。以下で3つのカテゴリーの詳細について説明しよう。

A．固定給
　固定給は定期的に特定の日に従業員に支払われる。固定給は基本給と呼ばれることもあるが，会社が支払いを保証する金額のことであり，従業員はそれが無条件に支払われることを期待する。そのような固定給は年，月，あるいは時間当たりのいずれかで示される。国によっては，固定給は，月ごとに等額で12回支払われるにもかかわらず，年額に換算して論ずることが通例となっていることもある。固定給が勤務した時間による場合には，それは時間給と表現

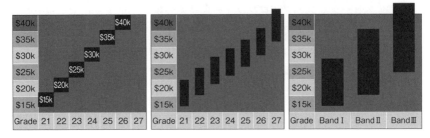

Figure 4.2
Pay Grade Structure Based
Upon a Salary Point

Figure 4.3
Pay Grade Structure Based
Upon a Salary Range

Figure 4.4
Broadband Pay Structure

the amount of payment is based upon actual hours of work performed, then the fixed salary may be quoted as an hourly wage.

In order to determine the fixed salary to pay to each employee, companies may establish a rational salary structure. Additionally, the salary structure may be aligned with a grade structure. Grades within the structure may be differentiated based upon requirements for competencies, experience levels or job functions.

Each grade may be assigned a salary point or a salary range. A salary point is a specific number such as $25,000. (See Figure 4.2.) In this case, all employees assigned to a specific grade are provided the same salary. A salary range is a range from the lowest to the highest salary levels for a particular grade; the specific salary paid to an employee is determined from within the range. For example, a range may be set from $13,000 to $20,000. (See Figure 4.3.)

For further flexibility in determining fixed salary, some companies have stopped using narrowly defined pay grade structures. Instead, pay grades are replaced by a broadband structure in which the range for different grades may overlap and the ranges themselves are rather wide. (See Figure 4.4.)

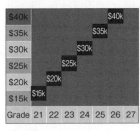

図 4.2
単一の給与額に基づく
報酬等級体系

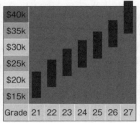

図 4.3
幅のある給与額に基づく
報酬等級体系

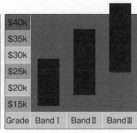

図 4.4
ブロードバンド報酬等級体系

される。

　各従業員に支給される固定給を決定するために，企業は，合理的な報酬体系を設定するであろう。この報酬体系は等級（グレード）体系と連動している。報酬体系の中の等級は，コンピテンシーの資格要件，業務経験値，あるいは職務の種類によって差がつく。

　それぞれの等級は，単一の給与額または幅のある給与額（サラリー・レンジ）で示される。単一の給与額は，例えば 25,000 ドルといった具体的な数値で示される（図 4.2 参照）。この場合，特定の等級に格付けされる全ての従業員は同額の給与が支給される。サラリー・レンジは，特定の等級に対して最低額から最高額にいたるまでの幅（レンジ）を示しており，その幅の中の特定の額が従業員に支給されることになる。例えば 13,000〜20,000 ドルのような幅で示される（図 4.3 参照）。

　固定給決定の自由度をさらに増すために，狭い範囲に設定された報酬等級体系の代りに，ブロードバンドと呼ばれる報酬等級体系を用いる会社もある（図 4.4 参照）。この体系を用いると，従業員の固定給の幅は，幅広いレンジの中で異なる等級が相互に重なり合うような形で設定することが可能となる。

When a salary range associated with a specific grade is wide (as in Figures 4.3 and 4.4), the company management has the discretion to determine the actual salary payment for employees on an individual basis; that is to say that employees who perform the same jobs may actually receive a different salary. Such a structure can be considered fair when the salary determinations account for individually impacted factors such as seniority, past performance results, skills or certifications that have been earned by the employee. Additionally, the structure allows for flexibility to respond to the results of any negotiations that may ensue between the company and employee regarding a salary offer.

However, when it is more desirable to maintain parity among employees at the same grade within the company regardless of the abovementioned individually impacted factors, the salary point in Figure 4.2 is most effective.

The internal salary structure that the company has adopted impacts the discussions to be carried out between the company and candidates for hire at the time of an initial job offer. In companies that maintain a salary structure in accordance with Figure 4.3 or 4.4, salary determinations may ensue through a negotiation process whereby the candidates and companies actively discuss the *best number*. In companies that adopt a salary structure as in Figure 4.2, the first offer from the company is most likely the only and final offer.

B. Allowances

In addition to fixed salary as described above, it is sometimes customary to provide additional allowances to employees. Although there is a social rationale for allowances, companies tend to provide allowances that have favorable tax benefits. Allowances that are sometimes provided include the following:

A) Housing Allowances
B) Family/Children Allowances

　給与額の幅を広く設けることで（図4.3，図4.4参照），企業の管理者は従業員それぞれに支給する給与を決定する際に裁量権を持つことが可能となる。つまり，同様の職務を与えられた従業員に異なる給与が支給されることも可能となる。この報酬体系は，年功，過去の成果，従業員が取得したスキルまたは資格などのような個人による要素を反映している場合には，公平なやり方と見なすことができる。同時に，この報酬体系は，給与の提示をめぐる企業と従業員の間の交渉の結果を反映した柔軟性を持つこともできる。

　しかし，上に記述した個人による要素に違いがあるにもかかわらず，社内で同じグレードの従業員を同等に扱うことがより望ましい場合には，図4.2のような単一の給与額に基づく報酬体系が最も有効である。

　採用に際して会社と求職者の間でなされる対話の仕方は，会社が用いる内部の報酬体系に影響される。報酬体系が図4.3，図4.4のようである企業においては，求職者と雇用者がそれぞれの「最善の数字」を積極的に交渉する中で，給与が決定される。図4.2の報酬体系を用いる企業では，会社が提示する最初の採用条件が唯一，最終のオファーとなる。

B．諸手当

　これまで検討してきた固定給に加えて，従業員に諸手当を支給する場合が通例となっている。諸手当にはそれぞれに社会的合理性があるが，企業は課税所得から控除される項目を諸手当の対象とする傾向がある。よく見られる諸手当には次のような項目が含まれる。

A）住宅手当
B）家族・子供に対する扶養手当

C) Regional Allowances

D) Position Allowances

E) Seniority Allowances

F) Commutation Allowances

(for train, bus, or a fuel allowance for private car)

In some companies/countries, allowances are not typically provided. This is because the provision of allowances may be construed as being discriminatory if the allowance provides certain employees with additional compensation for characteristics or factors that are not directly related to the employee's ability to conduct work for the company. For example, it may seem to be reasonable to provide Family/Children Allowances to employees with young children; however, those employees who choose not to have children may claim that the provision of higher compensation to fellow employees with children is a form of discrimination against those childfree employees.

C. Variable pay

The third component of cash compensation to discuss is variable pay. Variable pay may come in various forms depending upon the compensation philosophy. Herein, we will describe the mechanisms of a typical bonus plan. Generally speaking, a bonus is considered to be *extra* compensation contingent upon achievement of certain targets during the fiscal year as follows: a) Corporate revenue and profit attainment, b) Department performance (quantitative and/or qualitative) and c) Personal achievement. In such a scheme, the executive management first analyzes financial results versus previously determined goals and judges whether the minimum threshold for paying bonuses has been reached in the current fiscal year. If the threshold has been reached, then achievement of department goals will be reviewed and the bonus pool will be divided up accordingly among departments. Lastly, personal achievement is considered in

C）地域手当

D）役職手当

E）年功序列手当

F）通勤手当（電車，バス，または自動車の燃料手当など）

　会社あるいは国によっては，通常，手当が従業員に支払われない場合がある。なぜかといえば，ある手当は，仕事をする能力とは直接関係のない属性または要素に対して特定の従業員に支給されるため，その手当を受け取る資格のない従業員にとっては差別と見なすことができるからである。例えば，小さな子供を持つ従業員に家族・子供への扶養手当を支給することは一見合理的であると見えるかもしれないが，他方で，子供を持たないことを選択した従業員にとっては，子供を持つ同僚に対してより高い手当を支給することは，子供のいない従業員に対する一種の差別となる。

C．変動給

　検討すべき3つ目の金銭的報酬は変動給である。変動給はコンペンセーション・フィロソフィーに基づき，さまざまな形態をとる。ここでは典型的な賞与制度のメカニズムを検討する。一般的には，賞与は，年度内に次のような特定の業績目標値を達成することを条件に「追加的に」支給される報酬である。特定の業績目標には，a) 企業の売上高および利益の達成，b) 部門の成果（量的または／および質的），それに，c) 個人目標の達成，が含まれる。このような仕組みにおいては，経営幹部はまず，財務的成果と事前に定められたゴールとの乖離を分析し，それに基づいて，年度内のボーナス支給の最低限がクリアされたかどうかを判断する。最低限の水準がクリアされていたならば，部門ごとの目標の達成度を検討し，ボーナスの総額（ボーナス・プール）が部門の達成度合いに応じて配分される。そのあと，個人の達成度合いが検討され，各従業員に対する特定のボーナスの支払い額が決定される。

order to determine the specific bonus payments to be made to each employee.

The timing for payment of the bonus also depends upon corporate and cultural factors. For example, in the greater China region, a bonus may be considered as the 13th month's salary payable at the time of the Chinese New Year (Spring Festival). In some Western countries, the annual bonus which is paid in December is sometimes referred to as the *Christmas Bonus* as it is paid out prior to the Christmas holiday.

Advanced Monetary Compensation Schemes

The aforementioned monetary compensation components are typically standard for all levels of employees in the company, from staff to executives. The following are examples of more advanced schemes which differ from company to company and/or different hierarchal levels within a company.

Pension plans

Pension plans may be government-sponsored or company-sponsored. Government-sponsored plans differ from country to country. Company-sponsored pension plans may be classified as **defined benefit (DB) plans** or **defined contribution (DC) plans**. A DB plan is the "traditional" pension plan that provides employees with a pre-determined amount of after-retirement compensation. This kind of plan is becoming rare because the burden of maintaining such a plan is very high for companies. The DC plan is mainly based upon stock and mutual fund investments as determined by employees within their individually managed accounts. Returns are not guaranteed and companies do not retain liability for payment. A 401(k) plan, which originated in the USA and is becoming popular in other countries, is an example of a DC plan.

　賞与の支払い時期も企業の考え方や国の文化により異なる。例えば，中華圏の国々では賞与は 13 カ月目の給与が旧正月（春節）の時期に支給されるであろう。若干の西欧諸国では，12 月に年に 1 度の賞与が支払われ，クリスマス休暇前に支払われるため「クリスマス・ボーナス」と呼ばれることもある。

先進的な金銭的報酬の仕組み

　ここまで述べてきた金銭的報酬の構成要素は，担当職から経営幹部にいたる，会社の全ての職層に通常適応される。以下は，企業により異なり，そして／あるいは，社内の階層レベルの差異により異なる先進的な報酬の仕組みである。

年金制度

　年金制度には公的年金と企業年金がある。公的年金の内容は国によって異なる。企業年金制度には**確定給付型年金（DB）**と**確定拠出型年金（DC）**に分かれる。確定給付型は「従来型」の年金制度で，退職後の支給額が従業員に対して事前に示されている。このタイプの年金制度は，企業にとって制度維持が重荷であるため，少なくなってきている。確定拠出型は主に株式投資と投資信託投資を個人が行い，それを個人口座で管理する。収益は保証されておらず，企業は給付の責任を負わない。米国で開発され，他国でも普及している 401k プランは確定拠出年金の一例である。

Long-term incentive plan

A long-term incentive (LTI) plan is a performance-driven reward that pays compensation based on a three-to-five-year performance period. Performance may be evaluated based upon a variety of indicators. Such indicators may include a comparison of the relative position of the company to an industry peer group of other companies or the projection for long-term growth of the company versus actual results in the performance period. Rewards may be payable in cash, stock, stock options or a combination thereof.

For companies that are publicly traded, the stock option plan is popular because it gives employees a sense of ownership in the company by offering the right to buy a certain amount of company shares at a predetermined price for a specified period. It is intended to align employee interests with those of the management and external stockholders by providing employees a direct incentive to attain financial targets. Stock options are normally part of executive management compensation schemes but may be provided to all employees.

Additionally, employees may be provided the opportunity to purchase stocks directly under an **employee stock ownership plan (ESOP)**.

Retirement pay and severance pay

Another consideration for compensation schemes is whether a company provides additional payment when an employee retires from the company. In some countries, such payments may be mandated by law. In other countries, companies discretionally determine whether they will provide additional payments in the form of retirement pay (retirement allowance) upon departure of the employee from the company. Such payments may be made at a traditionally accepted retirement age such as 60 or 65 or, regardless of age, at any time that an employee leaves the company, provided that a minimum

長期インセンティブ・プラン

　長期インセンティブ (LTI)・プランは，3〜5 年の期間で成果が実現された場合に報酬が支給される成果追求型の報奨制度である。成果はさまざまな指標を用いて評価される。例えば，同業他社と比較した場合の自社の相対的位置づけの比較や自社の長期成長率の予測と結果の比較などがある。報酬は，現金，株式，ストック・オプション，あるいはそれらの組み合わせで支払うことができる。

　上場企業の場合には，ストック・オプション制度が導入されていることが多い。理由は，一定期間内に一定量の会社の株を事前に決められた価格で購入する権利を付与することにより，従業員の経営者意識（オーナーシップ）を高めることが可能だからである。ストック・オプション制度は，業績目標達成に関する直接的なインセンティブを従業員に与えることにより，従業員の利害を経営者や社外株主の利害と一致させることを狙っている。ストック・オプションは通常，経営幹部に対する報酬制度の一環であるが，全従業員に付与することも可能である。

　なお，従業員は**従業員持株制度（ESOP）**を利用して，自社株を購入することが可能である。

退職金と解職手当

　報酬制度で今ひとつ検討すべきは，従業員が退職する際に，企業が追加的支払いを行うかどうかという点である。退職金の支払いが法律で義務付けられている国もある。他方で，従業員の離職の際に，退職金（退職手当）を支払うかどうかは会社の裁量に任されている国もある。そのような支払いは，従業員が60 才あるいは 65 才の通常の退職年齢，あるいは年齢に関係なく最低限の雇用期間を経た後のあるタイミングで会社を辞める時に，支給されることになる。

number of years of employment has been served.

While **retirement pay** may be provided upon the voluntary termination of employment, **severance pay** may be provided when a company unilaterally terminates a person's employment. Severance pay is provided for various reasons. One such reason is to assist a person who has been let go from the company until new work is secured. Additionally, severance pay may be provided in exchange for the former employee's agreement not to sue or otherwise make claims against the company due to the termination of the employment.

Components of Non-Monetary Compensation: Benefits

Benefits normally refer to provisions of value made on behalf of employees and that are recorded as labor costs. However, benefits are not normally paid to employees directly as monetary compensation. Benefits may be divided into two categories: **standard (or customary) benefits** that are either legally required or company-elected and **fringe benefits** which are always company-elected. Standard benefits may include worker's compensation insurance, unemployment insurance, health insurance and **paid time off (PTO)**. The provision of PTO provides for regular payment of salary on days that the employee is excused from reporting to work. Typical categories of PTO include vacation, national holidays and sick leave. Depending upon statutory requirements, PTO may also cover time off to care for family, to vote in an election, to serve jury duty, or other reasons deemed necessary.

Fringe benefits, also referred to as *perks*, include gym membership, use of a corporate car, childcare facilities or special time off. Fringe benefits are *nice-to-have* but are not necessarily required when employees consider whether to join a company.

　退職金は従業員が自ら会社を辞める時に支払われるが，会社側が一方的に雇用を終了する場合には**解職手当**として支払われる場合もある。解職手当は，様々な理由で支払われる。そのような理由のひとつとして，雇用を打ち切られた人に対して新たな雇用を見つけるまでサポートするというものがある。さらに，離職に際して，さもなければ会社を訴えるという元従業員にその訴えをしないという旨の合意を得るのと引き換えに，解職手当が支払われる場合もある。

非金銭的報酬の構成要素：福利厚生

　福利厚生は通常，従業員のための引当金のことであり，労働コストの一部として計上される。しかし，福利厚生は多くの場合，従業員に直接金銭で支払われない。福利厚生は2つのカテゴリーに分けられることがある。すなわち，法定のものと企業独自のものに分けられる**標準的**（または**慣例的**）**福利厚生**と，企業独自のものに限られる**フリンジ・ベネフィット**がある。標準的福利厚生には，労働者災害保険，失業保険，健康保険，ならびに**有給休暇（PTO）**などがある。PTOの規定によって，従業員は仕事から離れた場合のその日数に応じて給与を通常通りに支払われる。PTOの典型的なものとして，休暇・休日，国民的祝日，それに病気休暇などがある。法的に求められる事項により異なるが，PTOはまた，家族の介護のための休み，投票のための休み，陪審員としての義務に伴う休み，あるいは，その他必要と考えられる休みが含まれる。

　フリンジ・ベネフィット，または「パークス」と呼ばれる場合もあるが，それはスポーツ・ジムの会員資格，社用車の利用，子供のための施設，あるいは特別の休暇などを含む。フリンジ・ベネフィットは「あれば有り難い」ものである。しかし，従業員がその会社に入るかどうかを考える際になくてはならな

References & Suggestions for Additional Reading

Gerhart, B. and I. Weller (2019), "Compensation", in Wilkinson, A., N. Bacon, S. Snell and D. Lepak (eds.), *The SAGE Handbook of Human Resource Management*, Second Edition, Sage, pp. 210-237, Chapter 13.

Emerson, L. and Y. Prang (2016), "Compensation and Benefits: Essentials of Benefits", in Zeuch, M. (ed.), Handbook of Human Resources Management, Springer-Verlag Berlin Heidelberg, pp. 931-938.

いものでもない。

さらに学びたい人のための参考文献

Gerhart, B. and I. Weller (2019), "Compensation", in Wilkinson, A., N. Bacon, S. Snell and D. Lepak (eds.), *The SAGE Handbook of Human Resource Management*, Second Edition, Sage, pp. 210-237, Chapter 13.

Emerson, L. and Y. Prang (2016), "Compensation and Benefits: Essentials of Benefits", in Zeuch, M. (ed.), *Handbook of Human Resources Management*, Springer-Verlag Berlin Heidelberg, pp. 931-938.

CASE STUDY 4.1

Target Achievement and Compensation Determination in the Sales Department of an Overseas Subsidiary

Question for consideration

When setting up a new subsidiary overseas, it is important to hire local managers based upon a clearly market-competitive compensation structure. **How should a new company structure its compensation, especially for sales professionals?**

Case study detail

Higashi Haruo, US representative office start-up chief
Sano Satoru, President, Nikkei Equipment, USA (NEUS)
Paul Mills, Vice President

When **Higashi Haruo** was sent to the USA to start the representative office for his manufacturing company in Japan, he was responsible for compiling information about local HR practices, namely the compensation of locally hired managers. From an introduction made via JETRO, Higashi contacted **Sano Satoru, President of Nikkei Equipment, USA (NEUS)**, a sales company located in the vicinity.

President Sano explained the following:

Sano: Here at NEUS, we have a few expatriates from Japan in the Corporate Administrative Department and the Research & Development Department.

CASE STUDY 4.1

海外子会社の営業部門における目標達成および報酬決定

本事例の着目点

　海外に新規子会社を設立する際には，市場で明確に競争力のある報酬体系に基づいて現地の管理職を採用することが重要である。**特に販売担当者に対して，新会社はどのようにその報酬を構築すべきだろうか？**

事例の詳細

米国駐在員事務所（立ち上げ期）所長：東晴夫氏

米国ニッケイ設備機器社長（NEUS）：佐野悟氏

副社長：ポール・ミルズ氏

　東晴夫氏が日本の製造会社の在米駐在員事務所を開設するために派遣された際には，彼は現地の人事慣行，すなわち現地採用の管理職の報酬に関する情報収集の責任を負っていた。JETRO の紹介を得て，東氏は，近隣に立地する販売会社である米国の**ニッケイ設備機器（NEUS）社長の佐野悟氏**に連絡を取ることになった。

　佐野社長は次のように説明した。

佐野：私共の NEUS では，本社管理部門と研究開発部門に日本から数人の駐在員が来ています。しかし，売上高の拡大は，**副社長のポール・ミルズ氏**の指

However, sales development is led by locally hired Americans under the direction of **Paul Mills**, the **Vice President**. As the sales activities are geared towards local businesses, from the outset, we thought that it would be better to leave the sales operations to the locally hired Americans rather than to have the Japanese be directly involved.

In the United States where the management of goals is typical, the goals setting process is indeed important. Even though I leave day to day sales operations to Paul, we set annual goals together in five areas: (1) sales and profit ratio, (2) market share, (3) headcount, (4) productivity (sales per capita), and (5) expenses (expense ratio for sales, etc.).

Upon hearing the abovementioned, Higashi asked the following of President Sano.

Higashi: What kind of compensation can Paul receive if he were to achieve the targets that you just spoke of?

Sano: As we have a long-term and short-term incentive system, Paul can receive a sizable bonus if he were to achieve the goals.

Higashi: Does this mean that Paul's staff members are also eligible for a bonus under this incentive system?

Sano: The incentive system is different for non-managerial staff, but yes, they also can receive a bonus based upon a calculation of corporate and individual performance. The level of achievement is evaluated at the time of the annual appraisals and then the bonus amount is determined. However, at our company, the minimum base salary is pre-determined and the bonus is paid

示のもとで，現地採用のアメリカ人により達成されたものです。営業活動は地元業界向けですので，わが社では当初から，日本人を営業の業務に直接関与させるよりも，現地採用のアメリカ人に任せた方が良いだろうと考えていました。

　目標による管理が一般的である米国では，目標設定プロセスは大変重要です。私は日々の営業の業務をポールに任せていますが，年間目標を5つの分野にまとめています。(1)売上高と利益率，(2)市場占有率，(3)人員数，(4)生産性（1人当たり売上高），(5)経費（対売上高経費率など）がそれです。

　東所長は上記のことを聞いて，佐野社長に次のような質問を行った。

東：あなたが話してくれた目標を達成した場合に，ポールはどのような報酬を受け取ることができますか？

佐野：私たちは長期および短期のインセンティブ・システムを準備しているので，目標を達成することがあれば，ポールはかなりのボーナスを受け取ることができます。

東：その場合に，ポールのスタッフもまたこのインセンティブ・システムの下でボーナスを受ける資格があることになりますか？

佐野：このインセンティブ制度は非管理職員のものとは異なっていますが，その通りです。企業ならびに個人の業績の計算に基づいて彼らもまた，ボーナスを受け取ることができます。達成度は年次考課時点で評価され，それに基づき賞与額が決定されます。ただし，当社では，最低限保障される最低基本給はあらかじめ決められており，ボーナスは基本給に加えて支払われます。

on top of the base.

Higashi: In the case that the targets are not achieved, what kind of rewards can Paul and his staff receive?

Sano: Of course, in that case there is no bonus.

Higashi: I can understand the mechanism for compensation. How do you determine the appropriate salary standard?

Sano: When the work of any department is assigned to locally hired managers, it is advisable to research the average salary levels offered within the industry. Consulting companies and headhunters have such data. The actual salaries of those staff who work below any manager can be determined by that manager. Even if you have to pay a high salary, it is quite important to hire top talent.

Learning points

In order to effectively tap into the local markets where the overseas subsidiaries are located, it is advantageous to hire local managers and staff who understand the customs and needs of local customers.

Additionally, it is important to align compensation incentives with the expectation in the local market. In many cases this means that the variable bonus and other incentives may make up a large percentage of total compensation.

While Japanese companies may rely upon locally hired sales personnel to bring in new business, the expatriates from Japan may retain the accountability for implementing and managing the HR system. Therefore,

東：目標が達成されなかった場合，ポール氏とそのスタッフはどのような報奨金を受け取ることができますか？

佐野：もちろん，その場合にはボーナスは出ません。

東：報酬の仕組みは理解できました。適正な給与水準をどのように決定しますか？

佐野：部門の仕事を現地採用のマネジャーに任せる場合は，業界内で支給されている平均給与水準を調査することをお勧めします。コンサルティング会社やヘッドハンターはそのようなデータを持っています。マネジャーの下で働くスタッフの給与は，マネジャーによって決定されます。高い給料を払ってでも，最高の才能を雇うことは非常に重要です。

学習ポイント

海外子会社が所在する現地市場に効果的に参入するためには，現地の顧客の慣習やニーズを良く分かっている現地の管理職やスタッフを採用することは好都合である。

さらに，報酬のインセンティブを現地市場での期待水準に合わせることが重要である。多くの場合，これは変動ボーナスやその他のインセンティブが総報酬の大きな部分を占めることを意味する。

日本企業は，現地採用の営業担当者に新規事業への参入を頼ることになるであろうが，他方で，日本からの駐在員は人事制度の実施と管理に関する責任を持つことになる。したがって，駐在員は採用候補者を面接し，選

the expatriates should be capable of interviewing and selecting people to hire. Then, they need to be able to communicate effectively with locally hired employees to manage performance through a goals setting and feedback process. Additionally, expatriates need to understand the compensation system and assess whether locally hired employees are satisfied or not with their level of compensation.

抜できる目利き力を持つ必要がある。次に，目標設定とフィードバック・プロセスを通じて業績を管理するために，現地採用の従業員と効果的にコミュニケーションを取れなければならない。さらに駐在員は報酬制度を理解し，現地採用の従業員がそれぞれの報酬水準に満足しているかどうかを見極める必要がある。

Career Development Planning & Employee Development

What Is a Career?

Over the course of one's working life, a person will carry out multiple roles in a variety of positions in different locations within one organization or across various organizations.

When such roles and positions are connected within a common area of pursuit and distinguished by related accomplishments, we can say that the person is following a particular career. While many people may work in similar jobs, a career is unique to each individual.

Careers follow different trajectory patterns. Some careers are seemingly vertical in that the worker may be promoted in an organizational hierarchy to increasingly higher positions of responsibility and authority within one functional area, such as sales or finance. Other careers may be horizontal as they seem to expand outward, whereby the worker attains a variety of experiences across different functional areas. Still, sometimes a career may be

キャリア・ディベロップメント・プラニング と人材育成

キャリアとは？

　自らの職業人生において，個人は，同じ組織内または複数の組織の様々な立場や場所で，数多くの役割を遂行する。

　そうした異なる役割や立場が，共通する職能分野において際立った成果に裏付けられている場合に，その個人は特別なキャリアを形成しているといえよう。複数の人がたまたま同様の仕事をしていても，個々人のキャリアには独自性があるのだ。

　キャリアは異なる経路パターンをたどる。あるキャリアは縦の経路をたどっているように見える。その場合，従業員は販売や財務などの単一の職種内の組織階層をより責任と権限のあるポジションへと昇進する。また，あるキャリアは横の経路をたどりながら拡大しているように見える。その場合，従業員は異なる機能分野（職種）での経験を積んでいく。しかし，時には，キャリアは，同じ職種の同じポジションに留まる場合もある。この場合には，従業員は，

characterized by work in the same functional area at the same position. In such a case, the worker may seem to have plateaued in career development, but the worker may be satisfied by the opportunity for deepening their skill and knowledge via focused experiences. In reality, a 40-to-50-year working career may demonstrate a combination of career trajectory patterns.

Career Development Planning

Career development planning is the deliberate consideration of one's anticipated career trajectory.

Career development planning may be conducted in steps as follows:

Step 1. Recognizing your preferences

Recognizing your preferences is to introspectively consider your career choices. Such choices include the selection of the type of work you like or dislike (i.e., analytical work, creative work, physical labor, to be interactive or solitary, etc.), consideration of the conditions that are most ideal (i.e., active or sedentary, full of travel or not, compensation level expectations, etc.), and identification of the unique contribution that you want to make through your efforts.

Preferences that affect career choices are sometimes referred to as **career anchors**.

Step 2. Researching opportunities

Upon conducting an inventory of personal preferences, it is then useful to research the existing opportunities towards which you would like to strive. In this case, a desirable opportunity may be a position currently held by somebody else in the same company or at another company. Or, if there is no

キャリア形成が停滞したと思うかもしれないが，焦点を絞った経験を積むことで自らの技能や知識を深化させる機会を得ることに満足することもある。実際には，キャリアは40年から50年に及ぶものであり，各種の経路パターンを含むものである。

キャリア・ディベロップメント・プラニング

　キャリア・ディベロップメント・プラニング（CDP）とは，個々人が期待するキャリア・パスを意図的に構想することである。

　キャリア・ディベロップメント・プラニングは次のような順を追って行われる。

ステップ1．自らの選好を把握する

　自らの選好を把握するということは，キャリアのための選択を内省的に考慮することである。そのような考慮には，自らがしたい，あるいはしたくない仕事のタイプは何か（例えば，分析的な仕事，創造的な仕事，肉体労働，他人と交わるものか否かなど），最も理想的な条件とはどういうものか（例えば，活動的なものか否か，出張が多い業務か否か，給与水準の期待値，など），さらには業務を通じて実現したい独自の貢献は何かなどが含まれる。

　自らのキャリアのための選択に影響を及ぼす選好の軸を，**キャリア・アンカー**と呼ぶことがある。

ステップ2．機会を模索する

　自らの選好軸を色々と検討した後ではじめて，自分が理想に向かって努力できる現実的な機会を探ることは有益である。この場合の望ましい機会とは，現在勤務している会社または別の会社で，他の社員が従事しているポジションかもしれない。あるいは，既存のポジションがない場合には，新たなポジション

pre-existing position, an opportunity may be the chance to mold and create a new position or area of pursuit.

Step 3. Recognizing gaps between one's current capabilities and the requirements for desired subsequent opportunities

After completing the abovementioned steps, it is now important to start some concrete planning by firstly considering the gaps between your current working situation and desired subsequent opportunities. It is necessary to ask yourself whether the new opportunity would be within your reach given your current level of education, demonstrated experience and knowledge. Furthermore, it is helpful to envision how someone in a position of authority to offer you a new opportunity may, at the current time, judge your qualifications for the new position.

Step 4. Filling identified gaps with personal development efforts

The final step of career planning is to fill such gaps with some type of effort for personal development. This may include any of the following combination of activities: conducting internet-based research, reading up on a topic in order to develop additional knowledge, attending an external seminar, networking to learn from others, receiving a formal degree, receiving coaching and/or learning via on-the-job-training.

Sometimes, however, the next opportunity in one's career may seemingly appear without forewarning or preparation when an acquaintance asks for your support and involvement or otherwise provides helpful unexpected advice. Therefore, while the abovementioned career planning process is advisable, career development should be approached flexibly and with an open mind.

または追求したい分野を構想し，生み出す機会となるかもしれない。

ステップ３．現在の仕事能力と望ましい今後の機会に求められる資格要件との差を認識すること

　上述のステップを経た後，自らの仕事の現状と将来の望ましい機会と間に存在するギャップをまずは検討し，具体的に計画を立て始めることが重要である。自分の現在の教育レベル，経験，知識が，新たなポジションに十分に到達可能か否かを自問自答すべきである。さらに，このギャップを把握するには，次の機会を与える権限を持つ人が，現時点における自分の資格要件が新たなポジションに相応しいかどうかをどのように評価しているかを予想することは有用である。

ステップ４．上で識別されたギャップを自己啓発の努力により埋める

　キャリア・プラニングの最終ステップとして，上述のギャップを補うための何らかの自己啓発の努力が必要となる。このプロセスには以下の各種の活動のいずれをも含む。すなわち，ウエッブ検索による調査の実施，特定の分野に関して不足している知識を得るための読書，社外のセミナーへの参加，他の人から学ぶためのネットワークづくり，学位取得，コーチングの受講や OJT を通じての学習などがある。

　しかし，時には，個々人のキャリアの次の機会が，前触れもなく，あるいは準備もしていない状態で，一人の知り合いから助けや協力を求められて始まることもあるし，あるいはそうでなくその人から有用で思いがけないアドバイスをもらって始まることもある。したがって，上述のキャリア・プラニングのステップは推奨されるが，一方で，キャリア開発は柔軟かつ強い先入観を持たずに取り組む必要がある。

Career Planning as a Corporate HR Initiative

As described in the previous sections, a career and its trajectory are unique to each individual. However, the practice of career planning may be an integrated part of the HR system within a company whereby an individual employee along with their direct supervisor and/or HR representative think towards their future together. Companies that integrate career planning with other elements of HR, such as performance management, succession planning and organizational development, recognize that the individual needs and aspirations of employees should be addressed in order to retain talented employees over the long run. In other words, career planning as an HR process is the effort to align corporate development goals with individual needs and aspirations.

When career planning becomes an internal HR initiative, *Step 2. Researching opportunities* (see above.) may be carried out as an activity for helping employees to envision as many growth opportunities within the company or corporate group structure as possible, in order to maximize the contribution of the employee to the corporate goals. When career planning is not conducted as an HR initiative, there is a risk that individuals will not envision how to continually contribute to the company over the long-term; in turn, talented employees who are necessary for the company may seek their next opportunity elsewhere.

Employee Development Interventions

Employee development as an HR activity is the planning and execution of interventions to provide employees with opportunities for expedited growth and maturity to hasten the achievement of corporate goals. Furthermore,

企業による人事施策としてのキャリア・プラニング

　前項で説明したように，キャリアとその経路は個々人により異なる。しかし，キャリア・プラニングの実践は企業の人事システムの一環である場合もあり，その場合，個々の従業員はその直属の上司や人事部の担当と共に自分たちの将来について考えをめぐらす。キャリア・プラニングを，パフォーマンス・マネジメント，後継者計画，組織開発などのような人事の要素に組み込んでいる企業では，優秀な従業員を長期にわたり定着させるために，従業員個々人の欲求や希望に応えるべきであると認識している。言い換えれば，人事施策としてのキャリア・プラニングは企業の成長目標と個々人の欲求や希望とを適合させるための工夫のことなのである。

　キャリア・プラニングが企業内人事施策である場合，「ステップ2. 機会を模索する」（上記参照）ということは，従業員が企業内，あるいは企業グループ内で出来る限り多くの成長機会を見込めるよう支援する行為として実施され，それを通じて従業員の企業目標への貢献が最大化されることになる。キャリア・プラニングが人事施策として実施されない場合には，従業員が会社に対して長期的にどのようにして継続的に貢献するかを見出せなくなるリスクがある。そして，その結果，会社に必要な優秀人材が次の機会を社外に求めることとなる。

従業員育成支援策

　人事活動としての**従業員育成**は，企業の目標達成を促進するために従業員の早期の成長・成熟の機会を提供するための支援策を計画し実施することである。さらに，このような支援策が，従業員にとって現在のスキルとキャリア願

when such interventions serve employees to fill the gaps between their current skills and requirements for fulfilling their career aspirations, the employee may appreciate the value of continuous work within the company.

Employee development interventions require time and financial resources that company leaders may be reluctant to invest, especially if it is believed that employees who benefit from such interventions may quit and move to other organizations. However, the very lack of development interventions inside of a company may signal employees to seek opportunities elsewhere. Therefore, the planning and provision of employee development interventions is an essential element for the long-term relations between companies and their employees.

Selecting Development Interventions

Nowadays, companies may select a variety of development interventions to help employees grow and mature to expand their capacity to perform. Interventions may be group-oriented or individual-oriented. The intervention may be mediated by a facilitator, trainer or coach who may be a colleague from within the company or an external professional. Or the learning may be self-led by the learning participants themselves.

Here is a sample of some widely used development interventions (See Figure 5.1.):

(Interventions in alphabetical order)
Classroom training

Classroom training is the traditional training method whereby participants gather in a physical setting together away from the regular workplace in order to focus their learning upon the subject matter at hand. Classroom training may provide a forum for multiple activities including lecture, facilitated

望のために必要な資格要件との間のギャップを埋めることになる場合，従業員
はその企業で継続して働く価値を実感することとなる。

　従業員育成支援策には時間ならびに資金という資源が必要だが，経営者はこ
うした投資に消極的になる可能性がある。これは特にそうした支援を享受した
従業員が退社し，他企業に移る可能性があると考えられる場合である。しか
し，企業内で育成支援策が欠如していると，そのこと自体が，従業員に対し他
企業に雇用機会を求めることを促進するかもしれないのである。したがって，
従業員育成支援策を作成し提供することは，企業と従業員の間の長期的な関係
にとって必要不可欠な要素となる。

従業員育成支援策の選択肢

　今日，企業は，従業員の成長・成熟を促し，職務遂行能力を向上させるため
の各種の従業員育成支援策を選択することができる。こうした支援策には複数
の社員を対象にするものもあれば，個々の社員を対象にするものもある。支
援策はファシリテーター（進行役），トレーナー，またはコーチにより実施さ
れるが，彼らは社内の同僚である場合もあれば，外部の専門家である場合もあ
る。あるいは，その学習は，参加者自身による自学自習の場合もある。

　次に示されているのは，広範に導入されている従業員育成支援策の一例であ
る（図5.1参照）：

（支援プログラム─アルファベット順）
室内座学研修
　室内座学研修は伝統的な訓練方法で，参加者はそれぞれの通常の職場を離れ
て一堂に会し，特定の課題に焦点を合わせて共に学ぶ。この研修では，講義，
ファシリテーターを入れての討論，アクション・ラーニング，自己反省などの
多様な活動の場を提供することができる。

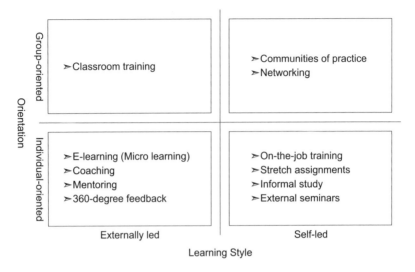

Figure 5.1 Sample of Employee Development Interventions

discussion, action learning and introspection.

Coaching

Coaching may be provided in an effort to help the person being coached to recognize their own points of learning, attain new levels of understanding and increase their motivation for overcoming challenges to optimize their work performance; coaching may be provided on a peer-to-peer basis or conducted by a professional who is experienced, and may be certified as a coach.

Communities of practice

Communities of practice refer to a group of people that engage together in learning and knowledge sharing around a common topic or pursuit of knowledge. Within such communities, members may possess disparate levels of experience, knowledge and insight. Therefore, the members shall take on alternating roles as teachers and learners.

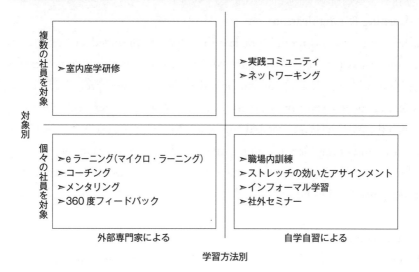

図5.1　従業員育成支援策の例

コーチング

コーチングは通常，コーチングを受ける人をサポートすることを通じて，彼らがそれぞれの学習すべきポイントを識別し，新たな理解度に到達し，さらに仕事のパフォーマンスを最適化するために課題を克服するモチベーションを高めるよう手助けする。コーチングは同僚間で行われる場合もあるが，他方で，経験豊かで，同時にコーチの資格を有する専門家により実施される場合もある。

実践コミュニティ

実践コミュニティとは，共通のテーマや知識の追求を目指して共に学習し，知識の共有を図るグループのことを指している。このような共同体は，テーマによって異なるレベルの経験，知識，洞察力をもったメンバーでしばしば構成される。そのため，メンバーは時には教える側の役割を果たし，時には学ぶ側の役割を果たすことになる。

E-learning & microlearning

E-learning refers to modules of learning that are provided to learners via computer-based technologies. While the content of an e-learning program is developed by an external content provider, the e-learning process can occur whenever or wherever the learner has access to a computer or device upon which the material can be viewed and heard. Microlearning refers to a learning process containing *short* learning activities which are normally provided by e-learning technologies and that range from a few seconds up to a duration of approximately 15 minutes.

External seminars

External seminars are non-degreed learning opportunities whereby people from different employment backgrounds gather to listen to, and interact with, a presenter who has experience and knowledge within the topic field. External seminars typically range from a couple of hours to a few days in length. Seminars may also be provided virtually through web-conferencing technologies.

Informal study

Informal study refers to a wide range of activities whereby the learner pursues knowledge autonomously. Informal study is characterized by daily research, reading, and thinking regarding topics in a field of interest. In this way, the learner tries to attain understanding that is up-to-date and relevant for responding to changes in the external environment.

Mentoring

Mentoring refers to a learning relationship between two people with different levels of experience whereby the person in the mentor role provides the learner with developmental support for identifying personal issues and overcoming challenges. A mentor may use similar processes as a coach. However, a mentor

eラーニングおよびマイクロ・ラーニング

　eラーニングとは，コンピューターを利用した技術により提供される学習の各モジュールのことである。eラーニングのプログラムのコンテンツは外部のプロバイダーにより開発されるが，他方で，学習者がコンピューターや端末などにアクセスし，そのコンテンツを見たり聞いたりできる場合には，何処でも何時でもeラーニング・プロセスが発生する。マイクロ・ラーニングとは，通常，eラーニング技術によって提供される数秒から15分程度の「短い」時間の活動の学習プロセスのことを指している。

社外セミナー

　社外セミナーとは，学位取得と無関係の学習機会のことであり，その場では異なる職業の人達が特定分野の経験や知識を持つ講師から話を聞き質疑応答を行う。社外セミナーは通常，数時間から長くて数日にわたり開催されるのが通常である。社外セミナーはまた，ウェブ・カンファレンス技術を用いてヴァーチャルに提供されることもある。

インフォーマル学習

　インフォーマル学習は，学習者が自主的に知識を追求する様々な学習活動を意味する。インフォーマル学習は，興味ある分野のトピックについて探索し，読書し，そして考えることである。このようにして，学習者は，外部環境における変化に対応するための最新かつ適切な理解を得ようとしている。

メンタリング

　メンタリングとは異なるレベルの経験を持つ二人の間の学習活動であり，メンターの役割を果たす側は，学習者が問題点を認識し課題を克服できるよう，学習者に対し，問題点を識別し，その課題を克服できるように育成のためのサポートを与える。メンタリングにおいてはコーチングと同様のプロセスを用い

may also provide advice and personal insight in a less objective manner than a coach in order to provide support to the learner from the mentor's own past experience.

Networking

Networking is the act of meeting new people in a professional context. Networking is not regularly associated with a learning purpose; however, the act of networking to expand one's connection with a community of peers as a form of *social capital* may lead to subsequent learning opportunities.

On-the-job training (OJT)

OJT is a learning process that recognizes the benefit of *learning by doing* rather than by simply observing or studying through books prior to conducting a set of tasks. When a person learns via OJT, it is recognized that output may not be perfect nor even acceptable at first; rather, through repetition and learning from making mistakes, the learner will ultimately be able to improve performance. Therefore, it is prudent to consider what kind of work OJT is appropriate for and what work should be learned more fully outside of the regular work environment.

Stretch assignments

A stretch assignment provides the learner with opportunities for growth and new insights through challenging experiences for handling tasks beyond the employee's current level of capability. By encouraging learners to *step out of one's comfort zone*, it is expected that learners should emerge more confident, competent and mature.

360-degree feedback

360-degree feedback is a tool for providing learners with insight about

るかもしれない。しかし，メンターは同時に，コーチとは異なりそれほど客観的でない方法で，自分の過去の経験から学習者をサポートするために，アドバイスや個人的な識見を伝えることもある。

ネットワーキング

ネットワーキングとは，仕事と関連する場面での，これまでとは異なる人たちとの出会いの活動を指している。ネットワーキングは通常，学習活動とは結びつけられてはいない。しかし，「ソーシャル・キャピタル」（社会的関係資本）の一形態として同類の人達との関係を拡大するためのネットワーキング活動は，後の学習機会に結び付くかもしれない。

職場内訓練（OJT）

OJTは，一連の課業（task）を遂行する前にただ単に観察したり本で学んだりするよりも，「実践により学ぶこと」の利点の認識に基づく学習プロセスである。人がOJTを通じて学習する際には最初のうちは出来上がったものが不完全であったり，受け入れがたいものであったりすることは，十分ありうることである。むしろ学習者は反復と失敗から学ぶことを通じて，最終的に成果を向上させることになるであろう。したがって，どのような仕事がOJTに適しているのか，またどのような仕事の場合に通常の仕事環境を離れてより周到に学ぶべきかを検討することは賢明なことである。

ストレッチの効いたアサインメント

ストレッチの効いたアサインメントは，学習者が挑戦的な経験を通じて成長と新たな視点を得るための機会を提供する。その経験は，学習者の現時点における能力を超える課業に取り組むというチャレンジをさせる。「自らのコンフォート・ゾーン（快適範囲）から抜け出す」ように促すことで，学習者はより大きな自信・能力・成熟度を身に付けた状態となることが期待されている。

360度フィードバック

360度フィードバックは，学習者に自らが行う意思疎通，相互交流，あるい

how their communication, interactions and behaviors impact others. With responses from multiple individuals in different relative positions to the learner (i.e., superior, colleague and subordinate), the 360-degree feedback provides the evaluated learner with a report containing quantitative and qualitative feedback.

When companies devise management and leadership development programs, a combination of multiple interventions as described above are employed in order to fast-track the learning and development of the participants.

Commentary on career planning and employee development interventions in Japanese companies

The topic of employee development interventions as presented in this chapter should be familiar to Japanese readers; Japanese companies have traditionally put emphasis on the development of individual capabilities for the long-term. In fact, the development of individuals is highly valued within the corporate philosophy of many companies.

However, the concept of career planning as an HR activity replete with mutual communication between the company and employees may not be as well recognized in Japanese companies. This is because, for many years since the end of WWII and the subsequent era of rebuilding, the company has planned for its future needs and unilaterally determined how employees should work within the company in order to achieve corporate goals; such planning has been predicated upon the assumption of life-time employment.

Nowadays, as the labor market in Japan is becoming as dynamic as it is overseas, employees may not automatically envision their long-term

は行動が他人に及ぼす影響を考察するための洞察力を提供する手段となる。学習者から見て異なる立場の人達（すなわち上司，同僚，部下）から回答を得ることで，360度フィードバックは被評価者である学習者に量的・質的なフィードバックを含むリポートを提供する。

　企業が経営管理及びリーダーシップの開発プログラムを企画する際には，上述の複数の支援策を各種組み合わせて，参加者の学習及び育成を加速するために導入される。

日本企業のキャリア計画および従業員の育成支援策に対する解説

　本章で示された従業員育成支援策に関するトピックは，日本の読者にはよく知られたことかもしれない。日本企業は従来から長期にわたる従業員個人の能力開発に力点を置いてきた。実際，個人の能力開発は，多くの企業の経営理念において極めて重要視されてきた。

　しかし，会社と従業員の間の双方向のコミュニケーションを伴う人事活動としてのキャリア計画の概念は，日本企業の中ではそれほど認識されていないかもしれない。というのも，第二次世界大戦の終結後，ならびにそれに続く復興期において，会社は，将来のニーズのために計画をし，会社の目標を達成するために一方的に会社の中で従業員がどのように働くべきかを決定した。そのような計画は，終身雇用の想定に基づいて立案されたものである。

　今日では，日本の労働市場が海外におけるように流動性が高くなってきているため，従業員は，定年までの一企業における長期のキャリアを当然

career with one company until retirement. We predict that, in order to retain and nurture their best employees, HR departments in Japanese companies will need to initiate more career planning discussions with employees as a means to envision a future of work together. It goes without saying that, at the overseas subsidiaries of Japanese companies, such career planning initiatives are essential for attracting, retaining and developing local talent.

References & Suggestions for Additional Reading

Hildebrand, U. (2016), "Performance and Talent: Essentials of Succession Planning", in Zeuch, M. (ed.), *Handbook of Human Resources Management*, Springer-Verlag Berlin Heidelberg, pp. 593-614.

Hughes, C. and M. Byrd, (2015), "Career and Performance Management", *Managing Human Resource Development Programs: Current Issues and Evolving Trends*, Palgrave Macmillan, pp. 97-110, Chapter 7.

Dickmann, M. and Y. Baruch (2011), "Managing careers: individual and organizational perspectives", *Global Careers*, Routledge, pp. 51-74, Chapter 3.

Schein, E. and J. Maanen (2013), *Career Anchors: The Changing Nature of Work and Careers*, Wiley.

のこととして想定することはないであろう。最優秀人材を確保し，育成するためには，日本企業の人事は将来の仕事をお互いに見通すために，従業員との間でキャリア計画に関する話し合いをより積極的に進める必要があろう。言うまでもなく，日本企業の海外子会社においても，そのようなキャリア計画の施策は，現地の優秀人材の引き付け，確保，そして育成のために不可欠なものである。

さらに学びたい人のための参考文献

Hildebrand, U. (2016), "Performance and Talent: Essentials of Succession Planning", in Zeuch, M. (ed.), *Handbook of Human Resources Management*, Springer-Verlag Berlin Heidelberg, pp. 593-614.

Hughes, C. and M. Byrd, (2015), "Career and Performance Management", *Managing Human Resource Development Programs: Current Issues and Evolving Trends*, Palgrave Macmillan, pp. 97-110, Chapter 7.

Dickmann, M. and Y. Baruch (2011), "Managing careers: individual and organizational perspectives", *Global Careers*, Routledge, pp. 51-74, Chapter 3.

Schein, E. and J. Maanen (2013), *Career Anchors: The Changing Nature of Work and Careers*, Wiley.

CASE STUDY 5.1

An Unwelcome Offer for a Position Transfer

Question for consideration

Providing employees with the opportunity to have various experiences across different positions within a company is typically assumed to be an effective method for developing the employee's skills and knowledge. **What happens when the intention of the company to provide such opportunities does not align with the personal vision of the employee?**

Case study detail

Company: Tozai Manufacturing Company, Inc. Canada

Suzuki Tsuyoshi, President

Ed Chan, Assistant Manager, Manufacturing Department

Over the course of his working career, **President Suzuki Tsuyoshi** of Tozai Manufacturing Company, Inc. Canada had various experiences across different departments within Japan and overseas. He thought that it would be important for local staff to similarly experience various departments as an element of their development. One day, he called **Ed Chan, Assistant Manager, Manufacturing Department** to his office for a discussion.

Suzuki: You have been highly evaluated within your work in the Manufacturing Department. And I am quite satisfied with the results you are producing.

CASE STUDY 5.1

ポジション異動という歓迎されない提案

本事例の着目点

　会社内の異なるポジションで様々な経験を積む機会を従業員に提供することは，通常，従業員のスキルと知識を向上させるための効果的な方法と考えられている。そのような機会を提供しようという会社の意図が，従業員個人の思いとかみ合わない場合，どうなるのだろうか？

事例の背景
会社名：カナダ東西製作所株式会社
代表取締役社長：鈴木剛氏
製造部副部長：エド・チャン氏

　これまでのキャリアを通じて，カナダ東西製作所株式会社の鈴木剛社長は，国内外の異なる部署で様々な経験を積んできた。彼は現地のスタッフも同様に，能力開発の要素として様々な部署を経験することが重要であると思っている。ある日，彼は話があるので自分のオフィスまで来るよう，**製造部副部長**である**エド・チャン氏**に電話をした。

鈴木：君は製造部門での仕事で高く評価されてきたよね。また私も，君の貢献による仕事成果には大いに満足している。さらに君は，弁が立つ。現在，人事

Furthermore, you are an effective communicator. As there is currently an opening in the HR Department for the HR Manager position, I think you should move into HR.

Chan: Such a position is out of my area of expertise. But since you are making this request of me directly, please give me some time to think this over. I will consult with my family and friends.

Suzuki: Okay. I understand.

Some time passed and the two spoke again.

Chan: President Suzuki, I appreciate that you had approached me directly with this opportunity. However, I am an engineer who has worked only in the Manufacturing Department until now. If I were to transfer to the HR Department, I would have to learn the work from the very beginning.

Suzuki: So, are you really that opposed to the HR Manager position?

Chan: Regrettably, I don't think I can do it.

Suzuki: Hmm . . . that is truly regrettable.

Learning points

In Japan, it is typical for employees to enter the company and experience various positions in different departments over the course of their working career as a means for expanding one's skills and knowledge. Of course, such a notion itself is not unique to Japan. However, the reason that such

部に部長ポストの空きがあるので，そちらに異動してくれないかな。

チャン：そのようなポジションは私の専門外の仕事です。でもせっかくの鈴木社長からのご依頼ですので，少し考えさせてください。家族や友人とも相談してみます。

鈴木：そうですね。では，よろしく。

　しばらく時間が経過し，二人はまた話し合いを持った。

チャン：鈴木社長，あなたがこのチャンスを直接，私に下さったことに感謝します。しかし，私は今まで製造部門だけで働いてきた一介のエンジニアです。もし私が人事部に異動するとしたら，一から仕事を覚えなければなりません。

鈴木：それだからといって，君は本当に人事部長のポジションを断るつもりなのか？

チャン：残念ですが，私にはその仕事が務まるとは思えません。

鈴木：うーん…それは本当に残念だ。

学習ポイント

　日本では，従業員は入社してからの長いキャリアの中で，スキルや知識を伸ばすための手段として，異なる部署で様々な役職を経験するのが一般的である。もちろん，そのような考え方自体は日本独自のものではない。しかし，このような人事異動が日本国内では許容され，海外子会社の外国

personnel transfers are acceptable within Japan and questionable among non-Japanese employees at overseas subsidiaries is due to a difference in the implicit understanding about the very basis of employment. In Japan, the implicit understanding about the expectation of *lifetime employment* (or more accurately *continual employment until retirement age*) enables companies to enact position transfers without much pushback from employees. In Japan, employees understand that the company will require employees to accept changes in working conditions (i.e., location or function) from time to time; the string of various working experiences forms the employee's career.

Outside of Japan, even at the overseas subsidiaries of Japanese companies, it is rare for employees to share in the implicit understanding that employment is expected to continue for the duration of the employee's entire working life.

Therefore, the offer that was made by Suzuki to Chan was not accepted full-heartedly by Chan. Mostly likely, when faced with such an offer, the employee may consider how the new position may impact—either positively or negatively—the prospects of working elsewhere if the need for finding work elsewhere were to arise. A job candidate with experiences in various roles but no clear area of expertise may be viewed as a less desirable candidate than someone who has a clear area of expertise from which he can contribute to a new employer.

If Suzuki would really like to persuade Chan to take the position, he needs to explain not only the merits to the company, but also the merits to Chan's overall career trajectory.

人従業員の間では疑念を持たれるのは，雇用ということに関して暗黙裡に根本的な理解の相違があるためである。日本では「終身雇用」（より正確には「定年までの継続的雇用」）の期待についての暗黙の理解があるため，企業は従業員からそれほど強い抵抗もなくポジションの異動を実施することができる。日本では，従業員は，会社が労働条件（すなわち，勤務場所，職務）の時折の変化の受容を彼らに要請するであろうことを理解している。こうして，そのような一連の各種の仕事経験が従業員のキャリアを形成しているのである。

　海外では，日本企業の海外子会社であっても，従業員の労働人生全てにわたって雇用が継続するであろうという暗黙の理解を従業員が共有することはほとんどない。

　そのため，鈴木社長がチャン副部長に行った提案は，チャン氏には全面的には受け入れられなかった。おそらくは，そのような提案に直面して当該従業員は，他の場所で仕事を見つける必要性が生じた場合，新しいポジションが他社で働くことの見通しにどのようにプラスまたはマイナスに影響するかを考えたのであろう。様々な役割での経験はあるが明確な専門分野のない求職者は，新しい雇用主に貢献できる明確な専門分野を持っている人よりも魅力に乏しい候補と見なされることになるかもしれない。

　もしも鈴木氏がチャン氏に，そのポジションに就くように本気で説得したいのであれば，彼は会社にとってのメリットだけでなく，チャン氏の生涯にわたるキャリアの軌跡に対するメリットについても説明する必要があるであろう。

Special note from the author, Bryan Sherman: I have facilitated career development seminars at the global HQ of Japanese companies for both Japanese and non-Japanese employees. In reality, among the non-Japanese employees from the overseas subsidiaries, I witness younger employees (under 35 years old) expressing a willingness to develop themselves through position transfers to other departments. Indeed, such aspirations do seem to diminish as the employees age and develop a sense of their own area of expertise.

Additionally, in my own experience, I have not witnessed an abundance of overseas subsidiary employees who raise their hands to be transferred to overseas positions. But I suspect that this is not a factor of being *non-Japanese* but rather that when the overseas subsidiaries recruit employees, they are not advertising the opportunities that may exist for overseas work. Therefore, the newly hired employees tend to be settled into their lives within the country of hire without much aspiration for global transfers.

ブライアン・シャーマンからの特別な注釈：私は，日本企業と外国人従業員の両方のために日本企業のグローバル本部でキャリア開発セミナーを支援してきました。実際には，海外子会社の外国人従業員のうち，他の部署への異動を通じて自分自身を成長させる意欲を表明している若い従業員（35歳未満）にも会っています。そのような願望は，従業員が年齢を重ねるにつれて確かに減少し，彼ら自身の専門分野の意識が強まっていくように思われます。

　また，私自身の経験では，海外のポジションへの移動を希望して手を挙げるような海外子会社の従業員をそれほどには見たことがありません。しかし，これは「外国人」であることの要因ではなく，むしろ海外の子会社が従業員を採用するときには，海外勤務というチャンスを奨励していないためです。したがって，採用された従業員は，グローバルな異動をあまり望まず，自国の中での生活に安住する傾向があります。

CASE STUDY 5.2

Quitting After Receiving Educational Assistance From the Company

Question for consideration

Companies routinely provide employees the opportunities for continual learning. Such training and development are often provided to employees at a high cost to the company but not to employees. **What should a company do when an employee who has recently received the benefits of a training initiative decides to resign from the company shortly thereafter?**

Case study detail

Company: Subsidiary of a Japanese company, Mumbai, India
Mizutani Morio, Senior Manager
Hanyu Takeo, Manager
Dalia Patel, Accounting Department staff

Let's listen in on a conversation between two expatriate managers working in an overseas subsidiary of their company in Mumbai, India.

Hanyu: The other day, **Dalia**, a **staff member in the Accounting Department**, announced that she would like to resign. She has an on-going family issue and would like to work at a company closer to her home.

Mizutani: What? Are you referring to Dalia who, just half a year ago, finished

CASE STUDY 5.2

会社から教育支援を受けた後の離職

本事例の着目点

　企業は，継続的な学習の機会を従業員に定期的に提供している。従業員に提供されるこのような教育訓練と人材開発は，多くの場合，会社には高い費用がかかり，従業員にはかからない。しかし，**教育訓練施策の便益を最近受けた従業員が，その後すぐに辞職することになった場合，企業はどうすべきだろうか？**

事例の背景

会社：日本企業のインド・ムンバイ子会社

シニア・マネジャー：水谷守夫氏

マネジャー：羽生武雄氏

経理部の職員：ダリア・パテル氏

　インドのムンバイにある海外子会社で働いている二人の駐在員マネジャーの間の会話を聞いてみよう。

羽生：先日，**経理部門スタッフのダリアが辞めたいと言ってきました。**彼女は現在，家族問題を抱えていて，自分の家の近くの会社で働きたいとのことです。

水谷：なにー？　わずか半年前にムンバイ大学で会計プログラムを終えたあの

the accounting program at the University of Mumbai?

Hanyu: Yes. I am afraid so. Dalia had only graduated from high school, but since she had such a go-getter attitude, the company helped her out with the tuition as we thought she would make some strong contributions to our accounting tasks.

Mizutani: Right, because there was a dearth of talent in the Accounting Department to begin with, we had her go to school. Was there anything put in writing between Dalia and the company regarding the tuition assistance she got from the company?

Hanyu: No. Nothing in particular was put in writing. It was the first time that the company provided tuition assistance for the purpose of receiving certification. And because Dalia was already working with the company for five years, we thought that she was a loyal employee, so we did not put any agreement in writing.

Mizutani: Hmm, that is a problem. In the future, if employees quit within a certain period of time after receiving tuition assistance, we need to have them return the tuition to the company or treat the tuition support as some kind of loan that can be deducted from salary.

Learning points

Companies that do not provide any training opportunities to employees will suffer from a lack of skills and a weak employer brand. Providing some level of educational support to employees is important not only to increase their skill level, but also to increase their commitment to the company. Yet, as this case demonstrates, employees do not always

ダリアのこと？

羽生：はい。残念ながら，そうなんですよ。ダリアは高校を卒業しただけでしたが，大変やる気のある態度を示していましたので，わが社としては，彼女は会計業務に何らかの形で多大な貢献をしてくれるものと考えて授業料を支援したのです。

水谷：そうだよね。もともと経理部では人材が不足していたので，彼女を学校に行かせたのだよ。ダリアが会社から受けた授業料援助に関して，彼女と会社の間に何か書いたものはなかった？

羽生：いいえ。特に何も書いたものはありません。わが社が資格取得の目的で授業料援助を提供したのは初めてでした。その上，ダリアはすでに5年間，わが社で仕事をしていましたので，彼女を忠誠心の高い従業員と考え，私たちは書面での契約を行いませんでした。

水谷：うーん，そこが問題だね。将来的には，授業料の援助を受けた後，一定期間内に辞職する従業員には授業料を会社に戻させたり，あるいは，授業料援助をある種のローンとして扱い，給与から控除したりすることが必要だね。

学習ポイント
　従業員に教育訓練機会を提供しない会社は，スキルの不足とエンプロイヤー・ブランドの弱さに苦しむことになる。従業員に対してある程度の教育支援を提供することは，彼らの技能レベルを高めるためだけでなく，また彼らの企業へのコミットメントを高めるためにも重要である。しかし，この事例が示すように，従業員はその投資を，当該従業員に長期間，会社

recognize or appreciate that the investment is an expression of the company's implicit desire for the employee to remain with the company for the long-term.

Therefore, it is advisable for the company and employee to have a career development meeting prior to the decision to invest in the educational advancement of the employee. In such a meeting, both the company representative and employee should discuss how the lessons from the education can be used by the employee to contribute to the company. As well, there may be a point of discussion about how the educational pursuit may impact the potential advancement of the employee in the company. As much as possible, it should be made clear to the employee that the company is undertaking the educational investment with a long-term perspective.

If the company would like to seek repayment from an employee who resigns within a specified period after receiving educational support, an agreement should be drafted before the company makes any payment.

However, the company needs to check first whether any expectations or limitations imposed upon the employee are legally defensible. (For example, if a company tells an employee that the employee cannot quit if the employee receives education support, such a limitation on the employee may not be legally defensible if the employee does actually quit.) In most cases, there is no legal recourse available to a company to prevent the employee from changing jobs after receiving educational assistance from a company. Therefore, the company needs to appeal to the employee's sense of ethics and loyalty to the company and hope that the employee feels appreciation for the opportunities provided.

に留まってほしいことを暗黙のうちに会社が望んでいることの表現であると，常に認識したり，感謝したりするわけではない。

　したがって，従業員の教育向上に投資することを決定する前に，会社と従業員がキャリア開発のミーティングを開くことをお勧めしたい。このようなミーティングでは，会社の代表者と従業員の双方が，従業員が教育を通じて学んだことを会社のためにどのように活用するかについて話し合うべきである。同様に，教育の継続が社内の従業員の能力向上にどのように影響を与えるかも議論のポイントとなるかもしれない。できる限り，会社が長期的な視点で教育投資を行っていることを従業員にはっきりと示すべきである。

　もし企業が，教育的支援を受けてから一定期間内に辞職する従業員からの返済を希望する場合は，会社が何らかの支援を行う前に契約書を作成しておく必要がある。

　ただし，会社は，従業員への期待や制限が法的に弁護可能かどうかをまず確認する必要がある（例えば，企業が，教育支援を受けた従業員は辞職できないと告げたとしても，当該従業員に対するそのような制限は，もし当該従業員が実際に辞職してしまった場合に，法的に守られないかもしれない）。多くの場合，会社から教育援助を受けた後の従業員の転職を防ぐために会社が利用できる法的手段は存在しない。そのため，会社は，与えられた機会に対して会社に感謝すべきであると従業員の倫理観と忠誠心に訴えていく必要がある。

Alternatively, the company may choose to provide reimbursement for expenses that are initially incurred by the employee after the employee attains a passing grade and/or after a specified period of time passes after receiving the educational certificate or degree.

　あるいは，会社は，従業員が及第点に到達した後，そして／あるいは，教育証明書または学位を受け取ってから一定の期間が経過した後に，当初に従業員が負担した費用の返還実施を選択してもよい。

Talent Management

What Is Talent Management (TM)?

If a company is not making efforts to acquire, develop and retain highly skilled and motivated employees, the company may not be able to continually prosper and meet the ever-changing needs of society. To support the achievement of business goals through the efforts of skilled and motivated employees, **talent management (TM)** has emerged in recent years.

Around 2009, the Association for Talent Development (ATD; formerly the American Society of Training & Development, ASTD) had defined *talent management* as follows:

TM is a holistic approach to optimizing human capital, which enables an organization to drive short- and long-term results by building culture, engagement, capability, and capacity through integrated talent acquisition, development and deployment processes that are aligned to business goals.

CHAPTER 6

タレント・マネジメント

タレント・マネジメント（TM）とは？

　もし企業が高い技能と高いモチベーションを保有する従業員の獲得，育成，そして確保に努めない場合には，当該企業は継続的に発展し，そして社会の常に変化する要請に応えられなくなるであろう。高い技能と高いモチベーションを有する従業員の頑張りを通じて事業目標の達成を支援するために，近年**タレント・マネジメント（TM）**が脚光を浴びてきた。

　ATD（元米国人材開発機構，ASTD）は，2009年頃に「タレント・マネジメント」を次のように定義している。

　TMとは人的資本を最大限に活用するための包括的なアプローチである。このアプローチは，事業の目標に沿ったタレントを獲得・育成・配置する一貫したプロセスを通じて企業文化および従業員のエンゲージメント，能力，才能を構築し，組織の短期・長期の業績を後押しすることを可能ならしめるのである。

Said more simply, TM consists of interconnected processes for analyzing, developing and using the skills and capabilities of employees to achieve corporate goals. To practice *talent management*, the HR Department must consider the inter-relation of HR functional elements such as hiring, career planning, assessment, succession planning, organization development, performance management, team and individual development, and retention.

While the practice of TM is still relatively new, TM incorporates traditional HR elements based upon the recognition that the HR function can positively impact business results.

Talent Management (TM) as Crisis Management

To say that TM is crisis management is to recognize that:

1. Good employees may leave the company and go to competitors, and
2. Employees may not have the skills necessary for the future if the company and employees do not begin identifying skill requirements and future development needs today.

In other words, companies need to make deliberate efforts to attract and retain the most talented employees. Otherwise, the most desired and necessary talented individuals may not stay within the company.

This crisis mindset assumes that employees are not loyal to their company unconditionally. Employees and companies have to endeavor to continually earn the trust and loyalty of each other throughout daily work.

　より簡潔に言えば，TMとは，企業の目標を達成するために従業員の技能と能力を分析・育成・活用するための一連のプロセスから成っている。「タレント・マネジメント」を実践するには，人事部門は，採用，キャリア計画，アセスメント，後継者計画，組織開発，パフォーマンス・マネジメント，チームと個人の育成，並びに人材の確保などの人事機能の諸要素の相互関係を考慮しなければならない。

　TMの実践はまだ新しいが，しかしそれは人事部の様々な伝統的人事要素を含んでおり，人事機能がビジネス成果にプラスの影響を与えるという認識に裏打ちされている。

危機管理としてのタレント・マネジメント（TM）

　TMは危機管理であるという指摘は次の認識に基づいている。

1. 優秀人材は会社を辞め，競合他社に移る可能性がある。
2. 会社と従業員双方が，将来必要とされる技能と将来の人材育成ニーズを現在において認識し始めていない場合には，従業員は将来必要とされる技能を持たないということになるかもしれない。

　すなわち，企業は最も優秀な従業員を獲得し，確保するためには意識して努力する必要がある。そうでないと，最も必要かつ重要な優秀人材は企業内に留まらないかもしれない。

　この危機意識は，従業員が会社対して持つ忠誠心は無条件ではないという想定に立っている。従業員と会社はお互いの信頼と忠誠心を日常の仕事の中で継続的に獲得する努力をしなければならない。

Does TM refer to all employees in the company?
There is debate within the literature on TM as to whether TM should be concerned with all employees in the organization (the inclusive approach) or whether TM exists as an approach to identifying the most necessary employees among the total of all employees (the exclusive approach).

In this book, we will define TM in terms of this exclusive approach as we understand it to be the more common. In this way, we can understand that Performance Management (See Chapter 3.) applies to the entire labor force whereas TM applies to an exclusive group of employees referred to as the **key talent pool**.

Developing and Managing a Key Talent Pool

The development and management of a *key talent pool* as the basis for TM involves three iterative phases:

Phase 1: Identification
Phase 2: Validation
Phase 3: Development

Firstly, in Phase 1: Identification, the HR Department conducts a review of the workforce of the company in an effort to gather information about the skills, capabilities, and career aspirations of employees. At the same time, based upon the business plans and goals, the HR Department, along with the executive management, needs to make assumptions about future skill and capability requirements. Through this inquiry, the HR Department can identify **high potential employees** (*high potentials, high-po's* or *HPP*) who

TM の対象は全従業員？

　TM の対象を企業内の全従業員とするアプローチ（包括的アプローチ）に関連するか否か，あるいは TM を全ての従業員全体の中の最も必要な従業員を識別するためのアプローチ（選抜的アプローチ）として存在するか否かに関する議論が，TM に関する文献の中でなされている。

　本書では，TM をより一般的に受け入れられていると考えられる，選抜的アプローチとして定義する。こうして，パフォーマンス・マネジメント（Chapter 3 参照）は従業員全体に適用され，他方で TM は**キー・タレント・プール**と呼ばれる選抜された従業員グループに適用されることになる。

キー・タレントプールの構築と管理

　TM の基礎としての「キー・タレント・プール」の構築と管理は，次の 3 つの反復フェーズを含む：

フェーズ 1．識別
フェーズ 2．検証
フェーズ 3．育成

　第 1 に，フェーズ 1．の識別では，人事部門は，従業員の技能，能力，キャリア願望に関する情報を収集すべく従業員全員の調査を行う。同時に，人事部は会社の経営幹部とともに，会社の事業計画・目標に基づき，将来，会社が必要とするスキルと能力を想定する必要がある。こうした検討を通じて，人事部は，**高能力従業員**（彼らは英語では「high potentials」，「high-po's」，「HPP」とも表現される）を見出すことが出来る。彼らはすでに優れたスキルを保有し，また会社のニーズに応じて成長できる潜在能力を持っている。このように

currently have superior skills and/or the potential of developing in accordance with the company's needs. This group of identified employees is referred to as the key talent pool.

Secondly, in Phase 2: Validation, the HR Department needs to validate whether those employees who have been identified as key talent are indeed qualified to have earned such a designation.

Validation occurs in two ways. One way is through direct observation and communication with the key talent by executives and HR representatives. Through formal or informal discussions, evidence may be gathered by executive management and HR representatives regarding the individuals' characteristics such as:

- Drive to achieve and make meaningful contributions
- Ability to learn new things and to apply such learning to work
- Other career factors (openness to new positions, desire to work in overseas locations, etc.)

The second way is through discussion about the key talent among executives and HR representatives. Discussion about the key talent may occur at specific intervals in a **talent review meeting**. In such a meeting, members of the executive management and HR Department gather to have strategic dialogue regarding the key talent. The meeting discussion may focus on pre-selected key positions and the incumbents in the positions. The following questions may be discussed:

- Is the incumbent struggling to fulfill the role of the position in any way? If so, what can be done to help the person overcome such issues?

識別された人たちをキー・タレント・プールと呼んでいる。

　第2に，フェーズ2.の検証では，人事部は，キー・タレントとして識別された従業員が実際にその指名に値するかどうか検証する必要がある。

　この検証作業は2つの方法で行われる。第1の方法は，経営幹部ならびに人事責任者がキー・タレントを直接観察し，また彼らとコミュニケーションを取ることである。フォーマルまたはインフォーマルな会話を通じて，経営幹部ならびに人事責任者により個々人の以下のような特徴に関する証拠が集められる。

- 達成への意欲ならびに重要な貢献への意欲
- 新しいことを学び，それを仕事に適用する能力
- その他のキャリア要因（新たな職務に対する前向きな姿勢，海外勤務への意欲，など）

　第2の方法は，経営幹部ならびに人事責任者の間でキー・タレントに関して話し合いを持つことである。キー・タレントに関する話し合いは，定期的に開催される**タレント・レビュー会議**で通常行われる。このような会議では経営幹部と人事責任者がキー・タレントに関する戦略的な議論を行う。会議は，事前に選ばれたキー・ポジションとそのポジションにいる現職者に関する議論に集中する。次のような問題点が議論されるであろう。

- 現職者は，理由はともかくとして役割の遂行上で苦戦しているかどうか？その場合には，課題を克服するためにその人に対してどのようなサポートが可能か？

- Or, is the incumbent ready for a new challenge in the current position or another position?
- Notwithstanding the above, is there any reason to believe that the incumbent should be considered as a **retention risk** (also, **flight risk**)?

Then, the following questions should be discussed regarding the level of succession readiness to assess the bench strength of a pool of successor candidates:

In the case that the incumbent was to vacate the position for any reason such as promotion or resignation:

- How many successor candidates currently possess the requisite skills and experience for the position?
- With some type of developmental intervention, how many successor candidates may be ready within the next year?
- Or, with some type of additional experience, how many successor candidates may be ready over the next three years?

In the case that there are no successor candidates who can be identified, discussion may move to the topic of **succession risk**. That is to say, discussion may focus upon how to mitigate any negative impact on the business in the case that the incumbent in the key position were to leave the company.

Once the current status of incumbents in key positions and the bench strength of successors are clarified, the meeting discussion may proceed to actual decision making regarding development interventions and/or organizational changes.

Thirdly, in Phase 3: Development, the people in the key talent pool are

- または，現職者は現在のポジション，あるいは別のポジションにおいて新たなチャレンジができるかどうか？
- 上記とは別に，現職者が**人材確保リスク**（または**人材流出リスク**）を抱えていると思わせる理由が存在するかどうか？

次に，後継候補者層の厚さを評価するために後継者準備状況に関する以下の点について検討する必要がある。

現職者の昇進あるいは辞職によりポジションが空席となった場合：

- 後継者候補として現時点で何名がその必要なスキルと経験を有しているのか？
- 何らかの育成支援策を通じて，1年以内に何名が登用可能となるのか？

- あるいは，何らかの追加的経験を積ませることにより，3年以内に何名が登用可能となるのか？

識別できる後継候補者がいない場合，議論は，**後継者リスク**のトピックに移ることになる。つまり，キー・ポジションにいる現職者が会社を去ることになった場合，議論はビジネスへの負の影響を軽減する方法に焦点を合わせることになる。

キー・ポジションの現職者の現状と後継者層の厚さがはっきりすると，議題は，人材育成支援および／または組織の変更に関する実際の意思決定に進むであろう。

第3に，フェーズ3.の育成においては，キー・タレント・プールの人には

provided with opportunities for professional growth.

Key talent development may consist of the following elements:

a. Stretch goals within current position
b. Special cross-functional project work
c. On-the-job training and coaching
d. Off-the-job training such as executive education opportunities and group training
e. The provision of other development interventions (Refer to Chapter 5 for further information.)

What Is Global Talent Management? (GTM)

The abovementioned TM approach may be carried out within one organization or be limited to group companies in one country. Or, the identification, validation and development phases of talent management may occur on a global basis. In this case, the practice may be referred to as **global talent management (GTM)**. Compared to TM as practiced within one single country, GTM is more complex. This is because of the need to gather and compare disparate information across global group companies. The practice of GTM places a high administrative burden on the HR function as HR professionals need to gather and analyze information and develop related initiatives. Additionally, it becomes necessary to support the smooth transfer of people across group companies and international borders according to a global mobility policy.

Globally standardized HR system for enabling GTM

It is necessary to instill some common standards within the global group so that the definition for key talent and key positions can be commonly

プロフェッショナルとしての成長の機会が提供される。

　キー・タレントの育成には次の要素が含まれる。

a．現ポジション内でのストレッチ目標
b．部門を跨ぐ追加的なプロジェクト業務
c．OJT とコーチング
d．エグゼクティブ教育の受講機会やグループ研修などの Off-JT

e．その他の育成支援策の提供（追加的情報は Chapter 5 参照）

グローバル・タレント・マネジメント（GTM）とは

　上述のタレント・マネジメント（TM）は一国内にある一企業内，あるいはグループ企業間に限定して実施されることもある。さらには，タレント・マネジメントの識別・検証・育成の諸段階がグローバル規模で実施されることもある。この場合の取り組みは，**グローバル・タレント・マネジメント（GTM）**と呼ばれる。GTM は一国内で実践される TM と比べて，より複雑である。その理由は，世界に散らばるグループ企業から様々な情報を収集・比較する必要があるためである。GTM の実践は，人事機能に対する運営負担を重くする。というのも，人事担当者は，情報を収集・分析し，関連する施策を立案する必要があるからである。さらに，グローバル・モビリティ・ポリシー（国際間人事異動政策）に従って，グループ企業間ならびに国境を横断する従業員のスムーズな異動を支援しなければならなくなる。

GTM を可能にするためのグローバルに標準化された人事システム

　キー・タレントとキー・ポジションに関する共通の定義の理解を促進するために，グループ企業間に何らかの共通の基準を導入する必要がある。このため

understood. For this, a globally standardized HR system is necessary. A global HR system generally includes the following components:

1) Globally standardized corporate credo/philosophy
   To instill a sense of respect for shared values and/or shared methods for cultivating and carrying out business.

2) Global organizational grading structure
   To globally classify employees into discrete levels based upon the expectations for their roles and the requisite skill sets thereof within the organizational hierarchy. When initially considering the key talent pool, employees who are assigned to the highest grades may be automatically deemed to be key talent due to their status as incumbents in key positions; thereafter, verification of their continuing status as key talent is necessary.

3) Global performance evaluation standards
   To carry out evaluations, in accordance with similar standards, of the results that employees are responsible for producing.

4) Global standards for promotion and/or demotion
   To ensure that employees move across positions based upon similar standards for growth within the group companies.

5) Global standards for compensation management
   To assist with administrative procedures for rewarding employees in the advent of a global transfer.

Global mobility policy

To institute a global-level talent management process, it is necessary for companies to conceive of and implement a **global mobility policy**.

に，グローバルに標準化された人事システムが必要となる。グローバルな人事システムは通常，以下の諸要素を含む。

1）グローバルに共通した企業の信条／理念

　　ビジネスの発展・遂行のための共通の価値観，そして／あるいは，共通の手法などへの尊敬心を浸透させること。

2）グローバルな組織内等級構造

　　組織内の階層の中での役割期待とそれに必要なスキル・セットに基づき，それぞれのレベルに従業員をグローバルに分類すること。最初にキー・タレント・プールを検討する際には，最も高いレベルのグレードに割り当てられている従業員は，キー・ポジションに居る現職者であるという立場の故にキー・タレントとして自動的に想定される。その後，キー・タレントとしてその地位を継続すべきかどうか検討される必要がある。

3）グローバルな業績評価基準

　　従業員は，同様の基準に従って，結果責任において評価を実施されること。

4）昇進そして／または降格に関するグローバルな基準

　　従業員に対して，グループ企業内での成長に関する同一の基準に基づいてポジション間の異動をさせること。

5）報酬管理に関するグローバルな基準

　　グローバルな人事異動の際には，従業員に対する報い方の業務手続を支援すること。

グローバル・モビリティ・ポリシー

　グローバルな規模でタレント・マネジメントのプロセスを制度化するには，企業は**グローバル・モビリティ・ポリシー**を制定し，実施する必要がある。

Even before this current era of GTM, many companies have managed the movement of employees from the home country to overseas subsidiaries under an expatriation system. Previously, expatriation had been viewed primarily as a means for managing group companies whereby nationals from the home country are sent overseas to develop and manage business. While such an expectation remains even today, under the rubric of GTM, overseas assignments are also viewed as a means for developing the skills and broadening the experiences of the expatriated individual, especially when that person is identified as key talent.

Furthermore, a comprehensive global mobility policy as conceived by the global headquarters is concerned not only with movement from the country of the headquarters to overseas subsidiaries but also from overseas subsidiaries to the country of the headquarters and from overseas locations to other overseas locations. To differentiate among these different movements, the following terms are regularly used.

Expatriate: a headquarters-based employee who is typically a home country national and who moves temporarily from the headquarters to an overseas subsidiary in a host country; may also be referred to as a *rotational employee* because employees in positions held by expatriates are normally *rotated* after about three to five years. (Refer to Chapter 9 for further information.)

Inpatriate: an employee of an overseas subsidiary who moves temporarily to a position in the headquarters or a group company in the home country.

Third-country national: an employee of an overseas subsidiary who moves temporarily to another overseas subsidiary in any country other than the country in which the headquarters is located.

　多くの企業は，今日のような GTM の時代以前から，それぞれの海外派遣制度の下に本国から海外の子会社へ従業員を派遣してきた。以前は，海外派遣はグループ企業を管理する主な方法とみられており，それにより，ビジネスを創出し管理するために本国籍従業員が海外に派遣されてきた。GTM という考え方の下，今日でもこのような役割は期待されているが，その人がキー・タレントと考えられている場合には，海外勤務は同時に，海外派遣者個人が技能を身に付け，経験を広める手段としても位置付けられている。

　さらに，グローバル本社により構築された包括的なグローバル・モビリティ・ポリシーは，本社の所在する国から海外子会社への異動のみならず，その逆の海外子会社から本社の所在する国への異動や海外子会社間の異動も含まれる。これらの様々な異動を区別するため，次のような用語がよく使われる。

海外派遣者：典型的には本国籍を有する本社の従業員であり，一時的に本社から受入れ国の海外子会社に異動する従業員。同時に「ローテーショナル・インプロイー」とも呼ばれる。というのも，海外派遣者により埋められるポジションにある従業員は，通常，3 年から 5 年で「ローテーション」されるからである（より詳しくは Chapter 9 を参照されたい）。

逆出向者：海外子会社から本社または本国にあるグループ企業に一時的に異動する従業員

第三国籍従業員：海外子会社の従業員で，本社の所在する国以外の国の海外子会社に一時的に異動する人

The abovementioned terms to describe globally mobile talent place the country in which the headquarters is located (*home country*) in the center of the metaphorical globally mobile group map. However, an *inpatriate* or *third country national* may personally refer to one's self as an *expatriate* as the individual is out of (*ex*) the person's own country (*patria*).

Commentary on TM in globalizing Japanese companies

More and more, Japanese companies are beginning to consider the need for a formal TM program. However, given the traditional practices of Japanese companies, TM has not been at the forefront of HR initiatives.

In Japan, it is common for large-size companies to hire new graduates out of college with the implicit understanding that employees are hired for the long-term duration of their working life. As a result, the crisis mindset of TM is not as well recognized in Japan as it is in other countries. Given this situation, Japanese companies have not felt the need to particularly identify and develop key talent from among all of their employees. Rather, they take a long-term approach in developing all people based on the idea that employees should receive equal opportunity for training and development according to their year of entry into the company or age. However, as the new generation of millennials is already demonstrating a stronger proclivity to change companies more than their predecessors had, the concepts of TM as presented in this chapter are becoming more relevant within the domestic Japanese market.

In terms of the overseas subsidiaries of Japanese companies, the need for GTM is ever present. Within the HR Departments at Japanese companies which recognize this sense of crisis, initiatives are underway to identify, validate and develop a key talent pool of national staff. Companies that

　グローバルに異動するタレント人材に関する上記の表現は，グローバルに異動する人たちの比喩的地図の中心に，本社が所在する国（「本国」）を据えている。しかし，「逆出向者」あるいは「第三国籍従業員」と呼ばれる従業員も自らを「海外派遣者」（"expatriate"）と呼ぶかもしれない。というのも，彼らも故国（"patria"）の外（"ex"）にいるからである。

グローバル化する日本企業における TM についての解説

　日本企業は，TM プログラムの必要性をますます感じ始めている。しかし，日本企業の伝統的慣行のために，TM は人事施策の中で優先的施策となるには至っていない。

　日本の大企業では長期に雇用するという暗黙の了解のもとに新卒を採用することが通例となっている。その結果，TM における危機意識が他国と比べると十分に意識されていない。こうした状況下，日本企業は全従業員の中から特別にキー・タレントを見出して，育成する必要性を他国ほどには感じていない。逆に，日本企業は，従業員は入社年次または年齢に応じて研修と能力開発で均等の機会を与えられるべきとの考えの下，長期志向に立って全ての従業員を対象に能力開発を行っている。しかし，ミレニアルと呼ばれる新しい世代は，前の世代と比べてすでに転職する傾向をより強く示しているので，本章で示された TM という概念は日本国内の労働市場においてより重要になりつつある。

　日本企業の海外子会社においては，GTM は常に必要である。このような危機意識を認識する日本企業の本社人事部では，現地スタッフのキー・タレント・プールを識別し検証し育成する施策に取り組んでいる。このような取り組みが進んでいる企業では，長年にわたり本社からの派遣者によ

are making progress have even been able to localize positions that were traditionally filled by expatriates from the headquarters. Additionally, some companies are even providing opportunities for national staff to take on positions in the Japanese headquarters or subsidiaries in other countries.

References & Suggestions for Additional Reading

Gallardo-Gallardo, E. and M. Thunnissen (2019), "Talent Management: Disentangling Key Ideas", in Wilkinson, A., N. Bacon, S. Snell and D. Lepak (eds.), *The SAGE Handbook of Human Resource Management*, Second Edition, Sage, pp. 164-178, Chapter 10.

Dries, N., R. D. Cotton, S. Bagdadli and M. Ziebell de Oliveira (2014), "HR Director's Understanding of 'Talent': A Cross-Cultural Study", in Al Ariss, A. (ed.), *Global Talent Management, Management for Professionals*, DOI 10.1007/978-3-319-05125-3_2, Springer International Publishing Switzerland, pp. 15-28.

Furusawa, M. (2014), "Global Talent Management in Japanese Multinational Companies: The Case of Nissan Motor Company", in Al Ariss, A. (ed.), *Global Talent Management: Management for Professionals*, DOI 10.1007/978-3-319-05125-3_2, Springer International Publishing Switzerland, pp. 159-170.

り埋められていたポジションの現地化が可能となっている。さらに，現地スタッフに対して日本本社や他国の子会社のポジションに就く機会を提供している企業も存在する。

さらに学びたい人のための参考文献

Gallardo-Gallardo, E. and M. Thunnissen (2019), "Talent Management: Disentangling Key Ideas", in Wilkinson, A., N. Bacon, S. Snell and D. Lepak (eds.), *The SAGE Handbook of Human Resource Management*, Second Edition, Sage, pp. 164-178, Chapter 10.

Dries, N., R. D. Cotton, S. Bagdadli and M. Ziebell de Oliveira (2014), "HR Director's Understanding of 'Talent': A Cross-Cultural Study", in Al Ariss, A. (ed.), *Global Talent Management: Management for Professionals*, DOI 10.1007/978-3-319-05125-3_2, Springer International Publishing Switzerland, pp. 15-28.

Furusawa, M. (2014), "Global Talent Management in Japanese Multinational Companies: The Case of Nissan Motor Company", in Al Ariss, A. (ed.), *Global Talent Management: Management for Professionals*, DOI 10.1007/978-3-319-05125-3_2, Springer International Publishing Switzerland, pp. 159-170.

CASE STUDY 6.1

Balancing New Talent Management Initiatives With Deeply Held Corporate Values

Question for consideration

Modern talent management practices call for the identification of key talent and the provision of opportunities for their growth and development. **What happens when such practices are not appreciated by all employees in the company?**

Case study detail

Company: Subsidiary of a Japanese Company, London

Sam Harris, General Manager, HR

Kato Hideyuki, President

Howard Cohen, veteran employee

Before **Sam Harris** was hired at the London subsidiary of a Japanese manufacturer as the **General Manager, HR** earlier this year, she had many years of experience in HR management at multiple European companies. Her initial mission was to stop the loss of an increasing number of the company's best employees to competitor firms.

Today she is providing some initial recommendations to **President Kato Hideyuki**.

Harris: If we want to try to prevent some of our best employees from being

CASE STUDY 6.1

タレント・マネジメントの新施策と深く保持されてきた企業の価値観とのバランスのとり方

本事例の着目点

　現代のタレント・マネジメントの実践では，キー・タレントの識別とその成長・発展のための機会提供の双方が求められている。**そのような実践が，社内の全ての従業員から歓迎されていない場合，どうなるのだろうか？**

事例の背景
会社：日本の会社のロンドン子会社
人事部長：サム・ハリス氏
社長：加藤英之氏
ベテラン従業員：ハワード・コーエン氏

　サム・ハリス氏は，今年初めに日系製造会社のロンドン子会社の**人事部長**に就任する前は，長年にわたり，複数のヨーロッパ企業で人事管理に携わってきた。彼女の最初の任務は，増加の一途を辿る社内の最優秀人材の競合他社へ流出を止めることであった。

　今日，彼女は**加藤英之社長**に最初のいくつかの提言をすることになっている。

ハリス：私たちが，最優秀人材の何人かを競合他社に引き抜かれるのを阻止し

lured away by our competitors, we should institute some drastic changes.

Kato: What sort of drastic change do you think is necessary?

Harris: In principle, we should bring our HR system more in line with those adopted by typical European companies.

Kato: Ok. What do you have in mind?

Harris: We should introduce programs for fast-tracking our young talent.

Kato: How would that work?

Harris: First we need to create a talent pool based upon current performance and an assessment of future potential. Then, we need to provide the talent with opportunities to grow and develop regardless of their age or how many years they have been working at the company. It is a very dynamic system with frequent intervals of evaluation.

Kato: I get what you are saying. How frequent are the evaluations?

Harris: Generally speaking, evaluations are not limited to the annual performance appraisal. Evaluations can be conducted on a project-by-project basis.

Kato: Sounds good. Let's get this in place as quickly as possible.

Harris went about implementing the program with some notable success. About six months after the program was announced though, there was a surprising turn of events.

ようとするなら，いくつかの抜本的な変化を起こすべきです。

加藤：どのような根本的変化が必要だと思いますか？

ハリス：原則として，我が社の人事システムをヨーロッパの代表的な会社のものに合わせるべきです。

加藤：なるほどね。で，そのためにどのようなアイデアがありますか？

ハリス：私たちは若い優秀人材の抜擢人事プログラムを導入すべきです。

加藤：それはどのように機能するの？

ハリス：まず，現在のパフォーマンス（成果）と将来の成長可能性の評価に基づいて，人材プールを作成する必要があります。それから，彼らの年齢やわが社での勤続年数に関係なく，成長し発展できる機会をそれらの優秀人材に提供する必要があります。それは，短い間隔での評価を伴うきわめて動態的な制度です。

加藤：私は君が言わんとしているところは分かりました。評価はどのくらいの頻度で行いますか？

ハリス：一般的に言って，評価は年に1回の業績評価に限定されません。評価はプロジェクトごとに行うことができます。

加藤：よさそうだね。できるだけ早くこれを実践することにしよう。

　ハリス氏はこのプログラムの実施に着手し，注目に値する成功を収めた。しかし，プログラムが発表されてから約6カ月後，事態の驚くべき急展開があった。

A **veteran employee** named **Howard Cohen** approached President Kato.

Cohen: I have worked here for over ten years and have been grateful for the opportunities I have had. But now, I am thinking of turning in my resignation letter.

Kato: Why? What has happened?

Cohen: These new HR policies that have been put in place have wrecked the company culture of teamwork and mutual trust.

Kato: What do you mean?

Cohen: We are becoming just like any other company out there. We are losing that family spirit which I and others have cherished. These young, up and coming guys—they are all about themselves. They do what they can do to get a good evaluation and to move up the hierarchy.

Kato: Ok. I hear what you are saying. We . . .

Cohen: And, if I knew this was coming, I could have changed jobs years ago and gotten paid more at a local firm. I weighed the sense of stability I got here against the potential of more pay elsewhere. But now . . .

Kato: Ok. We don't want to sacrifice that which employees have come to appreciate . . . hmm, please, don't resign yet. Let's figure this out together.

　ハワード・コーエン氏というベテランの従業員が加藤社長に申し入れてきた。

コーエン：私は10年以上ここで働いてきました。与えられた機会に感謝しています。しかし，今，私は辞職願を提出しようかと考えています。

加藤：なぜ？　どうしたの？

コーエン：今回の新しい人事施策が導入されたことで，チーム・ワークと相互信頼という企業文化が破壊されました。

加藤：それはどういう意味なの？

コーエン：うちの会社は他の会社と同じようになってきています。私も同僚も大事にしてきた家族的意識を失いつつあります。これらの若くて，これからの人間である彼らは，自分自身のことしか考えていないのです。彼らは良い評価を得て，キャリアの階段を上がるためなら何でもするという感じです。

加藤：なるほど。君の言っていることはよく分かるが，我々としては…

コーエン：その上，私は，こういうことになるのを知っていたなら，何年も前に転職して，地元の会社でもっと良い給料をもらうことも出来ましたよ。私はここで得られる安定感を他社でのより高い給料の可能性と比較考量し，こちらを選んだのです。でも今は…。

加藤：分かりました。私たちは，従業員がこれまで大事にしてきたことを犠牲にしたくありません…うーん，まずは辞職を思いとどまってよ，頼むよ。一緒にこの問題を解決しよう。

Learning points

When conducting business in a foreign country, it is reasonable to assume that the HR system should mirror that of other companies in the country in order to develop and retain the best employees. Furthermore, commonly accepted talent management practices which are becoming relatively standardized globally should be considered in order to remain competitive.

However, it should also be kept in mind that the introduction of new practices may have unforeseen consequences that run against long-held and important values. As we see in this case, veteran employees had come to appreciate the value of teamwork and a long-term perspective that the legacy system fostered.

As a word of caution to anyone who pursues change initiatives, it is necessary to ensure that the introduction of external best practices complement, and not destroy, pre-existing internal good practices.

学習ポイント

　外国で事業を行う場合は，優秀な従業員を育成し保持するために，自社の人事制度を国内の他の企業の制度に右に倣(なら)えと考えるのは理にかなっている。さらに，競争力を維持するためには，世界的に比較的標準化され，一般的に受け入れられつつあるタレント・マネジメント施策について考慮してしかるべきである。

　しかし，新しい施策の導入は，長期にわたる重要な価値観に反し，予期せぬ結果をもたらす可能性があることにも留意する必要がある。この事例に見られるように，ベテラン従業員たちは，チーム・ワークの価値と，これまで受け継がれてきた長期的な視点とを評価している。

　制度変革を追求する場合の注意点として，外部のベスト・プラクティスの導入は，内部の既存のグッド・プラクティスを補完し，破壊しないことが前提となる，と言っておこう。

Compliance & Risk Management

Corporate Compliance and Risk Management

While much of the work that is conducted in companies needs to be carried out with a high level of discretion and creativity, an area of corporate activity that requires obedience and strict adherence to standards is referred to as **corporate compliance**. Corporate compliance refers to the obligation of company employees to follow laws, regulations, standards, and ethical practices. On a global basis, effective corporate compliance encompasses adherence to international treaties and agreements on down to national, state and local laws.

In the realm of human resource related corporate compliance, laws and regulations may pertain to HR processes such as hiring, employment termination, compensation management and overtime payments, provision of employee benefits, provision of job-protected leave, workplace safety, privacy protection, discrimination and harassment prevention, and labor relations. The list is long and complex.

CHAPTER 7

コンプライアンスとリスク管理

企業コンプライアンスとリスク管理

　企業で行われる仕事の多くは，裁量度と創造性を高いレベルで維持しながら遂行される必要があるが，一方，基準への追従と基準の厳格な遵守とを求める企業活動の領域は，企業コンプライアンスと呼ばれている。**企業コンプライアンス**とは，会社の従業員が法令，規制，基準，および倫理慣行に従う義務のことである。グローバルな共通基盤において，効果的な企業コンプライアンスとは，国際的条約および協定から国，州，および地方の法律に至るまで，それらを遵守することを意味する。

　人事関連の企業コンプライアンスの領域では，法律や規制が様々に関連する。すなわち，採用，雇用終了，報酬管理，管理・残業手当，従業員福利厚生の提供，雇用保護休暇の提供，職場の安全，プライバシー保護，差別・ハラスメント（嫌がらせ）防止，それに労働関係などの人事プロセスに，法律や規制が関連する。このコンプライアンス領域のリストは長く複雑である。

Risk management refers to the assessment of threats and the efforts that should be taken to minimize or eliminate such threats. In the realm of HR, there are a multitude of risks that need to be addressed.

In this chapter, we will specifically address compliance and risk management in regard to four specific areas of interest: workplace discrimination, workplace harassment, data privacy, and immigration laws and employment.

I. Workplace Discrimination

Defining workplace discrimination

What constitutes workplace discrimination may differ from one country to another and change from time to time, making it necessary for HR departments to keep abreast of related laws and regulations. Generally speaking, **illegal discrimination in employment** refers to the following: *treatment or consideration of a person based on a group, class, or category to which the person is perceived to belong, rather than on individual attributes that are necessary for success in a job.* Specifically, HR professionals should be aware of applicable laws and regulations regarding discrimination in terms of categorical areas such as gender, age, ethnicity, marital status, disability status, pregnancy status, religion or sexual orientation.

Relevant discrimination laws

For the purpose of simplicity, we will limit discussion of relevant laws to the United States of America (USA), European Union (EU), People's Republic of China (China) and Republic of India (India) in this and subsequent sections.

Western countries, in general, have some of the strictest laws and regulations regarding workplace discrimination.

　リスク管理とは，脅威の評価と，そのような脅威を最小限に抑えるか無くすために取るべき行動とを指している。人事の領域では，対処する必要があるリスクが多数存在する。

　本章では，とりわけ4つのコンプライアンスとリスク管理について論じることにする。すなわち，職場における差別，職場におけるハラスメント，データ・プライバシー，そして，移民法と雇用について論じる。

I．職場における差別

職場における差別の定義

　職場における差別を構成する要素は，国によって異なり，時とともに変化する可能性があるため，人事部は関連する法律と規制の最新情報に常に注意を払う必要がある。一般的に，**雇用における違法な差別**とは以下のようなものを指す：「仕事で成功するために必要な個人の属性ではなく，その人が属していると考えられるグループ，階層，またはカテゴリーに基づいて，その人を取り扱うかまたは見なすことである」。具体的には，人事担当者は，性別，年齢，民族，婚姻状況，障害状況，妊娠状況，宗教あるいは性的指向など，カテゴリー別の分野ごとに差別に関して適用される法律と規制を認識する必要がある。

差別関連法

　簡略化のため，関連法の議論をアメリカ合衆国（米国），欧州連合（EU），中華人民共和国（中国），およびインド共和国（インド）に限定する。

　一般的に，西側諸国には職場における差別に関して最も厳しい法律や規制がある。

In an effort to prevent workplace discrimination, the USA has federal, state and local laws and regulations that clearly define what amounts to the violation of these rules. **Title VII of the Civil Rights Act of 1964** is the primary federal law which protects employees from discrimination based upon gender, race, color, national origin and religion.

By contrast, the **EU Anti-Discrimination Law** comprises two directives to which all member countries agreed in 2000, with each member obliged to incorporate these directives into their national legislations for enforcement.

In China, the **Labor Law of the People's Republic of China** and the **Labor Contract Law of the People's Republic of China** provide the foundation for the country's employment laws, with the primary goal of laying out the legal rights of workers and improving labor relations.

Regarding the country's anti-discrimination legislation, primary laws include the Labor Law of People's Republic of China, which prohibits discrimination of workers for reasons of their ethnicity, race, sex, or religion; the **Law of the People's Republic of China on Promotion of Employment**, which guarantees equality for women, all ethnic groups, and disabled workers to seek employment; and the **Law on the Protection of Women's Rights and Interests of the People's Republic of China**, which stipulates that women enjoy equal right to work and social security as men.

Furthermore, under the country's **Disabled Persons Security Law**, employers both in the public and private sectors must hire people with disabilities. It is mandated that large private-sector employers, including foreign companies, have at least 1.5 percent of their employees be persons with disabilities, with the exact percentage to be determined by the local government where the employer is located. Failing to meet its obligation, the employer is required to

　職場での差別を防ぐべく，米国には連邦，州，地方ごとの法律や規制があり，これらの規則に違反する金額を明確に定義している。**1964 年の公民権法のタイトルⅦ**は，性，人種，肌の色，出身国，ならびに宗教に基づく差別から従業員を保護する主要な連邦法である。

　対照的に，**EU の差別禁止法**は，全ての加盟国が 2000 年に合意した 2 つの指令から構成されており，各加盟国はこれらの指令を，強制力を持つ国内法に組み込む義務がある。

　中国では，**中華人民共和国労働法**と**中華人民共和国労働契約法**が，労働者の法的権利を整備し，労使関係を改善するという主要目標のもとに，同国の雇用法の基礎を提供している。

　同国の差別禁止法に関しては，民族，人種，性，宗教上の理由に基づく労働者の差別を禁止する中華人民共和国労働法が主な法律となっている。**中華人民共和国雇用促進法**は，女性，全ての民族，障害者が雇用を求める平等を保証している。さらに，**中華人民共和国女性の権利と利益の保護に関する法律**は，女性が男性と労働と社会保障を平等に享受することを定めている。

　さらに，同国の**障害者保障法**の下では，公的および民間部門双方の雇用者は，障害者を雇用しなくてはならない。外国企業を含む大規模な民間企業の雇用者は，従業員の少なくとも 1.5％が障害者とすべきであるとなっている。そのような人々の正確な割合は，雇用主が所在する地方自治体によって決定されることになる。その義務を果たせない場合，雇用者は**障害者雇用基金**への拠出が義務付けられている。

make contributions to the **Disabled Persons Employment Fund**.

In India, low-caste Indians are known to experience severe employment discrimination, despite the fact that the country's constitution outlaws the caste system. With some government job quotas now extended to low-caste citizens, a limited number of companies are reported to set aside some jobs for low-caste citizens, mainly to practice corporate social responsibility (CSR).

Managing the risk of discrimination claims

As the first step to manage the risks of workplace discrimination, companies may incorporate an anti-discrimination policy statement in their company regulations spelling out what constitutes discrimination and how a complaint can be lodged with the management if an employee experiences workplace discrimination.

This is an especially prudent step in countries that have established systems for employees to file claims against their employers when they believe any discrimination laws have been violated. For example, in the USA, employees who feel they have suffered discrimination can file a claim with the **Equal Employment Opportunity Commission (EEOC)**, an agency which enforces federal anti-discrimination laws, or directly in a court of law. When the employer is found to be at fault, the company may have to pay heavy compensation and suffer reputational damage.

If the company can investigate and address potential cases of discrimination internally before an employee files a claim with any external governing body or government agency, the associated legal risks may be minimized or eliminated. And of course, if the company appropriately responds by making strides to eliminate such discriminatory patterns of thinking, all employees may feel more comfortable within the company.

インドでは，同国の憲法がカースト制度を非合法化しているにもかかわらず，低カーストのインド人が厳しい雇用差別を経験することが知られている。一部の政府の雇用割り当てが低カースト市民に拡大される中，主として企業の社会的責任（CSR）を実践するため低カースト市民のために一部の雇用を確保する企業の数は，ごくわずかにとどまることが報じられている。

差別クレームのリスクの管理

職場における差別のリスクを管理するための第一歩として，企業は社内規則に，何が差別に当たるのか，また従業員が職場で差別を受けた場合に苦情を経営陣にどのように申し出ることができるかを明記する，差別禁止の方針宣言を組み込むことができる。

何らかの差別法に違反していると考える場合に，従業員が雇用主に対して申し立てを行うためのシステムが確立している国では，これは特に賢明な措置である。例えば，米国では，差別を受けたと感じる人は，連邦の差別禁止法を施行する機関である**男女雇用機会均等委員会（EEOC）**に申し立てを行ったり，あるいは直接，裁判所に申し立てを行ったりすることができる。雇用者側に過失が見つかった場合，会社は重い補償金を支払い，評判を落とすという損害を被る可能性がある。

従業員が外部の規制当局または政府機関に申し立てを行う前に，会社が内部的に差別の潜在的な問題を調査し，対処できる場合，それに付随する法的リスクを最小限に抑えるか，排除することができるであろう。もちろん，このような差別的な考え方をなくすために会社が積極的かつ適切に対応すれば，社員全員が社内でより快適に過ごせるであろう。

That being said, claims of discrimination may even be raised by individuals who are not even employed by the company; a candidate for a job interview who is not hired for a position may claim that the company illegally discriminated against the candidate if the interviewer had asked questions which did not pertain to the candidate's ability to fulfill the work requirements of the job. Therefore, companies may manage such risks by providing training to managers. Such training should provide managers with a deeper understanding of what constitutes illegal workplace discrimination and how they can avoid such claims.

II. Workplace Harassment

Defining workplace harassment

Standards of harassment and the definition thereof are not necessarily the same from country to country. However, we can generally understand harassment to be the *systematic and/or continued unwanted and annoying actions/behavior of one person or group of persons that may include threats or demands and result in physical or emotional harm to others.* Harassment may be manifested in many ways. In this text, we will be concerned with three distinct types: *sexual harassment, discriminatory harassment* and *bullying.* (*Power harassment* which is a term well-understood in Japan may not be universally understood; rather the term *bullying* is used herein.)

Sexual harassment includes behaviors or comments of a sexual nature. **Discriminatory harassment** includes intolerance of, or negative comments regarding any categorical area as discussed in the previous section of this chapter. **Bullying** includes any other type of harassment that causes psychological or physical harm. Recently, **cyberbullying**, the usage of email systems and/or SNS to belittle or embarrass another person, is a growing area

　とはいえ，差別の申し立ては，会社に雇われていない個人によっても提起されるかもしれない。求人面接の候補者は，もし面接官が仕事の要件を満たす能力に関係しない質問をした場合，会社が候補者に対して違法に差別したと主張する場合がある。したがって，企業は経営者にトレーニングを提供することによって，このようなリスクを管理することができる。このような研修は経営者に対し，何が違法な職場差別を生み出すのか，また，どのようにすれば彼らがそのような申し立てを回避できるのかについて，深い理解を促すものでなければならない。

Ⅱ．職場におけるハラスメント

職場におけるハラスメントの定義

　ハラスメントの基準とその定義は，必ずしも国を通じて同じではない。しかし，私たちは一般的にハラスメントとは「脅迫や要求を含み，他人に対し身体的または感情的な危害を引き起こす可能性のある1人またはグループによるシステマティックで（または）継続的な，不必要で迷惑な行為／行動」であると理解することができる。ハラスメントはいろいろと表現されるかもしれないが，本書では，3つの異なるタイプについて論じることにする。すなわち，「セクシャル・ハラスメント」，「差別的なハラスメント」，それに「いじめ」の3つである（日本でよく知られている用語である「パワー・ハラスメント」は一般的には理解されていないかもしれない。本書ではむしろ「いじめ」という用語を使用する）。

　セクシャル・ハラスメントには，性的な性質の行動やコメントが含まれる。**差別的なハラスメント**には，本章の前のセクションで説明したように，カテゴリー別の分野に対する不寛容，または否定的な意見が含まれる。**いじめ**には，心理的または身体的危害を引き起こす，その他全てのハラスメントが含まれる。近年，他人を軽蔑したり困らせたりするメール・システム，および（または）SNSの利用という**サイバーいじめ**は，職場におけるいじめの拡大分野で

of workplace bullying. These types are not mutually exclusive; discriminatory or sexual harassment may also be a form of bullying.

Harassment may be carried out in two specific manners: *quid pro quo* and *hostile work environment.*

Quid pro quo harassment occurs whereby an employee is pressured to do something in exchange for a favorable employment decision such as a salary raise, a promotion or a new job. *Quid pro quo* is derived from Latin and loosely means *something for something.* If, for example, in the case of sexual harassment, an employee is not provided a promotion because she refuses to have a private dinner with her boss, such a case may constitute *quid pro quo sexual harassment.* An example of bullying may be when an employee is forced to conduct excessive overtime work or extra work outside of work hours in order to get the approval of the boss. This kind of harassment is deemed to be an inappropriate use of power.

The second type is **hostile work environment harassment**, whereby an employee is subject to a pattern of unwanted behaviors in the workplace by another employee or group of employees. The word *pattern* here means that the harassment happens repeatedly. Such harassment may be caused by any employee, regardless of their position in the company. In the case of sexual harassment, this may include behavior such as telling sexual jokes, unwanted touching or staring, and asking inappropriate questions about private matters. Jokes or inappropriate questions concerning another employee's characteristics such as religion, marital status, or disability status may constitute discriminatory harassment. In the case of *bullying*, if the victim of the bullying feels any psychological or physical damage as a result of the on-going negative behavior targeted against the victim, such harassment can be viewed under the rubric of *hostile work environment.*

ある。これらのタイプは相互に排他的ではなく，差別的またはセクシャル・ハ
ラスメントもまた，いじめの一種である可能性がある。

　ハラスメントは，「代償型」（quid pro quo）と「敵対的な職場環境型」の2
つの具体的な形態で実施されている。

　代償型ハラスメントは，従業員が昇給，昇進，新しい仕事などの有利な雇
用決定と引き換えに何かをするよう圧力を受ける場合に発生する。「quid pro
quo」は，ラテン語に由来し，ほぼ「何かの代わりに何か」を意味する。例え
ば，セクシャル・ハラスメントの場合，もし女性従業員が上司とのプライベー
ト・ディナーを拒否すれば昇進を提供されないとすれば，このようなケースは
「代償型セクシャル・ハラスメント」とみなされる可能性がある。いじめの例
としては，上司の承認を得るために，勤務時間外の過度の残業や余分な作業を
強制された場合などである。この種のハラスメントは，権力の不適切な使用と
みなされる。

　2つ目は**敵対的な職場環境型ハラスメント**で，その場合，従業員は職場で他
の従業員や従業員グループによる望ましくない行動パターンに従わざるを得な
くなる。ここで「パターン」という用語は，ハラスメントが繰り返し起こるこ
とを意味する。このようなハラスメントは，会社の中のポジションにかかわ
らず，どのような従業員によってでも引き起こされる可能性がある。セクシャ
ル・ハラスメントの場合は，性的な冗談を言ったり，触れたり，じろじろ見
たり，私的な事柄に関する不適切な質問をするなどの行為が含まれる。宗教，
婚姻状況，障害状況など，他の従業員の特性に関する冗談や不適切な質問は，
差別的なハラスメントとみなされる可能性がある。「いじめ」の場合，いじめ
の被害者が被害者を対象とした継続的で否定的な行為の結果として心理的また
は身体的な被害を感じた場合，そのような嫌がらせは「敵対的な職場環境」の
範疇_{はんちゅう}に入ると見ることができる。

Relevant harassment laws

Many countries have adopted laws to prevent and protect employees from harassment.

From a legal standpoint, the financial risk of sexual harassment cases differs from country to country. In the USA, Title VII of the Civil Rights Act of 1964 laid the groundwork for a legal recognition of sexual harassment. Subsequent federal case law and specific state laws have further increased awareness about the illegality of harassing behavior. Furthermore, in some states such as California, companies are required to provide employees with training on sexual harassment prevention.

The United Kingdom and the European Union also recognize sexual harassment as discrimination under relevant laws.

China has several national and local statutes that prohibit sexual harassment; the **Law on the Protection of Women's Rights and Interests** is one of the national laws.

India passed a law in 2013 to protect women from sexual harassment.

Eliminating workplace harasssment

Harassing behavior has a negative impact on the workplace because it psychologically hurts employees. Therefore, as a core principle, HR professionals should work to develop a company environment based on trust and comfort through on-going awareness campaigns and training sessions to ensure that employees are fully aware of the implications of workplace harassment.

関連ハラスメント法

　多くの国では，従業員のハラスメントを防止し，保護するための法律が制定されている。

　法的な観点から見ると，セクハラ事件の金銭的リスクは国によって異なる。米国では，1964年の公民権法のタイトルⅦ（セブン）は，セクシャル・ハラスメントの法的承認のための基礎を築いた。その後の連邦判例法と特定の州法は，ハラスメント行為の違法性に対する承認をより高めている。さらに，カリフォルニア州などの一部の州では，企業は従業員にセクシャル・ハラスメント防止に関するトレーニングを提供することが義務付けられている。

　英国と欧州連合はまた，セクシャル・ハラスメントを法律の下での差別として認識している。

　中国にはセクシャル・ハラスメントを禁止する国家および地方の法律がいくつかあるが，中華人民共和国の**女性の権利と利益の保護に関する法律**は国家法の中のひとつである。

　インドは2013年，女性をセクシャル・ハラスメントから守る法律を可決した。

職場のハラスメントの排除

　ハラスメント行為は，従業員を心理的に傷つけるため，職場に悪影響を及ぼす。そのため，人事担当者は，中核的な原則として，継続中の啓発キャンペーンや研修会を通じて，信頼と快適性に基づく企業環境の整備に取り組み，従業員が職場のハラスメントのもたらすことの意味を十分に認識できるようにする必要がある。

The company should create policies and procedures so that employees can raise concerns about any on-going harassment. In turn, companies should employ trained personnel who can professionally investigate such claims, or develop relations with external professionals who can be called upon in the advent of a claim. As necessary, disciplinary measures inclusive of employment termination should be meted out for those individuals found culpable.

III. Data Privacy

Defining data privacy for personal data

According to the European Commission, **personal data** is *any information that relates to an identified or identifiable living individual. Different pieces of information, which collected together can lead to the identification of a particular person, also constitute personal data.* Personal data includes the following: a name and surname, a home address, an email address such as name.surname @company.com, an identification card number, location data (for example the location data function on a mobile phone), an Internet Protocol (IP) address, a cookie ID, or data held by a hospital or doctor, which could be a symbol that uniquely identifies a person.

Note about cookie IDs: Cookies are usually small text files, given ID tags that are stored on a computer's browser directory or program data subfolders. Cookies are created when a browser is used to visit a website that uses cookies to keep track of movements within the site, to help a user resume activity from a place previously left off, and to remember a registered login, theme selection, preferences, and other customization functions. The website stores a corresponding file (with the same ID tag) to the one set in the browser and in this file information on an individual's movements within the site can be kept and tracked inclusive of any information an individual may have voluntarily given while visiting the website, such as

　会社は，従業員が現在起こっているハラスメントに関する懸念を提起できるように，施策と手順を作成する必要がある。続いて企業は，そのような申し立てを専門的に調査できる訓練された人材を持つか，あるいは，申し立てが行われた際に依頼できる外部の専門家との関係を作る必要がある。当然ながら，解雇を含む懲戒措置は，過失が認められた個人に対して課されるべきである。

Ⅲ. データ・プライバシー

個人データのデータ・プライバシーの定義

　欧州委員会によると，**個人データ**とは「識別されるか，または識別可能な，生きている個人に関連する情報のことである。一緒に収集された様々な部分的情報も，特定の人物の識別につながる可能性があり，これもまた，個人データを構成する」。個人データには以下のようなものが含まれる。すなわち，個人を一意的に識別するシンボルとなる氏名，姓名，自宅住所，name.surname@company.com などのようなメール・アドレス，身分証明書の番号，位置データ（例えば携帯電話の位置データ機能など），インターネット・プロトコル（IP）・アドレス，クッキー ID，それに，病院や医師が保有するデータなどが含まれる。

　　クッキー ID：クッキーは通常，コンピュータのブラウザー・ディレクトリまたはプログラム・データのサブ・フォルダーに保存されている ID タグを指定した小さなテキスト・ファイルである。クッキーは，ブラウザーを使用してクッキーを使用するウェブサイトにアクセスしてサイト内の動きを追跡し，中断した場所から再開し，登録済みログイン，テーマ選択，設定，およびその他のカスタマイズ機能を記憶するときに作成される。ウェブサイトは，ブラウザーで設定したファイルに対応するファイル（同じ ID タグ）を保存する。このファイルでは，サイト内での個人の動きに関する情報と，例えばメール・アドレスとしてウェブサイトへのアクセス中に自発的に与えた情報を追跡および保持できる。

email address.

Data privacy, also called **information privacy**, is the aspect of information technology (IT) that deals with the ability of an organization or individual to determine what data in a computer system shall be shared with third parties.

Relevant data privacy laws

Privacy law is the area of law concerned with the protection and preservation of the privacy rights of individuals. Increasingly, various entities in both public and private sectors collect vast amounts of personal information for a variety of purposes. Laws regarding privacy regulate the type of information that may be collected and how it may be stored and used.

To that end, the EU had implemented the **General Data Protection Regulation (GDPR)** in 2018. This regulation in EU law regulates the usage and flow of personal data from within and outside the borders of the EU. In essence, any company that conducts business with entities in the EU is impacted by this law.

As of the writing of this chapter, the USA lacks a single, comprehensive federal law that regulates the collection and use of personal information. Instead, the government has approached privacy and security by regulating only certain sectors and types of sensitive information (e.g., health and financial). As a result, law in the USA is characterized by overlapping and contradictory protections.

The above notwithstanding, the **Fair Credit Reporting Act (FCRA)** of 1970 is a federal law that regulates the utilization of a person's information within the hiring process. It is common practice to seek and verify personal information of job candidates before hire by conducting a background check.

データ・プライバシーは，情報プライバシーとも呼ばれ，組織や個人がコンピュータ・システム内のデータを第三者と共有できる能力を扱う情報技術（IT）の特定の側面のことである。

関連データ・プライバシー法

プライバシー法は，個人のプライバシー権の保護と保存に関する法律の領域である。公的部門と民間部門の両方のさまざまな団体が，さまざまな目的のために膨大な量の個人情報を収集することがますます増大している。プライバシーに関する法律は，収集される可能性のある情報の種類と，その情報の保存方法および使用方法を規制している。

その目的に沿って，EU は 2018 年に**一般データ保護規則（GDPR）**を施行した。EU 法のこの規制は，EU の国境内外からの個人データの使用と流れを規制している。本質的に，EU 内の事業体と取引を行う企業は，この法律の影響を受けることになる。

この章の執筆時点では，米国は個人情報の収集と使用を規制する単一の包括的な連邦法を制定していない。その代わりに，政府は，特定の部門と種類の機密情報（例えば，健康や経済に関する情報）のみを規制することによって，プライバシーとセキュリティに対応している。その結果，米国の法律は，重複し，矛盾する保護施策の問題を抱えている。

上記にもかかわらず，1970 年の**公正信用報告法（FCRA）**は，採用プロセスにおける個人の情報の利用を規制する連邦法である。身元調査を行うことにより，採用前に求職者の個人情報を探索し，確認することが一般的に行われている。身元調査は，信用報告書，犯罪歴，運転記録，学歴などの公的記録に基

The background check draws upon public records such as credit reports, criminal records, driving records and academic records to name a few. In accordance with the FCRA, before an employer can get a consumer report for employment purposes, the company must notify the candidate in writing and get the candidate's written consent. If an employer decides not to hire a candidate due to the results of a report, the company is compelled to provide the candidate with a *pre-adverse action disclosure* that includes a copy of the report.

In China, it is reported that the legislative bodies are trying to emulate the GDPR (https://technode.com/2019/06/19/china-data-protections-law/). As of the writing of this chapter, there are more than 200 laws, rules, and national standards that have been brought up by the country's legislative bodies, government agencies, and cyberspace watchdogs. However, one comprehensive law that emulates the GDPR has not yet been passed, but is under development.

The current situation in India similarly reflects that in China as there are information security related laws in place, but not yet a comprehensive regulation such as the GDPR.

Handling personal data in companies

It is important for HR departments to protect the data security of employees and job candidates within the course of daily business.

When creating a global database of HR data, the HR Department must review the privacy laws concerned in order to ensure that the database is in compliance with those laws.

Since privacy laws are undergoing rapid changes across the world, it is prudent

づいて行われる。FCRA に従えば，雇用主が雇用目的のためにコンシューマー（個人データ）・リポートを得る前に同社は，書面で候補者に通知し，候補者の書面による同意を得る必要がある。雇用主が報告書の結果により候補者を採用しないことを決定する場合，同社は候補者に対して，同報告書のコピーを含む「不採用事前通知」を行うことが強いられている。

　中国では，立法機関が GDPR を模倣しようとしていると報告されている（https://technode.com/2019/06/19/china-data-protections-law/）。この章の執筆時点では，200 以上の法律，規則，国家基準が，同国の立法機関，政府機関，サイバースペース・ウォッチドッグによって提起されている。GDPR のような総合的な法律はまだ可決されていないが，開発中である。

　インドの現状は，中国と同様，情報セキュリティ関連法は制定されているが，GDPR などの包括的な規制は整っていない。

企業における個人データの取り扱い

　人事部門にとって，日常業務の中で従業員や求職者のデータ上の安全保障を守ることが重要である。

　人事のグローバル・データベースを作成する場合，人事部門は，データベースを確実にプライバシー法に準拠させるために，関連する法律を見直しておく必要がある。

　プライバシー法は世界中で急速に変化しているため，人事担当者は，従業員

for HR professionals to seek advice from legal experts from time to time on how to collect and store personal data of employees and job candidates.

IV. Immigration Laws and Employment

Defining the concern about immigration laws and employment

Another complex aspect of global HRM concerns the compliance with immigration regulations regarding work authorization and work permits/visas. Although business is conducted on a global basis using technologies that have broken down many barriers, the need for compliance with immigration laws still presents a formidable barrier to the complete freedom to employ any individual the company desires.

Considering immigration laws in employment

HR professionals firstly need to ensure that any individual employed by the company retains legal authorization to work within the country. Generally, citizens of the country in which the company operates are legally authorized to work within the country. If an individual is not a citizen of the country, employment may be legal upon confirmation that the individual has the status of permanent residence or other recognized work permit. While individual employees have the responsibility to ensure the legality of their own employability in any country, the HR Department should continually monitor the validity of the work authorization for their employees. As necessary, the HR representative should encourage the employees to re-apply for work authorization prior to the expiration of their status. If the legal status of an employee's work authorization were to lapse, the company may be forced to terminate the employment.

Additionally, HR representatives may need to take an active role in helping employees who will be expatriated overseas to receive a visa for entry into

や求職者の個人データを収集・保存する方法について，法律専門家から時折助言を求めることが賢明である。

Ⅳ. 移民法と雇用

移民法と雇用に関する懸念の定義

　グローバル HRM のもうひとつの複雑な側面は，仕事許可や労働許可／ビザに関わるような移民規制の遵守に関連する。ビジネスは，多くの障壁を取り除く技術を使用してグローバルに行われているが，移民法の遵守の必要性は，会社が欲する人を雇用できる完全な自由に対する大きな障壁となっている。

雇用における移民法の検討

　人事の専門家が，まず，会社で雇用されている全ての個人が国内で働く法的権限を保持していることを確認する必要がある。一般的に，会社が事業を行う国の市民は，国内で働くことを法的に許可されている。個人が国の市民でない場合，個人が永住権またはその他の認められた労働許可証を持っていると確認された段階で，雇用は合法となる。個々の従業員は，どの国においても自らの雇用権の合法性を確保する責任があるが，人事部は従業員の労働認可証明の有効性を継続的に監視する必要がある。必要に応じて，人事担当者は，従業員に対し，在留資格の満了前に労働認可証明を再申請するよう奨励する必要がある。もし従業員の労働認可証明の法的地位が失効することになった場合，会社は雇用を終了することを余儀なくされるであろう。

　また，人事担当者は，海外駐在員が労働認可証明と共に他国への入国ビザを受け取るのを支援する上で積極的な役割を果たす必要がある。

another country along with work authorization.

Implications of Compliance and Risk Management for Globalizing Japanese Companies

All HR issues contain two key aspects: global and area-specific. Whilst global HR professionals are usually equipped with a general understanding of what is the common-sense way of dealing with various HR issues, pitfalls emerge when they try to hastily apply those common-sense solutions to area-specific cases.

Therefore, it is imperative for HR professionals to be able to liaise with competent area-specific advisers such as labor lawyers in order to seek their advice when needed.

While the HR Department at the headquarters in Japan can provide a general vision and direction on how to align HR initiatives on a global scale, local expertise is an asset for tailoring global strategies to local requirements.

Data:

https://chapters.theiia.org/rochester/Events/Presentations%20Archive/HR%20Compliance%20Risk%20Presentation.pptx.pdf

https://i-sight.com/resources/11-types-of-workplace-harassment-and-how-to-stop-them/

https://www.eeoc.gov/eeoc/publications/fs-sex.cfm

https://i-sight.com/resources/11-types-of-workplace-harassment-and-how-to-stop-them/

https://ec.europa.eu/info/law/law-topic/data-protection/reform/what-personal-data_en

https://searchcio.techtarget.com/definition/data-privacy-information-privacy

https://www.cfr.org/report/reforming-us-approach-data-protection

https://www.thebalancecareers.com/fair-credit-reporting-act-fcra-and-employment-2059610

https://technode.com/2019/06/19/china-data-protections-law/

https://www.roedl.com/insights/india-eu-gdpr-data-privacy-law

グローバル化する日本企業にとってのコンプライアンスと
リスク管理の含意

　全ての人事課題には重要な2つの側面がある。すなわち，グローバルな側面とエリア固有の側面である。グローバル人事の専門家は通常，様々な人事課題に対処するための常識的な方策が何であるかを一応理解しているが，これらの常識的な解決策を地域固有の事例に軽率に適用しようとすると，落とし穴に落ちることになる。

　したがって，人事の専門家は，必要に応じて助言を求めるために労働弁護士などの資格のある地域固有のアドバイザーと連絡をつけられるようにしておくことが絶対に必要である。

　日本の本社人事部は，人事の新しい取り組みをグローバル規模でどのように浸透させていくかという一般的なビジョンや方向性は提供できるが，他方で，現地の専門家の知識は，グローバル戦略を現地の要件に合わせる際の強みとなる。

データ

https://chapters.theiia.org/rochester/Events/Presentations%20Archive/HR%20Compliance%20Risk%20Presentation.pptx.pdf
https://i-sight.com/resources/11-types-of-workplace-harassment-and-how-to-stop-them/
https://www.eeoc.gov/eeoc/publications/fs-sex.cfm
https://i-sight.com/resources/11-types-of-workplace-harassment-and-how-to-stop-them/
https://ec.europa.eu/info/law/law-topic/data-protection/reform/what-personal-data_en
https://searchcio.techtarget.com/definition/data-privacy-information-privacy
https://www.cfr.org/report/reforming-us-approach-data-protection
https://www.thebalancecareers.com/fair-credit-reporting-act-fcra-and-employment-2059610

References & Suggestions for Additional Reading

Cascio, W. F. and H. Aguinis (2019), "The Law and Talent Management", *Applied Psychology in Talent Management*, 8th Edition, SAGE, pp. 15-41, Chapter 2.

Courmadias, N., Y. Fujimoto, and C. E. J. Hartel (2010), "Japanese Equal Employment Opportunity Law: implications for diversity management in Japan", in Ozbilgin, M. F. and J. Syed, *Managing Gender Diversity In Asia: A Research Companion*, Edward Edgar, pp. 104-118, Chapter 7.

Barry, M. and A. Wilkinson (2019), "Regulation, Deregulation or Re-regulation? The Changing Regulative Framework for HRM", in Wilkinson, A., N. Bacon, S. Snell and D. Lepak (eds.), *The SAGE Handbook of Human Resource Management*, Second Edition, Sage, pp. 65-81, Chapter 4.

https://technode.com/2019/06/19/china-data-protections-law/
https://www.roedl.com/insights/india-eu-gdpr-data-privacy-law

---

さらに学びたい人のための参考文献

Cascio, W. F. and H. Aguinis (2019), "The Law and Talent Management", *Applied Psychology in Talent Management*, 8th Edition, SAGE, pp. 15-41, Chapter 2.

Courmadias, N., Y. Fujimoto, and C. E. J. Hartel (2010), "Japanese Equal Employment Opportunity Law: implications for diversity management in Japan", in Ozbilgin, M. F. and J. Syed, *Managing Gender Diversity In Asia: A Research Companion*, Edward Edgar, pp. 104-118, Chapter 7.

Barry, M. and A. Wilkinson (2019), "Regulation, Deregulation or Re-regulation? The Changing Regulative Framework for HRM", in Wilkinson, A., N. Bacon, S. Snell and D. Lepak (eds.), *The SAGE Handbook of Human Resource Management*, Second Edition, Sage, pp. 65-81, Chapter 4.

CASE STUDY 7.1

When "Mr. X & Mr. Y" Leads to a Claim of Discrimination

Question for consideration

Claims of discrimination often arise when something that is said by someone without any discriminatory intent is perceived to be discriminatory by another person. **How can claims of discrimination arise even when the perpetrator of the discrimination had no such intention to begin with?**

Case study detail

Company: European Regional Headquarters of a Japanese company in London

Iida Tatsuya, Regional HR Director

Terrence Fielding, HR Manager

Linda Murphy, Assistant Manager, Accounting

At the European Regional Headquarters of a Japanese company in London, **Iida Tatsuya, Regional HR Director**, and **Terrence Fielding, HR Manager** were having a meeting one day in a conference room with a whiteboard. They were having an active discussion regarding the organizational plans for the upcoming fiscal year. They wrote out an image of the new organization chart on the whiteboard. While there were no names specifically written, Iida wrote *Mr. X* and *Mr. Y* in the boxes of the organization chart to indicate that actual names should be filled in later. At the end of the meeting, they snapped

CASE STUDY 7.1

「ミスター X ならびにミスター Y」が，差別の申し立てに結び付く場合

本事例の着目点

　差別の意図を全く持たずに言った誰かの言葉が，別の人によって差別的であると認識され，その結果，差別であるという申し立てが行われることがしばしば起こる。そもそも，その差別の加害者がそのような意図を持っていなかったにもかかわらず，どのようにして差別であるという申し立てが生じるのだろうか？

事例の背景

会社：ロンドン所在の日本企業の欧州地域本社

地域本社人事ディレクター：飯田達也氏
人事担当マネジャー：テレンス・フィールディング氏
経理担当アシスタント・マネジャー：リンダ・マーフィ氏

　ロンドンの某日本企業の欧州地域本社で，**地域本社人事ディレクターの飯田達也氏**と**人事担当マネジャーのテレンス・フィールディング氏**が，ある日，ホワイトボードのある会議室でミーティングを行っていた。来年度の組織計画について活発な議論をした。ホワイトボードで，彼らは新しい組織図のイメージを描いた。特定の名前が書かれたわけではなかったが，飯田氏は，組織図のボックス内に実際の名前は後で記入することにして，「ミスター X」「ミスター Y」と書いた。会議が終わった後，彼らはホワイトボードの画像の写真を撮り，頑張って自分たちの仕事の形跡を無くした。

a picture of the whiteboard image and made their best efforts to erase their work.

However, as often happens, the words were still faintly visible on the whiteboard. A few hours later, when another meeting took place in the room, some female staff were able to make out the organization chart and were taken aback when they read what was still imprinted on the whiteboard.

The following day, **Linda Murphy, Assistant Manager in the Accounting Department** approached Fielding and exclaimed, "What is with this company? I saw the new organizational plan . . . all of the managerial positions in the new organization are to be held by men? Is there no opportunity for women in a Japanese company?"

Fielding attempted to explain what he had discussed with Iida and tried to assure Murphy that the usage of *Mr.* was not intended to be construed as a deliberate intention to limit opportunities for females.

Later in the day, Fielding recounted the concerns to Iida.

Iida retorted, "I really don't see the harm here. Clearly this is just a misunderstanding. And it is based upon information that was still confidential and not yet finalized. So why should anyone care?"

Fielding explained, "Yes, you are right, but we do need to be concerned with appearances. Now, when we finalize the new organization, we need to really make sure that we have a good number of qualified women in positions of management, or else these rumors will be proven to be true."

しかし，よくあることであるが，それらの文字はホワイトボード上でまだ何とか読み取れるくらいに残っていたのである。数時間後，その部屋で別のミーティングが開かれたとき，何人かの女性スタッフは組織図を何とか判読でき，彼らはホワイトボードにまだ消し残っているものを読んで驚嘆した。

翌日，**経理部門のアシスタント・マネジャーである**リンダ・マーフィ氏は フィールディング氏に連絡を取り，「この会社は何なんですか？ 私は新しい組織計画を見ました…新しい組織の管理職ポストは全て男性が担うべきなんですか？ 日本の会社では女性のための機会はないんでしょうか？」と叫んだ。

フィールディング氏は，彼が飯田氏と話し合ったことを説明しようと努力した。「ミスター」という表現を用いたのは，女性の機会を制限するということを意図していたわけでは決してないことをマーフィ氏に説得しようとした。

同日のその後，フィールディング氏はその懸念を飯田氏に再度説明した。

飯田氏は次のように返答した。「私には，本当にこのことで何が問題なのかが分からないね。これは明らかに単なる誤解だよ。そして，その誤解は，まだ内々の話で，確定もしていない情報に基づいている。結局そんなこと，だれが気にするの？」

フィールディング氏は次のように説明した。「あなたのおっしゃる通りかもしれません。しかし，私たちは兆候ということにもっと注意を払うべきです。今，私たちは新しい組織を完成させようとしていますが，管理職ポジションに優秀な女性が十分に配置されていることを確実に実現する必要があります。そうでなければ，これらの噂が真実であったことにされてしまいます」。

Learning points

This case highlights a significant example of how claims of discrimination can develop. While the intention to discriminate was far from the mind of Iida, the usage of the salutation *Mr.* can be said to represent an unconscious bias towards male managers.

However, it may also be said in the defense of the Japanese expatriate that there was no ill intent; in Japanese the salutation *san* is gender neutral. Therefore, the Japanese manager was not aware of the significance of the usage of *Mr.* vs. *Mrs.* or even *Ms.*

We may also assume that Fielding, who is a subordinate to Iida, had not immediately spoken up to Iida due to the organizational relationship between them.

Lastly, we can see that issues which occur in global workplaces occasionally stem from factors such as language differences and unconscious bias. While such factors may not be fully eliminated, open and direct communication among locally hired employees and expatriates is helpful for expediently addressing risky issues.

学習ポイント

　この事例は，差別の申し立てがどのように展開しうるかの重要な例に光を当てている。差別する意図は飯田氏の心からはほど遠いが，「ミスター」という敬称の使用は男性管理者を指向するという無意識の偏見を表していると言える。

　しかし，当該日本人駐在員を弁護して，そこに悪意はないと言う人がいるかもしれない。日本語では，敬称の「さん」は性別に中立である。そのため，当該日本人管理職は，「ミスター」対「ミセス」あるいは「ミズ」の用法の重要性を認識していなかったのだと言うかもしれない。

　また，飯田氏の部下であるフィールディング氏は，両者の組織的上下関係のゆえに，飯田氏にすぐには反論できなかったのかもしれない。

　最後に，言語の違いや無意識の偏見などの要因から，グローバルな職場で時折，問題が発生していることが分かる。このような要因を完全に無くすことはできないが，現地採用の従業員と海外派遣者との間の率直で直接的なコミュニケーションは，きわどい問題に早期に対処するのに役立つことになる。

CASE STUDY 7.2

Being Hit With a Claim of Discrimination After an Employment Interview

Question for consideration

Japanese companies tend to seek candidates for hire who have knowledge about, and an affinity with, Japanese culture. **What are the potential risks when an interviewer discusses a candidate's familiarity with Japan, but ultimately decides not to hire the candidate?**

Case study detail

Company: Overseas subsidiary of a Japanese electronics manufacturer
Suzuki Eiichi, Sales Manager
Pablo Kimura, job candidate
Maria Lopez, HR Manager

Suzuki Eiichi is a **Sales Manager** at the overseas subsidiary of a Japanese electronics manufacturer. At this subsidiary, each manager has the responsibility to interview and make hiring decisions for any open positions within their department. Today, Suzuki is going to conduct an interview with a person of Japanese ancestry named **Pablo Kimura**.

Kimura: Pleased to meet you.

Suzuki: Oh, I see that you are of Japanese ancestry. So, let's speak in Japanese,

CASE STUDY 7.2

採用面接の後での差別の申し立ての打撃

本事例の着目点

　日本企業は，日本の文化についての知識や親近感を持っている人を採用候補者にしようとする傾向がある。**ある面接担当者が，候補者が日本のことをよく知っていたため，そのことについて話し合ったが，最終的にその候補者を採用しないこととした。その場合の潜在的なリスクは何だろうか？**

本事例の背景
会社：日本の電子機器メーカーの海外子会社
営業担当マネジャー：鈴木英一氏
採用候補者：パブロ・キムラ氏
人事担当マネジャー：マリア・ロペス氏

　鈴木英一氏は，日本の某電子機器製造会社の海外子会社の**営業担当マネジャー**である。この子会社では，各マネジャーは，部署内の任意の空きポジションへの候補者を面接し，採用するかどうかを決定する責任がある。本日，鈴木氏は日系人である**パブロ・キムラ氏**の面接を行うことになっている。

キムラ：お会いできてうれしいです。

鈴木：おっ，あなたは日系人の方ですね。では，日本語で話しましょうか？

okay?

Kimura: Well, in fact, my parents were from Japan. But I was born here and actually have never formally learned Japanese. So, I would be happy if we could just speak English.

Suzuki: Really? But you look exactly like a Japanese person I would meet back home in Tokyo. By the way, what part of Japan did your parents come from?

Kimura: From Shikoku . . . umm, Tokushima I think.

Suzuki: Your parents have been here for a long time, eh? Was it that your father was sent over as an expatriate and decided to stay here?

Kimura: Yes. When I was born, my parents got permanent residency and decided to stay here.

Suzuki: Ok. That's quite interesting. Too bad you never learned to speak Japanese. Anyway, let's get on with the interview . . .

Kimura felt uncomfortable with how this interview started but as it progressed, he felt that Suzuki was indeed impressed with his qualifications. A few days later however, Kimura was informed that he was not going to be hired at this time. Dismayed and confused, he was overcome by an intense feeling that he was unfairly discriminated against. He recalled the discomfort he had with the interviewer's questions about his Japanese ancestry, and the comments about his appearance and his lack of Japanese language skills (despite the fact that Japanese language skills are not required to perform the job responsibilities of the position).

キムラ：はい，確かに私の両親は日本からの移民です。しかし，私はここで生まれ，実際に日本語を正式に学んだことはありません。ですので，英語で話せたら嬉しいです。

鈴木：そうですか。しかし，あなたは私が東京に帰ると見かける日本の人とまったく同じように見えますね。ところで，あなたの両親は日本のどちらのご出身ですか。

キムラ：四国の…えーと確か，徳島だと思います。

鈴木：あなたの両親は長い間ここに暮らしておられますね。あなたのお父さんは海外駐在員として派遣され，ここにとどまることにされたんですか？

キムラ：はい。私が生まれたとき，私の両親は永住権を取得し，ここに永住することを決めました。

鈴木：ほう，それはとても興味深い。でも，あなたが日本語を学ばれなかったのは残念ですね。ともあれ，それでは面接を始めましょうか。

　キムラ氏はこのインタビューの始まり方には違和感を持ったが，それが進むにつれて鈴木氏が間違いなく自分の持つ資格要件を理解してくれたと感じた。しかし数日後，キムラ氏は，この度は不採用という通知を受けた。落胆し困惑する中で，彼は自分が不当に差別されたという強い感情を抑えられなかった。彼は，自分が日系人であることに関してのインタビュアーからの質問，彼の容姿と日本語スキルの欠如（日本語のスキルは当該ポジションの職務遂行に必要ではなかったにもかかわらず）へのコメントに対する違和感を思い出した。

A few days later, **Maria Lopez, HR Manager**, approached Suzuki with an official looking document in hand. "Mr. Suzuki, we have received a complaint of discrimination. What did you say in the interview to have caused this to happen?"

Suzuki was shocked and unsure of the reasons.

Learning points

It is important to remember that employment interviews with candidates should be conducted with the utmost professionalism. Prior to the actual interview, the interviewer should prepare questions based upon a clear understanding of the nature of the position and the skills which are needed from a candidate. Questions should be appropriate, and job related; questions about nationality, gender, age, family conditions and other such personal characteristics should generally be avoided.

Of course, at times discussion may move away from the topic of the open position and information that is not relevant to the candidate's ability to perform the job may come up. In the case that the company makes an offer of employment to a candidate, the risk of discrimination claims is minimal. However, as in the case above, when the candidate is not offered employment, there is a risk that the candidate could misconstrue the interviewer's intentions and claim that the questions were discriminatory in nature.

As a general rule, it is best for line managers to conduct interviews with at least two interviewers present and to restrict conversation to the requirements for the position in order to assess all candidates in terms of their qualifications for the position. If any other information is deemed

　数日後，当該企業の**人事担当マネジャー**である**マリア・ロペス氏**は，公式文書のようなものを持参して鈴木氏に話を持ち込んだ。「鈴木さん，私たちは差別の訴えを受けました。面接の中で，どういう話をして，こういうことになったんですか？」

　鈴木氏はショックを受けて，なぜそうなるのか意味が分からなかった。

学習ポイント

　求職者に対する採用面接は最大限のプロ意識をもって行うべきであると自覚することが重要である。面接が実際に行われる前に，面接担当者は，どのような仕事内容を担当させ，そのためにどのようなスキルを必要とするかをきちんと理解したうえで，それに基づき質問を準備しておくことが重要である。質問は適切かつ仕事に関連するものに限定する必要がある。国籍，性別，年齢，家族状況など個人的特徴に関する質問は一般的に避けるべきである。

　もちろん，質疑のトピックが空席のポジションに関することから離れ，候補者の職務遂行能力に関連しない情報に結び付くこともあるかもしれない。会社が候補者に採用の申し出をする場合には，差別の申し立てを受けるリスクはほとんどない。しかし，上記のように候補者が不採用となった場合，候補者は面接担当者の意図を誤解し，質問が差別的なものであったと主張してくる可能性がある。

　原則として，ライン・マネジャーは，少なくとも2人の面接担当者同席の上で面接を行い，全ての候補者をそのポジションのための資格要件について評価するために，ポジションの要件に関することに会話を限定することが最善である。会社が採用申し出を行うかどうかの判断を行うために他

necessary to determine whether the company would like to make the offer of employment, it is prudent for the HR Manager (who is assumed to be familiar with local labor laws and regulations) to judge whether such information can lawfully be obtained or not.

Furthermore, it is not advisable to treat candidates of Japanese ancestry or even actual Japanese nationals different than other candidates from the host country.

の情報が必要であると判断した場合，人事担当マネジャー（彼は現地の労働法や諸規制に精通しているものと想定される）は，その情報が合法的に入手可能かどうかを判断するのが賢明である。

　さらに，日系人候補者であっても，あるいは実際に日本人であっても，受入国の他の候補者と異なるように取り扱うべきではない。

Employee and Industrial Relations

Note: The term *Employee Relations* refers to relations between the company and employees and efforts to maintain a positive and motivated workforce. The term *Industrial Relations*, while related in concept to employee relations, is a field of study that is concerned with the establishment of the employment relationship between organizations, individuals and the unions that represent individuals. For the purpose of providing general concepts that are not tied to the labor and union history of any one country, we will not create a strong distinction between employee relations and industrial relations within this chapter.

How Does a Person Become an Employee?

Why would one person be recognized as an employee of a company whereas another person is not? While this question seems simplistic, the definition of an employee is not always straightforward, nor is the process of becoming employed the same across companies and countries. In this chapter, we will consider the ways in which companies and the people who become their employees work towards developing a mutual understanding of *employment*.

CHAPTER **8**

エンプロイー・リレーションズと
労使関係

注：「エンプロイー・リレーションズ」という用語は，会社と従業員との関係を指しており，またそれは前向きで従業員を動機づけるための取組みも意味している。「労使関係」という用語は，エンプロイー・リレーションズという概念とも関連するが，以下のような研究分野を指している。すなわち，労使関係は，会社，個人，そして個人を代表する労働組合との関係を指している。特定の国の労働者と労働組合の歴史に関連しない一般的な概念を説明したいという目的のため，本章ではエンプロイー・リレーションズと労使関係とを明確に区別しないでおこう。

個人はどのようにして従業員となるのか？

　ある個人が特定の企業の従業員と見なされる一方で，他の個人がそうではないのはなぜか。この問いは単純に見えるが，従業員の定義は必ずしも単純なものではなく，また従業員となるためのプロセスも会社や国ごとに異なる。本章では，会社とその従業員になる人たちが「雇用」に関する相互理解をどのように形成していくかを考察する。

Establishing the Employment Relationship

The fundamental understanding of the nature of employment is based upon the **employment relationship** between employees and companies. Due to differences in culture, history and legal backgrounds, the nature of the employment relationship is not the same in all countries.

The employment relationship may be formalized through an employment contract. An employment contract may specify details such as work hours, work location, compensation amount, job position, and sometimes length of employment.

In some countries, employment is not based upon a contract. In the USA, for example, employment in non-union work environments is not contractually based. Rather, employment in the USA is based upon a legal doctrine known as **at-will employment**; accordingly, the company can terminate the employment of any employee without advance notice and without an expressed cause, so long as there is no unlawful reason such as a breach of laws related to discrimination or harassment. (While this doctrine remains relevant throughout most of the USA, a company's discretion to terminate employment, such as during a mass layoff, may be limited by factors that are outside the scope of this chapter's discussion.) Likewise, employees are free to resign whenever they want to leave the company. In the absence of a contract of employment, the first step towards initiating the employment relationship in the USA is normally made through the submission of an offer letter of employment to the individual. Then, upon beginning work at the company, the employee is provided with the employee handbook of rules and policies which is the basis for the formulation of the employment relationship.

雇用関係の形成

　雇用の性質に関する基本的な理解は従業員と会社の間の雇用関係に基づく。文化，歴史，法的な背景の違いにより，**雇用関係**の性質は全ての国々で同一とは限らない。

　雇用関係は雇用契約を通じて正式なものとなる。雇用契約には労働時間，勤務地，報酬額，職位，時には雇用期間などが明記されている。

　しかし，国によっては，雇用関係は契約に基づいていない。例えば，米国では，労働組合が結成されていない場合の雇用は，契約には基づいていない。むしろ米国における雇用は**随意雇用**として知られる法的な原則に基づく。したがって，会社は差別やハラスメントなどに関連する法律違反のような理由がない限り，事前の通告や理由の開示なく雇用関係を終了させることができる（この原則はほとんどのアメリカ合衆国の州で有効であるが，他方で，例えば多人数のレイオフの場合などの雇用の終了に関する会社側の裁量は，本章の議論の範囲を超える諸要因により制約を受けることもある）。同様に，従業員も自己都合により退社することができる。雇用契約がない中で，アメリカ合衆国における雇用関係構築への最初の一歩は通常，個人に対する雇用のオファー・レターの提示から始まる。その後，入社すると，当該従業員は，規則や規定が書かれたハンド・ブックが渡され，それが雇用関係形成の根拠となる。

In China, on the other hand, a labor contract law that went into effect in 2008, and that protects employees from dismissal without cause, requires that the contract be executed immediately upon hire. Prior to the passing of this labor law, employees were stricken with uncertainty about the continuation of their employment each year.

While the employment relationship is initially formed as stated above, it is also cultivated over time. That is to say that the employment relationship is not static; it is constantly evolving based upon the internal company circumstances.

For example, the employment relationship between employees and the company may become antagonistic; long-term trust and commitment towards the company may erode when employers tend towards restructuring and layoffs rather than maintaining employment for the long-term. As a result, employees may lose their vision of a long-term career with the company and some employees who were not originally targeted for restructuring may decide to leave the company on their own volition after all. However, in company environments that have such a history, the remaining employees come to understand that they must continue to perform their work well and contribute to the corporate mission in order to remain as a valued employee.

Conversely, when employers are not inclined to terminate employment so easily or there are legal restrictions on the right to restructure businesses, employees may be able to envision a long career with the company. As a result, trust and commitment may be high. However, in this case, employees may tend to lose a sense of urgency about producing results and may become complacent.

　一方，中国では2008年に施行された労働契約法により，採用直後に雇用契約を結び，その後従業員は正当な理由のない解雇から保護される。それ以前の労働法においては，従業員は毎年，雇用の継続に不安を抱えていた。

　雇用関係は当初は上記のような形で始まるが，同時に，その関係は時間をかけて醸成されてくるものでもある。すなわち，雇用関係は静態的なものではなく，それは企業内部の状況により，常に変化し続けるものである。

　例えば，会社が雇用の長期的な維持よりもリストラやレイオフを行う傾向がある場合には，会社・従業員間の雇用関係は対立的となり，会社に対して持つ従業員の長期的な信頼感やコミットメント（帰属意識）が損なわれる可能性がある。その結果，従業員は企業内で長期にわたるキャリアを見通せなくなり，もともとリストラクチャリングの対象となっていなかった従業員のうちの何名かは自分の意志で会社を去ることを決断することになるかもしれない。しかし，そのような歴史がある会社環境の中にとどまる従業員は，貴重な従業員であり続けるために職務を充分に遂行し，会社の使命に貢献し続けなければならないと認識するようになる。

　逆に，経営者が簡単には解雇を行わず，またリストラを行う権限が法的に制約されている場合には，従業員は会社との長期にわたる雇用関係を期待するかもしれない。その結果，信頼感とコミットメントが高くなる可能性がある。しかし，この場合には，従業員は結果を出さなくてはいけないという緊迫感を喪失し，現状に満足してしまう可能性がある。

Rights & Responsibilities of Employers and Employees

It is important for the HR Department to make the effort to effectively balance the rights and responsibilities between the employer and employees to support the cultivation of a favorable employment relationship.

The history of corporations is marked by conflict between *labor* and *management*. In the early days of the modern corporation, employees had few established rights and protections against abuse by employers. Over time, efforts to curb such abuses, to improve employee health and safety in the workplace (specifically in factories), as well as to empower employees to maintain a fair work-life balance have led to the establishment of labor laws, regulations and unionization.

As a result, rights and responsibilities of companies and employees have become established based upon a combination of explicit laws as well as implicit expectations that exist within the workplace. Certain rights and responsibilities are generally common worldwide; yet, certain rights and responsibilities may also be country-specific.

To understand the relationships of rights and responsibilities, let's consider the following example: See Table 8.1 below.

Table 8.1   Usage of Paid Time Off (PTO) From Work

	Rights	Responsibilities
Employee	To take time off from work for rest and recreation	To ensure that time off does not conflict with important work obligations
Employer	To determine a PTO policy that may exceed minimum legal requirements and to manage when and how long consecutively time off is taken by employees	To comply with legal requirements regarding time off and to ensure that employees are actually able to use time off that is allotted by the company's PTO policy

経営者と従業員の権利と責任

労使双方の権利と責任のバランスを効果的にとり，良好な雇用関係の醸成を支援することは，人事部の重要な仕事である。

企業経営の歴史は，「労働者」と「経営者」との間の紛争シーンを含むものである。現代企業初期の時代において，従業員には，経営者の不当な扱いに対する権利と保護はほとんど存在しなかった。時間の経過とともに，そのような不当な扱いを抑制し，職場（特に工場）での従業員の健康と安全を改善し，また，従業員に公正なワーク・ライフ・バランスを維持するための裁量権を与えようとする努力は，労働法，各種の規制および労働組合の導入，設立につながった。

その結果，会社と従業員の双方は，明文化された法律ばかりでなく職場内に存在する暗黙の期待に基づく権利と責任を確立するに至った。一定の権利と責任は，総じて世界に共通するものである。しかし，中には特定の国に固有なものもある。

権利と責任の関係を理解するため，表8.1を参照しながら以下の例を考えてみよう。

表8.1　有給休暇の取得

	権利	責任
従業員	休養やレクリエーションのため有給休暇が取得できる	有給休暇の取得は重要な仕事上の義務と対立しないことを確認する
雇用主	最低法的要件を上回るような有給休暇基準を決定し，従業員の有給休暇の取得時期・期間を管理する	有給休暇に関する法的要件を遵守し，従業員が会社の規則によって割り当てられた有給休暇を実際に活用できるようにする

The HR Department may oversee the administration of a time off policy that establishes rights and responsibilities of both the employees and the company. If either the employee-side or the company-side feels that there is an imbalance in the assertion of rights and execution of responsibilities, then the HR Department should act as a mediator to rectify the balance of rights and responsibilities.

Company Culture, Corporate Philosophy and Competency Frameworks

Company culture is formed as a result of the collective memory of beliefs, behaviors and decisions from the past that influence the current inter-relations among company members and how they respond to on-going business issues. The company culture is not normally written down nor explicitly stated. Rather, company culture is implicitly conveyed. A company culture can be an asset or a liability for conducting business depending upon the congruence between the internal beliefs and behaviors of employees and the needs within the external business environment. For example, if a company's culture emphasizes time consuming consensus-based decisions, the company culture may become a liability when the external market is changing rapidly. Conversely, company culture may be an asset in such a market if the company culture encourages quick decision making followed by necessary adjustments thereafter.

Oftentimes when companies maintain some strongly held beliefs from their past success cases, they try to turn the implicit expectations into explicit ideas that become the foundation for the **corporate philosophy**. The corporate philosophy may also be referred to as the **corporate credo, corporate values or corporate way**.

　人事部は，権利・責任を従業員・会社の双方に帰属させる有給休暇基準の運営を監視する。もし従業員側または会社側のいずれかが，権利の主張および責任の実行に不均衡があると感じた場合，人事部は，権利および責任のバランスを修正するための仲介者として行動するべきである。

企業文化，経営理念，および，コンピテンシー・フレームワーク

　企業文化は，会社のメンバー間に存在する現在の相互関係ならびにビジネス上の課題への対応方法に影響を与えてきた過去から続く信念，行動，そして意思決定についての集合的な記憶の結果として形成される。企業文化は，通常は明文化されておらず，明示的にも述べられていない。むしろ，企業文化は，暗黙のうちに伝達される。企業文化は，社内の従業員の信念および行動と社外のビジネス環境内のニーズとの間の一致性に応じて，事業を遂行する際の資産にも負債にもなりうるものである。例えば，もしある企業の文化が，到達に時間がかかる合意に基づく意思決定を重視するものであれば，外部市場が急速に変化している場合には，その企業文化は負債となることになる。逆に，もしある企業文化が迅速な意思決定とそれに続く必要な調整を奨励するものであれば，その企業文化はそのような市場においては資産となる可能性がある。

　しばしば，過去の成功事例から得られた強い信念を持つ場合に，企業はその暗黙の期待感を**経営理念**の基盤となる明示的な観念に転換しようとする。英語では経営理念は corporate credo, corporate values, あるいは corporate way などと表現されることもある。

The corporate philosophy may focus upon core concepts such as trust, challenge spirit, or respect. Or the corporate philosophy may describe a core business process that is followed within the company such as a variant of the PDCA process. Whatever the content of the corporate philosophy, it is explicitly written, and conveyed to all members of the organization. Then, employees are expected to behave accordingly to embody the ideals of the corporate philosophy within their work. A common method for disseminating the corporate philosophy throughout the organization is through classroom training programs. Such programs may include facilitated discussions about key corporate philosophy concepts, and challenge participants to consider how to embody the corporate philosophy via role plays and case studies. Additionally, on-the-job reinforcement initiatives delivered in the form of posters, special corporate philosophy event days and manager-led team discussions about corporate philosophy concepts are also common.

In recent times, the dissemination and embodiment of the corporate philosophy has been accelerated in various companies through the introduction of a corporate competency framework. In order to embody the ideals of the corporate philosophy, a competency framework puts forth a listing of the skills, knowledge and behaviors for employees to focus on continually developing. (Refer to Chapter 3 for more information about competencies.)

Employee Relations Initiatives

Effective employee relations initiatives foster mutual trust and respect among everyone in the company; additionally, they provide the foundation for honest, fair and equitable treatment for everyone in the company.

For relations between management and all employees to be smoothly

　経営理念は，信頼，チャレンジ精神，尊敬の念などの中核的な概念に焦点を
あてることがある。あるいは，経営理念は，一種の PDCA プロセスのように
社内で守られている中核的なビジネス・プロセスを表現することもある。経営
理念がどのような内容であれ，それは明確に記述され，全ての従業員に伝達さ
れる。組織全体に経営理念を普及させるための一般的な方法は，重要な経営理
念の概念についてのファシリテーターによる議論を含むクラスルーム・トレー
ニング・プログラムが含まれ，そこではロール・プレイやケース・スタディを
通じてどのようして経営理念を体現できるかを考えるよう参加者に求める。同
様に，ポスター，特別な経営理念イベントの日，そして，経営理念の概念につ
いてのマネジャー主導のチーム・ディスカッションという形で行われる職場内
の強化策も一般的である。

　最近では，経営理念の普及と体現化は，企業のコンピテンシー・フレーム
ワークの導入を通じて，様々な企業で加速化されている。経営理念の理想像を
体現するため，コンピテンシー・フレームワークは，従業員が継続的に成長す
ることに焦点を合わせた一連のスキル，知識および行動を提示する（コンピテ
ンシーについてのより詳細な情報は Chapter 3 を参照）。

エンプロイー・リレーションズ諸施策

　効果的なエンプロイー・リレーションズ諸施策は，社内の全ての人の間で相
互の信頼と尊敬の念を生み出す。同様に，全社の社員に対して，それは誠実，
公正かつ公平な扱いのための基礎を作る。

　企業の経営者と全従業員の関係を円滑に発展させるために，人事部は両者の

developed, the HR Department must take an objective stance between management and employees. As well, the HR Department needs to take a role in mediating relations among employees. To do this, HR professionals should keenly listen to what everyone says, and observe how everyone acts in the company and communicate actively at all levels.

When listening and making observations, the HR Department should take note of the following:

(Between management and employees)
• Are comments from employees about management generally respectful and trusting? Do the words and actions of management demonstrate trust and respect towards employees?
(Among employees)
• In what ways do employees interact with each other?
• How is information conveyed across departments?
• Do employees choose to socialize together or do employees move in cliques?

Based upon the abovementioned points, the HR Department may plan interventions for improving relations within the company via formal and informal methods.

A formal term to describe an informal method is **Management by Walking Around (MBWA)**. This term was coined by the famous business management *guru* Tom Peters to describe a fundamental human activity: walking around and talking with the people you meet. When an HR representative or manager practices this method, they should walk around to as many departments as possible, bring some good news, praise good work and criticize quietly or in private.

間で客観的な立場を取らなければならない。同様に，人事部は従業員間の関係も仲介しなければならない。この事を達成するためには，人事担当者は社内の全員の発言を慎重に傾聴し，また彼らがどのように行動するかを観察し，さらに全てのレベルで積極的にコミュニケーションをとるべきである。

　傾聴し，観察をする際には，人事部は以下の点に注意する必要がある。

（管理職と従業員の間）
• 管理職に対する従業員のコメントには，一般的に尊敬の念と信頼が含まれているかどうか？　管理職の言動は従業員に対する信頼と尊敬の念を含むものかどうか？
（従業員の間）
• 従業員どうしはどのように交流しているのか？
• 部門間で情報はどのように伝達されているか？
• 従業員は分け隔てなく交流しているのか，あるいはグループに分かれて行動をしているのか？

　上記に指摘したポイントに基づき，人事部は正式および非正式な方法によって会社内の人間関係を改善するための施策を計画することになる。

　非公式な方法を表現する正式な用語は**歩き回る経営（MBWA）**である。この用語は著名な「グル（尊敬される人物）」的経営コンサルタントであるトム・ピーターズの表現で，歩き回って会った人たちと話をするという基本的な人間の行動を意味している。この方法をとる場合には，人事担当者または管理者はできるだけ多くの部署を訪れ，良いニュースを伝え，良い仕事を誉め，そして，叱る場合には静かに，あるいは人前を避けてそれを行うべきである。

Another informal method for exchanging information is **the brown bag session**. In this setting, employees may bring their lunch (sometimes in a brown paper bag, hence the name) to an informal meeting with the HR Department or management to discuss specific issues of importance.

Some formal methods of communication include the following:

1. Employee satisfaction/engagement surveys

Employee satisfaction/engagement surveys, which may be conducted internally or by an external consulting firm, usually consist of a written, anonymous survey that questions employees about their satisfaction with managerial leadership, compensation, evaluation methods or level of engagement with their work. The survey results are then tallied and benchmarked against past results or external benchmarks. In addition to such surveys, interviews may be held with select employees to draw out feedback directly. Generally, a report is compiled with suggestions for improvement. Recently, with the growing ease of conducting surveys, short and frequent surveys called **pulse surveys** are being carried out in order to get information from employees at regular intervals.

2. Town hall meetings

A town hall meeting is an *all-hands* company meeting. At such a meeting, members of management typically lead the discussion while employees are free to ask questions and provide comments. When planning such town hall meetings in global companies, cultural issues should be taken into consideration. Depending upon the cultural norms, employees may be very vocal with questions and comments or employees may say nothing for fear of embarrassment or retaliation. Therefore, it may be necessary to employ various meeting facilitation methods in order to draw out ideas and opinions in a balanced and fair manner.

　情報交換のためのもうひとつの非公式な方法は**ブラウン・バッグ・セッション**である。この場合，従業員は昼食（時に茶色の紙袋に入っているので，このように呼ばれる）を持ち寄って人事部や経営陣とミーティングを持ち，特定の重要な問題について話し合う。

　公式的なコミュニケーションには次のようなものが含まれる。

1．従業員の満足度調査／エンゲージメント調査

　社内または社外のコンサルティング会社によって実施されることがある従業員満足度調査／エンゲージメント調査は，通常は匿名の記入式調査で構成され，管理職のリーダーシップ，報酬，評価方法に対する満足度，または仕事へのエンゲージメントのレベルについて質問する。調査結果が集計され，過去の結果または外部のベンチマークと比較される。そのような調査に加えて，直接フィードバックを引き出すために，特別に選抜された従業員との面接が行われることがある。一般的に，レポートは改善のための提案とともにまとめられる。最近，調査の実施が容易になってきたため，定期的に従業員から情報を得るために，**パルス調査**と呼ばれる短時間で頻繁な調査が行われている。

2．タウン・ホール・ミーティング

　タウン・ホール・ミーティングは「全従業員」を対象にした対話集会である。このような集会では通常，経営者が議論をリードし，従業員が自由に質問し，意見を述べる。グローバル企業でこのようなタウン・ホール・ミーティングを企画する場合には，様々な文化的な問題を考慮に入れるべきである。文化的規範によって，従業員は質問や意見を声高に発する場合もあるかもしれないが，他方で，困惑や制裁を恐れて口を噤む場合もあるかもしれない。したがって，バランスのとれた公正な方法でアイデアや意見を引き出すには，会議のファシリテーション上の様々な手法を用いる必要があろう。

3. Corporate memoranda/announcements

Electronic communication makes it possible to send messages to all employees with the push of a button. But the ease of the technology has not diminished the need to deeply consider the message being conveyed. A poorly developed message can have detrimental effects on relations with employees. Therefore, corporate memoranda, whether posted around the company such as on a board in employee breakrooms or sent to all employees globally via email, should be drafted, proofread, translated into foreign languages and then back-translated into the original language to ensure that the message is clearly and accurately conveyed.

4. Corporate newsletters

Unlike corporate memoranda which may be limited to current topics of importance, the newsletter is an often-used medium for sharing information about employees' lives, sharing information about strategic shifts in direction, and for also increasing a sense of pride in their company among employees. Newsletters can be colorful and creative and not cost much to produce nowadays. The cost of printing can be negligible if the newsletter is distributed primarily online.

5. Intranet

The intranet is the best method for posting up-to-date information about the company as well as for archiving past memoranda and newsletters. An added benefit of the intranet is that it can enable two-way communication. Employees can post questions and responses. However, in this case, it is important to designate a moderator within the HR Department to review and respond to comments.

6. Open-door dispute resolution policy

A final method of formal communication to consider is an open-door dispute

3．社内文書・社内通知

　電子通信は，ボタンひとつで全従業員にメッセージを送ることを可能にした。しかし，この技術の簡便さは，そうしたメッセージが伝達する内容を吟味することの重要性を減ずるものではない。中途半端なメッセージは従業員との関係にマイナスの影響を及ぼす。したがって，社内文書は従業員休憩室の掲示板に貼られるにしても，全世界の従業員に電子メールで送られるにしても，先ず，下書きし，推敲し，複数の外国語に翻訳し，その上でオリジナルの言語に逆翻訳して，意図する意味が明確かつ正確に伝達されるよう細心の注意を払わねばならない。

4．社内報

　時々の重要トピックに限定される社内文書とは異なり，社内報は様々な従業員の生活に関する情報を共有し，戦略的転換に関する情報を共有し，そして従業員の会社に対する誇りを高めるために，しばしば使用される媒体である。社内報はカラフルで，創造的で，昨今では安価に制作することができる。社内報をオンライン中心に伝達すれば，印刷費用はゼロに等しい。

5．イントラネット

　イントラネットは，会社に関する最新の情報を掲載するとともに，過去の社内通知や社内報を保管する最善の方法である。イントラネットのさらなる利点は双方向のコミュニケーションが可能なことである。従業員は疑問や反応をイントラネット上に掲載することができる。ただし，この場合，コメントを読み，それに返信するために，人事部門内のモデレータを指名することが重要である。

6．オープン・ドアによる紛争解決制度

　従業員との公式的なコミュニケーションの最後の方法はオープン・ドアによ

resolution policy. This is a policy whereby employees are encouraged to speak with representatives of management any time about any questions or issues of concern. Of course, speaking with one's direct supervisor first is desirable, but if the employee feels uncomfortable doing so, the employee may request time with the HR representative. If the HR representative cannot resolve the problem, the employee may escalate the issue to the top management level.

An effective open-door dispute resolution policy provides a route for resolving employee grievances internally before an employee may file grievances with external authorities. The very existence of this kind of policy can protect companies from externally filed claims. In the case that an employee files a claim with an external authority before seeking a resolution internally via the open-door dispute resolution policy, it may be determined by the external authority that the employee's claim cannot be investigated until the internal procedure is followed. However, the existence of such a policy may cause the HR Department and management to spend time responding to all employee concerns whether of high or low importance.

Emotional Well-Being of Employees

Studies in employee engagement, motivation, and satisfaction stem from the recognition that emotion affects the behaviors of employees and ultimately impacts the results of the company. An understanding of such concepts is crucial for HR professionals to assist in the resolution of problems which arise in the course of work.

Firstly, let's contrast the concepts of employee *engagement* and *motivation*.

る紛争解決制度である。この制度のもとでは，従業員が疑問や問題を抱えている場合にはいつでも，どんな内容であっても，経営陣の代表と面談することが推奨されている。もちろん，先ずは直接の上司と面談することが望ましい。しかし，そのことを気まずく感じる場合には，従業員は人事部の担当者とのミーティングを持つことができる。そして，人事部担当者が問題を解決できない場合には従業員は，トップ・マネジメント層にまでその問題を持ち上げることができる。

　効果的なオープン・ドアによる紛争解決制度は，申請人が外部の当局に苦情を申し立てる前に，従業員の苦情を社内で解決するための手段を提供する仕組みである。この種の制度が存在すること自体，まさに，外部の申し立てから企業を防衛することになる。すなわち，従業員がオープン・ドア紛争解決制度を介して内部的に解決を求める前に外部の当局に申し立てを提出した場合，内部の手続きに従うまでその従業員の申し立てを調査することはできないと外部の当局により判断される場合がある。ただし，そのよう制度が存在すると，人事部門や経営陣は，重要性の大小にかかわらず，全ての従業員の懸念に対応するために時間を費やすことになる。

従業員の精神的な幸福

　従業員のエンゲージメント，モチベーション（動機づけ），および満足度に関する研究は，感情が従業員の行動に影響を与え，最終的には会社の結果に影響を与えるという認識から生じている。そのような概念の理解は，人事の専門家が仕事の過程で発生する問題の解決を支援するためには必要不可欠である。

　まず，従業員の「エンゲージメント」と「モチベーション」の概念を対比しよう。

Employee engagement is a measure of the emotional commitment which employees have for their work. High levels of engagement among employees are associated with high levels of company performance. High workplace engagement is fostered through an effective performance management process whereby employees understand the company direction and their role within the company.

Motivation normally describes anything which employees are striving to receive for themselves. Motivation derives from the pursuit of a feeling that is received while doing some work task (intrinsic motivation) and/or the tangible benefit received from such work (extrinsic motivation). For example, intrinsic motivation derives from the pursuit of a sense of new inspiration, a sense of control/autonomy in one's work, or a sense of purpose. Extrinsic motivation may describe a desire to receive a promotion, the respect of others, new status, or to develop and deepen skills in a professional area.

In other words, motivation comes from a personal drive towards something. That drive is fueled by factors that may or may not impact levels of engagement. For example, while the desire to get a promotion may indeed be a motivating factor, this desire does not necessarily lead to overall better corporate performance. Highly motivated employees may be productive, but not necessarily highly engaged. That is to say that the employee may perform assigned tasks without any emotional connection to the work (low engagement) but may want to receive some self-serving benefit such as a promotion or salary increase (high extrinsic motivation).

In the most ideal cases, highly motivated employees are also highly engaged. That is to say that when an employee is motivated by a sense of new learning and the new learning is actively applied to the achievement of company goals,

　従業員のエンゲージメントは，従業員が自分の仕事に対して持つ感情的な傾倒の尺度である。従業員間の高レベルのエンゲージメントは，高レベルの企業業績に関連する。職場での高いエンゲージメントは，従業員が会社の方向性とその中での役割を理解する効果的なパフォーマンス・マネジメント・プロセスによって促進される。

　モチベーションとは通常，従業員が自分のために何かを受け取ろうとすることを表す。モチベーションは，ある仕事をしている間に受ける感覚（内在的モチベ─ション）や，そのような仕事から受ける有形の利得（外在的モチベーション）に由来する。例えば，内在的モチベーションとは，新しい着想，自分の仕事における統制心／自律心，または目的意識などを求める気持ちから生まれるものである。外在的モチベーションとは，昇進，他者からの敬意，新たな地位を求めようとすることであり，または職業上のスキルの上達・習熟を求めようとすることであろう。

　言い換えれば，モチベーションは何かに向かおうとする個人的な動機から来ている。その動機は，エンゲージメントのレベルに影響を与える場合もあれば，与えない場合もあるような諸要因によって左右される。例えば，昇進願望は確かに動機づけの要因であるかもしれないが，この願望は必ずしも全体的により良い企業業績につながるわけではない。モチベーションの高い従業員は生産的かもしれないが，必ずしもエンゲージメントレベルが高いわけではない。エンゲージメントの低い従業員が，仕事への情緒的なつながりが弱い（つまり低いエンゲージメント）中で，昇進や昇給などの利己主義的な利得を受けるというものに対するモチベーションが高い（つまり高い外在的モチベーションを有する）場合がある。

　最も望ましいケースは，高いモチベーションをもっている従業員がエンゲージメント度合も同時に高い場合である。例えば，ある従業員は新しい学びの感覚に動機づけられており，その新しい学びが会社の目標の達成に積極的に適用

then we can say that there is a strong connection between the motivation for something (will to learn) and the engagement for getting it done (commitment to work).

While it is often asked how it is possible to motivate others, it is instructive to recall the work of the psychologist Frederick Herzberg to understand that motivation derives from an internal feeling; the best that a company can do to increase levels of employee motivation is to cultivate an environment that nurtures feelings of motivation and minimizes dissatisfaction. According to **Herzberg's Motivation-Hygiene theory**, motivation derives from high-level factors such as a sense of achievement, recognition, or responsibility, and a belief in the value of the work itself. Conversely, a feeling of dissatisfaction may be felt by employees when lower level *hygiene factors* are not satisfactorily present in the work environment. Hygiene factors include consideration of the company policies, relationships with one's superior, work conditions, salary level or security. Improvement in the condition of hygiene factors may lead to a sense of *not being dissatisfied*, but not necessarily higher levels of satisfaction.

We can conclude that sufficient levels of satisfaction and the lack of dissatisfaction is what brings people to work, day in and day out. Motivation is what drives people to do work. High level engagement, which is the devotion that employees have towards their work, leads to personal and corporate growth.

Diversity & Inclusion (D&I)

There are two recognized categories of diversity that HR professionals should be aware of: demographic diversity and task diversity. **Demographic diversity** refers to the variety of personal characteristics that are intrinsic in the workforce of an organization such as race, ethnicity, gender, age, sexual

されている場合，何かに対するモチベーション（学習意欲）とその達成へのエンゲージメント（仕事への傾倒）の間に強い関連があると言える。

　他人のモチベーションをどのように引き上げることができるのかという問いがしばしば持ち出されることがあるが，動機づけが本質的に内的要因に基づいていることを理解するために心理学者フレデリック・ハーツバーグの仕事を思い出すことは有益である。従業員のモチベーションのレベルを上げるために会社ができる最善のことは，モチベーションの感覚を育み，不満を最小限に抑える環境を築くことである。**ハーツバーグの動機づけ－衛生理論**によると，動機づけは達成感，承認，責任，そして仕事そのものの価値に対する信念などの要求レベルの高い要因から派生する。他方で，それほど要求レベルの高くない「衛生要因」が職場環境に満足のいくレベルで存在していないと，従業員に不満感が感じられることがある。衛生要因には，会社の方針に対する評価，上司との人間関係，労働環境，給与水準，または給与保障などの考慮が含まれる。衛生要因の状態の改善は，「不満足ではない」という感覚につながるかもしれないが，必ずしもより高いレベルの満足度に繋がるわけではない。

　私たちは，満足度が十分なレベルにあり，また不満が存在しないことが人々を日々の仕事に向かわせていると結論づけることができる。動機は人々が仕事をするように駆り立てるものである。高位のエンゲージメントは，従業員が自分の仕事に打ち込むことにより，結果的に個人および企業の成長を促進することになる。

ダイバーシティとインクルージョン（多様性と包摂：D&I）

　人事のプロフェッショナルが知っておくべき多様性のタイプには，デモグラフィー型のダイバーシティとタスク型のダイバーシティの2種類が存在する。**デモグラフィー型のダイバーシティ**は，組織の社員に内在する人種，民族，性別，性的指向，障害状況などの個人的特性の多様性を意味する。**タスク型のダ**

orientation and disability status. **Task diversity** refers to the variety of experiences, values, skills and knowledges of the workforce.

Inclusion refers to the efforts made by the organization to ensure that the diversity which the collective of individuals brings to the company is appreciated, respected and accepted by the company. Likewise, when the level of inclusion is high, all employees feel comfortable in the company and are enabled to fully utilize their skills and capabilities. In any company, there may be a group of employees who are an identifiable minority, and unless there are efforts made to ensure inclusion for members of that minority, the members of the minority may not feel as if they are fully accepted into the company and provided opportunities as equally as the majority group within the company.

Employee Experience

To take the employee's perspective and describe how the employee feels and thinks about the company as a place to work, the term **employee experience** (abbreviated as **EX**) has come into usage in more recent times. As the usage of this term is currently evolving, it is difficult to identify a clear definition of what the EX entails. Generally, the EX includes consideration for each one of the interactions that are significant to employees of the company. For example, the starting point for EX is to consider how candidates for employment think and feel during the recruitment process. EX then extends into consideration of interactions during daily work. Considerations of EX may even extend beyond the employee's actual working period with the company to times when employees participate in alumni activities and reflect upon their former working experiences.

The EX concept has given way to an emerging area of HRM that is referred to as **employee experience management** (abbreviated as **EXM**). Based upon an

イバーシティは社員が持つ経験，価値観，技能，知識の多様性を意味する。

　インクルージョンとは，社内の各人の多様性が評価され，尊重され，受け入れようとする組織の努力を意味する。同様に，インクルージョンのレベルが高い場合，社内の全ての従業員が気持ちよく働くことができ，その結果，スキルや能力を最大限に発揮できることになる。何れの会社においても，社内で少数派となる社員グループが存在するであろう。そうしたマイノリティ・グループのインクルージョンを図る努力なしには，社内の少数派は多数派と比べて，組織に十分に受け入れられておらず，また平等な待遇も受けていないと感ずる可能性がある。

エンプロイー・エクスペリエンス

　従業員の視点から，従業員が会社を職場としてどのように感じ，考えているかを説明するために，最近ではエンプロイー・エクスペリエンス（従業員体験）（EX と略す）という用語が使用されるようになった。この用語の使い方は現在も進化中であるため，EX が何を意味するのかについて明確に定義することは困難である。通常，EX とは，会社の従業員にとって意味のある相互作用それぞれに思いを致すことを指している。例えば，EX の出発点は，募集プロセス中に採用候補者がどのように考え，感じるかに思いを致すことにある。EX はその後，日常業務中の相互作用についての思いに広がっていく。さらには，EX は会社での現役時代を超えて，退職後の元従業員による活動に参加し，会社での仕事経験を振り返る場合に広がっていくこともある。

　EX の概念は，エンプロイー・エクスペリエンス・マネジメント（従業員経験管理）（EXM と略す）と呼ばれる HRM の新しい分野に発展してきてい

understanding of the importance of the customer experience for developing a sense of loyalty of customers with a company's brand, EXM takes a look back into the company. As the quality of a customer's experience is thought to be directly correlated with the quality of the EX, EXM uses statistical tools and technology to qualitatively and quantitatively understand employee sentiment. Then, efforts are continually made to enhance the EX over the course of the **employee journey** with the company so that the customer experience may also be impacted in the end.

Trade/Labor Unions

A trade union (British English) or **labor union** (American English) is an organization of workers. The trade union, through its union officials, bargains with the employer on behalf of union members and negotiates labor contracts (**collective bargaining**) with employers. Union members are the **rank and file**, non-managerial workers. Issues that require union consideration may include the negotiation of wages, work rules, complaint procedures, rules governing hiring, firing and promotion of workers, benefits, and workplace safety. In some countries, unionization of employees is typical and common whereas in other countries, unionization is rare. It is sometimes possible to have unionized and non-union workers working within the same company. For example, white-collar office employees may not be unionized while blue-collar employees in a manufacturing department may be unionized.

In many countries, union members occasionally go on strike in an offensive against the company as a form of protest for winning more favorable conditions.

When a multi-national company establishes a subsidiary in a new country, it is important to understand the following about unions:

る。企業のブランドに対する顧客の忠誠心を育むためのカスタマー・エクスペリエンス（顧客経験）の重要性の理解に基づき，EXM は，社内にその視点を移す。カスタマー・エクスペリエンスの質が EX の質と直接相関していると考えられるので，EXM は，従業員の感情を定性的および定量的に把握するために，統計学的ツールやテクノロジーを使用する。会社との**エンプロイー・ジャーニー**（従業員の旅）の過程で EX を改善させる努力が継続的に行われる。その結果として，カスタマー・エクスペリエンスも影響を受けるかもしれない。

労働組合

労働組合（イギリス英語では**トレード・ユニオン**と呼ばれ，米国英語では**レーバー・ユニオン**と呼ばれる）とは，労働者の組織を表す。労働組合は，その組合リーダーを通じて，組合員を代表して雇用主と交渉し，雇用主と労働契約を締結する（**団体交渉**）。労働組合員は管理職でない**一般社員**である。労働組合が取り組むべき課題は，賃金，就業規則，苦情処理手続き，労働者の採用・解雇・昇進に関する規則，付加給付，それに職場の安全に関する交渉である。一部の国では，従業員の組織化は一般的で普通のことであるが，他の国では，組織化はまれである場合がある。時には，社内で組合労働者と非組合労働者が併存する場合がある。例えば，ホワイトカラーであるオフィス・ワーカーは組織されておらず，他方で，製造部門のブルーカラー従業員は組織されているかもしれない。

多くの国では，組合員がより有利な条件を勝ち取るための抗議の形として時折会社に対する攻撃でストライキを行う。

多国籍企業が新しい国に子会社を設立するときには，労働組合について次のことを理解することが重要である。

- History of unionization in the country: What is the traditional role of unions? Do unions generally exist independently of companies as trade unions or are unions tied to specific companies as enterprise unions?
- Strength of unions: To what extent does the union have negotiating power? Does the union have the right to strike?
- Negotiating points: In a union environment, what needs to be negotiated? (i.e., salary adjustments standards, evaluation methods, disciplinary procedures, etc.)

Employee Discipline

In an ideal world, every employee thinks and acts appropriately at all times. When employees do not do the right thing, however, disciplinary proceedings may be warranted in order to raise awareness of the issues and strongly request that an employee take remedial action. In the absence of clear improvement or cessation of undesirable behaviors, the offending employee's continuing employment with the company may be at risk.

The kind of ill-actions for which employees are disciplined include, but are not limited to, lateness, carelessness, rudeness to customers, failure to maintain standards of appearance and demeanor, use of drugs or alcohol, harassment, discrimination or violence.

The least severe infractions may warrant a verbal warning. A verbal warning may be explained by a manager to a subordinate employee without much forewarning. For example, the manager may simply ask the subordinate for a moment of time to speak in a relatively private setting. Such a verbal warning may consist of a description of the perceived problem, followed by a reference to the company's rules and regulations or a generally acceptable standard of conduct and a strong request from the manager for the employee to improve

- その国の組織化の歴史：労働組合の伝統的な役割は何か？　一般的に労働組合は企業とは独立的に存在するのか，それとも企業別組合として特定の企業と結びついているのか？
- 組合の強み：組合はどの程度交渉力を持っているのか？　労働組合はストライキをする権利があるのか？
- 交渉のポイント：労働組合のある場合，どのような要求事項を交渉すべきか？（例えば，昇給水準，評価方法，懲戒手続き，等）

従業員の懲戒

　理想的な世界では，全ての従業員が常に適切に考え行動する。従業員が正しいことをしない場合，問題の重要性に対する意識を高め，従業員に改善行為を取るよう強く要求するために懲戒手続きが必要となる場合がある。明らかな改善が見られず，望ましくない行動を止めない場合，問題のある当該従業員の社内での雇用継続は著しく困難になるかもしれない。

　従業員が懲戒処分を受けるような悪い行為には，遅刻，不注意，顧客への無礼，一定水準以下の外観や品行，薬物またはアルコールの常用，嫌がらせ（ハラスメント），差別または暴力が含まれるが，これら以外にもいろいろとありうる。

　最も軽度の違反行為には口頭での警告だけで十分かもしれない。口頭での警告は，ほとんど予告なく，上司から部下の従業員に発せられるかもしれない。例えば，マネジャーは，かなりプライベートな状況でほんの少しの時間，話そうかと言って部下を誘うだけかもしれない。このような口頭による警告は，認識された問題の説明から始まり，その後，会社の諸規則，または一般的に容認されうる行動基準への言及がなされ，さらにはその従業員に対して行動の改善または変更を当該マネジャーから強く要求されることにまで広がるかもしれ

or change behavior. Lastly, the consequences for not improving or changing behavior may be expressed as well. After the verbal warning has been provided, the manager should take notes to remember the content of the discussion (topic, reason, date, time, who was present, employee's response, etc.).

More severe infractions, as well as the failure to take adequate remedial action after an initial verbal warning, may be dealt with via the provision of a written warning. A written warning is customarily prepared on a disciplinary form in consultation with the HR representative or even external legal counsel and then signed by the manager of the employee to whom the written warning is provided. Once the written notice is passed to the employee, the written warning is signed by the employee. A copy is provided to the employee and another copy is retained by the company.

Disciplinary penalties may also be imposed by the company on the employee. Such penalties may include a reduction in salary, demotion, loss of certain privileges or benefits or temporary suspension from work. A suspension may also be imposed in order to provide the company time to investigate any grievances against the offending employee from other employees such as in a sexual harassment case.

Some incidents may warrant an immediate termination of employment. For example, in the case that an employee is violent or under the influence of illicit drugs, some countries allow companies to terminate employment immediately as a form of severe discipline. In the case that a crime has been committed, the company may be compelled to contact local law enforcement; the offending employee may also face prosecution under the law.

While local laws and regulations will dictate the extent to which disciplinary measures can be carried out, HR professionals, along with line managers and

ない。最後には，行動を改善または変更しない場合にはどのようなことになるかということも示されるであろう。口頭による警告を出した後，マネジャーは話し合った内容（テーマ，理由，日付，時間，同席者，従業員の返答内容，など）を記憶にとどめておくべく記録をとるべきである。

　最初の口頭による警告の後に適切な改善行動を取らなかった場合，あるいは，より深刻な違反があった場合は，書面による警告を発することによって対処することができる。書面による警告は，通常，人事担当者と協議するだけでなく，時には社外の顧問弁護士まで巻き込む形で，矯正的な形式で作成され，その後，警告が発せられた従業員の上司によって署名される。書面による通知が従業員に渡されると，書面による警告は従業員によって署名される。コピーが従業員に渡され，会社もそれを保持する。

　会社から従業員に懲戒処分が科されることもある。そのような罰則には，減給，降格，特定の特権または付加給付の喪失，または一時的な出勤停止が含まれる場合がある。セクシャル・ハラスメントの場合のように，苦情が従業員から寄せられた場合，それを犯しているとされる従業員に対する審査の時間を会社に与えるために，一時的な出勤停止が科されることもある。

　特定の出来事は即座の雇用終了に繋がるかもしれない。例えば，従業員が暴力的であるとか，違法薬物の影響を受けているとかの場合，一部の国では企業が厳しい懲戒処分の一環として即座の雇用終了を実施することを認めている。犯罪が起こった場合，会社は現地の警察に連絡することを余儀なくされるであろう。犯罪を起こした従業員もまた法律に基づいて起訴されるであろう。

　現地の法律ならびに規制は，社内での懲戒処分がどの程度まで実施されてよいかを定めている。一方で，特定の従業員が仕事中とはいえないような，また

executives, have the responsibility to protect the safety of other company employees when an employee is acting in a non-professional or immoral manner.

Employment Termination

Employment termination may be initiated by the employee or the company. Regardless of how the termination is initiated, the decision to terminate employment is rarely made lightly.

Employees who initiate their resignation to pursue opportunities at other companies and/or to make a change to their lifestyle customarily submit their notice of resignation to a company representative such as their direct supervisor or a member of the HR Department. Thereafter, a resigning employee customarily continues to work up to a period of two weeks or one month in order to assist with the transfer of responsibilities to other remaining employees.

Companies may initiate the termination of employment for a variety of reasons that normally fall into two broad categories: negative business conditions or individual concerns. Negative business conditions that lead to employee termination include economic downturns, the closure of a business unit, or downsizing in the short-term to realize efficiency and productivity gains in the medium-to-long-term.

As described in the previous section, employment termination for individual concerns may be a form of discipline. Or, employment termination may be the consequence of continually sub-standard work performance. The legality and cultural acceptability for initiating the termination of employment differs on a country-to-country basis. What is acceptable and sensible in one country

は不道徳な態度で行動している場合，人事担当者はライン管理者および役員とともに他の従業員の安全を守る責任がある。

雇用関係の終了

　雇用の終了は，従業員または会社のどちらかから持ち出される。その雇用の終了がどのようにして始まったかにかかわらず，雇用終了の決定の判断は，気楽になされることはほとんどない。

　他の会社での機会を追求するため，または／同時に，生活様式を変更するために退職を持ち出す従業員は，通常，直属の上司または人事部のメンバーなど，会社の担当者に退職願を提出する。その後，退職する従業員は，他の残りの従業員への業務引継ぎを行うために，通常2週間または1カ月までの期間，勤務を継続する。

　企業は，様々な理由で雇用の終了を持ち出すことがあるが，それらは通常，経営状況の悪化と個人の事情というほぼ2つのカテゴリーに分類される。従業員の雇用終了につながる一般的な経営環境には，景気後退や事業部門の閉鎖，あるいは，中長期的な効率性と生産性の向上を実現するための当面の規模の縮小が含まれる。

　前のセクションで説明したように，個人の事情に起因する雇用の終了は懲戒処分の一形態であるかもしれない。あるいは，雇用終了は，継続的に標準的な仕事成果を出せないことの結果かもしれない。雇用終了に入っていくための合法性および文化的許容性は，国ごとに異なる。ある国で受け入れられ，理にかなったことと考えられることが，他の国では前代未聞のことなのかもしれな

may be unheard of in another country.

Implications of Employee & Industrial Relations for Globalizing Japanese Companies

In this chapter, we have introduced some diverse concepts ranging from the employment relationship and employee experience (EX) to unions, discipline and employment termination. It is expected that the Japanese reader should find some of the concepts to be familiar and similar to practices within Japanese companies. However, some of the concepts may strike a different chord for Japanese readers.

The very concept that employee relations is necessary to handle strife between the company and employees may seem unfamiliar in modern Japan where relations are generally characterized by cooperation between the company and employees. While enterprise unions and company representatives engage in annual negotiations called *shunto* or **spring offensive**, it is rare to ever hear of labor strikes or strife in the news. In fact, the union representatives are often elected from the ranks of employees who have been hired by the company and are temporarily rotated out of the company to represent the union as a *senju*, only to return to the employ of the company after a stint in the union for about two to three years.

Furthermore, while the system of lifetime employment in Japan has been breaking down, many fresh recruits enter Japanese firms with the implicit understanding that they are joining a company in which they may pursue a full working career. Such implicit understanding amongst employees is rare outside of Japan. As a result, the understanding about rights and responsibilities in Japan may differ dramatically from the understanding in other countries. For example, in Japan, it is generally understood that employees have the

い。

エンプロイー・リレーションズと労使関係の
日本のグローバル企業への示唆

　本章では，エンプロイー・リレーションズ及びエンプロイー・エクスペリエンス（EX）から始まり，労働組合，懲戒処分，そして雇用の終了まで，様々な概念を紹介した。日本の読者はいくつかの概念が日本企業における慣行とよく似ていて類似していると感じるはずである。しかし，いくつかの概念は，日本の読者に対して違和感を感じさせるかもしれない。

　会社と従業員間のもめごとを処理するためにエンプロイー・リレーションズが必要であるという考え方というものは，会社と従業員の間の関係が協力関係によって一般的に特徴づけられる現代の日本ではなじみが薄いように見えるかもしれない。企業別組合や会社の代表者たちは，「春闘」，あるいは英語では**スプリング・オフェンシブ（春季闘争）**と呼ばれる年次交渉を行っているが，ニュースでストライキや紛争を耳にすることはめったにない。実際，組合の代表者は多くの場合，会社に雇われた一般従業員の中から選出され，会社から離れて約2〜3年という短い期間，「専従」として組合で勤務するが，その後に会社の雇用に戻ることになる。

　さらに，日本での終身雇用の制度は崩壊しつつあるが，多くの新入社員は，定年までの全キャリアを全うするかもしれない会社になるかもしれないという暗黙の了解のもとに，日本企業に入社する。従業員の間でのそのような暗黙の了解が存在することは日本以外では稀である。結果として，日本における権利と責任についての理解は，他の国々の理解とは劇的に異なるかもしれない。例えば日本では，自分の肉親や家族が国内に留まり，本人だけが新しい地域または国に転勤しなければならない場合でも，疑念の余地なくその人事異動を受け

responsibility to accept personnel transfers without question even if such transfers mean that the Japanese employee has to relocate to a new region or country while the employee's immediate family remains in the original location. In other countries, such a directive from the company may be met with opposition from an employee.

Therefore, globalizing Japanese companies need to be prepared for a different labor landscape when they expand overseas.

References & Suggestions for Additional Reading

Arenas, A., D. Di Marco, L. Munduate and M. C. Euwema (2017), "Dialogue for Inclusion: When Managing Diversity is not Enough", in Arenas, A., D. Di Marco, L. Munduate and M. C. Euwema (eds.), *Shaping Inclusive Workplaces Through Social Dialogue*, Springer, pp. 3-21.

Arenas, A., D. Di Marco, L. Munduate and M. C. Euwema (2017), "The Circle of Inclusion: From Illusion to Reality", in Arenas, A., D. Di Marco, L. Munduate and M. C. Euwema (eds.), *Shaping Inclusive Workplaces Through Social Dialogue*, Springer, pp. 261-272.

Dovidio, J. F., S. Abad-Merino and C. Tabernero (2017), "General Concepts About Inclusion in Organizations: A Psychological Approach to Understanding Diversity and Inclusion in Organizations", in Arenas, A., D. Di Marco, L. Munduate and M. C. Euwema (eds.), *Shaping Inclusive Workplaces Through Social Dialogue*, Springer, pp. 23-32.

M. Mor Barak (2014), "Discrimination, Equality, and Fairness in Employment", *Managing Diversity: Toward a Globally Inclusive Workplace*, 3rd ed., Thousand Oaks, California: SAGE Publications, pp. 55-75, Chapter 3.

Bebenrith, R. and D. Li (2011), "Expatriation and Performance", in Bebenrith, R. and T. Kanai (eds.), *Challenges of Human Resource Management in Japan*, Routledge, pp. 60-78.

入れる責任があると考えられている。他の国々では，会社からのそのような主張は従業員からの抵抗に合うかもしれない。

したがって，グローバル化する日本企業は，海外に進出するときには日本と異なる労働の状況に対応すべく準備をしておく必要がある。

さらに学びたい人のための参考文献

Arenas, A., D. Di Marco, L. Munduate and M. C. Euwema (2017), "Dialogue for Inclusion: When Managing Diversity is not Enough", in Arenas, A., D. Di Marco, L. Munduate and M. C. Euwema (eds.), *Shaping Inclusive Workplaces Through Social Dialogue*, Springer, pp. 3-21.

Arenas, A., D. Di Marco, L. Munduate and M. C. Euwema (2017), "The Circle of Inclusion: From Illusion to Reality", in Arenas, A., D. Di Marco, L. Munduate and M. C. Euwema (eds.), *Shaping Inclusive Workplaces Through Social Dialogue*, Springer, pp. 261-272.

Dovidio, J. F., S. Abad-Merino and C. Tabernero (2017), "General Concepts About Inclusion in Organizations: A Psychological Approach to Understanding Diversity and Inclusion in Organizations", in Arenas, A., D. Di Marco, L. Munduate and M. C. Euwema (eds.), *Shaping Inclusive Workplaces Through Social Dialogue*, Springer, pp. 23-32.

M. Mor Barak (2014), "Discrimination, Equality, and Fairness in Employment", *Managing Diversity: Toward a Globally Inclusive Workplace*, 3rd ed., Thousand Oaks, California: SAGE Publications, pp. 55-75, Chapter 3.

Bebenrith, R. and D. Li (2011), "Expatriation and Performance", in Bebenrith, R. and T. Kanai (eds.), *Challenges of Human Resource Management in Japan*, Routledge, pp. 60-78.

CASE STUDY 8.1

When the Collective Agreement With the Union Stymies Productivity

Question for consideration

A business professional wants to innovate in order to produce new efficiencies and raise productivity. However, when a company is unionized, it is necessary to consider how the provisions of the collective agreement may impact the business plan. **In what ways has the President of the Japanese subsidiary in this case study effectively considered the impact of the union on his business plans? How should the HR Manager ideally respond to the President and engage with the union chief?**

Case study detail

Company: Subsidiary of a Japanese company located in the USA

Yamada Daisuke, President

Dennis Price, HR Manager

Paul Sanchez, Union Chief

A Japanese company acquired a US-based company and started taking over most of its manufacturing facilities while maintaining many of the existing employees. While the company was unionized before the acquisition, labor relations were stable without major disputes. At the time of the acquisition, the **HR Manager** was an experienced professional named **Dennis Price** who was reputedly very adept at managing labor issues to the satisfaction of the company and union.

CASE STUDY 8.1

組合との労働協約が生産性を阻害する場合

本事例の着目点

　事業の専門家は，新たな効率を生み出し，生産性を高めるために革新を志向している。しかし，企業が組合に組織化されている場合は，労働協約の規定が事業計画にどのような影響を与えるかということを考慮する必要がある。ここで取り上げる日本企業の子会社の社長は，当該組合が自らの事業計画に与える影響に対して，どのように実質的に検討してきたのだろうか？　人事マネジャーは，社長にどのように対応し，また，組合委員長にどのように関わっていくのが理想的なのだろうか？

事例の背景

会社：在アメリカ日系子会社

社長：山田大輔氏

人事マネジャー：デニス・プライス氏

組合委員長：ポール・サンチェス氏

　ある日系企業が米国企業を買収したが，当初から，既存の従業員のうちの多くを継続雇用しながら，製造施設の大部分を引き継いだ。買収前は同社には労働組合が存在したが，大きな争いもなく労使関係は安定していた。買収時の**人事マネジャーはデニス・プライス氏**という経験豊富な専門家であり，彼は会社と組合の双方に満足をもたらすような労働問題のやり手で，これまでうまく対応してきたという評価を得ていた。

After some time passed since the US-based company was acquired by the Japanese conglomerate, it became necessary to assess the equipment and production lines in response to equipment deterioration and market changes. The company decided to promote efficiency within the production system by automating five out of the eight pre-existing lines and introducing a shift system whereby work hours fluctuate between day and evening shifts.

President Yamada Daisuke recognized that the union would need to understand and accept these changes. Therefore, he consulted with Price about how to communicate with the unions. In response, Price had only one point to make. He said, "**Paul Sanchez, the Union Chief** is a very conservative person and will not understand the need for a new production system."

President Yamada was undeterred. He invited the Union Chief to tour a factory in Japan. Upon seeing the line arrangement of the parent company and the employees working hard, the Union Chief was convinced. Sanchez expressed, "I understood the necessity for the review of the production system. Let's cooperate."

Thereafter, President Yamada decided to immediately implement the plan when he returned to the USA. He launched a project team for installing new production facilities and re-arranging shifts within the new work system. All seemed okay for a while.

However, after some time, some problems began to emerge. It was reported that quality problems were occurring frequently in the old line (even more than was ever experienced before the transformation). After examining the cause, it was apparent that a group of veteran workers who used to work the night shift and provide direction to the less experienced workers were primarily working now on the new automated lines during the day shifts.

　当該米国企業が日本のコングロマリットに買収されてからしばらくしてから，設備機器の劣化や市場の変化に対応して，機械設備や生産ラインを見直す必要があった。同社は，既存の8ラインのうち5ラインを自動化し，勤務時間が昼勤と夜勤の間で変化するシフト制を導入することにより，生産システム内の効率性を高めるという決定をした。

　山田大輔社長は，組合にはこれらの変化を理解し，受け入れてもらう必要があると認識した。そこで彼は，組合とどのようにコミュニケーションをとるべきかについてプライス氏に相談した。それに対して，プライス氏は1点だけ指摘した。彼は「**組合委員長**である**ポール・サンチェス氏**は非常に保守的な人で，新しい生産システムの必要性を理解しないでしょうね」と述べた。

　山田社長は怯まなかった。彼は労働組合委員長を日本の工場見学に招待した。親会社のライン配置と一生懸命働いている従業員を見て，組合委員長は納得した。サンチェス氏は「生産システムの見直しの必要性を理解しました。協力しましょう」と表明した。

　その後，山田社長はアメリカに戻った後すぐに計画を実行することにした。彼は，新しい生産施設を据え付け，新しい作業体制内でシフトを再調整するためのプロジェクト・チームを立ち上げた。全てはしばらくの間，順調に見えた。

　しかし，しばらくして，いくつかの問題が浮上し始めた。品質上の問題が旧ラインで頻繁に発生しているという（それは当該変革以前に経験したことがないほどの頻度であった）。原因を調査すると，これまで夜勤シフトで勤務し，経験の浅い労働者への指導を行っていたベテランの労働者のグループが，現在では昼勤シフトの主に新しく自動化されたラインで働くようになっていたことが明らかとなった。

President Yamada once again called for a meeting with Price.

"Take a look at this shift assignment chart. I suspect that the quality issues which are coming off the old lines are directly related to this shift pattern. Please rectify the situation."

Price retorted in response, "President Yamada. My hands are tied on this. You are aware of the company's collective agreement? In the collective agreement, the request for shifts is made according to seniority. Therefore, it is unavoidable that veterans who used to work at night will fill up the daytime shifts on the new lines."

President Yamada snapped back, "But don't the workers have any care about the quality from the old lines?"

To that Price firmly asserted, "Well, this is not an issue of quality. It is an issue about the collective agreement. We would need to revise the collective agreement. But the union won't go for it."

Exasperated President Yamada retorted, "Really? Aren't such personnel decisions within the scope of our management discretion?"

Price looked down at his shoes and remained silent.

Learning points

In a union environment, it is important to understand the restraints imposed by the collective agreements and to recognize that union agreements supersede or replace all company rules (and at times, even common sense in business). As a manager needs to be familiar with the

山田社長はもう一度，プライス氏と会合を持つことにした。

「このシフトの割り振り表を見てよ。古いラインから出てくる品質問題は，このシフト・パターンに直接関連していると思うよ。この状況を正常化してもらえる？」

それに対してプライス氏は答えた。「山田社長，これに関して私はお手上げなんですよ。会社の労働協約をご存じですか？　労働協約では，シフトの要求は先任権（勤続年数順）に従って行われます。したがって，夜間シフトで勤務していたベテランが，新しい生産ラインの昼間シフトに変わっていくことは避けられないんです」。

山田社長は，「しかし，労働者たちは古いラインの品質を気にしていないの？」と即座に言い返した。

その点に関してプライス氏はしっかりと主張した。「このことは品質に関する問題ではありません。労働協約に関する問題です。私たちは労働協約を改定する必要があります。しかし，組合はそれを受け入れないと思います」。

憤慨した山田社長は，「本当に？　そのような人事上の決定権は経営側の裁量権内にあるのではないの？」と言い返した。

プライス氏はうつむいて（自分の靴を見下ろして），沈黙を守った。

学習ポイント

　労働組合のある環境では，労働協約による制約を理解し，労働協約が全ての会社の規則（時にはビジネス上の常識）に優先するか，またはそれに取って代わるものであるということを認識すべきである。経営者は労働協約に精通している必要があり，労働協約や先任権に無関心であったという

collective agreement, in that respect President Yamada, who had been unconcerned with the collective agreement and the seniority rules, made a crucial error.

The nature of labor relations differs from country to country (or from industry to industry even within a country). Someone like President Yamada who comes from Japan where there is a history of stable and cooperative labor-management relations may be ill-prepared for the negotiations that should be conducted with a union.

That being said, we may also find fault with the behavior of Price in this case. Price could have acted more like a business partner. He could have proactively considered how to represent the business needs to the union so that a mutually acceptable agreement could be drafted up.

When existing collective agreements or labor practices, including seniority rules, present a major obstacle to the management of the business, it becomes necessary for the company representatives, including the HR Manager, to directly face the union and explain why such changes are desirable.

Given the differences between the labor environment in Japan and overseas, it is advisable to educate the managers who will be expatriated overseas regarding the actual conditions of labor relations and collective agreements at the assigned overseas subsidiaries, as well as regarding the labor-management relations, labor unions, and labor law.

点で，山田社長は重大な誤りを犯した。

　労使関係の性質は国ごと（同じ国内でも産業により）に異なる。安定した協力的な労使関係の歴史がある日本からやってくる山田社長のような人には，組合と必ず持たざるを得ない交渉に対して，どうしても準備不足となってしまうかもしれない。

　とは言いながらも，このケースにおけるプライス氏の態度には欠点があることも否めない。プライス氏はもっとビジネス・パートナーとして振舞うことができたのではないだろうか。ビジネス上の必要性を組合に説明し，相互に受け入れられる合意を構想することもできたのではないだろうか。

　先任権ルールも含めた既存の労働協約，あるいは労働慣行が，企業経営上，大きな障害になる場合には，人事マネジャーを含む経営側は「なぜ，このような変更が望ましいのか」を，労働組合に直接対面し，説明する必要がある。

　労働環境が日本と海外では異なるため，海外派遣予定者に対しては，赴任先現地法人における労働関係や労働協約の実情についてはもちろんのこと，派遣予定国の労使関係，労働組合，労働法の基本などについても教育することが望ましい。

CASE STUDY 8.2

When the Lack of Direct Communication Leads to a Lawsuit

Question for consideration

Problems in the workplace often arise when employees misunderstand each other's intentions. Ideally, if two employees can speak directly and confirm understanding of each other's intentions, problems can be stopped in their tracks. At the worst, employees may not seek to resolve the issues amicably. Rather, they may quit and even file a lawsuit against the company. **What do you think the managers did wrong in this situation and how could they have avoided a misunderstanding turning into a potentially damaging lawsuit?**

Case study detail

Overseas Subsidiary: Nihon Manufacturing UK

Onishi Takafumi, Production Engineering Manager

Robert Fulton, Production Control Supervisor

Jan Ainsworth, Administration Clerk

Emily Acton, HR Manager

Onishi Takafumi had been appointed to a subsidiary in the United Kingdom as the **Production Engineering Manager** in charge of both technology and management related to production. Although he was selected for this role based upon his deep technological skill, he admits that he was not prepared sufficiently for managing a team of people in an overseas subsidiary.

CASE STUDY 8.2

直接のコミュニケーション不足が訴訟につながった事例

本事例の着目点

　職場での問題は，しばしば，従業員どうしが互いの意図を誤解するときに起きるものである。理想的には，2人の従業員が直接話し合い，互いの意図を理解していることさえ確認できれば，問題はその場で解決できるであろう。最悪の場合，従業員は当該問題を友好的に解決しようとしないかもしれない。それどころか，彼らは辞職して会社に対して訴訟を起こすことすらある。この場合，マネジャーはどのような間違いを犯したのか，また，マネジャーは，潜在的に損害を与える訴訟に至るような誤解をどのようにすれば回避できただろうか？

事例の背景

海外子会社：日本マニュファクチャリング UK
生産技術マネジャー：大西貴文氏
生産管理スーパーバイザー：ロバート・フルトン氏
管理部門事務員：ジャン・アインスワース氏
人事マネジャー：エミリー・アクトン氏

　大西貴文氏は，生産に関する技術と管理の両方を担当する**生産技術マネジャー**としてイギリス子会社に任命された。彼は，彼の高い技術力に基づきこの役割に選抜されたが，海外子会社の人々を管理するために十分には準備できていなかったと自覚している。また，イングランド中部のアクセントを明確に理解し，しっかりとコミュニケーションを行うことは困難であると彼は感じて

Additionally, he felt that it was difficult to clearly understand the accents in central England and to communicate effectively. However, as a manager, he wasn't one to complain often as he tried to make the most of his situation. He felt lucky that his direct subordinate, **Robert Fulton, Production Control Supervisor,** would listen intently and patiently to try to understand Onishi's intentions. Oftentimes, Onishi would speak directly with Fulton first; then Fulton would communicate Onishi's intentions to the other employees in the department.

Within the Production Department, Production Technology and Production Control were divided into two areas. **Jan Ainsworth** was an **Administration Clerk** who would move back and forth between the two areas during her daily work. Onishi assessed her to be rather intelligent and capable of accomplishing work as needed, but not so efficient. He would often observe her to be standing around and talking with production engineers without a clear purpose. He wondered whether she was just killing time whenever she would come into the Production Technology section where Onishi had his seat.

After observing Ainsworth's behavior over the past few weeks, Onishi thought it was about time to say something. But as he was in the habit of speaking with many of the local staff through Fulton, he called Fulton over and commented, "Jan Ainsworth seems to be coming into this section too often for no reason. Please tell her something about this."

From the next day onward, Ainsworth was no longer seen coming into the Production Technology section. Onishi thought that Fulton had given her some type of directive and so he had forgotten about the matter thereafter.

However, a month later, **Emily Acton, HR Manager** requested Onishi and Fulton to come speak with her. Acton informed Onishi that Ainsworth had

いた。しかし，彼はよく苦情を言うような人間ではなく，マネジャーとして，自分の置かれた状況を最大限に活用しようと頑張っていた。彼の直属の部下である**生産管理スーパーバイザーのロバート・フルトン氏**は，大西氏の意図を真剣に聞き，辛抱強く理解しようとしてくれるので，ラッキーなことだと感じていた。しばしば，大西氏は最初にフルトン氏に直接話すことにしている。それからフルトン氏は大西氏の意図を部門の他の従業員に伝えてくれることになる。

　生産部門内では，生産技術と生産管理は2つのエリアに分かれていた。**ジャン・アインスワース氏は管理部門の事務員**であった。彼女は日常業務の中で2つのエリアを行き来する。大西氏は，彼女を，かなり知的で，必要に応じて仕事を成し遂げるだけの能力はあるが，それほど効率的でもないと評価していた。彼は，彼女が明確な目的もなく歩き回り，生産技術者と立ち話をしているのをよく見かけた。彼は，彼女が，大西氏の席がある生産技術課に来るのはいつもただ暇つぶしをしに来ているだけではないのかと考えた。

　アインスワース氏の行動を過去数週間観察した後，大西氏は何かを言うべき時期が来たと考えた。しかし，彼はフルトン氏を通して現地スタッフの多くと話す習慣があったので，彼はフルトン氏を呼んで，「ジャン・アインスワースは理由もなくあまりにも頻繁にこのセクションに来ているようだね。これについて彼女に何か言ってやってよ」。

　翌日から，アインスワース氏が生産技術課に足を踏み入れることはもはや見られなくなった。大西氏は，フルトン氏が彼女に何らかの指示をしたのだと考え，その後はその問題について失念していた。

　しかし，1カ月後，**人事マネジャーのエミリー・アクトン氏**が，大西氏とフルトン氏に話があるので，彼女のところ来てほしいと言ってきた。アクトン氏

submitted her resignation letter and will no longer be coming to work. Acton queried Onishi, "Do you know what may have caused Jan to quit?" Neither Onishi nor Fulton had heard anything directly from Ainsworth that they could speak about at that time. The meeting was ended and once again Onishi thought that the issue was resolved.

Two weeks later, Onishi was summoned again by the HR Manager. Acton explained, "We have received a letter from a legal representative that Jan Ainsworth is engaging. According to the letter, she quit because she was banned from entering the Production Technology section. Although she voluntarily quit, it is asserted that this is a **constructive dismissal*** because she had been prevented from carrying out her work duties due to the restrictions placed on her movement within the workplace. We have to respond to this allegation."

* when an employer creates a condition that leaves the employee with no choice but to quit.

Onishi sighed in exasperation as he wondered why things got to this point.

> **Learning points**
>
> Work in a foreign country is complicated by language barriers. While Onishi's reliance upon Fulton to handle some of the communication with other department employees may be acceptable in certain cases, Onishi may have become too complacent in the thought that he could manage others through Fulton.
>
> This case illustrates the need for having as much direct communication with others as possible, especially when performance-related feedback and/or disciplinary measures need to be taken.

は大西氏に，アインスワース氏が辞職願を提出したため，彼女はもう仕事には来ないと伝えた。アクトン氏は大西氏に「何でジャンが辞職をしたのかわかりますか？」と尋ねた。大西氏とフルトン氏は，アインスワース氏からは直接何も聞いていなかったので，その場で言えることはなかった。そのミーティングは終わり，再度，大西氏は問題が解決したと思った。

　その2週間後，大西氏は再び人事マネジャーに召喚された。アクトン氏はこう説明した。「ジャン・アインスワースが依頼している弁護士から文書を受け取りました。その文書によると，彼女は生産技術課に入ることを禁じられたので辞めるとのことです。彼女は自発的に辞任しましたが，これは**疑似解雇***であると弁護士は主張しています。なぜなら，彼女は職場内での動きに対する制限のために仕事を遂行することができなかったからです。我々はこの訴えに対応しなければなりません」と述べた。

*雇い主によって退職せざるをえない状況に追い込まれる不当な解雇のことを指す。

　大西氏は，どうしてこういうことになるのか疑問に思ったので，憤慨し，ため息をついた。

学習ポイント

　外国での仕事は言葉の壁によって複雑になっている。他の部署の従業員とのコミュニケーション対応の一部を大西氏がフルトン氏に頼っていたが，大西氏がフルトン氏を通して相手を管理できると思って自己満足に陥り過ぎていたのかもしれない。

　このケースは，特にパフォーマンス関連のフィードバックおよび／または懲戒処分を行う必要がある場合に，相手とできるだけ直接コミュニケーションをとる必要性を示している。

To avoid such problems, what could Onishi do differently in the future?

(1) If he chooses to continue to communicate through Fulton, he should ensure that Fulton has accurately grasped his intention and knows what to convey to others. After explaining his intentions, Onishi may say something like the following. "I want to make sure that I was clear with you. Kindly tell me what you will express to others based upon what I have just directed."

(2) Alternatively, Onishi should directly communicate with others, but do so with Fulton or the HR Manager present. The presence of another person during such conversations can help to ensure that Onishi is effectively expressing his ideas.

(3) Additionally, any manager should realize that their perceptions of others may not be fully accurate. Before asserting that another person's behavior is inappropriate, it is always advisable to firstly have a discussion together to understand that person's way of thinking which has led to such behavior.

In short, while it is irrefutable that language barriers can be frustrating, the lack of language skill does not justify the failure to communicate appropriately as a manager.

　このような問題を回避するために，大西氏はこれまでと異なり，将来どうすべきだろうか？

(1)　彼がフルトン氏を通してコミュニケーションし続けることを選ぶならば，彼はフルトン氏が彼の意図を正確に理解して，相手に何を伝えるべきかを知っていることを確実にするべきである。自分の意図を説明した後，大西氏は次のように言う必要があろう。「私はあなたと確実に意思疎通ができていることを確認したい。私が今指示したことに基づいて，相手にあなたがどのように説明するのかを教えてくれますか」。

(2)　あるいは，大西氏は相手と直接コミュニケーションをとるべきであるが，フルトン氏あるいは人事マネジャーの立会いの下にそうすべきである。そのような会話で第三者が立ち会うことは，大西氏が彼の考えをしっかりと表現することを確実にする助けになるであろう。

(3)　また，いかなるマネジャーも，相手に対する自分の見方が完全に正確ではないかもしれないことを認識すべきである。他人の行動が不適切であると断言する前に，まずはその人と話し合い，その人の考え方および／または行動を理解することをお勧めする。

　要するに，言葉の壁が欲求不満をもたらす可能性があることは否定できないとはいえ，語学力の欠如という理由でもって，マネジャーとしての適切なコミュニケーションの失敗を正当化することはできないのである。

CASE STUDY 8.3

Responding Effectively to an Employee Who May Be Abusing the Paid Time Off Policy

Question for consideration

When benefits are provided to employees, the employees have the right to use the benefits as long as they are in compliance with any stipulated regulations. **How should a company maintain employee satisfaction with benefits while eliminating any abuse of a benefits policy?**

Case study detail

Company: Southeast Asian subsidiary of a Japanese company
Nakata Jiro, Sales Manager
Kevin Lee, Sales Associate

At the Southeast Asian subsidiary of a Japanese company, most of the employees assert their rights to use all of the 20 days of *paid time off* (PTO) that they are allotted each year. In addition to this regular paid leave, employees are provided with optional sick leave in the case that they fall ill and cannot come to work. In order to substantiate the sickness and have their time off covered under the sick leave policy rather than deducted from the 20-day PTO bank, the employee is compelled to submit a note from a physician usually called an MC (medical certificate).

Today **Kevin Lee**, a **Sales Associate**, approached **Nakata Jiro, Sales Manager** and announced, "I will need to take a medical leave next Wednesday. Thank

CASE STUDY 8.3

有給休暇制度を悪用している可能性のある
従業員への効果的な対応

本事例の着目点

　従業員に福利厚生が提供される場合，従業員は，規定の規則に準拠している限り，その福利厚生を享受する権利を有する。**会社は福利厚生規定の悪用を排除しつつ，従業員の福利厚生に対する満足度をどのようにして維持すべきだろうか？**

事例の背景
会社名：日本会社の東南アジア子会社
セールス・マネジャー：中田二郎氏
営業担当者：ケビン・リー氏

　日本企業の当該東南アジア子会社では，ほとんどの従業員が，毎年割り当てられる 20 日間の「有給休暇」（PTO と略す）の全てを使用する権利を主張する。通常の有給休暇に加えて，従業員は，病気になって仕事に来られない場合に備えて，任意の病気休暇が与えられている。20 日間の PTO の蓄えから差し引かれるのではなく，病気を裏付け，休暇を病気休暇規定の下でカバーするために，従業員は通常 MC（診断書）と呼ばれる医師による文書を提出しなくてはならない。

　今日，**営業担当者**であるケビン・リー氏が**セールス・マネジャー**の**中田二郎**氏に連絡を取り，次のように表明した。「来週の水曜日，病気休暇を取る必要

you in advance for your understanding."

Nakata was a bit shocked as he first wondered whether Lee had a health issue. He said, "Oh, is everything okay?"

Lee said, "Yes, but I have to go to the doctor on that day."

Nakata had no reason to deny the request, so he grudgingly agreed.

But more so, he wondered why Lee knew so far in advance that he would need to take medical leave. Was Lee really sick, or was he misusing the company's generous policy?

Curious as to the general trends in time off usage among all employees in his department, Nakata requested the HR Department to send him the records for the past three years.

It was clear that all of the employees used up their 20 days of available regular PTO. As well, a majority of the employees also made use of the medical leave.

Nakata shook his head back and forth and thought to himself, "Well, these trends seem to be quite different from Japan."

Learning points

In some countries, employees view their benefits as entitlements. That is to say that employees feel entitled to use any time off provided to them. Time off is a form of non-monetary compensation. Not taking advantage

があります。ご理解いただけますと幸いです」。

　中田氏は，まずリー氏が健康上の問題を抱えているかどうか疑問に思ったので，ちょっと驚き，次のように言った。「それは，それは。でも，仕事のことなどいろいろ大丈夫なの？」

　リー氏は，「はい，何とか。その日はどうしても医者に行かなければなりませんので」と返答した。

　中田氏はその要求を否定する理由がなかったので，しぶしぶ同意した。

　しかし，それ以上に，彼は，なぜリー氏がそんなに前から医療休暇を取る必要があると分かっていたのか疑問に思った。リー氏は本当に病気なのだろうか，あるいは彼は会社の寛大な規定を悪用しているのだろうか？

　部門内の全従業員の休暇の使用状況の一般的な傾向が気になり，中田氏は，人事部門に過去3年間の記録を送付するよう要請した。

　従業員全員が，利用可能な通常のPTOを20日間使い切っていることは明らかであった。同様に，大多数の従業員は医療休暇も利用していた。

　中田氏は首を前後に振って，「まあ，このような傾向は日本とはかなり違うようだな」と自分に言い聞かせた。

学習ポイント

　一部の国では，従業員は福利厚生を権利と見ている。つまり，従業員は自分に与えられた休暇全てを使い切る権利があると思っていると言える。休暇は，ある種の金銭以外の報酬である。福利厚生を利用しないというこ

of the benefit is akin to throwing away a form of compensation.

In some countries, such ways of thinking are supported by law whereby companies are obliged to pay the value of an unused paid time off day in monetary compensation at the end of the fiscal year.

It is advisable not to discourage employees from utilizing the benefits provided by the company in order to maintain favorable employee relations. Nor is it advisable to penalize employees who take medical leave and substantiate the need for the leave with a doctor's note. Oftentimes, the labor law has been designed to protect the rights of employees in such cases.

However, to avoid the administrative burden of managing multiple time off policies and the need to question the motives of employees who want to take time off, it is sometimes advisable to *lump* all time off categories into one general PTO (paid time off) policy rather than having different policies for different types of leave requirements. For example, it used to be common in the United States for companies to designate different types of time off as follows: vacation days (days off for rest or leisure as planned in advance), personal days (days off to handle sudden personal or family affairs) and sick days (days off when fallen ill). Nowadays, companies tend to simply offer PTO and trust their employees' discretion. In this case, an occasional check of employee usage of time off is advisable.

Or, some companies have even eradicated the policy of allotting time off. In such companies, employees are able to work flexibly and take unlimited time off as long as they carry out all of their work responsibilities.

とは，報酬の一形態を放棄することに似ている。

　国によっては，そのような考え方が法律によって支持されているため，企業は会計年度末に未使用の有給休暇の価値を金銭的に補償する義務がある。

　良好な従業員関係を維持するために，従業員が会社から提供された福利厚生を利用することを妨げないことをお勧めする。医療休暇を取得し，医師の文書で休暇の必要性を立証する従業員に罰を課すこともお勧めできない。多くの場合，労働法はそのような場合に従業員の権利を保護するように設計されている。

　ただし，複数の休暇規定を運営し，休暇を取りたいという従業員の動機をチェックするという管理上の負担を避けるために，各種の休暇要求に対して異なる方針を持つのではなく，全ての休暇カテゴリーをひとつの包括的PTO（有給休暇）制度に「一まとめにすること」をお勧めする。例えば，バケーション・デイ（事前に計画された休息やレジャーのための休み），パーソナル・デイ（突然の個人または家族の問題に対処するための休み），シック・デイ（病気になった時の休み）などのように，使用目的別に休日を認めることが米国の会社ではこれまで一般的であった。今日では，企業はPTOを簡便に提供し，従業員の裁量権を信認する傾向にある。その場合には，従業員の有給休暇の利用に対する時折のチェックが望ましい。

　あるいは，会社によっては，休暇割り当て施策を撤廃したところさえある。このような企業では，従業員は全ての仕事上の責任を遂行する限り，フレキシブルに仕事をし，制限を受けない休暇を享受することができる。

Therefore, it is important to consider local cultural tendencies and expectations to design time off policies that are administratively easy to manage and do not create an adversarial relationship between company managers and subordinates.

　したがって，管理が容易で，社内で上司と部下の間に敵対的な関係を作り出さないような休暇制度をデザインする際には，現地の文化的傾向や希望を考慮することが重要である。

CASE STUDY 8.4

When Coming to Work with Makeup Is Against the Company Rules

Question for consideration

In manufacturing environments, as conditions in a factory sometime adversely impact the quality of the products produced, the company needs to enact rules and procedures that may be troublesome to employees. **In what ways is the Factory Manager in this case acting appropriately? How could he have better managed the roll out of the new prohibition against the usage of cosmetic products in the factory?**

Case study detail

Company: Overseas subsidiary of a Japanese precision machinery manufacturer

Horiuchi Haruo, Factory Manager

Female employees in the factory

At the Japanese subsidiary of a precision machine manufacturer in Southeast Asia, it is essential for the factory environment to remain clean and free of any contamination from foreign substances. Employees are strictly required to wear protective hats to prevent hair from getting into the parts, and uniforms are particularly designed to hamper the conduction of static electricity.

Even having taken these kinds of measures, quality management is a challenge. Recently, **Horiuchi Haruo, Factory Manager**, received a report from the

CASE STUDY 8.4

化粧をして仕事に来ることが
社内規則に違反する場合

本事例の着目点

　もの作りの環境では，工場内の状況がそこで生産される製品の品質に悪影響を与えることがあるため，会社は従業員にとっては面倒な規則や手順を制定する必要がある。**この事例の工場長はどのような方法で適切に対応しているのだろうか？　また，彼は工場内の化粧品の使用に対する新しい禁止の導入をどのようにすれば，よりうまく管理できたのだろうか？**

事例の背景

会社：日本の精密機械メーカーの海外子会社

工場長：堀内治夫氏

工場内の女性従業員たち

　某日系精密機械メーカーの東南アジア子会社では，工場環境が清潔で異物による汚染が一切ないことが不可欠となっている。従業員は，部品に髪の毛が入らないように保護用の帽子を着用し，特に静電気の伝導を妨げるユニフォームを着ることが，厳格に求められている。

　このような対策を講じたとしても，品質管理は難題である。最近，**工場長の堀内治夫氏**は検査員から不良品の発生数が減少していないという報告を受け

inspection staff that the occurrence of defective products has not diminished. Therefore, Horiuchi immediately formed a project team and launched a full-scale survey. Eventually, it was determined that fine particles from the cosmetics used by female employees were causing the quality issues.

Horiuchi immediately decreed that female employees would now be forbidden from coming into the factory with any cosmetic products applied on their faces. Horiuchi drafted a policy that warned any female employee found to be wearing makeup would be asked to immediately wash her face or be sent home for the day without pay. The site managers were obliged to enforce the new rule immediately. However, the ban caused an uproar. The female employees were gathering and starting to stir up various ideas about quitting and even taking legal action against the company for such a discriminatory policy.

Learning points

Generally, companies have the right to change the rules of the company at any time as long as there is no law or regulation that supersedes the company rules. In this case, Horiuchi was taking steps that were rational and necessary for ensuring quality, so declaring a new rule can be deemed reasonable from a business standpoint.

However, it is important to communicate effectively with employees before a new rule goes into effect, by informing employees about changes in advance and by leaving some room for discussion. If Horiuchi made efforts to respectfully explain the report findings to all employees first and even provide a *transition period* for the female employees to get accustomed to the new rule, he may have been able to eliminate the negative reaction from employees.

た。そこで，堀内氏はすぐにプロジェクト・チームを編成し，本格的な調査を開始した。最終的には，女性従業員が使用する化粧品からの微粒子が品質の問題を引き起こしていると判断された。

　堀内氏は直ちに，女性従業員が顔に化粧品を塗ったまま工場に入ることを禁じると宣言した。堀内氏は，化粧をしていると判断された女性従業員には直ちに顔を洗うか，従わない場合はその日は無給で帰宅させると警告する施策を策定した。工場の管理職は，新しい規則を直ちに施行せざるを得なかった。しかし，その禁止は騒動を引き起こした。女性従業員は集まって，そのような差別的な方針をとるような会社は，辞めるばかりでなく，法的措置で対抗しようというような様々なアイデアを出して騒ぎだした。

学習ポイント

　一般的に，会社は，社内の規則に優先する法律や規制がない限り，社内の規則をいつでも変更する権利を有する。今回のケースでは，堀内氏は品質を保証するために合理的かつ必要な手段を講じたのであり，このため新しい規則を宣言することはビジネスの観点から合理的であると考えることができる。

　ただし，変更を事前に従業員に通知し，議論の余地を残すことによって，新しい規則が施行される前に従業員と効果的にコミュニケーションをとることは重要である。もし堀内氏が，報告書で明らかになった結果を先ずは全従業員に丁寧に説明し，女性従業員が新しい規則に慣れるための「移行期間」を提供する努力をしていたとすれば，彼は従業員の反発を排除できたかもしれない。

Thereafter, the requirement for adherence to such rules should be clearly notified to employees before hire as a condition for employment.

　今後においては，そのような規則の順守という要件は，採用条件のひとつとして，採用の前に従業員に明確に通知されるべきである。

Expatriation

What Is an Expatriate Assignment?

Expatriation often refers to the dispatch of employees on a temporary basis from one organizational entity such as the global headquarters or a subsidiary within a multi-national corporate group to another organizational entity in a foreign country. An expatriate assignment may be for as little as one year, but typically extends from three to five years.

The Roles of an Expatriated Individual

Individuals dispatched overseas are tasked with carrying out a variety of roles. While the tasks undertaken by any one expatriate depend on the characteristics of the overseas subsidiary, and the position of the expatriate in the organization, it is possible to make some generalizations about the roles of an expatriate.

When employees are sent from the global headquarters of a multi-national company to an overseas subsidiary, we can refer to the dispatched employee as

海外派遣

海外駐在とは何か？

海外派遣とは多くの場合，グローバル本社や多国籍企業グループ内の子会社などの組織から，海外に所在する別の組織への，一時的な従業員の派遣を意味する。海外駐在の期間は短くて1年程度であるが，通常は3年から5年である。

海外派遣者の役割

海外に派遣される個人は，様々な役割を果たす責任がある。海外派遣者の役割は海外子会社の特性，および海外派遣者の組織内のポジションによって異なるが，海外派遣者の役割について，ある程度一般化することもできる。

従業員が多国籍企業のグローバル本社から海外子会社に派遣される場合，当該派遣者のことを**本国籍人材（PCNs）**と呼ぶ。PCNsは，海外子会社の従業

parent-country nationals (PCNs). The PCNs work directly with employees of the overseas subsidiary who are referred to as **local employees, national staff** or **host-country nationals (HCNs)**. (In this chapter, we will use PCNs and HCNs specifically to refer to both groups of employees.)

Traditionally, PCNs have become expatriates for the purposes of taking on various roles involved with: (1) managing the overseas subsidiaries, (2) coordinating affairs between the overseas subsidiary and the headquarters, (3) transferring technology and management know-how from the headquarters to the overseas subsidiary and (4) providing various developmental opportunities for direct subordinates among the HCNs.

Nowadays, it is emphasized that the role of an expatriate is to identify and cultivate potential successors among the HCNs. In this way, the position which is currently filled by that expatriate may become filled by a locally hired HCN rather than by another subsequent PCN from the headquarters. This is referred to as the process of **localization**. Such an HCN should attain a deep understanding of the corporate philosophy of the multi-national group and familiarity with the global direction for the group.

According to the seminal work of Howard V. Perlmutter published in 1969, when PCNs work in overseas subsidiaries, often in top management or senior management positions, there are both recognized advantages and disadvantages. The advantages of assigning PCNs, who generally have extensive work experience in the parent company, to manage the operation of overseas subsidiaries include the following points: (1) They are familiar with the business philosophy of the headquarters, business direction and internal business practices. (2) They possess competencies such as management know-how, technological skills and knowledge that can be transferred to overseas subsidiaries. (3) They have developed a rich professional network

員と一緒に働くことになる。その海外子会社の従業員は，**現地従業員，ナショ
ナル・スタッフ，**あるいは**現地国籍人材（HCNs）**とも呼ばれる（本章では，
両グループの従業員のことを，特に PCNs，HCNs と呼ぶことにする）。

　　通常，PCNs は，次のような様々な役割を達成するために海外派遣者とな
る。すなわち，(1)海外子会社の統制，(2)海外子会社と本社との間の調整，(3)
本社から海外子会社への技術および経営ノウハウの移転，ならびに，(4)HCNs
のうち直近下位の部下に対する様々な育成機会の提供，である。

　　今日，海外派遣者の役割は，その海外派遣者によって現在満たされているポ
ジションが本部からの後任の PCNs ではなく現地採用の HCNs によって充足
されるように，HCNs の中から後任候補者を識別し育て上げることであるとい
うことが強調されている。これは**現地化**のプロセスと呼ばれる。そのような
HCN は，多国籍グループの企業理念を深く理解し，グローバルなグループの
方向性についても精通する必要がある。

　　1969 年に公刊されたパールミュッター（Howard V. Perlmutter）の独創的
な論文によると，PCNs が通常，トップ・マネジメントまたは上級管理職とし
て海外子会社に勤務する場合には，有利な点と不利な点の両方が存在する。親
会社での業務経験が豊富な PCNs を海外子会社の運営管理に割り当てることの
有利な点は，次の通りである。すなわち，(1)本社の経営理念，経営方針，社内
の業務慣行などを体得し，熟知している。(2)高度で海外子会社に移転すべき経
営ノウハウ，技術・知識などのコンピテンシーを保有している。(3)本社での人
脈が豊富で，親会社・子会社間の連絡やコミュニケーションを効果的に行うこ
とができる，という点である。

within the headquarters and are thereby able to facilitate collaboration and communication between the headquarters and subsidiaries.

On the other hand, the disadvantages of relying upon PCNs to manage overseas subsidiary operations are also notable. (1) PCNs generally require time to adapt to the living and working environment in other countries, and sometimes individuals are unable to effectively adapt. (2) There are high costs associated with dispatching employees overseas. (3) The very act of dispatching an expatriate from the headquarters prevents qualified HCNs from ascending to the position held by the expatriate. (4) The accompanying family of the expatriate may experience problems acclimating to the local society and daily life.

Conversely, the merits and demerits of leaving the operations of overseas subsidiaries to HCNs are the reverse of the merits and demerits associated with the overseas dispatch of PCNs described above. In addition, leaving the operations of overseas subsidiaries to HCNs may deprive young headquarters employees of the experience to work abroad.

An alternative option in the debate about whether positions should be assigned to PCNs or HCNs is to consider the utilization of **third-country nationals (TCNs)**. TCNs are similar to HCNs to the extent that they are employees of the overseas subsidiaries of a multi-national company. Similar to the merits of PCNs, TCNs may be dispatched from one overseas subsidiary to another overseas subsidiary when they possess management know-how, technological skills and knowledge not readily available at the subsidiary to which the TCN is dispatched. In this case as well, promotion opportunities for HCNs may be limited by the arrival of the TCN. However, the policy of utilizing TCNs is an indication to the HCNs that they themselves may one day become a TCN and have the chance to work internationally within other subsidiaries. (For more information refer to Chapter 6: Global mobility policy.)

　他方，海外子会社の経営に際して PCNs に依存することの不利な点には以下のようなものがある。(1)全般的に PCNs が外国での生活や仕事の環境に適応するには時間がかかり，時には効果的に適応できない人も出る。(2)従業員を海外に派遣するには高いコストがかかる。(3)本社から海外派遣者を送るという行為そのものが，資格要件を満たす HCNs が，海外派遣者が就いていたポジションに昇進する機会を奪うことになる。(4)海外派遣者の帯同家族は，派遣先の現地社会や日常生活への適応に問題を抱えることがあり得る。

　逆に海外子会社のオペレーションを HCNs に任せる場合の有利な点，不利な点は，上記の PCNs の海外派遣に伴う有利な点と不利な点と逆の関係になる。ちなみに，海外子会社のオペレーションを HCNs に任せきりにすると，本社の若年スタッフの海外勤務経験の機会を奪うことになるかもしれない。

　職位を PCN と HCN のどちらに割り当てるべきかについての議論に対する別の選択肢は，**第三国籍人材（TCNs）**の活用を検討することである。TCNsは，多国籍企業の海外子会社の従業員であるという点で HCNs と似ている。PCNs の有利な点と同様に，TCNs が派遣先の子会社では容易に利用できない管理ノウハウ，技術，および知識を持っている場合，TCNs はひとつの海外子会社から別の海外子会社に派遣されることがある。この場合も同様に，子会社内での HCNs の昇進の機会は TCNs の出現によって制限されるかもしれない。ただし，TCNs を活用するという方針は，HCNs 自身がある時には TCNs となり，国際的に他の子会社内で働く可能性を HCNs に示すものである（詳細については，Chapter 6「グローバル・モビリティ・ポリシー」を参照されたい）。

Selecting Employees to Be Expatriated

Upon deciding whether to dispatch a PCN or a TCN, it is essential to select the best individual for the expatriate assignment. A poor candidate selection may lead to any number of potentially damaging outcomes.

Therefore, it is essential for the HR Department to consider the fit of candidates for overseas assignments. While the assignment may be presented as a growth opportunity for the expatriated individual, the lack of an essential level of aptitude may result in the expatriate needing to return home in the middle of an assignment. In such cases, the local business operations may also be detrimentally impacted.

The research published in 1981 by Rosalie Tung provides relevant guidance. Tung cautions HR Departments to assess the following:

1. Given the stated mission of the assignment, does the candidate possess sufficient work knowledge and experience (competency) already to achieve the mission of the assignment?
2. To what extent does the individual demonstrate the presence or absence of aptitude and ability to adapt to a cross-cultural environment and situations of varying degrees of difference from the home country environment?
3. How might the individual's family situation/conditions impact the individual's ability to work overseas at the present time?

Various assessment tools have been devised in order to assist in the difficult judgment of aptitude and ability of an individual for work abroad.

The risk of *failures* in expatriate assignments is considered to be relatively

海外派遣者の選抜

　PCN と TCN のどちらを派遣するかを決定する際には，海外派遣者の任務に最適な個人を選定することが不可欠である。不適切な候補者の選定は，潜在的に有害な結果をもたらす可能性がある。

　したがって，人事部は，候補者が海外での任務に適しているかどうかを検討しなくてはならない。赴任は海外派遣された個人の成長の機会と見えるかもしれないが，本質的なレベルでの適性の欠如は海外派遣者の赴任途中での帰任という結果となるかもしれない。このような場合，現地の事業運営も悪影響を受ける可能性がある。

　ロザリー・トン（Rosalie Tung）が 1981 年に発表した研究は，重要な方向性を提供している。トンは次の点を評価するよう人事部門に警告している。

1．海外派遣のミッションが明示的に示されていることを前提として，当該候補者が派遣中のミッションを達成するのに必要な仕事上の十分な知識および経験（コンピテンシー）を有するかどうか。
2．母国の環境と異なる度合いが様々である異文化環境や状況に適応する適性ならびに能力の有無を，個人はどの程度まで示しているか。

3．個人の家族の状況や条件は，現時点で海外で働く場合に個人の能力にどのように影響するか？

　個人の海外で働く適性や能力を判断するという難しい判断をサポートするために，様々な評価ツールが考案されている。

　海外派遣の「失敗」のリスクは，操業年数の長い現地法人に比べ，それの短

less in newly established subsidiaries where the expatriated PCNs retain an absolute advantage in technological skills and management know-how. Conversely, when the subsidiary company has a long operational history and the locally hired HCNs have had the time to develop and accumulate technological and/or managerial ability, the expatriate's skills and experience may not be seemingly required by the subsidiary. In such cases, the expatriated individuals will need to assess the situation to determine what unique contribution they can make in order to justify the decision to send a PCN to the overseas subsidiary.

Phases of the Expatriation Process

Once an employee is selected to be dispatched overseas as an expatriate, the expatriation process commences. The process can be considered across three phases as follows: (1) Preparation for expatriation, (2) Expatriation, and (3) Return (repatriation). Let's review each of these phases in detail.

(1) Preparation for expatriation

It is desirable to provide for a period of preparation of at least six months to one year from the announcement of the assignment to the individual's actual departure to become an expatriate. The individuals need time to gather relevant information about the expectations for their work overseas and to become psychologically ready for the work. They also need to handle personal affairs related to making a move abroad, including considerations of housing, as well as medical and family concerns. (At times, they may make a preliminary business trip to the overseas subsidiary site to start organizing affairs.) As well, they may need to ensure that current work responsibilities are adequately handed over to others in the home country.

The HR Department should make provisions for pre-departure training.

い現地法人においては相対的に少なくなると考えられる。操業年数の短い現地法人においては本社からの派遣者には技術，経営ノウハウにおける絶対的優位性が存在するためである。逆に，現地法人が長い操業期間を有し，現地採用のHCNs が技術能力および／またはマネジメント能力を長きにわたり開発し，蓄積している場合には，海外派遣者のスキルや経験は表面上，それほどには必要とされないかもしれない。このような場合，海外派遣者個人は，海外子会社にHCN を派遣しているという決定を正当化するために，現地の事情を見極め，自分が独自にどのような貢献ができるかを決める必要があるだろう。

派遣のプロセス

　従業員が海外派遣者として海外に派遣されることが決まって初めて，海外派遣プロセスが始まる。派遣のプロセスは，(1)派遣前の準備，(2)赴任中，(3)帰国（帰任）という3段階を踏むことになる。そこでその段階ごとに詳しく検討しよう。

(1)　派遣前の準備

　海外派遣の内示から派遣実現までには十分な準備期間を置くことが望ましく，理想的には少なくとも1年くらいが必要であろう。個人はそれぞれ，海外での仕事への期待に関する関連情報を収集し，心理的に仕事をする準備をする時間を必要とする。彼らはまた，住宅，医療，家族の事柄など，海外への移動に関連する個人的な問題への対応を行う必要がある（時には，問題への対応を開始するにあたり，海外子会社の所在地に事前に出張することもある）。同時に，現在の仕事の責任が国内の他の人に適切に引き継がれるよう，しっかりと対応する必要があるかもしれない。

　人事部は，派遣前研修を準備する必要がある。通常，派遣前研修の内容に

Topics of pre-departure training typically include language training (English and/or other languages typically used in the target country), compliance, risk and crisis management, safety training, health management and disease control, and other topics of concern such as how to express the corporate philosophy to overseas colleagues.

It is also advisable for expatriates to envision working with the HCNs. To do this, expatriates should prepare their own self-introductory message to make a positive first impression on the HCNs upon arrival at the overseas subsidiary. While the HCNs may be familiar with having new managers arrive from overseas, HCNs are typically anxious to understand why the expatriate has been assigned to the role. For the expatriate to make a positive first impression upon their arrival, the expatriate should be prepared to explain the following:

a) Their understanding of their own mission
b) How their previous experience qualifies them for this assignment
c) How they intend on working with the HCNs
d) Appropriate personal information about themselves

(2) During expatriation

An expatriate assignment is deemed to be successful when the dispatched employee sufficiently adapts to the local work and living environment and makes a positive contribution to the company, both to the business results and relations with the HCNs.

The speed and level to which expatriates adapt to the local work and living environment differs from person to person based upon the individual's ability to handle stress and difficulties working in a foreign country. There are four generally accepted phases of adjustment that people go through when they begin to live and work in a country that has a culture quite different from their

は，言語研修（英語および／または派遣先国で通常使用される英語以外の言語），コンプライアンス，リスクおよび危機管理，安全対策研修，健康管理および疾病対策，およびこれら以外の重要なテーマ，例えば海外の同僚に企業理念をどのように表明するのかなどが含まれる。

　また，海外派遣者が HCN と一緒に働くということをイメージすべきであろう。これを行うには，海外派遣者が海外子会社に到着した時点で，HCN に積極的な第一印象を与えるような自分自身の自己紹介の挨拶を準備する必要がある。HCN は親会社から新しいマネジャーが赴任するということに慣れているかもしれないが，他方で，HCN は通常，海外派遣者が何故その役割で派遣されてきたのかという理由を知りたがっている。派遣者が着任直後，最初の好印象を与えるためには，以下の点を説明するために準備しておくべきである。

a）自分たちの使命をどのように考えているか
b）以前の経験が当該任務にどのように役立つか
c）どのように HCN と一緒に働こうとしているのか
d）適切な個人情報

(2) 赴任中

　派遣社員が現地の仕事や生活環境に十分に適応し，事業の業績と HCN との関係という両方の側面でプラスに貢献した場合，海外派遣の任務は成功したと見なされる。

　海外派遣者が現地の仕事や生活環境に適応する速さと程度は，外国で働くことによる個々人のストレスや困難さへの対処能力によって異なる。とはいえ，彼らは自国の文化とはかなり異なる文化を持つ国に住み，仕事を始める際には，一般的によく知られている4つの調整期を通り抜けることになる。カルチャー・ショックの4つの期は次のとおりである。

home culture. The four stages of culture shock are as follows:

1) Honeymoon stage: when everything is new and positively exhilarating
2) Frustration stage: when the difficulties of understanding have built up and the individual is hitting some emotional walls
3) Adjustment stage: when the individual has learned new behaviors and ways of dealing with difficulties and the frustration starts to subside
4) Acceptance stage: when the individual has come to terms with the differences in culture by recognizing and respecting the differences and similarities in cultural norms between the host country and one's native country

An expatriate makes a positive contribution by accomplishing tasks, creating new processes, bringing a new product to market, and/or by ensuring that operations are smooth. In most cases, it is impossible to produce such results without close communication, and collaboration with the HCNs and other stakeholders within the host country. Therefore, the success of an expatriate can be measured by the extent to which the expatriate develops positive working relations with the HCNs and gets to know and understand the HCNs on an individual basis. While HCNs may be skeptical about the new expatriate upon their initial arrival in the country, over time, successful expatriates are able to overcome such skepticism and prove the value of their assignment to the HCNs.

The success of an assignment may be minimized if the expatriate fails to recognize and deal with various managerial risks while overseas. While expatriates are compelled to act ethically and in compliance with all legal and company regulations, the expatriate should also maintain awareness at all times of their role as a representative of the company. Accordingly, the expatriates need to protect the company from any kind of wrongdoing by the HCNs

1）ハネムーン期：全てが新鮮で，気分が高揚する時期
2）フラストレーション（欲求不満）期：理解の困難度が蓄積し，個人が感情
　　的な壁にぶつかる時期
3）調整期：個人が困難に対応するための新しい行動や方法を学び，フラスト
　　レーションが収まり始める時期
4）受け入れ期：受入国と自国との文化規範における違いや類似点を認識し，
　　尊重することによって，文化の違いを受容するようになる時期

　海外派遣者は，タスクの遂行，新しいプロセスの創設，新製品の市場投入
により，および／または，業務の円滑化を図ることにより，プラスの貢献を
する。ほとんどの場合，密接なコミュニケーション，および受入国内の他の
HCN および他の利害関係者との協力なしには，このような結果を生み出すこ
とは不可能である。したがって，海外派遣者の成功は，海外派遣者が HCN と
積極的な協力関係を築き，個別に HCN を知り理解することができる程度に
よって測定することができよう。HCN は入国時に新しい海外派遣者について
懐疑的であるかもしれないが，時間の経過とともに，成功する海外派遣者はそ
のような懐疑論を克服し，結果として HCN への彼らの赴任の価値を証明する
ことになる。

　もし海外派遣者が赴任中の様々な管理上のリスクを認識し対処することに失
敗するならば，彼らの赴任の成功も最小限に抑えられることになろう。海外派
遣者は倫理的に行動し，全ての法律および会社の規制を遵守しなければならな
いが，海外派遣者は会社の代表としての役割について常に認識する必要もあ
る。そのため，海外派遣者は，HCN ならびに海外派遣者自身による，あらゆ
る種類の不正行為から会社を保護する必要がある。そのような不正行為には，

and even by themselves. Such wrongdoing includes, but is not limited to, unlawful discrimination, causing and/or not discouraging harassing behaviors, and inappropriate usage of financial resources. The point is that even if the expatriate is not doing wrong, but fails to recognize and stop wrongdoing by others, any scandal or incident that occurs during the expatriate's assignment may negatively impact the evaluation of the expatriate's level of success.

(3) Return (repatriation)

After working abroad for several years, the expatriate is scheduled to return to the home country. Repatriation comes with stress and difficulty as well. Ideally the returnee is assigned to a role that capitalizes upon the individual's work experience overseas. For example, the individual may be assigned to a role with responsibilities to continue to oversee the business of subsidiaries from the global headquarters. However, many times, the returnee may feel that their experience overseas is not adequately being put to use. Or, the returnee may suffer from a period of reverse culture-shock. Having learned new ways of doing things while overseas, the returnee gets frustrated because others continue to do things in the *old ways*. Or, conversely, in the time that the individual has been overseas, the headquarters may have undergone some major changes of which the individual may not be aware. In addition to being provided with a new assignment and direct supervisor, there may be major changes in company policy, business procedures and/or the business itself. Therefore, it can be said that the individual needs to adapt once again to a new environment.

In extreme cases, the returnee has difficulty reacclimating and decides to quit the company in order to pursue opportunities elsewhere.

To assist the returnee in the process of reacclimating, advanced companies implement pre-return training to provide information on matters expected

違法な差別，嫌がらせ行為を引き起こすこと，および／または，それを抑制しないこと，ならびに財源の不適切な使用が含まれるが，これらだけに限定されない。重要なポイントは，海外派遣者が不正行為をしなかったにもかかわらず，他人の不正行為を認識しながら阻止できなかったとすれば，海外派遣者の赴任中に発生したスキャンダルや事件が海外派遣者の成功レベルの評価に悪影響を及ぼす可能性があるということである。

(3) 帰国（帰任）

　海外で数年間仕事をした後，海外派遣者は本国に戻ることになっている。帰任は，ストレスと困難も伴っている。理想的には，帰任者は海外での仕事経験を活用できる役割に割り当てられることになる。例えば，当該個人は，グローバル本社で子会社の事業を引き続き監督する責任を有する役割に割り当てられることがある。しかし多くの場合，帰任者は海外での経験が十分に活用されていないと感じているかもしれない。あるいは，帰任者は逆カルチャー・ショックの期間に苦しむかもしれない。海外で新しいやり方を学んできたことで，帰任者は他の人々が「古いやり方」でやり続けることに不満を感じるようになる。あるいは，逆に，その人が海外に赴任中に，本社は，その人が知らないうちに，大きな変化を経験していたのかもしれない。新しい任務および直属の上司の変更に加えて，会社の方針，業務手続，および／または，事業自体に大きな変化が起こっているかもしれない。したがって，派遣者個人はもう一度新しい環境に適応する必要があるといえよう。

　極端な場合には，帰任者は再適応するのが難しく，他での機会を求めて会社を辞めることになる。

　このため，先進的な企業では，再適応プロセスにある帰任者をサポートするために，例えば，金融・税務に関するカウンセリングとともに，キャリア計

when returning to work, such as career planning, and updates on changes in the company, along with financial/tax counseling.

Determining Appropriate Compensation Schemes for Expatriates

While many multi-national companies adopt global standards for determining how compensation is paid across group companies, compensation for expatriates falls within a separate category. This is because an expatriate assignment is a temporary transfer overseas at the behest of the dispatching organization. Furthermore, it is a commonly accepted principle that the expatriate should not suffer any financial losses as a result of the assignment. Whether the expatriate is entitled to financial gain, however, in exchange for the individual's willingness to live and work overseas, is an issue generally determined by the managerial philosophy of the dispatching organization.

Therefore, the HR Department of the dispatching organization needs to determine policies for handling the associated costs during the expatriate's overseas assignment such as housing, transportation, schooling for accompanying children, or annual home leave.

In addition, schemes for determining the calculation of the expatriate's compensation must be determined. There are two widely recognized approaches: **the going rate approach** and **the balance sheet approach**.

The going rate approach is to directly link the base salary of an expatriate with the pay structure of the receiving organization, thus matching the local market rate. In other words, the compensation standards applied to the expatriate are the same standards that apply to the HCNs. As a result, the expatriate is treated the same as an HCN during the assignment. However, in the case that

画，会社の変化に関する情報提供など，仕事への復帰に際して期待される事項に関する情報提供を中心とする帰任前研修を実施している。

海外派遣者に対する適切な報酬スキームの決定

　多国籍企業の多くは，グループ会社間で報酬がどのように支払われるかを決定するために世界的な基準を採用しているが，海外派遣者に対する報酬は別のカテゴリーに分類されている。これは，海外派遣が派遣元組織の要請による海外への一時的な異動であるためである。さらに，海外派遣者が，赴任の結果として経済的損失を被るべきではないことは，一般に認められている原則である。しかし，海外に住んで仕事をしたいという個人の意欲と引き換えに，海外派遣者が経済的利益を得る権利があるかどうかは一般的に，派遣元組織の経営理念によって決定される問題である。

　したがって，派遣元組織の人事部は，住居，交通手段，帯同子弟の学校教育，年次のホーム・リーブ（帰国制度）など，海外派遣者の赴任中の関連費用の取り扱いに関する方針を決定する必要がある。

　同時に，海外派遣者の報酬算出の制度も決定されなくてはならない。基本的には，2つのよく知られた方法が存在する。**現行レート・アプローチ**と**バランス・シート・アプローチ**がそれである。

　現行レート・アプローチは，海外派遣者の基本給を受け入れ企業の給与構造に直接リンクさせ，したがって，現地の市場レートに合わせるというものである。つまり，海外派遣者に適用される報酬基準は，HCN に適用される基準と同じとなる。その結果，海外派遣者は赴任中，HCN と同様に扱われる。ただし，本国より低い給与水準の国に赴任する場合には，企業によっては異なる給

an expatriate is assigned to a country with a lower standard compensation level than that of the dispatching organization, some organizations may choose to continue to pay a differential amount.

By **the balance sheet approach**, the focus is on maintaining the expatriate's economic purchasing power, living standards and savings rates at a level comparable to that enjoyed prior to the assignment overseas. For this reason, when adopting a balance sheet approach, it is necessary to maintain changing price data on cost of living in each country/region.

The balance sheet approach has been more common generally. However, with global mobility on the rise and pressures to cut costs, the going rate approach is becoming popularized.

Implications for Japanese Companies

Japanese companies have been sending PCNs on overseas assignments from the headquarters in Japan for decades.

It should be noted that the nationality of expatriates sent from a parent company does not necessarily need to be limited to nationals of the country in which the parent company is located. Starting with a consideration of nationality, characteristics within the pool of candidates should be diverse, as long as the candidates can embody the business philosophy of the company, possess know-how of the parent company and have the skills to take on roles in management, or to lead various functional areas of the overseas operations. However, as a matter of fact, in most cases, expatriates sent from the parent company of Japanese companies are predominantly Japanese nationals, particularly Japanese males.

与額を支給し続けることを選択する場合がある。

　それに対して**バランス・シート・アプローチ**は，どこに赴任するかは関係なく，赴任前と遜色ないだけの海外派遣者の購買力，生活水準，貯蓄率を保障するという点に焦点が当てられている。このため，バランス・シート・アプローチを採用する場合には，各国・地域における生活費に関する物価データを常に最新のものに更新する必要がある。

　現在，バランス・シート・アプローチの方が，より一般的である。しかし，世界的なモビリティの高まりとコスト削減への圧力により，現行レート・アプローチが普及してきている。

日本企業への含意

　日本企業は何十年もの間，日本の本社からPCNを派遣してきている。

　親会社から送られる派遣者の国籍は，必ずしも親会社が所在する国の国籍に限定される必要はないことに注意してほしい。候補者が会社の経営理念を具現化し，親会社のノウハウを持ち，管理職での役割を担うか，または海外オペレーションでの様々な機能分野をリードできるスキルを持っている限り，候補者のプールは，国籍をはじめとする属性は多様でなければならない。しかし実態として，日本の多国籍企業からの海外派遣者は日本人（しかも男性）である場合がほとんどである。

The overseas subsidiaries of Japanese companies are characterized by the use of TCNs at a much lower rate than multinational companies from the USA and Europe, especially in their operations in Asia. (See Shiraki, 2006, and Shiraki, 2014.) In other words, overseas organizations of Japanese companies (especially in Asia and in North America) are "bi-national" type companies (**bi-national corporations (BNCs)**: a phrase coined by the author of the aforementioned reference) consisting of only Japanese PCNs and HCNs.

Additionally, global mobility practices whereby employees can move from an overseas subsidiary into the headquarters in Japan as a so-called **inpatriate** have been rare until very recent times.

Given the abovementioned, it can be said that there has been an excessive burden placed on Japanese national PCNs to work within the global operations of Japanese companies (Shiraki, 2006).

Despite this reliance on Japanese males to become expatriates, many expatriates remain poorly prepared for the transition to working overseas.

Problems arise throughout the expatriation process.

At the time of initial selection, the expatriate's family situation may be overlooked by the dispatch company. For this reason, Japan's expatriates are known to go on assignment overseas having left their family back in Japan. (In Japanese, this situation is referred to as *tanshin funin*.) Such family situations may be a cause of stress for the expatriate.

While it is reasonable to expect that the expatriate's previous experience has sufficiently prepared the individual for working overseas, oftentimes, the managerial and leadership experience of the Japanese expatriate is insufficient

　日本企業の海外オペレーション，とりわけアジアでのオペレーションでは，欧米系の多国籍企業と比べて，TCNs の活用がきわめて少ないという特徴を有している（白木著，2006 年，ならびに白木編著，2014 年参照）。すなわち，日本企業の海外組織（とりわけアジア，北米）では，日本人 PCNs と HCNs のみから成る**二国籍型企業 (BNCs)**（これは上記の著者の造語である）となっている場合が多い。

　さらに，従業員が海外子会社から日本の本社にいわゆる**逆出向者**として移動できるグローバル・モビリティの実践は，ごく最近まで稀であった。

　上記のような限界があることを考慮すると，日本企業のグローバルなオペレーションの中で働く日本人海外派遣者には過剰な負担がかかっていると考えられる（白木著，2006 年）。

　海外派遣者を日本人男性に依存しているにもかかわらず，多くの海外派遣者は海外勤務への移行への準備が整っていない。

　諸問題は海外派遣プロセス全体で発生している。

　最初の選抜の時点で，派遣者の家族の事情は見過ごされるか，派遣元の親会社によって見過ごされている場合がある。このため，日本の海外派遣者は家族を日本に残したまま海外に赴任すること（日本語で「単身赴任」と呼ばれている）が知られている。このような家族の状況は，派遣者のストレスの原因となっているかもしれない。

　派遣者の以前の経験が，個人が海外で働くための十分な準備となっていると考えることは合理的であるが，多くの場合，日本人派遣者の管理職およびリーダーシップの経験は新しい役割には不十分である。

for the new role.

Although the majority of expatriates hold positions at the section or department managerial level prior to overseas dispatch, the assignment overseas is akin to the provision of a promotion by as much as two ranks. This is because the expatriate often takes on top managerial roles with a wider range of duties than were previously assigned back in Japan (Labor Policy Research and Training Organization, March 2008).

Although the size of the overseas group company may be considerably smaller than the parent company in Japan, top management is required to have top management-specific qualities such as leadership ability. It is important to note that there is a considerable difference in the scope of work and the weight of responsibility between the requisites for competent middle-level management and the requirements for top management.

Therefore, in addition to cross-cultural training for expatriates, lessons are needed on the topic of *leadership for being an expatriate who is part of top management.*

At the end of an overseas assignment, certain repatriation issues may occur. Upon return to Japan, it is normal for the returnee to be essentially demoted down one-to-two position ranks. As a result, job areas and job responsibilities will become comparatively smaller for the returnee. Furthermore, if the post-return position cannot make full use of the experience and knowledge gained by the individual from working abroad, the returnee may start to lodge complaints, and in the worst case, decide to resign from the company.

It goes without saying that leaving the company upon return from overseas represents a certain loss for the returnee; moreover, the company shall lose

　国内における派遣前の職位は過半数が課長・部長クラスであるが，海外派遣に伴い職位上，約2ランクの昇格が行われることになる。これは，派遣者が赴任前に日本で割り当てられていたよりも職務の範囲が広いトップ・マネジメントを務めるようになることが多いためである（労働政策研究・研修機構，2008年3月）。

　海外グループ企業の規模は日本の本社と比べると格段に小さくなるものの，トップ・マネジメントにはトップ・マネジメント特有の資質が要求される。その最たるものが，リーダーシップ能力である。ここでの重要なポイントは，優秀な中間管理職に必要とされる要件とトップ・マネジメントに必要とされる要件とには，その職域の範囲と職責の重さにおいて大きな差があるということである。

　したがって，海外派遣者の異文化トレーニングに加えて，「トップ・マネジメントとなる海外派遣者のためのリーダーシップ」というテーマによる研修は必要である。

　海外での任務の終了時には，帰任の問題が付随するかもしれない。日本への帰任に伴いポジションが1−2ランク下がることにより実質的に降格となるのが普通である。その結果，帰任者の職域，職責が狭く小さくなる。さらに，帰任後のポジションが海外勤務で得た経験や知見を十分に活用できない場合には，不遇を託つか，最悪の場合には離職ということにもなる。

　帰任後の離職は本人にとって一定の損失であることは言うまでもない。同様に，企業にとっても帰任者の蓄積した経験・知見，ならびに幅広い人的ネット

out on the benefits of the returnee's accumulated experiences, knowledge and expansive human network.

It is necessary to adequately consider how to treat returnees and provide them with continual career development support along a suitable career path.

References & Suggestions for Additional Reading

Black, Stewart J., Hal B. Gregerson, Mark E. Mendenhall and Linda K. Stroh (1999), *Globalizing People Through International Assignment*, Addison-Wesley.

Cerdin, J. L. and C. Brewster (2014), "Talent Management and Expatriation: Bridging two streams of research and practice", *Journal of World Business*, 49, pp. 245-252.

Haslberger,A., C. Brewster and T. Hippler (2013), "The Dimensions Of Expatriate Adjustment", *Human Resource Management*, May-June 2013, Vol. 52, No. 3. pp. 333-351.

Harzing, A. and A. H. Pinnington (2015), *International Human Resource Management* (4th Ed.), London: Sage Publications, Chapter 5.

Labor Policy Research and Training Organization (2008), *Results of the Survey on Work and Life of the 7th Overseas Dispatched Workers*, March. (in Japanese)

McNulty, Y. and C. Brewster, (2018), "Management of (Business) Expatriates", in Machado, C. and J. P. Davim, (eds.), *Organizational Behaviour and Human Resource Management: Management and Industrial Engineering*, Springer International Publishing, pp. 109-137.

Perlmutter, H. V. (1969), "The Tortuous Evolution of the Multinational Corporation," *The Columbia Journal of World Business*, January-February, pp. 9-18.

Shiraki, Mitsuhide (1995), *International Human Resource Management of Japanese Companies*, Japan Labor Research Organization. (in Japanese)

Shiraki, Mitsuhide (2006), *A Comparative Analysis of International Human Resource Management*, Yuhikaku. (in Japanese)

Shiraki, Mitsuhide ed. (2014), *Development and Evaluation of Global Managers*, Waseda University Press. (in Japanese)

Tung, Rosalie L. (1981), "The Selection and Training of Personnel for Overseas Assignments", *The Columbia Journal of World Business*, Spring, pp. 68-78.

Tung (https://beedie.sfu.ca/profiles/RosalieTung).

ワークという利得を失うであろう。

　帰任者をどのように処遇し，また適切なキャリアパスに沿って継続的なキャリア開発支援を提供するかについての適切な検討が求められる。

さらに学びたい人のための参考文献

白木三秀著（1995）『日本企業の国際人的資源管理』日本労働研究機構。

白木三秀著（2006）『国際人的資源管理の比較分析』有斐閣。

白木三秀編著（2014）『グローバル・マネジャーの育成と評価』早稲田大学出版部

労働政策研究・研修機構（2008）『第 7 回海外派遣勤務者の職業と生活に関する調査結果』2008 年 3 月。

Black, Stewart J., Hal B. Gregerson, Mark E. Mendenhall and Linda K. Stroh (1999), *Globalizing People Through International Assignment*, Addison-Wesley.（ブラック他著，白木・永井・梅澤監訳『海外派遣とグローバルビジネス』白桃書房，2001 年。）

Cerdin, J. L. and C. Brewster (2014), "Talent Management and Expatriation: Bridging two streams of research and practice", *Journal of World Business*, 49, pp. 245-252.

Harzing, A. and A. H. Pinnington (2015), *International Human Resource Management* (4th ed.), London: Sage Publications, Chapter 5.

Haslberger, A., C. Brewster and T. Hippler (2013), "The Dimensions Of Expatriate Adjustment", *Human Resource Management*, May-June 2013, Vol. 52, No. 3. pp. 333-351.

McNulty, Y. and C. Brewster, (2018), "Management of (Business) Expatriates", in Machado, C. and J. P. Davim, (eds.), *Organizational Behaviour and Human Resource Management: Management and Industrial Engineering*, Springer International Publishing, pp. 109-137.

Perlmutter, H. V. (1969), "The Tortuous Evolution of the Multinational Corporation," *The Columbia Journal of World Business*, January-February, pp. 9-18.

Tung, Rosalie L. (1981), "Selection and Training of Personnel for Overseas Assignments," *The Columbia Journal of World Business*, Spring, pp. 68-78.

Tung (https://beedie.sfu.ca/profiles/RosalieTung).

CASE STUDY 9.1

When an Employee Attempts to Negotiate Conditions for an International Assignment

Question for consideration

When an employee is transferred within a global group from one company to another, it is helpful to have an international mobility policy to govern the transfer. However, not all companies have made preparations for such cases and so decisions need to be made on an ad hoc basis. **How do you think President Torii and her HR Manager should respond to the conditions requested by the employee to be transferred?**

Case study detail

Company: UK subsidiary of a Japanese company
Torii Taeko, President of UK subsidiary
Heinrich Becker, President of German subsidiary
Otto Mueller, German technical advisor
Stacy Mayweather, HR Manager, UK subsidiary

Torii Taeko, President of a Japan-based subsidiary in the United Kingdom is in the middle of a project to transfer technological know-how from its German subsidiary. German engineers have been traveling back and forth between London and Dusseldorf to provide training and support. However, since the German engineers are coming to London on business trip no more than once or twice a month, the pace of the technology transfer has not progressed as expected.

CASE STUDY 9.1

従業員が国外赴任の条件を交渉してくる場合

本事例の着目点

従業員をある企業から別の企業にグローバル・グループ内で異動させる場合，その異動を管理するための国際的な異動規定を策定しておくことが役に立つ。しかし，全ての企業がそのような場合に備えているわけではないので，決定は臨機応変に行われる必要がある。**異動予定の従業員から要求された条件に対して，鳥居社長とその人事マネジャーはどのように対応すべきだろうか？**

事例の背景

会社名：日本企業の英国子会社

英国子会社の社長：鳥居妙子氏

ドイツ子会社の社長：ハインリッヒ・ベッカー氏

ドイツの技術顧問：オットー・ミューラー氏

英国子会社の人事マネジャー：スターシー・メイウエザー氏

英国の日系子会社の社長である鳥居妙子氏は目下，ドイツの子会社から技術ノウハウを移転するプロジェクトに取り組んでいる。ドイツのエンジニアたちは，トレーニングと支援のためにロンドンとデュッセルドルフの間を行き来している。しかし，ドイツの技術者はせいぜい，月に 1，2 回程度の出張でロンドンにやってくるに過ぎないので，技術移転のペースは予想通りには進んでいない。

President Torii thought that it would be beneficial for one of the German technical advisors to be temporarily transferred to the London plant until the new manufacturing line was up and running. So, President Torii made an inquiry with the **President of the German subsidiary, Heinrich Becker.**

President Torii asked, "I would like to talk to you about **Otto Mueller.** He is a superb **technical advisor** who provides clear and helpful advice to our technical staff, but since the technology transfer is delayed due to the travel schedule, I was wondering if you would agree to having him transfer to London for a year or so until the new line is up."

In response, President Becker answered, "We are also working with a limited number of personnel in Germany and it wouldn't be easy. Let me discuss the issue internally and we will get back to you shortly."

One week later, President Becker informed President Torii that the transfer can be approved. However, Mueller has some *conditions* that he would like to discuss with the London-based HR Manager.

President Torii called upon **Stacy Mayweather, the Human Resources Manager**, to have a video conference as soon as possible in order to understand the meaning of the *conditions.*

In response, Mayweather asked President Torii, "Hmm, before I speak with Mr. Mueller, it would be good to have an idea of the International Transfer Policy from Japan. Can you provide it to me?"

To that, President Torii replied, "Well, we don't have a policy in English because whatever we do in Japan only covers expatriate transfers of Japanese people from Japan to subsidiaries. Anyway, please talk with Mr. Muller and

鳥居社長は，新しい製造ラインが稼働するまで，ドイツの技術アドバイザーの一人に一時的にロンドンの工場に転勤してもらうことが有益であると考えた。そこで，鳥居社長は**ドイツの子会社のハインリッヒ・ベッカー社長**に問い合わせを行った。

鳥居社長は，「**オットー・ミューラー氏**についてお話ししたい。彼は私達の技術スタッフに明確で有用な助言を提供してくれるすばらしい**技術顧問**ですね。しかし，技術移転は出張ベースによるために遅れているので，彼が1年かそこらの間，新ラインが立ち上がるまで，ロンドンに異動することを認めてもらえないでしょうか」と依頼した。

これに対してベッカー社長は，「我々ドイツの方でも限られた数の人員で働いているので，それは容易ではないと思いますよ。その問題について社内で話し合わせてください。その後で早めにお返事するようにします」と答えた。

1週間後，ベッカー社長は鳥居社長にその異動を承認し得ることを通知した。しかし，ミューラー氏はいくつかの「条件」を持ち出しており，彼はロンドンの人事マネジャーと話し合いたがっていると述べた。

鳥居社長は，**スターシー・メイウエザー人事マネジャー**に，その「条件」の意味を理解するためにできるだけ早くビデオ会議を開くよう求めた。

それに対してメイウエザー氏は鳥居社長に，「そうですね，ミューラー氏と話をする前に，日本本社の国際間異動規定についての考え方を知っておきたいと思います。私にそれを提供していただけますか？」と尋ねた。

それに対して鳥居社長は，「ええと，英語で書かれた規定は持っていないんだよ。何らかの形であれ日本本社が持っているものは，日本から海外子会社への日本人の海外派遣のみをカバーしているだけでね。とにかく，ミューラー氏

then let's consider what to do. We do not have to worry ahead of time."

A week later, Mayweather approached President Torii to explain the conditions that Mueller presented. Mayweather explained that Mueller was emphatic that these conditions need to be met in order for him to be willing to accept the transfer.

The following conditions were listed on the paper that Mayweather passed to President Torii:

1. Maintain payment of wages in Germany at the same level while offering a payment in British pounds to cover all living expenses plus a hardship stipend in recognition that I will be separated from my family for the period of the assignment.
2. Furnish a residence in the UK with all-expenses paid.
3. Allow for me to take *an extended weekend* in Germany once per month or allow for my wife and son to travel to the UK once monthly; airfare shall be considered as a company expense.
4. All actual moving costs shall be reimbursed by the company.
5. I want a transfer allowance of about one month's salary.
6. I would like you to compensate for the actual costs of consulting for tax filing in the UK.
7. I want annual paid leave to be granted according to German standards.
8. The health insurance system in the UK is not sufficient for my needs; allow for a supplemental plan as well.
9. Provide a company car for the duration of my transfer.

Mayweather explained her analysis, "There are some conditions which are rather excessive in my opinion, but in light of the fact that this is an

と話をしてくれる。それからどうしたらいいのか考えてみようよ。前もって心配する必要はないよ」と答えた。

1週間後，メイウエザー氏は鳥居社長に会ってミューラー氏が提示した条件を説明した。メイウエザー氏は，異動を前向きに受け入れるためには以下の条件を満たしてほしいとミューラー氏が強く主張していると説明した。

メイウエザー氏が鳥居社長に渡した書類には以下のような条件が列挙されていた。

1．ドイツでの給与と同じレベルを維持してほしい。それと同時に，英国ポンドで，全ての生活費をカバーするとともに，それに加えて，赴任期間中は家族と別れて暮らすことを考慮してハードシップ手当を支払ってほしい。

2．英国での住居に必要な備え付きの家具は全額会社負担でお願いしたい。

3．月1回，ドイツで「土日を絡めた連休」を私に許可するか，妻と息子が月1回，英国に来ることを認めてほしい。航空運賃は会社の費用とする。

4．実際の引越し費用は全て会社が負担してほしい。

5．給与約1カ月分に相当する赴任手当が欲しい。

6．英国での納税申告のためにかかるコンサルティング費用の実費を補償してほしい。

7．ドイツの基準に従って年次有給休暇の取得を認めてほしい。

8．英国の健康保険制度は私の要求水準よりも低い。補完的施策も同時に準備してほしい。

9．私の赴任期間中，社用車を提供してほしい。

メイウエザー氏の分析は以下の通りである。「私の意見ではかなり過剰な条件がいくつかあります。しかし，これが国際的な異動であるという事実に照ら

international transfer, we should flexibly consider his requests."

President Torii was taken aback as she had not anticipated such strong requests from Mueller.

"Hmm, what shall we do?"

Learning points

In many countries it is acceptable and common for company representatives and employees to negotiate employment conditions, especially when international assignments are under consideration. In Japan, the company makes a transfer decision—oftentimes unilaterally without much (or any) prior notification to or discussion with the employee—and the employee is expected to accept the decision as a requirement of employment. Employees in Japan normally accept the decision without much hesitation or debate.

This is not because Japanese employees are necessarily more loyal or obedient. Rather, it is due to the fact that the employee and the company have an implicit understanding about the long-term nature of employment; an overseas transfer is one of many assignments that the Japanese employee will experience during a long working career with the company.

In other countries, the situation is different for two primary reasons: (1) long-term employment is conditional based upon factors such as company and employee performance, and is not based upon an implicit understanding of long-term employment; and (2) as international transfers are life events that impact both one's working and private life, it is normally

して，私たちは彼の要求に対し柔軟に考えるべきです」。

鳥居社長はミューラー氏からのそのような厳しい要求が来るとは予想していなかったので，驚いてしまった。

「うーん，どうしたらよいものか？」

学習ポイント

多くの国では，特に国際的な赴任が検討されているときには，会社の代表者と従業員が雇用条件について交渉することは容認されており，また一般的でもある。日本では，会社は多くの場合，事前の通知や従業員との話し合いをそれほど多く（時にはまったく）持たずに，一方的に異動の決定を下し，従業員はその決定を雇用条件のひとつとして受け入れることが期待されている。日本の従業員は通常，それほどの躊躇や議論をすることなく決定を受け入れる。

これは，日本人の従業員が必ずしも，より忠実で従順だからというわけではない。むしろ，それは，従業員と会社が長期的な雇用の性質についての暗黙の了解をしているという事実によるものである。海外への異動は，日本の従業員が社内の長いキャリアの中で経験する多くの任務のうちのひとつであるためである。

他の国々では，状況は２つの主な理由によって異なる：(1)長期雇用は，会社ならびに従業員のパフォーマンスのような要因に基づいており，長期雇用に関する暗黙の理解に基づいていない。(2)国際的な赴任は，仕事と私生活の両方に影響を与えるライフ・イベントであり，そのような決定は会社によって一方的になされるべきではなく，むしろ相互の議論と交渉にお

expected that such a decision should not be made unilaterally by the company but rather in mutual discussion and negotiation.

In this case, the initial request by the company to transfer the employee to the UK for one year signifies that the employee's skills and influence are necessary for the company; this means that the employee is put into a position of advantage to seek out conditions that are favorable to himself. For that reason, he feels justified in making requests to the company for conditions of transfer.

In the end, through mutual discussion, some of his demands will be accepted by the company whereas some of the demands will not. This is the nature of negotiating employment conditions. When managers are expatriated from Japan to overseas countries, Japanese managers should not feel that the local employee is being disloyal or rude for making such demands. Rather the expatriate should engage in a negotiation of sorts to come to a win-win agreement between the company and the employee.

Hereafter, there is an element of uncertainty about whether Japanese companies can continually determine overseas assignments unilaterally as has been done to this point. For example, in Japan, the number of married couples with two working spouses is increasing. Therefore, it may be difficult to mandate the overseas assignment of an employee without considering the working career of the employee's spouse as well. In addition, because of the declining birthrate and aging population, it is expected that there will be an increase in the number of employees who need to provide parental-care and cannot be away from Japan for a long period of time.

いてなされるべきであると通常は期待されている。

　このケースでは，従業員を英国に1年間派遣するという会社からの最初の要求は，従業員のスキルと影響力が英国の会社に必要であることを意味している。これは，従業員が自分にとって有利な条件を引き出すのに有利な立場に置かれていることを意味する。そのため，彼は会社に異動のための諸条件を要求することは正当であると感じることになる。

　結局，相互の議論を通して，彼の要求のいくつかは会社によって受け入れられ，他方で，要求のいくつかは受け入れられないことになろう。これが雇用条件を交渉するということの本質である。日本から海外に赴任した場合，日本の管理職は，現地の従業員がそのような要求をすることに対し，忠誠心がないとか無礼であるとか感じてはいけない。むしろ，海外派遣者は，会社と従業員の間で双方にとってウイン・ウインとなるある種の合意を得るための交渉を行うべきなのである。

　日本の海外派遣においても今後，これまでのように会社側からの一方的な通知だけで事が進むかどうかわからない面がある。例えば，日本において，夫婦共働きが増えているため，配偶者のキャリアを考慮せずに海外赴任を命ずることは困難になるかもしれない。また，少子高齢化のゆえに，親の介護などの理由で日本を長くは離れられない状況が今後より多くなることも考えられる。

CASE STUDY 9.2

Who Is Looking Out for the Mental Health of Expatriates While They Are Working Abroad?

Question for consideration

While it is expected that an expatriate sent from Japanese HQ to an overseas subsidiary should be able to work effectively while overseas, it is well known that people often experience difficulties that negatively impact their overall mental health. **What kind of role do you think the GHQ (Global Headquarters) HR function should play in minimizing the negative impact on the health of expatriates sent from Japan?**

Case study detail

Company: Singapore branch of a Japanese financial institution
Kato Takayoshi, Assistant Manager
Sudo Akio, friend

Kato Takayoshi joined a leading Japanese bank upon graduation from university ten years ago. Last April, he was assigned to the Singapore branch as an **Assistant Manager**. With an outstanding score on English proficiency exams, he was confident in his skills to communicate and work successfully overseas. His wife was excited to go with him as well. She thought that Singapore is a clean, safe and well-developed country. And given Singapore's relative proximity to Japan and the large number of expatriates from Japan, she thought that there couldn't be any better place for an overseas assignment. Along with their two-year old daughter, they were excited to make the move.

CASE STUDY 9.2

海外派遣者の赴任中の精神衛生（メンタル・ヘルス）：誰が彼らの面倒を見るのか？

本事例の着目点

　日本の本社から海外の子会社に派遣される海外派遣者は，海外でもしっかりと働いてしかるべきであると期待されている。しかし，良く知られているように，彼らはしばしば，メンタル・ヘルス全般に悪影響を及ぼすような困難に直面するものである。**日本から派遣された海外派遣者の健康への悪影響を最小限に抑えるために，世界本社の人事部門（GHQ HR）が果たすべき役割にはどのようなものがあるだろうか？**

事例の背景
会社：日本の金融機関のシンガポール支店
アシスタント・マネジャー：加藤貴義氏
友人：須藤昭夫氏

　加藤貴義氏は，10年前に大学を卒業して日本の大手銀行に入社した。昨年4月，彼は，**アシスタント・マネジャー**としてシンガポール支店に配属された。彼は英語能力試験で優れた点数を得ており，海外でのコミュニケーションと仕事の成功に自信を持っていた。彼の妻も一緒に行けるということで興奮していた。彼女は，シンガポールは清潔で安全で発展している国だと思っていた。また，シンガポールと日本は相対的に近く，日本からの海外派遣者の数が多いことを考えると，彼女は海外駐在の場所として，これ以上良い場所はあり得ないと考えていた。彼らは，2歳の娘と一緒に転勤することにうきうきしていた。しかし，6カ月が経過した頃，加藤氏は身体的な問題を訴え始めた。仕事に行

However, after six months had passed, Kato started complaining of physical problems. It became hard to get up to go to work. He was often late to report to the office and days of sudden absence increased.

On the occasion of a business trip to Japan, Kato had a heart-to-heart discussion with his close friend, **Sudo Akio**.

Kato: Recently, when I get up in the morning, I still feel so lethargic and sometimes I hate going to work.

Sudo: Hmm, are you having stress at work? Or do you have some issue getting along with your Singaporean counterparts? I've heard that everyone going overseas gets a dose of culture shock.

Kato: I don't think so. After all, I am surrounded by a lot of other Japanese people and there are many Japanese restaurants nearby, so I don't think I am suffering from culture shock. And the Singaporeans in the office are used to working with Japanese expats, but . . .

Sudo: But what? What is it?

Kato: The pressure coming to me from the HQ in Japan and my boss is getting me down. Because Singapore acts as a regional sales company, we have to report to Tokyo headquarters frequently. Besides, my boss and I are always going for lunch and dinner together. I am under the gun to produce results. Last week, I did not get home until really late each night.

Sudo: That's more intense than it is here in Japan.

くために起床するのが難しくなってきた。遅刻と突然の欠勤が増加した。

　日本へ出張した際に，加藤氏は親友の**須藤昭夫氏**と腹蔵なく話し合った。

加藤：最近，朝起きると，倦怠感が強く，時には仕事に行くのが嫌になるんだよ。

須藤：うーん，仕事でストレスがある？　それとも君はシンガポールの同僚とうまくいっていないのか？　海外に行くと誰でも多少はカルチャー・ショックを受けると聞くけどね。

加藤：そうじゃないと思うんだ。何しろ，僕はたくさんの日本人の中にいて，また日本食レストランが周りにいっぱいあるんで，カルチャー・ショックに苦しんでいるわけではないんだ。そして，オフィスのシンガポール人は日本人海外派遣者と仕事をすることに慣れているんだけど，しかし…。

須藤：しかし，何？　何だろう？

加藤：日本の本社と上司からのプレッシャーに打ちのめされているんだよ。シンガポールは地域の販売会社として機能しているため，東京本社に頻繁に報告する必要がある。その上，上司といつも一緒に昼飯と夕飯を食べている。結果を出すようプレッシャーをかけられているんだよ。先週は，毎晩夜遅くまで家に帰れなかったよ。

須藤：確かにそれは日本にいるよりも激しいね。

Learning points

While HR professionals are not generally qualified to treat mental health issues, HR professionals should be aware that there is an increased risk of mental health issues when an employee is working abroad. Difficulties experienced in acclimating to the overseas environment (both for the expatriate and the expatriate's family) are typical causes. In this case however, we see that cultural factors may not be the primary source of difficulty. Rather, work stress is getting Kato down.

This case presents a warning of sorts to GHQ HR departments. In many companies, the GHQ HR staff and management have little to no contact with expatriates while they are overseas. The GHQ HR Department generally takes responsibility for preparing expatriates to go overseas but does not actively communicate with expatriates while they are working overseas. Furthermore, the local HR Department may not see it as their responsibility to look after the expatriates as accountability falls to handling issues with the national staff. Given such a case, no one is looking out for the Japanese expatriate.

To recognize and minimize such problems, it may be necessary for the GHQ HR Department to occasionally check up on the expatriates, to check in with the local HR Department or make an inquiry to the local top management to ensure that the expatriate is doing well, not just in terms of work performance, but also in terms of the level of acclimation to the environment and overall health.

Additionally, in cases where there are many expatriates being sent to a particular country, it may be advisable to send Japanese expatriates from

学習ポイント

　人事の専門家は一般的に，メンタル・ヘルス問題を治療するような資格
はないものの，彼らは，従業員が海外で勤務する際にはメンタル・ヘルス
問題が発生する危険性が高まるということを認識すべきである。海外の環
境に順応する際に経験する困難（海外派遣者およびその家族の両方にとっ
て）がよくある原因である。しかし，この事例では，文化的要因は問題の
主たる原因ではないと思われる。むしろ，仕事上のストレスが加藤氏を蝕
んでいる。

　この事例は，世界本社の人事部門に対し，ある種の警告を発している。
すなわち，多くの企業では，世界本社の人事部門スタッフや管理職は，海
外で勤務する海外派遣者と接触することはあってもそれはほんの少しで，
ほとんどの場合，接触することはない。世界本社の人事部は一般的に，海
外派遣者の派遣前の準備については責任を負うが，彼らが海外で勤務して
いる間は積極的に連絡を取ることはない。さらに，現地の人事部は，自ら
の責務は現地スタッフの問題への対応にあると考えているため，海外派遣
者の世話をすることは自分たちの責任ではないと考えるであろう。そのよ
うな場合，誰も日本人海外派遣者の面倒を見ていないことになる。

　このような問題を認識し，問題を最小限に抑えるために，世界本社の
人事部は時折，海外派遣者に問い合わせをする，または，海外派遣者が上
手く行っていることを確認するために，現地の人事部と連絡を取り合った
り，あるいは現地のトップ・マネジメントへの問い合わせを行ったりすべ
きかもしれない。その場合，仕事のパフォーマンスの面でだけでなく，環
境への順応の程度と全般的な健康面も照会する必要がある。

　なお，特定の国に日本人海外派遣者が多く駐在する場合には，人事部か
らも海外派遣者を出すことをお勧めする。

the HR Department overseas as well.

Even if there are just a few Japanese expatriates and the need for the aforementioned support role is minimal, the expatriation of a member of the HR Department shall be beneficial for increasing the global work experience of that individual and shall also impact the level of sensitivity overall of the HR Department to global work issues.

　日本人駐在員の数が少なく，前述のサポートの役割の必要性が小さい場合でも，人事部のメンバーの海外派遣は，当該派遣者のグローバルな仕事経験を増やすという利点があり，また同時に，人事部全体のグローバルな仕事関連の問題に対する感度を高めることになろう。

The Activities of the HR Department Within the Global Headquarters

The HR Department within the global headquarters (hereinafter referred to as the *GHQ HR*) is at the center of the global HR function as the business partner to the top management executives. Therefore, it is expected that the employees of the GHQ HR take on its work as stewards of the company, as employees themselves and integral members of the society that the company serves. In order to act professionally in this regard, it is necessary to have the understanding and cooperation of internal organizational stakeholders from the top management, down to each business department, each functional department, and overseas subsidiaries. That is to say that the GHQ HR must forge strong connections with stakeholders on a global level.

For this reason, it is an essential requirement that all GHQ HR employees firstly make continual efforts to establish the legitimacy for their roles by carrying out the following core activities across the global group (See Figure 10.1.):

CHAPTER 10

グローバル本社における人事部の活動

　グローバル本社の人事部門（以下では「GHQ HR」という）は，トップ・マネジメントのビジネス・パートナーとしてのグローバル人事機能の中心にある。したがって，GHQ HR の従業員は，従業員自身として，また会社が奉仕する社会の不可欠なメンバーとして，会社のスチュワード（世話役）としてその役割を果たすことが期待される。この点で専門的に行動するためには，トップ・マネジメントから各事業部門，各機能部門，そして海外子会社までの組織内部のステークホルダーの理解と協力を得ることが必要である。つまり，GHQ HR は，世界レベルでステークホルダーとの強いつながりを築く必要がある。

　このため，不可欠の要件となるのは，グローバル・グループ全体で以下の中核的業務を実行することによって，全ての GHQ HR の従業員がまずもって自らの役割の正当性を確立するための継続的な努力をすることである（図 10.1 参照）。

Figure 10.1   Core Activities of the GHQ HR for Establishing Legitimacy

1. Efforts to Disseminate the Corporate Philosophy

Firstly, the GHQ HR should be the corporate bellwether for promoting a corporate philosophy which includes some combination of the corporation's overarching mission, vision and values. The GHQ HR should spearhead the development of tools, methods and activities for the in-house dissemination of the corporate philosophy. This is essential for encouraging all employees to rally around shared values and ideas that form the identity and corporate culture of the organization. The initiatives for instilling understanding about the corporate philosophy may be carried out independently, but in many cases, will often be carried out in conjunction with various trainings and events.

On a global basis vis-à-vis the overseas subsidiaries, the GHQ HR should exert its influence to insist upon adherence to the corporate philosophy in order for all of the employees within the group to be unified by ideas that transcend national cultural differences. That being said, the GHQ HR should be patient and flexible when carrying out initiatives globally. For example, the cases used in training events may need to be customized and/or created newly within each region or subsidiary to deepen the HCN's understanding of, and increase

1. 企業理念の普及のための努力	2. パフォーマンス・マネジメントの基準およびプロセスの伝達	3. グローバル・タレント・マネジメント（GTM）の方法とプロセスの統括	4. グローバルな学習と人材育成の実施

5.HR 情報システム（HRIS）の実施

6. ビジネス上の問題とリスク軽減の支援

7. グローバル HR ネットワークの開発と強化，ならびに HR プロフェッショナルの継続的な育成

図 10.1　正当性を確立するために必要な GHQ HR の中核的業務

1．企業理念の普及のための努力

　第 1 に，GHQ HR は，企業の包括的な使命，ビジョン，価値観の組み合わせを含む企業理念を推進するための企業の先導者となるべきである。GHQ HR は，企業理念を社内に広めるためのツール，方法，および活動の開発を主導すべきである。これは，組織のアイデンティティと企業文化を形成する共有された価値観やアイデアを全ての従業員が賛同するよう誘導するために不可欠である。企業理念についての理解を浸透させるための施策は単独で実施することもできるが，多くの場合，様々なトレーニングやイベントと組み合わせて実施される。

　グループ全体の従業員全員が国の文化の違いを超えた観念によって統一されるためには，GHQ HR は海外子会社に対しグローバルな規模で企業理念の遵守を主張するようにその影響力を発揮すべきである。とはいえ，グローバルに施策を実行する場合，GHQ HR は忍耐強く柔軟に対応する必要がある。例えば，研修イベントで使用される事例は，HCN の理解を深め，企業理念との共鳴を高めるために，各地域または子会社内でカスタマイズしたり，新たに作成したりする必要があるかもしれない。

the resonance with, the corporate philosophy.

2. Promulgation of Performance Management Standards and Processes

Secondly, the processes and mechanism for performance management should be made clear and visible within the departments of each group company. For performance management processes to be established in such a way, both the GHQ HR and internal stakeholders must mutually support the system. To that end, the GHQ HR should implement processes for performance management which enable managers and subordinates to communicate openly and fairly during the performance management period. In other words, the processes that the GHQ HR puts in place should facilitate business and not create administrative burden.

The GHQ HR should develop directives and guidelines for the implementation of a viable HR system within each overseas subsidiary. While it may not be possible for the GHQ HR to dictate exact processes within each overseas subsidiary, it is feasible for the GHQ HR to provide oversight for the development of an HR system. For this purpose, the GHQ HR should devise global guidelines. Such guidelines may include high level principles about the aim and significance of performance management within the company as well as templates of commonly used forms (i.e., MBO form, performance evaluation form) and process specifications (i.e., how to provide feedback effectively, how to conduct a performance appraisal).

3. Overseeing Global Talent Management (GTM) Methods and Processes

The third core activity of the GHQ HR to mention is the planning and

2．パフォーマンス・マネジメントの基準およびプロセスの伝達

　第2に，パフォーマンス・マネジメントのプロセスとメカニズムは，各グループ会社の部門内で明確かつ可視化されるべきである。このようにしてパフォーマンス・マネジメント・プロセスを確立するには，GHQ HR と内部利害関係者の双方が協力し合ってこのシステムをサポートしなければならない。そのために，GHQ HR は，管理職と部下がパフォーマンス・マネジメント期間中に率直かつ正直にコミュニケーションをとることを可能にするパフォーマンス・マネジメントのためのプロセスを実施すべきである。言い換えれば，GHQ HR が導入するプロセスは，ビジネスを促進するものであり，管理上の負担を増やすものであってはならない。

　GHQ HR は，各海外子会社内で実行可能な人事システムを導入するための指令とガイドラインを作成する必要がある。GHQ HR が海外子会社内それぞれに的確なプロセスを指図することは不可能かもしれないが，GHQ HR が HR システムの開発のための監視を行うことはできる。この目的のために，GHQ HR は，パフォーマンス・マネジメントのグローバルなガイドラインを策定すべきである。そのようなガイドラインには，企業内のパフォーマンス・マネジメントの狙いと意味についての高次の方針，一般的に使用されるフォーム（MBO フォーム，パフォーマンス評価フォーム）のテンプレート（雛型），および，プロセスの詳細な記述（すなわち，フィードバックをどのように効果的に提供するか，パフォーマンス評価をどのように行うかなど）が含まれる。

3．グローバル・タレント・マネジメント（GTM）の方法と　　　プロセスの統括

　言及すべき GHQ HR の第3の中核的業務は，広義の**グローバル・タレント・**

practice of **Global Talent Management (GTM)** in a broad sense. With an eye towards the future of the entire corporate organization, the HR system, training & development methods and the retention of employees are concerns at the heart of GTM. Within the practice of GTM, it is firstly necessary to envision how talent should be attracted, retained and developed with a long-term point of view. Then the gap between the envisioned state of being and the current state of affairs shall be minimized via initiatives to train and develop current employees, and efforts to attract and hire external talent within the short-term. When adopting such practices, it will also be necessary to ensure consistency with other HRM measures and practices within the company.

4. Enabling Global Learning & Development

Next, GHQ HR should formulate methods and content for the provision of **learning and development (L&D)** initiatives on a global, group-wide basis. The GHQ HR may establish an internal L&D entity that is often referred to as the **corporate university** or **academy**. Within this corporate learning entity, a combination of methods may be used such as the following: (1) optimal usage of technology (on-line, virtual), (2) focused learning (classroom training), and (3) experiential learning in the field (factory tours, historical site tours, external company visits, etc.).

Topic areas of learning may be determined as follows: fundamental business skills training, functional specific training, global leader development, and corporate philosophy and strategy sessions. Depending upon the topic area, the primary accountability for practically executing L&D programs may be assigned on a global, regional or subsidiary-level basis. Additionally, the language of instruction is a point of consideration when determining how to assign accountability. While the language of instruction for global programs is typically English, regional or subsidiary-level programs may be conducted in

マネジメント（GTM）の計画と実践である。全社組織の将来を見据えて，人事制度，トレーニングと人材育成の方法，そして従業員の定着は，GTMの核心である。GTMの実践の中では，長期的な観点から才能をどのように引き付け，確保し，育成すべきかを第1に考える必要がある。そして，現在の内部従業員を訓練し育成する施策を通じ，同時に他方で，短期間に外部の才能を引き付け，採用すべく努力するという施策を通じて，望ましい状況と現在の状況との間のギャップを最小にすべきである。そのような実践策を採用する際には，社内の他のHRM対策および慣行との整合性を確保することも必要であろう。

4．グローバルな学習と人材育成の実施

次に，GHQ HRは，グローバルにグループ企業を巻き込む規模での**学習および人材育成（L&D）**施策の提供方法およびその内容を策定する必要がある。GHQ HRは，しばしば**コーポレート・ユニバーシティ**または**アカデミー**と呼ばれる内部のL&D事業体を設立するかもしれない。このコーポレート・ラーニング事業体においては，例えば次のような方法を組み合わせて利用している。(1)テクノロジーの最適な活用（オンライン，バーチャル），(2)集中的な学習（クラスルーム・トレーニング），および(3)現場での体験的学習（工場見学，史跡見学，外部企業訪問など）。

学習分野は以下のように決められるであろう。すなわち，基本的なビジネス・スキル・トレーニング，機能別トレーニング，グローバル・リーダーの育成，そして企業理念と戦略の授業などであろう。L&Dプログラムの現場での実施に関する主な責任は，その役割により，世界レベルまたは地域レベル／子会社レベルのいずれかに割り当てられる。さらに，教育での使用言語は，実施責任の割り当て方を検討する際の考慮事項である。グローバル・プログラムの教育での使用言語は通常英語であるが，地域レベルまたは子会社レベルのプログラムは現地の言語で実施されるであろう。

local languages.

For example, *marketing skills* training, a functional skill topic, may be conducted on a unified, global basis in English because concepts in marketing are universal. However, in the case that the marketing skills training should be developed to target specific regional or subsidiary-specific needs, the training program may be carried out on a regional or subsidiary-level basis in local languages.

Global leader development programs, which are global by definition, are normally designed and executed under the oversight of the corporate HQ L&D entity. The content of such programs may be designed internally and carried out with a combination of internal and external instructors, or the program may be outsourced to a traditional university and led by the university faculty. The cost of programs of this caliber may be borne by the overseas subsidiary that is sending participants, or the cost may be partially or fully funded by the corporate HQ. The overseas subsidiary may be compelled to send participants to such programs or retain discretionary judgment about the value of participation. The language of instruction of such programs is typically English, even in cases when the local language of the corporate HQ is not English.

5. Implementing HR Information Systems (HRIS)

Fifth, in order to efficiently carry out and execute processes for performance management, GTM, and learning management, the GHQ HR needs to take the lead in selecting and implementing HR technologies for building the **HR information systems (HRIS)** infrastructure. Such HR technologies enable the company to manage employee-related data, to grasp the current state of employees (human resources) within the company and to ascertain the

　例えば，「マーケティング・スキル」トレーニングは，マーケティングの概念が普遍的であるため，英語により，統一されたグローバル・ベースで行われることがある。しかし，特定の地域または子会社固有のニーズをターゲットにして展開される場合，マーケティング・スキル・トレーニングは，現地の言語により，地域または子会社で実施されることもある。

　本来グローバルであるべきグローバル・リーダー開発プログラムは通常，本社 L&D 事業体の監督の下で設計され，実施されている。そのようなプログラムの内容は内部的に設計され，内部と外部のインストラクターの組み合わせで実行されるであろう。あるいは，プログラムは伝統的な大学に外部委託され，そこの教員によって主導されるかもしれない。このレベルのプログラムの費用は，参加者を派遣している海外の子会社が負担することもあれば，本社が部分的または全面的に費用負担をすることもある。海外子会社は，そのようなプログラムに参加者を派遣することを強制されることもあるし，参加の価値について裁量的判断を保持する可能性もある。このようなプログラムの教育での使用言語は，本社での使用言語が英語ではない場合でも，通常は英語である。

5．HR 情報システム（HRIS）の実施

　第 5 に，パフォーマンス・マネジメント，GTM，およびラーニング・マネジメントのプロセスを効率的に実行し，実施するために，GHQ HR は，**HR 情報システム（HRIS）**のインフラストラクチャーを構築するための HR テクノロジーの選択と実装において主導権を握る必要がある。このような HR テクノロジーにより，会社は従業員関連のデータを管理し，社内の従業員（人的資源）の現状を把握し，各人の育成上のニーズを確認することができる。このイ

developmental needs of each person. In this infrastructure construction, it is beneficial when the system enables the users to understand information about key positions in the global organization, incumbents in such positions and successor candidates. To this end, it will be necessary to build and introduce an information system that is transparent and enables users to get a snapshot of the organization's situation.

As of the writing of this chapter, developments and utilization of Artificial Intelligence (AI) are still in the early stages. In the near future, we can anticipate that the GHQ HR will need to take the lead in assessing how AI technologies should be best utilized to enhance data analysis and decision making within the realm of HR affairs.

6. Supporting Business Issues & Risk Mitigation

Sixth, the day-to-day work of GHQ HR is to contribute to the business divisions and overseas subsidiaries by providing specialized knowledge and know-how for handling business affairs from the HR perspective. Generally, the GHQ HR provides ideas and solutions for condition-specific issues regarding attraction, retention, management and development of the workforce. At the same time, GHQ HR should have an eye on compliance and management risk mitigation concerns (harassment, discrimination) as well as labor relations.

To have an impact in this way, the management and the staff of the GHQ HR must always keep their finger on the pulse of internal and external trends, to grasp various problems, to identify the bud of potential future problems, and to offer effective solutions.

ンフラストラクチャー構築において，システムが，グローバル組織における重要なポジション，現職者および後継候補者についての情報をユーザが確認することを可能にする場合，有益であるといえる。そのためには，透明で組織の状況を即座に把握できる情報システムを構築し，導入することが必要になる。

　本章の執筆時点では，人工知能（AI）の開発と利用はまだ初期段階にある。近い将来，GHQ HR が主導して，人事問題の領域内でデータ分析と意思決定を強化するために AI テクノロジーをどのように活用するのが最適かを評価する必要があると予想できる。

6. ビジネス上の問題とリスク軽減の支援

　第6に，GHQ HR の日常の仕事は，人事の観点からビジネス上の問題に対処するための専門的な知識とノウハウを提供することにより，事業部門および海外子会社に貢献することである。一般的に，GHQ HR は，労働者の採用，確保／管理，および育成に関して各条件に固有の問題についてのアイデアと解決策を提供する。同時に，GHQ HR は，コンプライアンスとマネジメントのリスク（嫌がらせ，差別）軽減の問題，さらには労使関係にも注目すべきである。

　このように貢献するには，GHQ HR の管理職ならびにスタッフは，常に内外の動向に関する最新の情報に通じることにより，様々な問題を把握し，将来の潜在的な問題の芽を見極め，そして効果的な解決策を提供する必要がある。

7. Developing and Strengthening the Global HR Network and Continual Development of HR Professionals

Lastly, the GHQ HR should take the initiative to develop and continually strengthen the professional network among HR professionals working within the group. GHQ HR can practically do this by planning and facilitating **group-wide HR meetings (conferences)** on a regional and/or global basis. Such meetings serve multiple purposes including (1) creating a sense of team cohesion among the HR professionals working across the group, (2) providing an opportunity for expressing the expectations of the GHQ HR to the subsidiaries, and (3) sharing information amongst all participants so that common issues can be drawn out, and initiatives for collaborative efforts may be planned.

Additionally, such a meeting may provide all participants with the opportunity to study topics of concern in HR (i.e., employer branding, utilization of AI in recruiting, retention methods, etc.) and to develop skills for representing HR priorities to other stakeholders. (i.e., how to explain the performance management process to employees, what to say during a company information session on a university campus, etc.)

Such meetings provide a unique opportunity for the learning and development of the GHQ HR professionals. The GHQ HR management and staff need to exert leadership in the planning and execution of the meeting. Additionally, they may need to make presentations to overseas colleagues during the meeting and facilitate global communication via active discussions. Such a forum provides the GHQ HR with opportunities not experienced otherwise.

Beyond the abovementioned meeting events, it is essential for the GHQ HR

7．グローバル HR ネットワークの開発と強化，ならびに HR プロフェッショナルの継続的な育成

　最後に，GHQ HR は，グループ内で勤務する人事担当者間の専門家ネットワークを作り，継続的に強化するためのイニシアチブをとるべきである。GHQ HR は，地域的および／または世界的規模で**グループ全体の人事ミーティング（会議）**を計画し，サポートすることにより，事実上それ（イニシアチブをとること）を実現できる。このようなミーティングは，次のような複数の目的に資することができる。(1)グループ全体で活動する HR 専門家間のチームの結束感の創出，(2) GHQ HR の期待を子会社に表現するための機会の提供，および(3)全ての参加者間で情報を共有することにより，共通の問題が引き出され，協力的努力のための施策が企画されるようになる。

　さらに，そのようなミーティングは，全ての参加者に，人事における関心のあるトピック（すなわち，エンプロイヤー・ブランディング，募集・確保の手法における AI の活用，など）を研究する機会を提供し，また，他の利害関係者に人事の優先事項を表すためのスキル（すなわち，パフォーマンス・マネジメント・プロセスを従業員にどのように説明か，大学キャンパスにおける会社説明会の間に何を言うか，など）を開発する機会を与える。

　このようなミーティングは，GHQ HR の専門家の学習と人材育成にもユニークな機会を提供する。GHQ HR の管理職とスタッフは，ミーティングの計画と実施においてリーダーシップを発揮する必要がある。その上に，彼らは，ミーティング中に海外の同僚にプレゼンテーションを行い，また活発な議論を通じたグローバル・コミュニケーションの進行役を務める必要がある。このような討論の場は，GHQ HR に対し，他では経験できない機会を提供する。

　上記のミーティングのイベント以外にも，GHQ HR は，時には自組織内に

to shift its attention inward at times and to ensure that the HR professionals can continually grow and develop. One effective method is to plan and carry out personnel rotations of corporate GHQ HR members to become embedded HR representatives within business divisions or to experience working overseas as an expatriate in a group company subsidiary. Or, companies may choose to send their most promising HR talent back to school to earn an advanced degree in HRM. Participation in global HR conferences or local seminars is also highly recommended.

And it goes without saying that studying about, discussing and comparing practices regarding important concepts in global HR, both via Japanese and English text, is an essential method for increasing the awareness of HR professionals!

References & Suggestions for Additional Reading

Johnston, S. (2015), *Headquarters and Subsidiaries in Multinational Corporations: Strategies, Tasks and Corporations*, Palgrave Macmillan UK.

Kostova T, V. Marano and S. Tallman (2016), "Headquarters-subsidiary relationships in MNCs: fifty years of evolving research", *J World Bus*, 51, pp. 176-184.

Kunisch, S., G. Müller-Stewens and D. J. Collis (2012), "Housekeeping at corporate headquarters: international trends in optimizing the size and scope of corporate headquarters", in Survey report, University of St.Gallen/Harvard Business School, St.Gallen/Cambridge.

Rickard, Cat, et al. (2009), "Globalisation and HR", *Going Global: Managing the HR Function Across Countries and Cultures*, Routledge, Chapter 1.

Dickmann, Michael and Yehuda Baruch (2010), "The organizational context: exploring strategic international HRM", *Global Careers*, Routledge, Chapter 2.

注意を払い，HR の専門家が継続的に確実に成長し発展できるようにする必要
がある。効果的な方法のひとつは，企業の GHQ HR メンバーの人事ローテー
ションを計画し実行することにより，事業部所属の人事担当者にするか，また
はグループ企業内子会社の海外派遣者として海外で仕事経験を積ませることで
ある。または，企業は，最も有望な HR 人材を HRM の高度な学位を取得させ
るために教育機関に戻らせる選択をすることもできる。グローバルな人事会議
や地元のセミナーへの参加も強くお勧めする。

　そして，日本語と英語の両方で書かれたテキストを通して，グローバル HR
の重要な概念に関する実践について学び，議論し，比較することは，HR の専
門家の意識を高めるためには不可欠な方法である！

さらに学びたい人のための参考文献

Johnston, S. (2015), *Headquarters and Subsidiaries in Multinational Corporations: Strategies, Tasks and Corporations*, Palgrave Macmillan UK.

Kostova T, V. Marano and S. Tallman (2016), "Headquarters-subsidiary relationships in MNCs: fifty years of evolving research", *J World Bus*, 51, pp. 176-184.

Kunisch, S., G. Müller-Stewens and D. J. Collis (2012), "Housekeeping at corporate headquarters: international trends in optimizing the size and scope of corporate headquarters", in Survey report, University of St.Gallen/Harvard Business School, St.Gallen/Cambridge.

Rickard, Cat, et al. (2009), "Globalisation and HR", *Going Global: Managing the HR Function Across Countries and Cultures*, Routledge, Chapter 1.

Dickmann, Michael and Yehuda Baruch (2010), "The organizational context: exploring strategic international HRM", *Global Careers*, Routledge, Chapter 2.

CASE STUDY 10.1

Which Comes First: Promotion of Local Talent or HQ's English Skills?

Question for consideration

Globalization provides various challenges and opportunities for Japanese companies overseas. In fact, globalization provides challenges for Japanese companies even in Japan. **Should a locally hired employee be promoted at an overseas subsidiary into a position that requires close communication with the Japan HQ even if the counterparts in Japan do not speak English well enough to communicate actively with the subsidiary employees?**

Case study detail

Company: Malaysian subsidiary of a Japanese company
Kawasaki Yuriko, General Manager
Shimizu Osamu, Accounting & Finance Manager
Lou Li, Sales Manager
Kato Tsuyoshi, Sales Director

At a subsidiary of a Japanese company in Malaysia, two expatriates from Japan are engaged in conversation.

Kawasaki: As some time has passed since we started up our operations primarily under the leadership of managers from Japan, it is now time to start promoting more localization of key positions.

CASE STUDY 10.1

どちらが優先されるべきか？
現地の優秀人材の昇進か本社の英語スキルの向上か？

本事例の着目点

　グローバリゼーションは，海外の日本企業に様々な課題と機会をもたらす。 実際のところ，グローバリゼーションは日本国内に所在する企業に対しても課題を提示する。**カウンターパートとなる日本本社の従業員が現地採用の従業員と頻繁にコミュニケーションをとるのに十分な英語を話せない場合においてもなお，現地採用の従業員は，日本の本社との緊密なコミュニケーションを必要とする海外子会社のポジションに昇進してもよいものだろうか？**

事例の背景
企業：日本企業のマレーシア子会社
部長：川崎友里子氏
経理・経理財務課長：清水修氏
セールス・マネジャー：ルー・リー氏
セールス・ダイレクター：加藤剛氏

　マレーシアの日本企業の子会社で，日本からの二人の駐在員が話をしている。

川崎：基本的に日本からの管理職のリーダーシップの下で事業を立ち上げてから，かなりの年数が経ちました。そこで，今こそ主要なポジションの現地化を促進し始める時ですね。

Shimizu: Yes. I agree.

Kawasaki: For example, how about considering **Mr. Li**, our top locally hired **Sales Manager**, to replace **Kato san** as the **Sales Director** once Kato san returns to Japan?

Shimizu: Yes. Mr. Li has been working since the very early days of the company, so this could be a reasonable plan, but . . .

Kawasaki: But what?

Shimizu: In the senior manager role, he has been taking care of sales issues quite well here in Malaysia and across the ASEAN region, but as the Sales Director, there will be a need to communicate with Japan often.

Kawasaki: And is that so difficult?

Shimizu: A main role of the Sales Director position is to develop sales strategies with the Tokyo office. Mr. Li is fluent in Malay, Chinese and English, but unfortunately his Japanese is quite rudimentary.

Kawasaki: However, our company is a company with the very slogan *a company for a global society*. Shouldn't the overseas subsidiary management be able to communicate with the HQ in English by now?

Shimizu: Yes. I have tried to have English-only meetings with the Malaysian sales guys and the HQ people many times. But it never goes so smoothly. The Japan side always asks to have information explained in Japanese.

清水：ええ。賛成です。

川崎：例えば，加藤さんが帰国したら，現地採用の**トップ・セールス・マネ ジャー**である**リーさん**を，**加藤さん**に代わって**セールス・ディレクター**に起用 したらどうでしょうか？

清水：ええ。リーさんは会社の初期の頃から働いていたので，これは妥当な線 かもしれません。でも…。

川崎：でも，何ですか？

清水：彼は，上級部長として，ここマレーシアと ASEAN 全域でのセールス の問題に非常によく対応してきました。しかし，セールス・ディレクターとな ると，日本と頻繁にコミュニケーションをとる必要があるでしょうね。

川崎：それは難しいですか？

清水：セールス・ディレクターのポジションの主な役割は，東京オフィスと一 緒になって，販売戦略を展開することです。リーさんはマレー語，中国語，英 語に堪能ですが，残念ながら彼の日本語はかなり初歩的な段階にとどまってい ます。

川崎：しかし，私たちの会社はまさに，「グローバル社会のための会社」とい うスローガンを掲げた会社です。海外子会社の経営管理職は今でも，英語で本 社と意思疎通することができないんですか？

清水：はい。私は今まで，マレーシア人の営業担当者と本社スタッフとの間で 英語のみのミーティングを何度も試みました。しかし，それはそれほどスムー ズに行ったためしはありません。日本側は常に日本語での情報を要求してきま す。

Kawasaki: Okay, but should we hold up the promotion of talented local employees just because of the HQ's inability to communicate effectively in English?

Shimizu: Well, that is a good point, but still, we have to make decisions that are practical and won't slow down our business growth . . .

Learning points

We can see that globalization is not just an issue for business in overseas locations. In fact, the situation in the headquarters has an impact on the very business overseas.

In an ideal world, language issues would not be a barrier to communication. But, for many globalizing Japanese companies, the lack of English language communication skills does cause difficulty. Emphasizing the need to speak English within the HQ is of course necessary. That being said, success in global business requires the overseas counterparts to also have the patience and skill to communicate with people in the HQ and overcome language barriers.

Therefore, to consider the promotion of an employee such as Li to a position that requires interaction with the headquarters, an employee like Li may need to do any of the following:

1) Spend some time in Japan on a business trip or short-term assignment to get to know the people in the HQ
2) Study Japanese
3) Try to communicate logically and simply

川崎：それでは，本社が英語で効果的にコミュニケーションを取れないという理由のゆえに，優秀な現地従業員の昇進を延期すべきということですか？

清水：確かに，おっしゃる点が肝です。それでもなお，現実に即して，またビジネスの成長を遅らせることのないような決断をしなければなりませんしね…。

学習ポイント

　グローバリゼーションは単に海外事業にとっての問題だけではないことが分かる。実際には，本社の状況はまさに海外事業に影響を与えるのである。

　理想的な世界では，言語の問題はコミュニケーションの障害にはならない。しかし，グローバル化を進める多くの日本企業にとって，英語によるコミュニケーション・スキルの欠如こそが文字通り，困難を引き起こしている。本社内で英語を話す必要性を強調することはもちろん必要である。そうは言いながらも，グローバル・ビジネスで成功するには，海外のカウンターパート側も，本社の人々とコミュニケーションするための忍耐力とスキルを持ち，言葉の壁を乗り越える必要がある。

　したがって，リー氏などの従業員を本社とのやり取りが必要なポジションに昇進させようとする場合には，リー氏のような立場の従業員は次のいずれかを実行する必要がある。

1）本社の人々と知り合うために出張または短期的な駐在の形でしばらく日本に滞在する
2）日本語を勉強する
3）論理的かつ平易なコミュニケーションを心がける

Additionally, to enable Li to be promoted into the Sales Director position, a young trainee who already speaks English well could be expatriated to assist Li's interactions with the Japan side.

It is clear that English proficiency alone will not produce results, but it is also clear that the lack of English proficiency will hamper the production of desired results. It can be said that the efforts to polish up one's English skills from as young an age as possible will bear fruit in the long-term.

また，リー氏がセールス・ディレクターの地位に昇進することを可能にするために，すでに英語を上手に話す若い研修生を，リー氏の日本側とのやり取りを支援するために現地に派遣するという方法もある。

　英語能力だけで成果が出るというものでないことは明らかである。とはいえ，英語能力がないと出たであろう成果を得ることができないことも明らかである。出来るだけ若いうちから英語能力に磨きをかけるということは，長期的には成果に繋がることになるといえよう。

Supplement:
Communicating From an Appropriate "Stance" for Good Relations Between the GHQ HR and Overseas Subsidiaries

Note: the content of this chapter's supplement has been derived from the consulting work conducted by the author (Bryan Sherman) for global Japanese organizations.

Communicating With Counterparts in Overseas Subsidiaries

On a daily basis, the GHQ HR management and staff in Japan communicate with their counterparts at overseas subsidiaries via email and/or videoconference, while on business trips as well as during global HR meetings. When I speak with the GHQ HR management and staff about their experiences communicating with their overseas counterparts, I often hear of their frustrations.

Here is a short story to help introduce the frustration experienced by an HR manager (We'll call him Mr. Saito.) in the GHQ HR of a company with which I worked.

補論：
GHQ HR と海外子会社との
良好な関係には適切な「スタンス」に
基づくコミュニケーションが重要

注：この章の補論の内容は，グローバルな日本の組織のために著者（ブライアン・シャーマン）が実施したコンサルティング作業に基づいている。

海外子会社のカウンターパートとのコミュニケーション

　日本における GHQ HR のマネジャーやスタッフは，日常的に，出張中やグローバル HR ミーティング中に，電子メールやビデオ会議を介して，海外子会社のカウンターパートとコミュニケーションを行っている。私が，GHQ HR のマネジャーやスタッフと彼らの海外のカウンターパートとのコミュニケーションの経験について話を交わすと，往々にして彼らのフラストレーションを耳にすることになる。

　これは，私が働いていた会社の GHQ HR で，HR マネジャー（彼を斉藤氏と呼ぼう）が経験したフラストレーションを紹介するための短い話である。

Mr. Saito explained, "We asked our overseas HR managers to share with us their performance management process forms so that we could *support* them . . . but they really are not too cooperative."

Then, I queried, "Well, did you explain your purpose for asking?"

"Hmm, well . . . yes, my purpose had been to *support* them," he said.

Can you understand why the overseas subsidiary HR counterparts may not have acted as cooperatively as Mr. Saito expected?

While the English expressions used by Mr. Saito were acceptable, his communication was not effective because he mixed up different types of *stances* when speaking from his position in the GHQ HR.

What Is a *Stance*?

For our purposes, we will refer to *stance* as to how entities/people with high levels of power (i.e., GHQ HR) choose to relate to others with less power (i.e., overseas subsidiary) for carrying out a certain task. We can identify three categories of stances as explained below. Each stance is associated with various *interaction types* which describe how the entities/people with high power communicate with others who have lower power.

　斉藤氏は，「海外子会社の『サポート』をしたいので，海外子会社の人事部に
パフォーマンス・マネジメント・プロセスのフォームを我々と共有してほしい
と依頼したところ，…実際には，彼らはあまり協力的ではなかった」と述べた。

　そこで私は，「ところで，依頼の目的を説明しましたか？」と尋ねた。

　「うーん，えーと，…はい，私の目的は彼らを『サポート』することでした
が」と彼は言った。

　読者は，なぜ，海外子会社のカウンターパートは斉藤氏の期待どおり協力的
に行動しなかったのかを理解できるだろうか？

　斉藤氏が使用した英語の表現は適切であったが，彼が GHQ HR における自
分のポジションから話す際に，様々なタイプの「スタンス」を混同したため，
彼のコミュニケーションは効果的となるには至らなかった。

「スタンス」とは何だろうか？

　この目的のために，特定のタスクを実行するに際して，権力の高い事業体／
人（例えば GHQ HR）が，権力の低い他の事業体／人（例えば海外子会社）
とどのように関係するかについて，「スタンス」という用語を用いて表現す
る。以下で説明するように，スタンスにおいて３つのカテゴリーを識別でき
る。各スタンスは，高い権力を持つ事業体／人が，権力の低い他の事業体／人
とどのように対話するかを記述する様々な「インタラクション（接触）型」に
関連づけられている。

Three Categories of Stances (See Figure 10-Supplement 1.)

Category 1: Authoritative power stance
Compelling action from an authoritative power stance

A person in power decides to utilize their power position to get something from others; in such a case, the person in power communicates from a higher power position (*top down*) to compel others to action.

Category 2: Neutral power stance
Working collaboratively from a neutral power stance

A person in power decides to be *power neutral*; in this case, the person in power communicates openly and equally with others in lower power positions to seek out new ideas and solutions with counterparts.

Category 3: Bottom up power stance
Being responsive to others based upon a bottom up power stance

A person in power firstly defers to the needs/wants of counterparts in lower

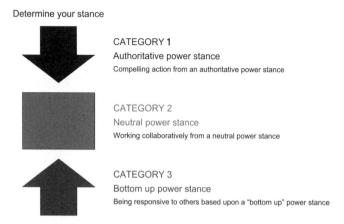

Determine your stance

CATEGORY 1
Authoritative power stance
Compelling action from an authoritative power stance

CATEGORY 2
Neutral power stance
Working collaboratively from a neutral power stance

CATEGORY 3
Bottom up power stance
Being responsive to others based upon a "bottom up" power stance

Figure 10-Supplement 1   Three Stance Categories

スタンスの３つのカテゴリー（図10-補.1 参照）

カテゴリー１：権力行使スタンス
権力行使スタンスからの行動の強制

　権力を持つ者は，自分の地位を利用して他の人から何かを得るという決定ができる。そのような場合，権力を持つ者はより高い地位から（「トップ・ダウン」で）他の人に行動を強制するようなコミュニケーションを行う。

カテゴリー２：権力中立スタンス
権力中立スタンスからの協働

　権力を持つ者は「権力中立的」である立場を取ることができる。この場合，権力を持つ者は権力的により低い立場にいるカウンターパートと率直かつ対等な立場でコミュニケーションを取り，新たなアイデアや解決策を模索する。

カテゴリー３：権力委譲スタンス
権力委譲スタンスに基づく他者への対応

　権力を持つ者は，何らかの行動を起こす前にまず，権力的により低い立場に

スタンスを決定

カテゴリー１：
権力行使スタンス
権力行使スタンスからの行動の強制

カテゴリー２：
権力中立スタンス
権力中立スタンスからの協働

カテゴリー３：
権力委譲スタンス
権力委譲スタンスに基づく他者への対応

図10-補1　スタンスの３つのカテゴリー

power positions before taking any actions; in this case, the person in power respects the discretion of others in lower power positions and aims to be helpful only when appropriate.

Let's now understand each of the interaction types under each category and consider how the GHQ HR may interact with overseas subsidiaries in each case.

Category 1: Authoritative power stance (See Figure 10-Supplement 2.)
Three interaction types
A. Directive type: *Do as we say!*
When communicating from a *directive* interaction type, the GHQ HR provides a clear order with which the subsidiary should comply.

B. Leading type: *Follow us and do as we do!*
When communicating from a *leading* interaction type, the GHQ HR expresses that the subsidiary should do something based upon similar actions which have already been taken by the GHQ HR.

C. Managing type: *Do it and report on the progress!*
When communicating from a *managing* interaction type, the GHQ HR provides guidelines for what should be done, but may leave procedural

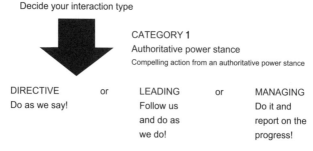

Decide your interaction type

CATEGORY 1
Authoritative power stance
Compelling action from an authoritative power stance

DIRECTIVE   or   LEADING   or   MANAGING
Do as we say!   Follow us   Do it and
                               and do as   report on the
                               we do!   progress!

Figure 10-Supplement 2   Category 1, Three Interaction Types

いるカウンターパートの要求や欲求に譲歩する。この場合，権力を持つ者は，権力的により低い立場にいる者の裁量権を尊重し，適切な場合にのみ援助しようとする。

　次に，各カテゴリーの中の複数のインタラクション型を理解し，GHQ HRがいろいろな場合に海外子会社とどのように対話するかを考えてみよう。

カテゴリー1：権力行使スタンス（図10-補2参照）
3つのインタラクション型
A．指示命令型：「言った通りにせよ！」

　「指示命令型」インタラクションによりコミュニケーションをとる場合，GHQ HRは，子会社が遵守すべき明確な命令を下す。

B．先導型：「私たちに従い，私たちと同じようにせよ！」

　「先導型」インタラクションによりコミュニケーションをとる場合，GHQ HRは，子会社がGHQ HRによってすでに実行された同様のアクションに基づいて何を行うべきかを表明する。

C．管理型：「実行し，その後の進捗を報告せよ！」

　「管理型」インタラクションによりコミュニケーションをとる場合，GHQ HRは何をすべきかについてのガイドラインを提供するが，手続き上の決定は

インタラクション型を決定

カテゴリー1：
権力行使スタンス
権力行使スタンスからの行動の強制

指示命令型	又は	先導型	又は	管理型
言った通りにせよ！		私たちに従い，私たちと同じようにせよ！		実行し，その後の進捗を報告せよ！

図10-補2　カテゴリー1，3つのインタラクション型

decisions to the subsidiary; however, the subsidiary usually needs to report on progress to the GHQ HR periodically.

Category 2: Neutral power stance (See Figure 10-Supplement 3.)
One interaction type

In category 2, there is only one interaction type to introduce:

Collaborative type: *Let's think and work together!*

When communicating from a *collaborative* interaction type, the managers and staff in the GHQ HR work together with counterparts in the subsidiary-level HR Department for purposes such as the co-creation of a tool, determination of a new standard or implementation of a new process.

Determine your interaction type

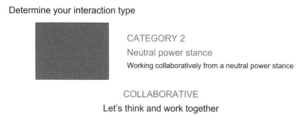

CATEGORY 2
Neutral power stance
Working collaboratively from a neutral power stance

COLLABORATIVE
Let's think and work together

Figure 10-Supplement 3   Category 2, One Interaction Type

Category 3: Bottom up power stance (See Figure 10-Supplement 4.)
Three interaction types

A. Consultative type: *Let us know if you need any advice.*

When communicating from a *consultative* interaction type, the GHQ HR provides consultation, comparative information, and opinions to the subsidiary when requested or otherwise appropriate.

子会社に任せるであろう。ただし，子会社は通常，進捗状況を定期的に GHQ HR に報告する必要がある。

カテゴリー2：権力中立スタンス（図 10-補 3 参照）
ひとつのインタラクション型

　カテゴリー2では，以下の通り，インタラクション型はひとつだけである。

協働型：「共に考え，共に働こう！」

　「協働型」インタラクションによりコミュニケーションをとる場合，GHQ HR のマネジャーやスタッフと子会社レベル人事のカウンターパートは，ツールの共同制作，新しい標準の決定，または新しいプロセスの実施などの目的で協働する。

インタラクション型を決定

カテゴリー2：
権力中立スタンス
権力中立スタンスからの協働

協働型
共に考え，共に働こう。

図 10-補 3　カテゴリー2，ひとつのインタラクション型

カテゴリー3：権力委譲スタンス（図 10-補 4 参照）
3つのインタラクション型

A．相談型：「何らかのアドバイスが必要な場合は知らせてほしい。」

　「相談型」インタラクションによりコミュニケーションをとる場合，GHQ HR は，要求があった場合などには，子会社の相談に乗り，比較可能な情報や意見を子会社に提供する。

B. Supportive type: *Let us know if you need any assistance or resources.*

When communicating from a *supportive* interaction type, the GHQ HR performs work in lieu of a subsidiary when the subsidiary does not have the capacity or capability to do something on its own.

C. Delegative type: *We leave things up to you.*
When communicating from a *delegative* interaction type, the GHQ HR expresses trust in the subsidiary management's ability to handle an issue based upon its own discretion without any oversight/direct involvement by the GHQ.

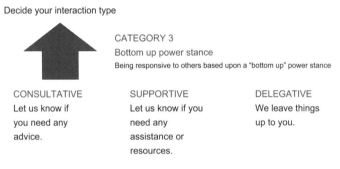

Decide your interaction type

CATEGORY 3
Bottom up power stance
Being responsive to others based upon a "bottom up" power stance

CONSULTATIVE
Let us know if you need any advice.

SUPPORTIVE
Let us know if you need any assistance or resources.

DELEGATIVE
We leave things up to you.

Figure 10-Supplement 4   Category 3, Three Interaction Types

Let's return to the topic in the conversation I had with Mr. Saito at the GHQ HR. Hopefully it is now clear to the reader that this manager, Mr. Saito, was communicating from two different stances within the same topic of conversation. The GHQ HR manager's intention was to convey a message based upon a **category 1 stance, directive type**, but actually, what was understood by the subsidiaries was primarily of a **category 3 stance, supportive type**.

Upon hearing of the GHQ HR manager's message, the subsidiary HR

B．縁の下の力持ち型：「何らかの支援やリソースが必要な場合は知らせてほしい。」

　「縁の下の力持ち型」インタラクションによりコミュニケーションをとる場合，GHQ HR は，子会社が独自に何かを行う力量または能力を持っていない場合，子会社の代わりにリソースを提供する。

C．委任型：「皆さんに仕事を任せる。」
　「委任型」インタラクションによりコミュニケーションをとる場合，GHQ HR は，子会社の経営力への信頼を表明する。子会社は，GHQ による監視または直接の関与なしに，独自の裁量に基づいて問題を処理する。

インタラクション型を決定

カテゴリー3：
権力委譲スタンス
権力委譲スタンスに基づく他者への対応

相談型　　　　　　又は　　　縁の下の力持ち型　　又は　　委任型
何らかの　　　　　　　　　　何らかの支援や　　　　　　　皆さんに
アドバイスが　　　　　　　　リソースが　　　　　　　　　仕事を任せる。
必要な場合は　　　　　　　　必要な場合は
知らせてほしい。　　　　　　知らせてほしい。

図 10-補4　カテゴリー3，3つのインタラクション型

　GHQ HR での私が斉藤氏と話し合ったという件のトピックに戻ろう。このマネジャー（斉藤氏）が，同じ会話のトピック内で2つの異なるカテゴリーのスタンスからコミュニケーションを行っていたことが，読者に明確になったと思う。GHQ HR マネジャーの意図は，**カテゴリー1のスタンスの中の「指示命令型」インタラクション**に基づいてメッセージを伝えることであったが，実際に子会社が理解したのは，主に**カテゴリー3のスタンスの中の「縁の下の力持ち型」インタラクション**であった。

　GHQ HR マネジャーのメッセージを聞いて，子会社の HR マネジャーは次

managers probably thought to themselves: "Well, we do not need the support of the GHQ HR with our performance management process. Therefore, I do not need to provide any information to the GHQ HR."

Based upon an understanding about the different categories of stances and interaction types, Mr. Saito came to understand how to communicate in the future with overseas subsidiary counterparts. For example, he could now clearly indicate the following:

(First, express category 1 stance, directive interaction type.)

"The GHQ HR is currently reviewing the performance management processes at each of our subsidiaries so that we can determine some global best practices and standards. Please send us a copy of all of the performance evaluation forms currently being used in your company.

(Then express category 3 stance, supportive interaction type.)

As well, please feel free to ask us if you need any support to implement an effective process in your company."

To minimize frustration when communicating from the GHQ HR in English with colleagues that reside overseas and work at your company's subsidiaries, firstly, please consider which stance would be the most appropriate for your issue. Then respectfully and appropriately communicate the intention of your chosen stance with the best interaction type.

のように考えた。「パフォーマンス・マネジメント・プロセスで GHQ HR からのサポートを必要としていません。したがって，GHQ HR に情報を提供する必要はありません」。

　様々なスタンスのカテゴリーおよびインタラクション型の理解に基づいて，斉藤氏は海外子会社の HR カウンターパートとコミュニケーションをとる方法について理解した。例えば，彼は次のように話すであろう。

（まず，カテゴリー 1 の指示命令型のインタラクションで表現する。）

「現在，GHQ HR は，グローバルなベスト・プラクティスと基準を決定するために，各子会社のパフォーマンス・マネジメント・プロセスをレビューしています。現在貴社で使用されている全てのパフォーマンス評価フォームのコピーをお送りください。

（次に，カテゴリー 3，縁の下の力持ち型インタラクションで表現する。）

　また，効果的なプロセスを実施するためにサポートが必要かどうかお気軽にお問い合わせください」。

　海外に居住し，子会社で働く同僚と英語で GHQ HR からコミュニケーションする際のフラストレーションを最小限に抑えるために，まずどのスタンスが当該問題への対応に最も適しているかを検討する。その後，選択したスタンスを最適なインタラクション型を通じて，敬意を込めて適切にコミュニケーションしていただきたい。

Useful Expressions

Here are some expressions for each interaction type so that you can communicate respectfully and appropriately:

Category 1 stance
Directive type

- [ ] Please do this . . .
- [ ] Please comply with this directive by . . .
- [ ] Please make sure that you follow this . . .

Leading type

- [ ] Please follow our lead by doing . . .
- [ ] Please do as we do by . . .

Managing type

- [ ] Please report to us on the status about . . .
- [ ] Please use these guidelines to implement . . .

Category 2 stance
Collaborative type

- [ ] Let's think together in order to develop a new initiative for . . .
- [ ] Let's collaborate on developing . . .
- [ ] Let's work together to do . . .

Category 3 stance
Consultative type

- [ ] If necessary, we would like to explain our experiences about . . .

有用な表現例

　敬意を込めて適切にコミュニケーションをとるための表現を，各インタラクション型からいくつか例示する。

カテゴリー1
指示命令型
　　□　この・・・をしてください。
　　□　・・・により，この指示命令を遵守してください。
　　□　この・・・に従っていることを確認してください。

先導型
　　□　私たちのリードに従って・・・をしてください。
　　□　私たちが・・・によって示すようにしてください。

管理型
　　□　・・・についての状況について報告してください。
　　□　このガイドラインを利用して・・・を実施してください。

カテゴリー2
協働型
　　□　・・・のための新しい施策を開発するために一緒に考えましょう。
　　□　・・・の開発で協働しましょう。
　　□　・・・をするために一緒に仕事をしましょう。

カテゴリー3
相談型
　　□　もし必要でしたら，・・・についての我々の経験を説明したいと思います。

☐   We would like to provide advisement if needed about . . .

Supportive type

☐   Let us know how we can best support you . . .

☐   We would like to support you in this endeavor by . . .

Delegative type

☐   We leave the next steps up to your judgment . . .

☐   Please do what you think is best for . . .

□　もし・・・について必要でしたらアドバイスをしますよ。

縁の下の力持ち型

□　どのように支援するのが最適か教えてください。

□　・・・により，この事業で皆さんをサポートしたいと思います。

委任型

□　次のステップをどうするかはあなたの判断に任せます。

□　・・・のために最適だと思うことをしてください。

Sample Conversations

サンプル・カンバセーション

Introduction

In order for you to succeed in your endeavors as a global human resources professional or global business manager, you should first understand the theories, concepts and case studies presented in Section I of this book. However, that understanding alone is not sufficient; you need to be able to communicate appropriately and naturally with various counterparts in order to deal with human resource-related issues of relevance to your company.

With English being the de facto lingua franca in today's business world, it is advisable for you to study how to communicate in English; the study of the following sample conversations shall be instructive in this endeavor.

The sample conversations presented in this section take place within Kindai Systems Kabushiki Kaisha (abbreviated as KSK)—a fictional company that manufactures automotive components. KSK has its headquarters in Tokyo, Japan and is developing a network of subsidiaries across North America, Asia and Europe. (Refer to the following KS Group organization charts (Exhibit 1a-e) which contain a list of characters who appear in those conversations.)

序　論

　　グローバル人事の専門家またはグローバル・ビジネスのマネジャーとしての
あなたの努力に報いるには，本書の Section I で書かれている理論，概念なら
びに事例研究を最初に理解する必要がある。ただし，その理解だけでは十分で
はない。会社にとって重要な人事関連の問題に対処するために，様々なカウン
ターパートと適切かつ自然にコミュニケーションを行う必要がある。

　　今日のビジネス界では英語が事実上の共通語であるため，どのように英語で
コミュニケーションをとればよいのかについて学ぶことが望ましい。以下に続
くサンプル・カンバセーションで学ぶことは，このような取組みにおいて，有
益であろう。

　　この章で紹介するサンプル・カンバセーションは，自動車部品を製造する架
空の会社である近代システムズ株式会社（略称 KSK）内で行われる。KSK の
本社は日本の東京にあり，北米，アジア，ヨーロッパに子会社ネットワークを
構築している（これらのカンバセーションに登場する登場人物のリストを含む
KS グループの組織図（Exhibit 1a-e）は以下を参照されたい）。

Note on the usage of names in the sample conversations: when characters are first introduced, their full names and job titles are provided in **bold** text.

Thereafter, the following standards have been followed to denote the names of characters:

In recognition of recent trends and developing preferences for representing Japanese names in English, the names of Japanese characters have been written with the family name before the given name.

To indicate a speaker within the sample conversation script, speakers are indicated by family names regardless of nationality.

Within the explanatory text and throughout the dialogues of the sample conversations, Japanese characters are referred to by their family names. Non-Japanese characters are referred to by their given name or their family name depending upon what is natural within the context of the situation. Salutations such as *Mr.*, *Mrs.*, or the Japanese *san* and *shi* are attached to family names when appropriate.

Additionally, after each sample conversation, we have included a part called *Key Phrases & Expressions*. In this part, we explain the usage of selected phrases and expressions that appear in **bold** text throughout the sample conversation.

It is hoped that Section II will provide you with a new level of familiarity with the style of communication in real-world business settings.

　サンプル・カンバセーションに登場する氏名の使い方についての注意事項は以下のとおりである。登場人物が最初に紹介される際にはフル・ネームと役職が**太字**で記載される。

　その後，次の標準に従って登場人物の名前を示すことにする。

　日本人の名前は英語でもこの形式で書くべきであるという最近の傾向と選好の変化を折り込み，日本人の登場人物の名前は，苗字を名前の前に置く形で示されている。

　サンプル・カンバセーションのせりふを話すスピーカーを示すために，スピーカーは国籍に関係なく，苗字（ファミリー・ネーム）で示される。

　解説の文章およびサンプル・カンバセーションの対話全体を通じて，日本人の登場人物は苗字で表すこととする。日本人以外の登場人物は，状況に応じて自然となるように，名前（ギブン・ネーム）または苗字で示される。「Mr.」，「Mrs.」，または日本語の「さん」及び「氏」の敬辞は，必要に応じて苗字のみにつける。

　さらに，各サンプル・カンバセーションの後に「重要表現」というコーナーを設けている。このコーナーでは，サンプル・カンバセーションを通じて**太字**のテキストで表示される重要フレーズと表現の使用法について解説する。

　読者のみなさんが，この Section II により，実際のビジネス現場でのコミュニケーションのあり方についてこれまで以上に精通して下さることを期待する。

KS Group Companies

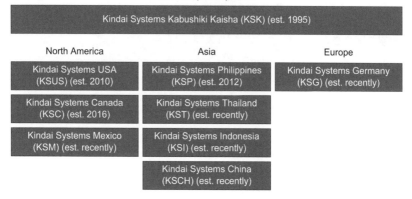

Figure 1a   KS Group Companies

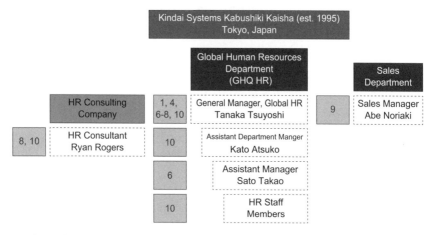

Numbers in the boxes indicate the number of the sample conversation in which the character appears.

Figure 1b   KSK Partial Organization

KS グループ会社の一覧

近代システムズ株式会社（KSK）（1995 年設立）

North America	Asia	Europe
米国近代システムズ (KSUS)（2010 年設立）	近代システムズ・フィリピン (KSP)（est. 2012）	近代システムズ・ドイツ (KSG)（最近設立）
近代システムズ・カナダ (KSC)（est. 2016）	近代システムズ・タイ (KST)（最近設立）	
近代システムズ・メキシコ (KSM)（最近設立）	近代システムズ・インドネシア (KSI)（最近設立）	
	中国近代システムズ (KSCH)（最近設立）	

図 1a　KS グループ会社の一覧

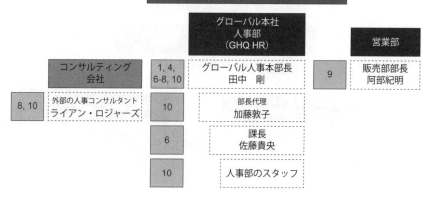

ボックス内の数字は，登場人物が登場するサンプル・カンバセーションの番号を示す。

図 1b　KSK の組織（一部）

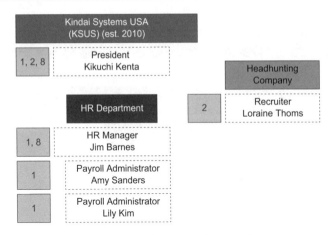

Numbers in the boxes indicate the number of the sample conversation in which the character appears.

Figure 1c   KSUS Partial Organization

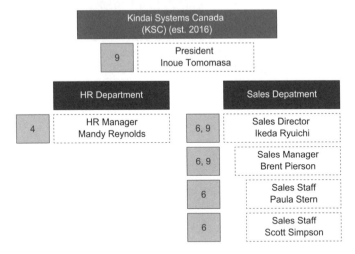

Numbers in the boxes indicate the number of the sample conversation in which the character appears.

Figure 1d   KSC Partial Organization

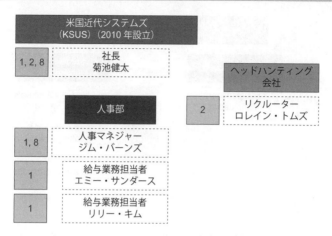

ボックス内の数字は，登場人物が登場するサンプル・カンバセーションの
番号を示す。

図 1c　KSUS の組織（一部）

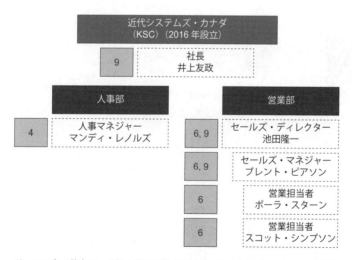

ボックス内の数字は，登場人物が登場するサンプル・カンバセーションの番号
を示す。

図 1d　KSC の組織（一部）

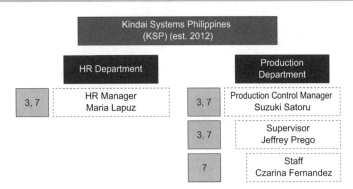

Numbers in the boxes indicate the number of the sample conversation in which the character appears.

Figure 1e   KSP Partial Organization

You will be able to download PDF of Figure 1a to Figure 1e from following URL.

http://www.bunshin-do.co.jp/catalogue/book5072.html

近代システムズ・フィリピン
（KSP）（2012 年設立）

人事部		生産部	
3, 7	人事マネジャー マリア・ラプス	3, 7	生産管理マネジャー 鈴木　悟
		3, 7	スーパーバイザー ジェフリー・プレゴ
		7	スタッフ ザリーナ・フェルナンデス

ボックス内の数字は，登場人物が登場するサンプル・カンバセーションの番号を示す。

図 1e　KSP の組織（一部）

図 1a ～図 1e の PDF は，下記の URL からダウンロードできます。

http://www.bunshin-do.co.jp/catalogue/book5072.html

Hiring a New HR Manager to Strengthen HR Functions

Background Information

When Kindai Systems USA (KSUS) had grown in size to more than 20 employees, **President Kikuchi Kenta** decided it was time to hire an HR manager to oversee the company's HR functions. The company already had two staff members handling payroll and administration, but he wanted to increase the scope of the HR function beyond administrative tasks.

Against this backdrop, KSUS considered hiring **Jim Barnes** as its first **HR Manager**. Although Barnes was still relatively young at the age of 29, President Kikuchi thought that the combination of his study abroad experience in Japan while in college and his work experience at a small HR consulting firm would make him a suitable hire. Before making the offer of employment, President Kikuchi consulted with **Tanaka Tsuyoshi, General Manager of Global HR** at the Tokyo headquarters of KSK. Both agreed that Barnes would fit well into KSUS.

Three months after Barnes joined KSUS, President Kikuchi requested that Tanaka speak with Barnes and encourage him to hasten the development of the HR function at KSUS.

人事担当責任者の採用により
人事機能強化を図る

背景情報

　米国近代システムズ（KSUS）が社員数で20名を越す規模にまで成長した時点で，**社長の菊池健太氏**は人事機能を統括する責任者を採用することにした。会社は，給与の支払いやその他の人事関連業務の担当者をすでに2名雇用しているが，人事の機能の範囲を，人事業務を超えてさらに拡大したいと考えた。

　こうした背景の下，KSUS は**ジム・バーンズ氏**を同社の初代**人事マネジャー**として採用することを検討していた。バーンズ氏は29歳と比較的若年であったが，菊池社長は，彼が大学時代に日本に留学した経験があり，また小規模な人事コンサルティング会社での勤務経験もあることから採用者として適任と考えた。バーンズ氏の採用を決定する前に，菊池社長は KSK 東京本社の**グローバル人事本部長**である**田中剛氏**に相談した。両者は，バーンズ氏が KSUS でうまく馴染んでいけるだろうという点で一致した。

　バーンズ氏が KSUS に入社して3カ月後，菊池社長は田中氏に対し，バーンズ氏と連絡をとり，彼に KSUS の人事機能の充実を急がせてほしいと要請した。

(Having accepted this request, Tanaka is now holding a video conference with Barnes. After greetings have been exchanged, Tanaka starts off by querying Barnes.)

• •

Tanaka: Now that you have been working at KSUS for 3 months, please tell me about how the HR Department at KSUS is beginning to provide new value under your direction.

Barnes: Well, I think **I started off on the right foot**. I mean, everything is going all right for now.

Tanaka: Okay. That's good to know. **Tell me more, please**. In what ways is your HR Department providing such good value to the company?

Barnes: Well, my staff is competent when it comes to the back-office functions such as the administration of payroll and benefits.

Tanaka: Okay. That is important, of course. Is there anything else?

Barnes: Well, I am still new here and therefore trying to get to know as many KSUS employees as possible. But, I don't think that employees feel comfortable yet coming to HR for support or advice. I want to create more open relations to support employees.

Tanaka: I hear what you are saying. I can agree that you and your team need to be proactive . . . to approach employees, to get to know what motivates them and to understand how they feel about their work, workload, and responsibilities.

（これを受けて，田中氏がバーンズ氏とビデオ会議を行っている。挨拶を交わした後，田中氏はバーンズ氏に質問を始めた。）

・・・

田中：KSUSで仕事を始めてから3カ月になりますが，あなたの指揮のもと，KSUSの人事部はどのような価値を生み出し始めたかを説明してもらえますか。

バーンズ：そうですね，**良いスタートが切れた**と思っています。つまり，現時点では全てうまくいっています。

田中：ほお，それは良かった。**もう少し聞かせてくれますか**。どのような面で，あなたが属する人事部が，会社に良い価値を生み出しているのですか？

バーンズ：はい，私の部下は人事のバック・オフィス機能，例えば，給与や福利厚生などの業務に関して，有能です。

田中：なるほど。そうした業務はもちろん重要です。その他にはどうですか？

バーンズ：ええ，入社して間もないので，なるべく多くのKSUS社員と知り合いになるべく努めています。しかし，彼らはサポートやアドバイスを求めて気軽に人事部にコンタクトを取ることはまだないようです。社員を支援できるように，よりオープンな関係を作れるようにしたいと思います。

田中：**言いたいことは，わかりました**。あなた方が積極的に行動すべきという点では一致していますね…社員に近寄り，彼らのモチベーションを知り，彼らの仕事内容，仕事の量，責任に関してどう感じているのかを理解する必要がありますね。

But at the same time, HR also needs to fully understand the business strategy pursued by the company and consider how to provide support from the HR perspective.

Barnes: Yes. I have been thinking about that. I know that, based upon the company's mid-term business plan, we are gearing up to expand the business significantly. For that purpose, the HR Department will need to not only hire new employees, but also provide training to existing employees.

Tanaka: Yes, President Kikuchi has explained the same to me. Well, **it seems like you are off to a good start** there and have ideas for how to improve the value of the HR function. **Let me suggest that you** come up with some more concrete initiatives for how you can enhance the HR function there. Then, I would be happy to speak with you again and provide you with any advice or assistance that you may need.

Barnes: Thank you very much. I will have a meeting with my staff and come up with some ideas. I will reach out to you again soon.

(A week later, Barnes is holding a meeting with **Amy Sanders** and **Lily Kim**, two staff members in charge of **payroll and administration** at KSUS HR Department.)

Barnes: Thank you for your time today. As I wrote in today's meeting invitation, I had a videoconference with Mr. Tanaka from the Japan HQ recently. Since then, I have been considering how we as an HR Department can enhance the value that we provide to the organization.

Sanders: What do you mean? I spend most of my time making payroll calculations and ensuring that the salary payments are made on time and

　しかし同時に，人事部は会社が追及している事業戦略を十分に理解し，それを人事の観点からいかに支援すべかを考えていく必要もありますよね。

バーンズ：はい，そのことについて考えていました。会社の中期事業計画に基づいて，当社でもビジネスを大幅に拡大する態勢を整えていることを知っています。その目的に沿って，人事部は新入社員を採用するだけではなく，現有従業員の研修も行わねばなりません。

田中：はい，私も菊池社長から同様のお話を聞いています。さて，そちらで**良いスタートを切ったようですね**。そして，人事機能の価値をどのように高めるかに関してもいろいろとアイデアを持っているようですね。そちらでの人事機能を高めるためのより具体的な施策をいくつか**考案してみてはどうでしょうか**。その上で，再度お話しし，必要に応じてアドバイスや援助を喜んでさせてもらいます。

バーンズ：有難うございます。部下とミーティングを持ち，何か良いアイデアが出ないか探ってみます。なるべく早くご連絡するように致します。

（一週間後，バーンズ氏は KSUS の人事部で**給与**ならびに**アドミニストレーション業務**を担当する**エミー・サンダース**と**リリー・キム**の２名の部下とミーティングを行っている。）

バーンズ：今日は時間を取ってくれて有難う。今日の会議の開催通知に書いたように，先日，日本本社の田中さんとビデオ会議を行いました。その後，我々人事部として会社に提供する価値をどのように高めることができるか考えてきました。

サンダース：それはどういうことですか？　私は従業員の給与を計算し，予定通りに正確な給与支給がなされるようほとんどの時間を費やしていますよ。こ

accurately. What kind of work could be more important than that?

Barnes: That's a good point. But what if there was a way to decrease the amount of time it takes to prepare those payments? Then, what could we do as the HR Department with the extra time to further contribute to the strengthening of the company's business?

Sanders: Hmm, that's something I haven't thought much about until now. Have you, Lily?

Kim: Not really . . . I thought we were doing everything that we were expected to do.

Barnes: And yes, that is so. I appreciate everyone's efforts. So **please don't misunderstand my intentions for this discussion**. What I want to do in this and follow-up meetings is to brainstorm with you how to streamline our administrative responsibilities and to then consider how to strengthen the function of our HR Department. For example, we could devote the freed-up time to talking with our employees in order to gain more insight into what really motivates them. Such insight would enable us to implement more effective HR initiatives that could make it easier to achieve the company's business goals.

In short, we, the HR Department, need to become the business partner which President Kikuchi expects us to be!

Commentary on sample conversation
In this sample conversation, we have encountered an exchange between

れ以上に大事な仕事があり得ますか？

バーンズ：それはよい指摘です。しかし，給与支払業務に関わる時間を減らす方法があるとしたらどうでしょう？　その場合に，人事部として，生み出された時間を用いて，会社の事業を強化するためにどのような貢献ができますかね？

サンダース：ウーン，そのことについてはこれまで余り考えて来ませんでした。リリー，あなたは考えてた？

キム：いや，別に…。私たちに期待されていることは全て実行していると思っていましたよ。

バーンズ：はい，それはその通りです。私は皆さんの努力に感謝していますよ。で，**このミーティングでの私の意図を誤解しないでください。**このミーティングとこの後に続くミーティングにおいて，どのようにして我々の人事のアドミニストレーション業務を簡略化するのか，そしてその結果として，どのようにして人事部の機能を強化するのかという点に関して，皆さんとブレインストーミングしたいのです。例えば，業務の簡略化によって得られた時間を使って，従業員とよく話し合い，彼らのモチベーションを上げるのは何かについての洞察を得ることが可能となります。このような洞察によって，会社の事業目標の達成に資するより効果的な人事施策を実施することが可能になります。

　つまり，我々人事部は，菊池社長が期待しているビジネス・パートナーとなる必要があります！

サンプル・カンバセーションに関するコメント

　本サンプル・カンバセーションでは，日本に本社がある自動車部品メー

the global HR general manager at the Japan-side headquarters and the local HR manager at its U.S. subsidiary. As is often seen in global companies, managers at overseas subsidiaries usually have more than one boss to report to—in the case of Jim Barnes, one is Kikuchi Kenta of KSUS and the other, Tanaka Tsuyoshi of KSK. This kind of management structure is called the *matrix organization structure*, which is adopted by many globalized companies to varying degrees, because of their needs to cater to both local and global business environments.

Key Phrases and Expressions

Tell me about . . . ; Tell me more, please . . .

In his conversation with Barnes, Tanaka used these expressions in order to ask him to provide additional information. Such expressions are called *imperatives* and are used to give an order, warning or advice. Note however, that in a business environment, it is advisable for an imperative to be preceded or followed by *please*.

I hear what you are saying . . .

This expression is useful for demonstrating that you are listening to what another person is saying, but this expression does not indicate agreement unless agreement is explicitly stated. To indicate agreement, say the following: "I hear what you are saying and I completely agree with you."

Off to a good start/started off on the right foot

Both of these idioms signify that some endeavor which has recently begun is currently going well. Note that the opposite meaning can be expressed with the idioms "off to a bad start", "off to a slow start" or "didn't get started off on the right foot."

カーのグローバル人事本部長とその米国子会社の現地採用の人事マネ
ジャーの間のコミュニケーションを主に考察した。グローバル企業にしば
しば見られるが，管理職は通常，二人以上の上司を持つ。本事例ではバー
ンズ氏にとっての上司は，KSUS の菊池健太社長と KSK 本社の田中剛本
部長である。このような管理形態は「マトリックス組織」と呼ばれ，ロー
カルとグローバルなビジネス環境への適応を必要とする多くのグローバル
企業により程度の差こそあれ採用されている。

重要表現

Tell me about . . . ; Tell me more, please . . .

　田中さんはバーンズ氏との会話で追加の情報を得るためにこれらの表現を用
いている。「imperatives」（命令形と呼ばれる表現方法）は通常，指示，警告，
あるいは助言を与えるために用いられる。但し，ビジネスの状況においては，
文頭または文末に「please」を付けることが望ましい。

I hear what you are saying . . .

　この表現は，相手の発言を聞いていることを示すのに役立つが，この表現
は，同意が明示的に述べられていない限り，同意を示すものではない。同意を
示すためには，以下のように述べる必要がある。「あなたの言いたいことは分
かります。また，私はあなたとまったく同意見です」。

Off to a good start/ started off on the right foot

　これらのイディオムは両方とも，最近始まったいくつかの努力が現在順調
に進んでいることを示している。反対の意味は，「悪いスタートを切る」，「ス
ロー・スタートを切る」，「良いスタートを切れなかった」というイディオムで
表現できることに注意してほしい。

Let me suggest that you (verb) . . .

The phrase is used to politely request someone to do something that the speaker believes is necessary to carry out or accomplish. When using this phrase, the speaker is seemingly advising the listener to take the action, rather than strongly requesting or compelling such action.

Please don't misunderstand my intentions . . .

In the sample conversation, Barnes said to his staff, "I appreciate everyone's efforts. So please don't misunderstand my intentions for this discussion." The phrase "please don't misunderstand" is quite useful for de-escalating rising tensions as you deal with a difficult issue with others.

Let me suggest that you (verb) . . .

このフレーズは，話し手が実行または達成することが必要であると考えることを相手に丁寧に要求するために使用される。このフレーズを使用する場合，話し手は，そのようなアクションを強く要求または強制するのではなく，聞き手にアクションを実行するようアドバイスしているようにみえる。

Please don't misunderstand my intentions . . .

本サンプル・カンバセーションでは，バーンズ氏は部下に対して，「このミーティングでの私の意図を誤解しないでください」と述べている。この「私の意図を誤解しないでください」という表現は，難しい問題に対応する際に，相手側との間に発生する緊張を緩和するために極めて有用な表現である。

Talking With a Headhunter

Background Information

KSUS has now grown in size from the time when Kindai Systems Kabushiki Kaisha established Kindai Systems USA (KSUS). In the early years, **President Kikuchi Kenta** needed to spearhead hiring initiatives on his own, although he was still new in the USA and had little knowledge about the local labor market. With his first important HR task being to hire local talent in order to start the business, he fortunately received a reference to a headhunting company that had a good reputation among local Japanese companies.

(Let's revisit the time when President Kikuchi was a new arrival in the USA. On one fine day, he picked up the phone and called **Loraine Thoms**, a **recruiter** at a headhunting company.)

• •

Kikuchi: Hello. My name is Kikuchi. I am calling from a company called KSUS, a newly established subsidiary of a Japanese company. May I speak with Ms. Thoms?

SAMPLE CONVERSATION 2

ヘッドハンターと打ち合わせをする

本会話の背景

　近代システムズ株式会社が Kindai Systems USA（KSUS）を設立したとき
からみると現在，規模が拡大している。初期の頃，**菊池健太社長**は，米国に来
てまだ間がなく，地元の労働市場についてほとんど知識がなかったものの，採
用の施策を独力で主導する必要があった。最初の重要な人事関連業務は，会社
を立ち上げるために現地の優秀な人材を採用することであったが，幸いにし
て，現地の日系企業から高い評価を得ていたヘッドハンティング会社を紹介さ
れた。

（菊池社長がアメリカに来て間もない頃に戻ってみよう。ある日，彼は電話を
取り，ヘッドハンティング会社の**リクルーター**，**ロレイン・トムズ氏**に電話を
かける。）

・・・

菊池：もしもし，菊池と申します。日本企業の新参者の子会社である KSUS
からご連絡しております。トムズさんをお願い致します。

Thoms: Yes, that's me. How may I help you?

Kikuchi: I am calling at the recommendation of Mr. Saito from the Misono Bank. He recommended your company as a reliable headhunting firm that could possibly help us in our search for top talent.

Thoms: Ah yes, Mr. Saito. He is very kind for recommending our company to you.

Kikuchi: Shall I explain the position which we hope you can help us fill?

Thoms: Sure. May I ask you first if you have a job description for the position?

Kikuchi: Umm, no. Is it necessary?

Thoms: Not necessary. But it would be helpful. Please explain to me verbally then.

Kikuchi: Okay, let me explain the position we want to fill and the type of person we are seeking.

Thoms: Fine. Just hold on for one moment so that I can grab my pen . . . I am ready now.

Kikuchi: Thank you. As we have recently set up operations here in the USA, we will be hiring people for management and staff positions in the next few months. Initially we are interested in meeting with candidates for the Operations Manager position.

トムズ：はい，私です。何の御用件でしょうか。

菊池：三園銀行の斉藤さんの**ご紹介でお電話しております**。弊社はトップ・クラスの人材を求めていますが，貴社をこの場合の信頼に足るヘッドハンティング企業としてご紹介頂きました。

トムズ：はい，斉藤さんですね。弊社を推薦して頂き有難く存じます。

菊池：貴社にサポート頂き，埋めたいと思っているポジションについて説明してもいいでしょうか？

トムズ：もちろんです。先ずお聞きしたいのですが，そのポジションに関する職務記述書はありますでしょうか？

菊池：いいえ。必要でしょうか？

トムズ：なくても良いのですが，あれば助かります。では，口頭でご説明頂けますか？

菊池：分かりました。弊社が埋めたいポジションと求めている人材を説明します。

トムズ：分かりました。ペンを取って来ますので，少々お待ちください…ではお願い致します。

菊池：有難う御座います。弊社は米国で最近設立したばかりなので，今後数カ月で管理職と担当職の社員を採用しなければなりません。先ずは，オペレーション・マネジャーの候補者何名かと面談できればと思っています。

Thoms: Okay. Please let me know more about your needs.

Kikuchi: Well, I think we need to hire a male between the age of 35 and 45.

Thoms: Hmm. Mr. Kikuchi, of course I want to help you by finding the most qualified candidates for that position. However, if we limited our search to males in that age range it would be inappropriate . . . and even present potential grounds for discrimination. May I suggest that you firstly explain the necessary qualifications for the position?

Kikuchi: Oh. I understand. Well, candidates for this position should have experience in business development and sales with manufacturers in the automotive industry.

Thoms: Okay. **Is there anything else I should know?**

Kikuchi: Well, I think candidates should be able to speak Japanese.

Thoms: Well, if you required Japanese language skills outright, the candidate pool, I am afraid, would be rather small. What if we were to introduce candidates who have had some type of experience in Japan or have knowledge of Japanese business practices, but are not necessarily fluent in Japanese? Would that be acceptable?

Kikuchi: Okay. That would be reasonable. At the very minimum, we are looking for candidates who can work well with expatriates from Japan and communicate directly with management at our headquarters.

Thoms: Sure. That is to be expected. Is there anything else you want me

トムズ：了解いたしました。ご希望条件をより詳しく説明していただけますか？

菊池：はい，35〜45才くらいの男性を採用したいと思っています。

トムズ：ウーン…菊池様，もちろん，そのポジションに最も適した候補者をお探ししたいと思っていますが，候補者を特定の年齢枠の男性に制限することは適切ではありません。差別の根拠にさえなる可能性がありますよ。先ず，このポジションに必要な要件をご説明頂けますか？

菊池：なるほど，分かりました。そうですね。この役職の候補者は自動車業界のメーカーでの事業開発と販売の経験が必要です。

トムズ：承知致しました。**他に理解しておくべきことはありますか？**

菊池：そうですね，候補者には日本語を話す能力が必要です。

トムズ：さて，日本語能力を絶対条件とすると，候補者が少なくなる可能性があります。日本語能力は高くなくても日本に関する何らかの経験，あるいは日本のビジネス慣行についての知識を持つ人を候補者としてご紹介するということで如何でしょうか？　それでよろしいでしょうか？

菊池：はい。それが妥当と思います。最低限，日本からの駐在員と上手く仕事ができ，日本本社の管理職とも直接，意思疎通を図れる候補者を探しています。

トムズ：かしこまりました。ごもっともです。他に留意すべき点はあります

to know?

Kikuchi: Umm, lastly, of course, we want to hire someone who will work for a long time at our company and already has **a proven track record**, both personally and professionally. So, we would like to understand each candidate's experience in making important decisions and producing results.

Thoms: Okay. I understand your priorities. Shall I send you a contract draft for your review so that we can get to work on seeking candidates for this important position as quickly as possible?

Kikuchi: Yes, that would be fine.

Thoms: Okay. Please tell me your email address . . .

Commentary on sample conversation

In this sample conversation, we encounter a newly expatriated President Kikuchi having to communicate with a recruiter for the first time. Having just arrived in the USA without much understanding about how to recruit talent, he initially started to describe his ideal candidate as a *male between the ages of 35 and 45 with Japanese language skills*. Ms. Thoms redirected the conversation in order to avoid the appearance of discrimination and to ensure that she could seek out a broad pool of candidates. In the end, the communication that occurred between President Kikuchi and Ms. Thoms was sufficient for starting a working relationship together.

Note as well that it is generally standard practice to develop a job description that can be provided to recruiters and/or posted on recruitment websites. Such job descriptions should be reviewed to ensure that there is

か？

菊池：そうですね，最後に，当然ですが，弊社に長く勤めてくれる方で，個人的にも仕事の上でも**優れた経歴**を有する候補者を採用できればと思います。したがって，各候補者がどのような重要な意思決定をこれまで行い，どのような結果を生み出して来たのかを知りたいと思います。

トムズ：承知致しました。優先される要件が理解できました。私どもができる限り早く候補者探しに取り掛かれるよう契約書のドラフトをお送りしますので，ご確認頂ければ幸いです。

菊池：結構です。よろしくお願い致します。

トムズ：では，メール・アドレスをお教え頂けますか…

サンプル・カンバセーションに関するコメント

　この会話のサンプルで我々は，新しく着任した菊池社長が，リクルーターと初めて会話せざるを得ない場面に直面する。タレントの募集方法についての理解不足のままで米国に到着したばかりの彼は，当初，理想的な候補者を「日本語能力のある 35〜45 歳の男性」と表現した。トムズ氏は，幅広い候補者を探し出すために，また差別とならないようにしながら，会話の流れを誘導した。最終的に，菊池社長とトムズ氏との間で行われたコミュニケーションは，協力関係を開始するのに十分であった。

　さらに，採用担当者に提供したり，採用 Web サイトに掲載したりすることができる職務記述書を作成することは，一般的に標準的な慣行であることを理解する必要がある。このような職務記述書には，差別的またはそ

no content which may be construed as being discriminatory or otherwise illegal in any way.

Key Phrases and Expressions

I am calling at the recommendation of . . .

This is a common alternative to the expression "Mr. X recommended that I call you . . ." Similarly, "Mr. X suggested that I write to you about . . ." can otherwise be expressed as "I am writing to you at the suggestion of Mr. X about . . ."

Is there anything else I should know?

This is a good expression for checking if there is any additional information that should be discussed. An alternative expression is, "Is there anything else you would like to tell me?" To such a query, the response may be, "I think we have covered what needs to be discussed for now."

track record

The expression refers to the facts known about the past successes and failures of a person, company or product. When the performance in question shows positive results, adjectives as follows are used: *good, proven, successful* or *impressive track record*. But in opposite situations, the track record may be described as being *poor*.

の他の方法で違法であると解釈される可能性のある内容が含まれていない
ように確認する必要がある。

重要表現

I am calling at the recommendation of . . .

　この表現は「Mr. X recommended that I call you . . .」をより簡潔に表現
したものである。同様に，「Mr. X suggested that I write to you about . . .」
は，「I am writing to you at the suggestion of Mr. X about . . .」と表現する
ことが可能である。

Is there anything else I should know?

　この表現は相手との会話において，取り上げるべき情報が他にあるかどう
かを確かめる際に有用な表現である。代替表現として「Is there anything else
you would like to tell me?」などもあるが，この質問に対する返事は例えば，
「I think we have covered what needs to be discussed for now.」（現時点で議
論すべきポイントはカバーしたと思います）のようになろう。

track record

　この表現は個人，企業，製品などに関する過去の成功や失敗といった事実を
表現している。当該の実績が良好な場合には，track record の前に「good」
（良い），「proven」（証明された），「successful」（好結果の），「impressive」
（優れた）のような形容詞が使われる。反対の場合には「poor」（弱い）といっ
た形容詞が使われる。

How to Effectively Communicate Feedback

Background Information

Suzuki Satoru is a newly assigned expatriate at Kindai Systems Philippines (KSP), where he is the **Production Control Manager**. Prior to this assignment, he did not have any direct subordinates, but now he is responsible for managing a team of local workers and supervisors.

While reviewing KSP's latest production report one day, Suzuki noted that, in recent weeks, an increasing number of defective products had been coming off a line supervised by **Jeffrey Prego, Production Supervisor**. Although the percentage of defective products was still within the limit set by his department, Suzuki was alarmed by the rising numbers and decided to talk to Prego straight away.

Suzuki found Prego on the factory floor engaged in discussion with his workers. But Suzuki decided to interrupt them, because he felt that his concern was urgent and needed to be addressed immediately.

フィードバックの効果的な伝達方法

本会話の背景

　鈴木悟氏は近代システムズ・フィリピン（KSP）に最近赴任した。そこでの役職は**生産管理マネジャー**である。フィリピンに赴任する前は，部下を持ったことはなかったが，今は現地採用の従業員やスーパーバイザーを管理する責任を負っている。

　鈴木氏はある日，KSP 社の直近の生産報告書に目を通していて，**スーパーバイザーであるジェフリー・プレゴ氏**が管理する生産ラインで過去数週間，不良品の数が増えていることに気付いた。不良品率は生産管理部が設定した範囲内には収まってはいるが，鈴木氏はその増加傾向に懸念を覚え，直ちにプレゴ氏と話すことにした。

　鈴木氏は工場でプレゴ氏を見つけた。彼は部下の作業員と話をしていたが，鈴木氏は自らの懸念事項が緊急を要し，直ちに対応が必要と考え，プレゴ氏と作業員の話を遮ることにした。

Suzuki: Jeffrey, the latest production report indicates that there are too many defective products coming off of your line. **I expect that you** improve your line's work process. **You had better research the problem and report to me.**

(In response, Prego first looked confused. Then he responded in a way that Suzuki did not expect.)

Prego: Sorry, I am busy. I don't have time right now.

Suzuki: But this is urgent . . .

Suzuki and Prego continued talking for another five minutes until Suzuki started to feel a wave of frustration overcome him. Then he walked away from Prego wondering why the local employees were so unconcerned about product quality.

(Early the next morning, **Maria Lapuz, HR Manager,** visited Suzuki in his office.)

Lapuz: Suzuki san, could you spare a moment to talk about an issue of importance? It has to do with Jeffrey Prego.

Suzuki and Lapuz moved into a conference room to talk. She began explaining the situation.

Lapuz: I am afraid that Jeffrey came to me late yesterday afternoon with a concern about a conversation he had with you earlier. You spoke with him regarding defective products coming off his line in rising numbers lately, correct?

鈴木：ジェフリー，直近の生産報告書によると，あなたの生産ラインの不良品の数が急増しているね。ラインの作業プロセスを改善すること**を期待しているよ。問題点を調査して私に報告するように頼むよ。**

（これに対して，プレゴ氏は当初，困惑したような顔をし，その後，予期もしない返事をした。）

プレゴ：すみません。取り込み中なので，今時間がありません。

鈴木：でもね，これは急を要するんだよ…。

　鈴木氏とプレゴ氏はさらに5分間話し続けたが，鈴木氏のいら立ちが高じてきたのでそこで話を止めた。そして，彼は現地従業員がなぜ製品の品質にそれほど無頓着でいられるかと疑問に思いながら，プレゴ氏から離れた。

（翌朝一番で，**人事マネジャーのマリア・ラプス氏**が鈴木氏に会いにオフィスへやって来た。）

ラプス：鈴木さん，大事なお話しがあるのですが，お時間を少々頂けますか。ジェフリー・プレゴの件です。

（鈴木氏とラプス氏は話をするために，会議室へ移動した。彼女が説明を始めた。）

ラプス：鈴木さん，ジェフリーが昨日の午後遅く，私のところにやって来ました。昨日のあなたとの会話に不満を訴えていました。彼が管理する生産ラインで不良品が増えていることについて話をされましたね？

Suzuki: Yes, I mentioned that to him because we must improve the situation immediately.

Lapuz: I can understand your intention. However, he felt that you were verbally reprimanding him in front of others and that you demanded him to do additional work for which he was not ready.

Suzuki: Well, if the issue is not resolved quickly, we will lose the trust of our customers. I wanted him to understand the urgency of the situation and take immediate action.

Lapuz: Sure, I think that it was reasonable for you to speak to him about this. But was there anything you may have said or done to upset him so much that he came to speak with me?

Suzuki: I am not sure, but he seemed irritated about something when I talked to him yesterday. Should I speak with him again?

Lapuz: That may be a good idea. To avoid having this situation worsen, let's consider how you could effectively speak with him.

Suzuki: Well, I will tell him that I did not intend to make him upset; instead, I wanted him to look into the possible problems in his production line and try to find a solution.

Lapuz: Okay. Then why don't you both first discuss the data on the increasing number of defective products coming off his production line lately. Remind him of our quality standards and ask him what can be done to fix the problem. If he doesn't have an immediate answer, give him some time to propose a possible solution.

鈴木：ええ，そのことを彼に言いました。状況をすぐに改善する必要があるためです。

ラプス：あなたの意図は理解できます。しかし，彼は皆の前であなたから叱正され，また，あなたから予定していない追加の仕事をするよう要求されたと受け取ったのです。

鈴木：そうかもしれませんが，もしこの問題を直ちに解決しないと，客先の信用を失うことになります。彼に状況の緊急性を理解してもらい，大至急対策を講じて欲しかったのですよ。

ラプス：もちろん，本件に関してあなたが彼に話をするのは当然です。しかし，あなたの発言や行動で彼が大変気分を害して，その結果，私に話に来ることになったことに何か思い当たりませんか？

鈴木：良く分かりませんが，昨日話した時に彼は苛立っているようでしたね。私の方から再度コンタクトしましょうか？

ラプス：その方が良いかも知れません。但し，事態を悪化させないよう，彼とよりきちんと話す方法を考えてみましょう。

鈴木：分かりました。そうですね，次のように言いましょう。私には彼の気分を害する意図があったわけではなく，彼の生産ラインにどのような問題点があり得るのかを調べ，解決策を見出して欲しかったのだ，と。

ラプス：そうですね。では，彼の生産ラインで最近，不良品が増えているというデータに関して先ずお二人で話し合ってはいかがですか？　彼に当社の品質基準を改めて示して，この問題をどうすれば解決できるか問いかけてみてはいかがですか？　もし即答が得られない場合は，可能な解決策を提案するための時間を与えてはいかがでしょうか？

Suzuki: Hmm, that approach sounds like what we learned about *coaching* in a recent workshop you organized.

Lapuz: Well, yes. *Critical feedback* delivered in a coaching style is non-threatening and could even help you improve working relation with your staff.

Suzuki: Okay. I see.

Lapuz: One more thing. Jeffley said that you approached him suddenly and started speaking with him in front of his subordinates in such a way that he felt uncomfortable. While it may not be necessary to sit down and have a lengthy discussion at first, let him know that you have something of urgency to discuss and do confirm his availability to speak. Even though he is your subordinate, let's try to create a corporate culture that respects the time of everyone. Does that sound reasonable?

Suzuki: Yes, I understand. Thank you.

Commentary on sample conversation

In this sample conversation, we encountered the difficulties experienced by the Japanese Production Control Manager as he tried to communicate with his subordinate who supervises a production line that is turning out rising rates of defective products.

The difficulties arose when the Japanese manager abruptly interrupted the conversation the supervisor was having with his workers on the factory floor, and then gave him what sounded like a reprimand in front of everybody else. Although the Japanese manager acted out of good

鈴木：ウーン，そのアプローチは人事部の企画による最近の研修で学んだ「コーチング」と似ていますね。

ラプス：その通りです。コーチングで使われる「（改善を要求するための）クリティカル・フィードバック」は，相手に脅威を与えるものではなく，部下との仕事上の関係を改善することさえ可能となるのです。

鈴木：分かりました。

ラプス：もうひとつあります。ジェフリーは，貴方が突然やってきて，彼が部下の前で当惑させられるような話し方で話し出したと言っています。当面はじっと座って長い議論をする必要はないかもしれませんが，急いで話し合う必要があることを伝え，その場ですぐに話せるかどうかを確認してください。確かに彼はあなたの部下ですが，彼の都合を尊重するという企業文化を作っていきましょうよ。いいでしょうか？

鈴木：了解です。有難う。

サンプル・カンバセーションに関するコメント

　本サンプル・カンバセーションでは，日本人の生産管理マネジャーが，不良品比率が上昇し続ける生産ラインを管理する現地のスーパーバイザーとのコミュニケーションに苦戦する様子を考察した。

　事の発端は，スーパーバイザーが製造現場で部下の作業員たちと会話をしているところを日本人マネジャーが突然遮り，皆の前でスーパーバイザーに対し，叱責と思える指示を出したことにある。日本人部長の言動には悪意はなく，生産ラインの改善を目指していたものであるが，同氏の

intentions in order to improve the performance of the production line, the way he approached and spoke to the supervisor created unintended results.

Thanks to the advice given him by the local HR manager, the Japanese manager is now likely to develop more effective communication with the supervisor and succeed in lowering the rising rates of defective products.

Key Phrases and Expressions

× **I expect that you . . .**

○ **There is a need to . . .**

Suzuki approached Prego and initially stated, "I expect that you improve your line's work process . . ." While Suzuki may not have intended to seem impolite, in English the expression, "I expect that you . . ." is highly authoritative and direct. A better alternative is to say, "There is a need to . . ." Suzuki may say, "There is a need to improve your line's work processes." Such an expression is objective and focuses the conversation on the desired outcome rather than a *top-down* directive from the boss to the subordinate.

× **Research the problem and report back to me.**

○ **(Please) let me know what you can do in order to improve the situation.**

When Suzuki approached Prego, he overbearingly directed Prego to "research the problem and report back to me." Such a directive can lead to two impasses: (1) the subordinate only focuses on the past problem rather than the future solution and (2) the subordinate is made to feel as if he is working to satisfy the manager's need for information rather than working to determine actual improvement. Such a directive may delay or prevent the employee from recognizing how to improve the situation.

スーパーバイザーへのアプローチの仕方と話し方が意図せぬ結果をもたらすこととなった。

　しかし，現地の人事マネジャーの助言により，日本人の生産管理マネジャーはスーパーバイザーとよりしっかりとした意思疎通を図り，上昇する不良品比率の低減に成功する可能性が高くなっている。

重要表現

× **I expect that you . . .**

○ **There is a need to . . .**

　鈴木氏はプレゴにアプローチし，最初に「ラインの作業プロセスを改善することを期待している…」と言った。鈴木氏は失礼に振舞おうは思わなかったかもしれないが，「I expect that you . . .」この英語表現はきわめて権威主義的で，単刀直入すぎるのである。より良い代替案は，「There is a need to . . .」と言うことである。むしろ，鈴木氏は「There is a need to improve your line's work processes.」（ラインの作業プロセスを改善する必要がある）と言うべきであった。そのような表現は，上司から部下への「トップ‐ダウン」的指示命令ではなく，客観的で，望ましい結果に会話の焦点を向けさせる。

× **Research the problem and report back to me.**

○ **(Please) let me know what you can do in order to improve the situation.**

　鈴木氏は，プレゴ氏に近づき，頭ごなしに，プレゴ氏「問題を調査し，私に報告するように」と指示した。このような指示は，2つの行き詰まりにつながる可能性がある。⑴部下は，将来の解決策ではなく，過去の問題にのみ焦点を合わせる。⑵部下は，実際の改善策を見つけるためではなく，マネジャーの情報に対するニーズを満たすために働いているかのように感じさせられる。こういう場合には，従業員が状況を改善する方法を認識するのを遅らせたり，妨げたりすることになるであろう。

Alternatively, Suzuki could have asked, "Please let me know what can be done in order to improve the situation." With such an expression, Suzuki would communicate in a positive, future-oriented manner and convey a sense of trust to Prego. In turn, Prego may not have reacted so negatively to Suzuki's request.

....

Provided the above two key phrase explanations, critical feedback from Suzuki to Prego may be more effective as follows:

Suzuki: Jeffrey, can I have a moment to talk with you about an issue of urgency?

Prego: Um, sure.

Suzuki: Jeffrey, the latest production report indicates that there are too many defective products coming off of your line. There is a need to improve your line's work processes. Please let me know what can be done in order to improve the situation.

Prego: Okay. Um, let me look into it and get back to you shortly.

Suzuki: Thank you. In order to maintain the trust from our customers, we really need to resolve these issues. Let's talk again tomorrow about your ideas, okay?

Prego: Okay. I understand.

　他方で，鈴木氏は「状況を改善するために何ができるか教えてください」と尋ねることができたかもしれない。そのような表現で，鈴木氏は建設的かつ前向きな方法でコミュニケーションし，プレゴ氏に信頼感を伝えることができる。一方，プレゴ氏も鈴木氏の要求にそれほど否定的に反応しなかったかもしれない。

．．．

　もし上記の2つの重要なフレーズについての説明があったならば，鈴木氏からプレゴ氏への建設的なフィードバックは，次のように効果的なものとなっていたかもしれない。

鈴木：ジェフリー，急いで話したいことがあるんだけど，今，大丈夫？

プレゴ：ええ，大丈夫ですが。

鈴木：ジェフリー，最新の生産レポートは，君の担当するラインからの欠陥製品がきわめて多いことを示しているんだよ。ラインの作業プロセスを改善する必要があるね。状況を改善するために何ができるか教えてもらえる？

プレゴ：分かりました。それでは，調べてから，すぐにご連絡します。

鈴木：有難う。お客さんからの信頼維持には，これらの問題を絶対に解決する必要があるんでね。明日，君のアイデアについてもう一度話そうよ。

プレゴ：分かりました。了解です。

Revising the Compensation System

Background Information

Tanaka Tsuyoshi, General Manager of Global HR, at the global HQ of Kindai Systems Kabushiki Kaisha (KSK), in Tokyo, is having a video conference with **Mandy Reynolds, HR Manager** of Kindai Systems Canada (KSC), about Reynolds' concerns regarding the subsidiary's current compensation system.

• •

Reynolds: Thank you for your time. We recently have had a few key employees leave the company to go to work for some of our competitors. **We suspect that** this was due to their dissatisfaction with their salary.

Tanaka: What makes you say so?

Reynolds: In the exit interviews, the resigning employees all commented that their current salary was below the market. One engineer even said that he was offered a starting salary that is more than ten-thousand dollars higher annually than what he was making here at our company.

SAMPLE CONVERSATION 4

報酬体系の改定

本会話の背景

　東京にグローバル本社のある近代システムズ株式会社（KSK）の**グローバル人事本部長**である**田中剛氏**が，近代システム・カナダ（KSC）の**人事マネジャー**である**マンディ・レイノルズ氏**と打ち合わせしている。二人がビデオ会議で議論しているのは，レイノルズ氏が KSC の報酬体系に関して持っている懸念についてである。

● ●

レイノルズ：時間をお取りいただき有難うございます。こちらでは最近，数名の重要な社員が当社を辞めてライバル企業に転籍しました。給与に不満があったのでは**と推測しています**。

田中：なぜ，そう思うんですか？

レイノルズ：退社時の面接で，彼らは口をそろえて給与が市場水準を下回っていると言っていました。あるエンジニアは，彼がこの我が社で得ている給与よりも年間 10,000 ドル以上高い初任給を提示されたとさえ言いました。

Tanaka: Hmm. Given the current business conditions . . .

Reynolds: I understand that we need to maintain tight control on labor costs, but if salaries do not remain competitive in the market, then even more employees may start to seek work elsewhere.

Tanaka: Well, how can you be sure that salary is the real concern for employees?

Reynolds: Other than obtaining comments from exit interviews, we conduct an employee satisfaction survey annually. While employees who have worked with the company for three years or less do not seem to have any issues with their salary, dissatisfaction spikes upward from employees working four years or longer.

Tanaka: That's a noteworthy trend. **How do you account for these results?**

Reynolds: We have hired experienced engineers each year for the past few years. In order to attract top engineers, we had to make competitive salary offers in an effort to win the war for talent.

Tanaka: Okay. And that sounds reasonable. So, what's the problem?

Reynolds: Well, the starting salary for most of these engineers is at the top of the salary range for their assigned grade . . .

Tanaka: Okay.

Reynolds: Well, that's where we have a problem. Initially the salary offer has been competitive enough to attract top-notch engineers. But, because the

田中：ウーン。今のビジネス環境では…。

レイノルズ：労働費用を厳しくコントロールする必要があることは分かるのですが，しかし給与が市場での競争力を維持できない場合には，さらに社員が転職活動を始める可能性があります。

田中：**と言っても，**給与そのものを社員が本当に気にしている**と断言できるの？**

レイノルズ：退社時面接でコメントを得るだけでなく，毎年，社員の満足度調査も実施しています。入社後3年以内の社員は給与レベルに関する問題を意識していないようですが，入社4年目以降の社員の不満は急上昇しています。

田中：それは顕著なトレンドだね。**このような結果を君はどのように解釈していますか？**

レイノルズ：過去数年間，毎年，経験豊富な技術者を採用してきました。そして，トップ・クラスのエンジニアを引き付けるために，私たちはタレント・ウォーに勝つために，競争力のある給与を提供しなければなりませんでした。

田中：そうですね。適切な考え方と思います。では，何が問題なのですか？

レイノルズ：ええ，これらのエンジニアのほとんどの人の初任給は，割り当てられたグレードの給与幅の最上位に置かれました…。

田中：なるほど。

レイノルズ：さて，そこにこそ，問題があります。当初，給与の提示額は一流のエンジニアを引き付けるのに十分な競争力がありました。しかし，その初任

starting salary has been set at a high level within the salary range associated with the employee's job grade, the engineer is essentially not eligible to receive a salary raise until a promotion to the next grade is granted. Since it is difficult to grant a promotion to all engineers every year, some inevitably fall behind others in salary raises.

Tanaka: Over time, most employees will earn a promotion and get a salary raise, right?

Reynolds: Yes. But since the external market demand for engineers is high, especially for those specializing in artificial intelligence needed for the autonomous emergency braking technology which we are trying to commercialize, the lack of a raise in salary for a period as long as three years leads employees to become disgruntled.

Tanaka: Have you conducted any salary surveys recently to get data on other companies?

Reynolds: Well, we try to gather information about competitors in the local market, but have not requested any consulting firms to provide benchmark data that we'd have to pay for.

Tanaka: Hmm, engineers in Japan rarely voice out such concerns and, umm, what was that expression . . . Ah, *jump ship*—they rarely *jump ship* so easily. How many engineers have you lost in the past year?

Reynolds: . . . about ten. But in a department of thirty-five engineers, that's sizable. As we have seen over the years, it's not that employees here lack loyalty to the company. They appreciate the working environment and understand

給与は，従業員の職務等級に連動する給与幅の中で高いレベルに設定されているため，エンジニアは基本的に次の等級への昇進が認められるまで昇給を受ける資格がないんですよ。毎年全てのエンジニアに昇進を認めることは難しいため，何名かは昇給で他の人に遅れをとることは避けられません。

田中：時間が経てば，ほとんどの従業員が昇進することになり，昇給も伴うよね？

レイノルズ：はい。しかし，エンジニアに対する外部市場の需要が多いため，特に私たちが商業化しようとしている自律ブレーキ技術に必要な人工知能に特化した人たちにとって，3年の期間にわたって昇給がないと，彼らの不満を招きます。

田中：最近，他社のデータを得るための給与調査を実施しましたか？

レイノルズ：ええと，私たちは地元市場の競合他社に関する情報を収集しようとしていますが，コンサルティング会社に有料のベンチマーク・データを得るための依頼はしてはいません。

田中：うーん，日本のエンジニアはそんなことを口に出すことはめったにないね。また，えーと，あの表現は何だったかな…あ，「ジャンプ・シップ」―彼らはそんなに簡単に「転職する」ことはめったにありません。過去1年間に何人のエンジニアが辞めましたか？

レイノルズ：…10人くらいです。しかし，35人のエンジニアからなる部門としては，かなりの規模です。長年にわたって見てきましたように，ここの従業員は会社に対する忠誠心に欠けているわけではありません。彼らは職場環境を

that the company cares for them, especially with the generous benefits package. However, when they don't see a salary raise for as long as three years, they start to wonder whether the company truly cares for employees as much as we say.

Tanaka: I understand your concerns now. What do you want to do in order to deal with this problem?

Reynolds: It may be necessary to establish broader salary ranges within each grade in order to provide managers with the discretion to grant salary raises, even if employees are not promoted to the next grade.

Tanaka: Yes, that seems reasonable for positions which are experiencing high turnover. But even still, I hope that you can find ways to control fixed labor costs while motivating employees for the long term.

Reynolds: And **I understand your perspective.** Another idea I have is to institute a new bonus plan. I recently spoke with the HR representative at another company. She explained to me about how they have designed their bonus structure in order to provide variable pay to employees who produce strong results. Maybe their structure would be worthy of our review.

Tanaka: Good. Thank you for explaining the current situation. I recognize that compensation planning cannot be centrally controlled by the HQ in Japan. However, the HQ perspective is that we must institute the right mechanisms for effectively managing labor costs on a global basis. So please inform me soon about what you and President Inoue would like to do in this regard.

Reynolds: I will surely do so. Thank you for your time today.

高く評価し，特に寛大な福利厚生で会社が彼らを大切にしていることを理解しています。しかし，3年間も昇給が見られない場合，彼らは会社が言うほど従業員を本当に気遣っているのかと疑問に思うようになります。

田中：**私はあなたの懸念をよく理解していますよ。**この問題に対処するために何をしたらいいと思う？

レイノルズ：従業員が次のグレードに昇進しない場合でも，マネジャーに昇給を認める裁量を与えるために，各グレード内でより広い給与の幅を設けることが必要かもしれませんね。

田中：そうだね。それは高い離職率を経験しているポジションにとっては理にかなっているよね。しかし，それでも，従業員の長期的な動機づけを行いながら，固定的な人件費を抑制する方法を見つけられないかねえ。

レイノルズ：そうですね，**あなたの言おうとされていることはよくわかります。**私のもうひとつのアイデアは，新しいボーナス・プランを導入することです。最近，別の会社の人事担当者と話をしました。彼女は，良い成果を生み出す従業員に変動給を支給するために，彼らがどのようにボーナス体系を設計したかについて説明してくれました。たぶん，同社の体系は検討に値すると思います。

田中：なるほど。現在の状況を説明してくれて有難う。日本の本社が報酬計画を一元管理することはできないことを認識していますよ。ただし，本社の観点からは，人件費をグローバルで効果的に管理するための適切なメカニズムを採用する必要があるよね。ですから，この点について，あなたと井上社長が何をしたいのかについて近いうちに報告してください。

レイノルズ：きっとそうします。本日はお時間をいただきまして，有難うござ

Commentary on sample conversation

In this sample conversation, we encounter an exchange between the GHQ HR in Japan and an overseas subsidiary regarding issues of employee compensation. While it is possible for the GHQ HR to provide the overseas subsidiaries with general direction and guidelines for instituting a compensation structure, it is advisable to provide the overseas subsidiary with the flexibility to respond to local market trends and pressures. In this sample conversation, Tanaka insists that KSC institute mechanisms for controlling fixed labor costs, but does not insist upon any particular methods.

In many countries outside of Japan, employees may come to expect an annual salary raise. Salary raises are provided to keep up with inflation, and to maintain general motivation; even if a promotion is not provided, a salary raise within the current grade provides recognition of the employee's growth within, and value to the company. However, when an employee's current salary level reaches the maximum of the salary range, it is common to freeze salary raises until the employee is promoted.

However, we can see that the compensation structure in the case of highly competitive positions such as engineers is sometimes out of step with the market realities. To control fixed labor costs while motivating employees for the long-term, the following points are considerable:

1) Institute a variable bonus plan which is determined and payable after the results of the fiscal year are known; a variable bonus does not increase fixed costs and is payable based upon the company's actual

いました。

サンプル・カンバセーションに関するコメント

　本サンプル・カンバセーションでは，従業員の報酬問題に関して，日本のグローバル本社人事部と海外子会社との間の意見交換の場面に直面している。グローバル本社人事部は，海外子会社に対して特定の報酬体系を導入するための一般的方針やガイドラインを提供することは可能であるが，他方で，海外子会社に現地市場の動向と圧力に対応するための柔軟性を持たせることも必要である。このサンプル・カンバセーションでは，田中氏は，KSC が固定的な人件費を制御するためのメカニズムを設けることを主張しているが，特定の方法に固執しているわけではない。

　日本以外の多くの国では，従業員は毎年の昇給を期待するようになるかもしれない。インフレに対応し，全般的な動機を維持するために，昇給が実施される。たとえ昇進が認められない場合でも，現在のグレード内の昇給は，従業員の社内での成長とかれらの会社にとっての価値を示すことになる。しかし，従業員の現在の給与レベルが給与幅の上限に達した場合，従業員が昇進するまで昇給を凍結することはよくあることである。

　ただし，エンジニアのようなきわめて競争の激しいポジションにおける報酬体系が，市場の実態からかけ離れている場合がある。従業員を長期的に動機づけながら固定的な人件費を抑制するには，次の点を考慮すべきである。

1) 会計年度の結果がわかった後に決定・支給される変動ボーナスプランを導入する。変動ボーナスは固定費を増加させずに，会社の財務状況に基づいて支払われる。

financial situation.

2) Conduct a salary survey for key positions and adjust the salary ranges upward when the salary surveys indicate that the company standards are below market.

3) Ensure that employees understand the value of their total compensation package inclusive of all types of monetary and non-monetary rewards. For example, if the company pays a substantial amount for social insurance (including health insurance), the cost that the company bears should be open to employees.

Key Phrases and Expressions

We suspect that . . .

This is a good expression to use when there is some evidence available for expressing a point of view, but it is still difficult to come to a final conclusion.

What makes you say so?

This expression is useful for drawing out more information about the reason(s) behind a person's opinion and to gather the available evidence.

Well, how can you be sure that . . . ?

How do you account for these results?

These expressions are useful for politely questioning the opinion or assertion of another person. With these expressions it is possible to draw out more objective evidence regarding the reason or cause of something.

I understand your concerns now.

I understand your perspective.

These expressions are useful for demonstrating that the listener has grasped the ideas/opinions of the speaker. However, these expressions do not necessarily

2）キー・ポジションの給与調査を実施し，その給与調査によって会社の基準が市場を下回っていることが示されている場合，給与幅を上げるべく調整する。

3）全ての種類の金銭的および非金銭的報酬を含む報酬総額の価値を従業員が理解していることを確認する必要がある。例えば，もし会社が社会保険（健康保険を含む）で多額の金額を支払っている場合，会社が負担している費用を従業員に公開すべきである。

重要表現

We suspect that . . .

　これは，ある見解を表現するための何らかの証拠はあるが，最終的な結論に達することが依然として困難な場合に使える適切な表現である。

What makes you say so?

　この表現は，人の意見の背後にある理由に関する詳細情報を引き出したり，利用可能な証拠を収集したりするのに役立つ。

Well, how can you be sure that . . . ?
How do you account for these results?

　これらの表現は，他人の意見や主張に対して丁寧に質問するのに有用である。これらの表現により，何かの理由や原因に関するより客観的な証拠を引き出すことができる。

I understand your concerns now.
I understand your perspective.

　これらの表現は，聞き手が話し手のアイデアや意見を把握していることを示す場合に役立つ。しかし，これらの表現は必ずしも，同意を示すものではな

denote agreement.

い。

Career Planning

Background Information

Ikeda Ryuichi is the **Sales Director** at Kindai Systems Canada (KSC). **Brent Pierson** is a **Sales Manager** who reports to Ikeda. While Ikeda appreciates the contribution that Pierson is making to the department, he does not fully understand Pierson's desired career development plan (CDP). Therefore, Ikeda has decided to have a career planning discussion with Pierson.

• •

(After some greetings have been exchanged)

Ikeda: What do you find to be most interesting in your current work?

Pierson: Recently, you remember that we had a customer complaint, right? While none of us liked receiving the complaint, I felt a strong sense of mission to resolve the problem along with the entire team.

Ikeda: Yes, I remember. You took swift action to gather members from various

キャリア・プランニング

本会話の背景

池田隆一氏は近代システムカナダ（KSC）の**セールズ・ディレクター**である。**ブレント・ピアソン氏は**，池田氏にリポートする立場の**セールズ・マネジャー**である。池田氏は営業部門へのピアソン氏の貢献を評価しているが，他方で彼は，ピアソン氏のキャリア開発計画（CDP）の希望に関して十分には把握していなかった。そこで，池田氏はピアソン氏とキャリア計画に関する話し合いを持つことにした。

● ●

（若干の挨拶を交わした後）

池田：君は現在の業務の中で何に最も関心を持っている？

ピアソン：最近，お客様から苦情がありましたよね？　誰もあのような苦情を受けたくなかったのですが，私は皆と共に協力してその問題を解決することに強い使命感を感じました。

池田：はい，よく覚えていますよ。あなたは速やかに色々な部署からメンバー

departments and then led discussions to resolve the issue.

Pierson: Yes, and when we were able to propose the change in product specifications, we succeeded in transforming our relationship with the customer. Walking out of that meeting with the customer, I felt a strong sense of accomplishment.

Ikeda: I am happy to hear about that. So, is there anything else you would like to be able to do?

Pierson: Well, now that you ask, I guess . . .

Ikeda: Please go ahead. Let me know what's on your mind.

Pierson: I have been working here now for about five years. While I enjoy the work, as I just explained, I have difficulty envisioning my next step in this organization . . . I mean, what could my next position be?

Ikeda: Why do you say that?

Pierson: Well, I report to you directly and you are an expatriate from Japan. Before you came here, I reported to Mr. Sato, who also came from Japan. So, I am not sure if there is any room for growth beyond my current position . . . you know, umm, room for a locally hired manager like myself to go up in the organization.

Ikeda: Okay, and you are saying that you are interested in progressing upward within the company?

Pierson: Sure, if possible.

を集め，議論をリードして問題を解決してくれたよね。

ピアソン：はい。製品の規格変更を提案することで，そのお客さんとの関係を大きく改善することに成功しました。そのお客さんとの会議が終わった時，大きな達成感を感じました。

池田：それを聞いてうれしいね。で，他にもっとやりたいことはありますか？

ピアソン：はあ，そうやって聞かれますと，えーと…。

池田：**遠慮しないでよ。思っていることを聞かせてよ。**

ピアソン：ここで働き始めて5年になります。先程申し上げましたように，仕事は楽しいのですが，この会社で自分の次のステップを描くことが難しいなあと…つまり，自分の次のポジションが何か？　ということですが。

池田：それはなぜですか？

ピアソン：ええ，私の直接の上司はあなたで，日本からの駐在員の方ですよね。あなたの前任者もやはり，日本から来られた佐藤さんという上司でした。ということで，今のポジションを超えて私のキャリアを伸ばす余地があるのかどうか…えーっと，私のような現地採用のマネジャーに社内でさらに上に行ける余地があるのかどうか分からないんですよ。

池田：**分かりました。この会社での昇進に関心があるということですね？**

ピアソン：可能であれば，もちろんです。

Ikeda: Well, such a higher position requires coordination with counterparts at the HQ . . . tell me this then . . . over the past three years, how much opportunity have you had to communicate directly with counterparts in Japan and other worldwide subsidiaries?

Pierson: Not too much actually. I have had conversations with some people from the HQ when they traveled here on business, but I wouldn't know who to contact in Japan regarding concerns such as QC.

Ikeda: Hmm, **it may be beneficial for you to** participate in a global training program. I heard that the GHQ HR has some plans to start up a training program in Tokyo for subsidiary managers like you. Or even, if there's the chance, maybe you could go work in Tokyo for a while.

Pierson: Oh, either of those options would be quite interesting.

Ikeda: I will inquire about the timing of the program and the necessary requirements for participation in the program. Also, next week, we will be having some visitors from Tokyo. I will arrange a meeting so that introductions can be made.

Pierson: Thank you so much. I really appreciate that you are thinking about my growth within the company.

Ikeda: Sure. However, **I can't make any promises now, but** let's do what we can for your future by providing you with necessary exposure within the organization.

Pierson: I am thankful for your support.

池田：そうですね，今以上に高いポジションでは本社の人達との調整業務が必要になるよね…ちょっと教えてくれる？　過去３年間に日本の本社や世界各地の子会社の人たちと直接コミュニケーションを取る機会はどれくらいあった？

ピアソン：実際にはそれほどありませんでした。本社から何人かの人がここに出張して来られた時に会話を交わしたことはありますが，品質管理（QC）のような問題に関して本社のどなたと連絡を取るべきか，分かっておりません。

池田：そうか…じゃあ，グローバル研修プログラムに参加することは**君には有益かもなあ**。本社人事部（GHQ HR）が君のような子会社のマネジャーを対象にした研修プログラムをいくつか開始する予定があると聞いているよ。あるいはねえ，チャンスがあれば，しばらく東京で仕事をしてみるのもいいと思うな。

ピアソン：本当ですか。どちらにもとても興味がありますね。

池田：そのプログラムの実施時期と参加者に必要な資格について問い合わせてみよう。また，来週，東京本社から数名の出張者が来ることになっているんだ。君の紹介になるようにミーティングを手配するよ。

ピアソン：誠に有難う御座います。この会社での私の成長を考えてくださっていることに，心底から感謝いたします。

池田：いやいや。ただし，**現時点では何も約束できませんよ。**しかし，君の将来のために，必要とされている社内での登場機会をできるだけ作るようにしましょう。

ピアソン：ご支援に感謝いたします。

Commentary on sample conversation

In this sample conversation, we encounter an interaction between an expatriate from Japan and the locally hired subordinate as they consider the subordinate's future within the company. Discussing the future with employees is essential for maintaining the engagement and motivation of top talent over the long-term. It is important to note, however, that Ikeda does not make any direct promises about Pierson's future positions. He simply comments that he could seek out information regarding the new global training program and that he would introduce Pierson to HQ representatives. In career planning discussions, it is necessary to speak about future possibilities, but it is advisable not to make any direct promises.

Key Phrases and Expressions

What do you find to be most interesting in your current work?

This expression is useful for asking someone about their satisfaction with their work. An alternative expression that seeks an answer about a person's passion is, "What gets you out of bed each morning to come to work?"

Please go ahead. Let me know what's on your mind.

This expression is useful for encouraging someone who seems hesitant or reluctant to speak out.

Okay, and you are saying that . . . ?

This expression is useful for the listener to ask in order to confirm their understanding of the speaker's intentions.

サンプル・カンバセーションに関するコメント

　本サンプル・カンバセーションでは，日本からの派遣者と現地採用の部下との間で，部下の社内での将来のあり方についての場面に直面している。社員と一緒に将来について議論することは，長期にわたってトップ人材のエンゲージメントとモチベーションを維持するために極めて重要である。しかし，注意すべき重要なことは，池田氏がピアソン氏の将来のポジションに関しては何ら直接的な約束をしていないことである。池田氏は，新たなグルーバル研修プログラムに関する情報を入手し，本社からの出張者にピアソン氏を紹介することについて述べているだけである。キャリア計画に関する話し合いでは，将来の可能性について言及する必要はあるものの，直接的な約束をすることは避けるべきである。

重要表現

What do you find to be most interesting in your current work?

　この表現は，仕事に満足しているかどうかを質問する際に役に立つ。仕事への熱心さを尋ねる別の表現として，「仕事に来るように毎朝ベッドから出させるものは何ですか？」がある。

Please go ahead. Let me know what's on your mind.

　これは，発言することを躊躇したり，嫌がったりする人に発言を促す際に役に立つ表現である。

Okay, and you are saying that . . . ?

　これは，話し手の意図が何であるかについての自分の理解を確認するために，聞き手が尋ねるのに役立つ表現である。

It may be beneficial for you to . . .

This expression is useful for politely providing an opinion or advice about what someone else should do.

I can't make any promises now, but . . .

This expression is useful for decreasing the expectations of others regarding the level of certainty about some future decision or event. It helps the speaker to express an intention without an explicit expectation of the outcome.

It may be beneficial for you to . . .

　これは，相手がすべきことについて意見や助言を丁寧に述べるのに役立つ表現である。

I can't make any promises now, but . . .

　この表現は，将来の決定や出来事に関する確実性のレベルに関する相手の期待値を下げるのに役立つ。結果への明確な期待を示さずに，話し手がある種の意図を表現するのに役立つ。

Talent Review Committee

Background Information

The Global HR Department (GHQ HR) of Kindai Systems Kabushiki Kaisha (KSK) has started to conduct a Global Talent Review Meeting to identify key positions and successor candidates at overseas subsidiaries.

The Global Talent Review Meeting is attended by the CEO, functional directors and HR Department managers from within the group. Although the Global Talent Review Meeting occurs in Japan, the meeting is conducted in English, as there are now two non-Japanese speakers present. The meeting is facilitated by **Tanaka Tsuyoshi, General Manager of Global HR**.

• •

Tanaka: Thank you everyone for joining this second Global Talent Review Meeting. Let's take a look at the next slide in order to ensure understanding of the purpose of this meeting.

(While showing the slide of the Purpose of Today's Meeting, Tanaka explains the agenda.)

タレント・レビュー・コミッティー

本会話の背景

　近代システムズ株式会社（KSK）のグローバル本社人事部（GHQ HR）は，海外子会社におけるキー・ポジションおよび後継者候補を識別するためのグローバル・タレント・レビュー会議を開始した。

　グローバル・タレント・レビュー会議には，最高経営責任者，各機能の取締役，グループ内の各企業の人事マネジャーが出席する。同会議は日本で開催されるが，この会議には日本語が話せない参加者が2名出席するため，会議は英語で行われる。会議の進行役は**田中剛グローバル人事本部長**が務める。

• •

田中：第2回目のグローバル・タレント・レビュー会議にご出席いただき有難うございます。皆さんと本会議の目的を共有するため，次のスライドを見ていただきたいと思います。

（田中氏は「本日の会議の目的」に関するスライドを示しながら，アジェンダを説明する。）

Excerpted from slide

Purpose of Today's Meeting

Part I. Regarding talent

A. To identify potential changes to **incumbents** in key positions over the next twelve months

B. To assess the **level of succession readiness** and/or succession risks for key positions

Part II. Development interventions for successor candidates

To discuss development interventions as follows:

• The new Global Management Training Program (GMTP) for key talent to be held annually in Tokyo

• Stretch assignments for the development of successor candidates

• Other efforts to develop successor candidates

Tanaka: In the first part of this meeting, we want to review the incumbents in the key positions and identify those who are eligible for promotion. Then, we want to discuss any other changes that may be on the horizon within the next twelve months. For example, let's consider the **retention risks** posed by any incumbents who may leave the KS group or otherwise vacate their current positions.

Once we identify the positions that may have a change in incumbents, then we will discuss the **succession bench strength** to identify any existing **succession risks**.

In the second part, we want to focus on development interventions for people that have been identified as candidates for succession.

Prior to this meeting, we had selected four key positions for today's discussion;

（スライドからの抜粋）

本日の会議の目的

第1部 人材について

A．キー・ポジションにいる**現職者**の今後12カ月以内に起こりうる変化についての特定

B．キー・ポジション**後継者の準備状況**，および後継リスクの把握

第2部 後継候補者のための育成支援策

育成支援策についての議論は以下の通り。

・東京で開催予定のキー・タレントのための新しいグローバル・マネジメント・トレーニング・プログラム（GMTP）

・後継候補者を育成するためのストレッチの効いたアサインメント

・その他，後継候補者を育成するための取り組み

田中：この会議の前半では，キー・ポジションの現職者を検討し，昇進の可能性のある人を識別したいと思います。その後，今後12カ月以内に起こりうる変化を議論したいと思います。例えば，現職者がKSグループから退職するか，または，その他の理由で現在のポジションが空席となるに伴い発生する**人材確保リスク**を検討します。

　現職者に関して変化が起こりうるポジションが特定された場合，その際には，現在の**後継リスク**を特定するために**後継候補者層の厚さ**を議論したいと思います。

　第2部では，後継候補者に上がった社員の育成支援策を中心に議論したいと思います。

　この会議に先立ち，本日議論する4つのキー・ポジションを選びました。時

if we have any time remaining, we may focus on others as well.

Does anyone have any questions or comments? If not, then let's start off by reviewing the Sales Director position at KSC. Sato san, please explain.

Sato: Hello everyone. My name is **Sato Takao**. As I am the **HR manager** overseeing the North America region from the GHQ HR, I will explain. At KSC, the current **Sales Director** is **Ikeda Ryuichi**. He reports to **President Inoue Tomomasa**. There is a high possibility that Ikeda san will be transferred back to Japan within the next year. Therefore, most likely we will need to send another expatriate to replace him. However, if we can delay Ikeda san's return to Japan for at least two years, President Inoue and Ikeda san explained to me that there could be a locally hired successor candidate for the position. The candidate's name is **Brent Pierson**. He is a trusted and loyal **Sales Manager** who has demonstrated interest in expanding the scope of his work within the KS Group.

Tanaka: Okay. Assuming that Brent Pierson was to be promoted, what about the succession bench strength for his current position, the Sales Manager position?

Sato: Well, that's the problem. Ideally, we would have three or more such candidates. Right now, we have one clearly identified candidate and one distant second candidate. The clearly identified candidate, **Paula Stern**, has a degree from a prestigious university, more than two years of work experience in the company and is well-respected as a leader in her current team. However, she has had little cross-functional experience so far and has a very weak human network across the KS group.

間が許せば，他のキー・ポジションについても取り上げましょう。

　ご質問，ご意見はありますでしょうか。なければ，KSC のセールズ・ディレクター・ポジションの検討から始めたいと思います。佐藤さん，説明をお願いします。

佐藤：皆さん，こんにちは。**佐藤貴央**です。私は GHQ HR から北米地域をみている**人事課長**ですので，私からご説明申し上げます。KSC の現在の**セールズ・ディレクター**は**池田隆一**さんです。彼は**井上友政社長**の直属の部下です。池田さんは今後 1 年以内に日本に帰任する可能性が高いです。したがって，日本から後任を派遣する必要が出てくる可能性が大きいと思われます。しかし，池田さんの日本への帰任を少なくとも 2 年遅らせることができれば，井上社長と池田氏からの説明では，現地採用の後任候補が出てくる可能性があります。その候補者の名前は**ブレント・ピアソン**です。彼は信頼できる誠実な**セールズ・マネジャー**で，KSK グループ内で自らの職務範囲を拡大することに関心を示しています。

田中：分かりました。ブレント・ピアソン氏がセールズ・ディレクターに昇進した場合に，彼の現在のポジション，つまりセールズ・マネジャーの後継候補者層の厚さはどうなっていますか？

佐藤：それが問題点です。理想は 3 名以上の候補者がいることですが，現時点では 1 名のはっきりと識別できる候補者と，もう 1 名のかなり離れて第 2 順位の候補者しかおりません。前者は**ポーラ・スターン氏**で一流校から修士号を取得しており，当社で 2 年以上の勤務経験を持ち，所属グループのリーダーとして高く評価されています。しかし，彼女はこれまで，機能横断的な経験がほとんどなく，KS グループ内の人的ネットワークがきわめて弱いですね。

The second candidate, **Scott Simpson**, also has a strong educational background, but had just joined KSC last year. Additionally, it seems that his 360 evaluation identified some issues regarding his team development skills. He may not be ready in time to be promoted upward.

Tanaka: Okay. So, we need to identify some development interventions in order to ensure that the first successor candidate can become ready within two years to be promoted. At the same time, it may be necessary to identify at least two additional successor candidates to be safe.

Let's focus on discussing developmental opportunities in more detail during the latter part of this meeting. Now, let's move the discussion to the next position . . .

Commentary on sample conversation

In this sample conversation, we encounter the agenda of a global talent management review meeting and the opening statements that may be made by the meeting facilitator. The conversation demonstrates how the GHQ HR may think about global talent management inclusive of both expatriates from Japan and HCN. When the global talent review meeting incorporates information about the expatriates from Japan with information about the employees in the overseas subsidiaries, it becomes possible to enact a dynamic global talent management system. Such a system is an example of how the GHQ HR can directly impact rates of retention within overseas subsidiaries.

Key Phrases and Expressions

In this sample conversation, we introduce some specific terms that may be used in a global talent review meeting:

　2番目の候補者である**スコット・シンプソン氏**も高い学歴を有しておりますが，昨年，KSC に入社したばかりです。また，360 度評価によると，彼のチーム形成能力にはやや難点が見られるようです。したがって，彼の昇進は時期尚早であると思われます。

田中：分かりました。最初の後継候補者が2年以内に昇進できるよう，能力開発プログラムを準備しましょう。また，念のため，少なくともさらに2名の後継候補を探しましょう。

　能力開発機会については，この会議の後半で集中的に検討することにしたいと思います。それでは次に，ポジションに関する議論に移りましょう…

サンプル・カンバセーションに関するコメント

　本サンプル・カンバセーションでは，グローバル・タレント・レビュー会議の議題，ならびに，会議の進行役が行う冒頭の発言の場面に直面している。このカンバセーションは，GHQ HR が日本からの駐在員と現地国籍社員（HCN）の双方を含むグローバル・タレント・マネジメントをどのように考えているかを示している。グローバル・タレント・レビュー会議で，日本からの駐在員に関する情報と，海外子会社の従業員に関する情報とが共に検討されるようになれば，ダイナミックなグローバル・タレント・マネジメント・システムを実行に移すことが可能になる。こうしたシステムは，GHQ HR がどのようにして海外子会社の社員の確保率に直接的な影響を与えうるかを示す例である。

重要表現

　本サンプル・カンバセーションではグローバル・タレント・レビュー会議で使用されるかもしれない若干の特有な表現をいくつか紹介する。

Incumbent

the employee who is currently in a specific position

Retention risks

refers to level of possibility that a key employee may voluntarily choose to leave the company in a specified period such as the next 12 months

Level of succession readiness

refers to the match between a position's requirements and the qualifications of a particular successor candidate to take on the position

Succession bench strength

refers to the quality and quantity of successors for key positions; sufficient succession bench strength is characterized by the existence of clearly identified successor candidates who are currently ready to be promoted into the key position; alternatively, insufficient succession bench strength refers to conditions where there are clearly identified successors who need to have more experience or development interventions before being judged to be qualified for promotion

Succession risk

refers to the negative impact on the business that may occur in the case that a qualified successor is not available to take on a key position if that position were to be suddenly vacated by the incumbent

現職者

現在，特定のポジションの職務を担当している従業員。

人材確保リスク

主要な従業員が，例えば次の 12 か月以内などの一定の期間内に自発的に退職することを選択する可能性のレベルを指す。

後継者の準備状況

ポジションに必要な要件と，ポジションに就く予定の特定の後継候補者の資格要件との一致度を指している。

後継候補者層の厚さ

キー・ポジションへの後継者の質量を指す。それにより，十分な後継候補者層の厚さであるということは，現在キー・ポジションに昇進する準備ができていると明確に識別された後継者候補が存在することによって特徴づけられる。他方で，後継候補者層の厚さが不十分であるということは，後継候補者が昇進の資格があると判断される前に，より多くの経験または能力開発プログラムを必要とする場合である。

後継リスク

現職者のポジションが突然空席となった際に，そのキー・ポジションを引き受けることができる適格な後継者がいない場合のビジネスへのマイナスの影響を指している。

A Potential Case of Harassment

Background Information

The Global HR Department (GHQ HR) of KSK carried out the Global Employee Satisfaction Survey recently. Employees at its headquarters in Japan and at the overseas group companies responded.

While most of the survey responses were positive, those from the Production Department at KSP in the Philippines caught the attention of **Tanaka Tsuyoshi, General Manager of Global HR** in the Tokyo Headquarters.

In the Production Department of KSP, responses regarding overall satisfaction with the relations between manufacturing line workers and the management were notably lower than in other departments around the global group.

Particularly, there was an anonymous comment written by an employee who may be alluding to an instance of on-going harassment in the workplace.

The comment was, "I think my boss is just playing around with us, so I don't want to create a fuss, but I really wish the company could do a better job to

ハラスメントの潜在的可能性

本会話の背景

　KSK のグローバル本社人事部 (GHQ HR) は最近，グローバル従業員満足度調査を実施した。日本本社および海外のグループ会社の従業員が回答した。

　調査への回答は総じて肯定的な内容であったが，フィリピンの KSP 製造部からの回答は東京本社**グローバル人事本部長**の田中剛氏の注目を引いた。

　KSP 製造部の製造ライン従業員からの回答によると，管理職との関係に関する彼らの満足度が KSK の他の全世界に所在する子会社の他部門よりも際立って低かった。

　特に，ある従業員による匿名のコメントがあり，その中では現在，職場で起きているハラスメント行為に言及していると思われる文章があった。

　コメントは，「上司は単に私たちをからかっているだけだと思うので，あまり大騒ぎはしたくはありません。しかし，皆が安全で快適な職場と思えるよ

ensure everyone feels comfortable and safe at work. Sometimes joking around goes too far."

Such a comment was not sufficiently clear for Tanaka to understand the employee's claim, so he decided to conduct a video conference with **Maria Lapuz, HR Manager** at KSP.

• •

(After greetings have been exchanged, Tanaka expresses the following.)

Tanaka: Thank you for your recent cooperation in carrying out the Global Employee Satisfaction Survey. My team here in Tokyo is compiling the results. We will share a report with all of the subsidiaries in a few weeks.

Lapuz: Thank you. I was happy to assist. I am interested in seeing the results and understanding how KSP compares with other group companies.

Tanaka: Well, that is why I wanted to speak to you right away.

Lapuz: Oh, is something wrong?

Tanaka: To be honest, I am not yet sure. So, **I would like to bring something to your attention right away.**

Lapuz: Hmm, what is it?

Tanaka: Well, results from the Production Department seem to indicate that employee satisfaction is lower than in other departments of KSP and compared to other group companies.

う，会社として一層努力して欲しい。時には冗談が行き過ぎる場合があります」という内容であった。

　田中氏にとって，この社員の苦情を理解するにはこのコメントだけでは不十分であった。そこで，KSP の**マリア・ラプス人事マネジャー**とビデオ会議を持つことにした。

・・

（挨拶が終わった後で，田中氏は以下のように述べた。）

田中：最近のグローバル従業員満足度調査の実施に際してご協力頂き感謝します。東京本社の私のチームで現在結果を取りまとめ中です。数週間後に報告書を全子会社にお送りします。

ラプス：有難うございます。ご協力できて幸いです。調査結果を見て，KSP が他のグループ企業と比較してどのような状況であるかを理解したいと思っています。

田中：実は，そのことで，直ぐにお話したいことあったのですよ。

ラプス：えー，何か問題がありましたか？

田中：正直申し上げて，現時点では未だ確かではありません。そこで，**先ずは報告だけしておきます。**

ラプス：はい。何でしょうか？

田中：実は，KSP の製造部の従業員満足度の結果は，KSP の他部門よりも低く，また，他のグループ企業よりも低いことを示しているようです。

Lapuz: Oh, why is that?

Tanaka: Responses to the question about *satisfaction with the relationship with your superior* demonstrate that operators in the Production Department of KSP are much less satisfied with their relationship with superiors than similarly positioned employees at other KS group subsidiaries.

Lapuz: Oh. That is disappointing to hear.

Tanaka: And also, there was one anonymous comment that I felt we should look into immediately. I will read the comment to you.

(Tanaka reads the previously mentioned comment.)

Lapuz: I don't think the comment is a complaint against the expatriates from Japan as Suzuki san is rather serious-minded; rather, I think that whoever wrote the comment is expressing dissatisfaction with their locally hired direct supervisor. Kindly send me a copy of this response by email. Then, give me a few days to look into this and I will get back to you.

Tanaka: Sure, I will send you the email. Shall I also cc: Suzuki san in Production Control so that he knows in advance about the situation?

Lapuz: Yes, I think that is okay.

Tanaka: Fine, I will send the email right away.

(Lapuz is meeting with **Suzuki Satoru, Production Control Manager**. She started to inquire with Suzuki.)

ラプス：それはなぜでしょうか？

田中：「自分の上司との関係に対する満足度」に関する質問への回答は，KSP
の製造部のオペレーターが，他の KS グループ子会社の同様の立場にある従業
員よりも，上司との関係において極めて低い満足度を示しています。

ラプス：えー。それは残念です。

田中：そして，直ちに検討すべきと思われる匿名のコメントがひとつありまし
た。読んでみます。

（田中氏は上記に示したコメントを読む。）

ラプス：そのコメントは日本からの派遣者に対する苦情ではないと思います。
というのは，鈴木さんは真面目な性格だからです。むしろ，このコメントを書
いた人が誰であれ，現地採用の直属の上司に対する不満を述べていると思いま
す。すみませんが，そのコメントのコピーを E メールで送っていただけませ
んか。調べてご連絡をいたしますので，数日間お時間をください。

田中：了解です。E メールをお送りします。生産管理マネジャーの鈴木さんも
前もって状況を把握できるよう，彼もメールの cc に入れておきましょうか？

ラプス：はい，それで結構です。

田中：分かりました。すぐに E メールを送ります。

（ラプス氏は，**生産管理マネジャーの鈴木悟氏**とミーティングを持っている。
彼女は鈴木氏への質問を始めました。）

Lapuz: So, do you have any idea about why such a comment might be raised by someone?

Suzuki: Well, not really. I thought that everyone was getting along well in the factory.

Lapuz: Hmm, is there anything you've seen or heard until this point that you can recall?

Suzuki: I see and hear a lot of non-job-related discussions going on. If this was Japan, I would expect the staff and managers to not speak about topics unrelated to their work, but since this is the Philippines, I thought I needed to be a bit less strict in this regard.

Lapuz: Sure, we like to talk with each other on friendly terms even at work. But still, there are professional standards that should be upheld. Does anything come to mind?

Suzuki: Well, we hired a new **supervisor** a few months back—**Jeffrey Prego**.

Lapuz: Sure, we had spoken together about him previously.

Suzuki: He, umm . . .

Lapuz: What is it?

Suzuki: He tells jokes a lot. I don't always understand his jokes, so I don't laugh. When he tells jokes, some people laugh along. But there are some people who don't laugh too much either.

ラプス：さて，誰から，どうして，このようなコメントが出されるか，お気づきの点はありますか？

鈴木：いや，あまりよく分かりませんね。工場では皆は上手くやっていると思っていましたが。

ラプス：そうですか…これまで何か気になるようなことを見たり聞いたりしていませんか？

鈴木：仕事と関係のない話が行われるのを見聞しますね。日本であれば，スタッフと上司が仕事とは関係がない話をすることは控えるものでしょうね。しかし，ここはフィリピンなので，この点で，それほど厳しくするものではないと思っていました。

ラプス：確かに，私たちは仕事中でもスタッフと上司が打ち解けた雰囲気で話をすることを好みます。とは言っても，職業人として守るべき基準はあります。この点で何か心当たりはありますか？

鈴木：そう言えば，数カ月前に新しいスーパーバイザーを雇いました。ジェフリー・プレゴ氏です。

ラプス：もちろん，以前に一緒に彼について話しましたよね。

鈴木：彼は，あの…。

ラプス：何ですか？

鈴木：彼は頻繁に冗談を言います。私はいつも彼の冗談を理解できるわけではないので，笑いません。彼が冗談を言うと，一緒になって笑う人もいます。しかし，それほど笑わない人もいますね。

Lapuz: Are the ones who don't laugh typically men or women?

Suzuki: Both I think . . . but, **come to think of it**, there is one female staff member—**Czarina Fernandez**—who may be laughing the least. I spoke with her recently about the problem of her attendance.

Lapuz: Oh?

Suzuki: Well, she arrives late, and starts to get ready to leave the workplace a few minutes early each day. She wasn't like this previously.

Lapuz: And she works with Jeffrey, right?

Suzuki: Yes . . .

Lapuz: Okay. Just from this conversation alone, we cannot be certain whether the comment came from Czarina or not, but please do observe the nature of the interaction between Jeffrey and his subordinates, especially Czarina. I will make an effort to walk through the factory with some more frequency too. Shall we have a follow-up meeting early next week?

Suzuki: Sure, I understand.

Lapuz: Thank you for your time today.

A few days after this conversation, Suzuki observed Prego joking around with his staff. Suzuki caught a glimpse of the flushed face of Fernandez. Her eyes seemed glassy, as if she may burst into tears. Later, he approached her and asked how her work is going. She said things are okay, but not as good as before. After some more probing, she opened up about her discomfort with

ラプス：笑わないのは通常，男性と女性のどちらですか？

鈴木：両方いると思いますね…でも**考えてみると**，ほとんど笑わない女性スタッフが一人います。**ザリーナ・フェルナンデス**さんです。私は最近，彼女と出勤関連の問題について話し合いました。

ラプス：あ，そうですか？

鈴木：いや，まあ，彼女は遅刻し，毎日定時よりも数分早く職場を離れる準備を始めます。以前は，こんな感じではなかったんですよ。

ラプス：また，彼女はジェフリーと一緒に仕事をしていますよね？

鈴木：ええ…。

ラプス：分かりました。この会話だけでは，投稿者がザリーナかどうか断定できませんが，ジェフリーと彼の部下，特にザリーナとのやり取りがどの程度か確かめてください。私はもう少し頻繁に工場に行くようにします。来週初めに再度ミーティングを持ちましょう。

鈴木：はい，わかりました。

ラプス：本日は時間をとって頂き有難うございました。

　この会話の数日後，鈴木氏はプレゴがスタッフとからかっているところを見た。鈴木氏はフェルナンデスを見かけたが，彼女は赤面していた。彼女の目は潤み，今にも泣き出しそうであった。その後，彼はフェルナンデスに近づき，仕事の状況を尋ねた。彼女の返事は，何とかやっているが，以前ほど順調ではないというものであった。鈴木氏はその後の質問を通じて，彼女がプレゴの冗

some of the jokes that Prego tells.

Unsure about the right corrective action, Suzuki suggested that Fernandez could have a conversation with Lapuz in the HR Department about the matter. Fernandez showed relief and gratitude for Suzuki's interest in her concern.

Lapuz and Fernandez spoke together the next day. During the conversation, Fernandez revealed that she was the one who wrote the comment into the survey. Given her religious upbringing, Fernandez explained that Prego's joking made her uncomfortable. But she did not want to get him into trouble with the company. Lapuz thanked Fernandez for her openness and expressed the company's commitment to ensuring a comfortable workplace for everyone.

Thereafter, Lapuz and Suzuki had a meeting with Prego. While Prego reacted at first with defensiveness, he came to understand the negative impact of his joking and committed to be more careful in the future.

Commentary on sample conversation

In this sample conversation we encounter the GHQ HR spearheading an initiative to conduct a global employee satisfaction survey and to closely review the results. We see how the GHQ HR and the overseas subsidiary HR Managers can work hand-in-hand to deal with important issues of concern.

The topic of this sample conversation is related with the chapter on discrimination and harassment. While the behaviors described herein may not be illustrative of illegal, high-risk harassment, there is an important point to be recognized: when the behaviors of one employee, especially, the behaviors of a manager, have a negative impact upon the comfort and work satisfaction of others, the company has a responsibility to take

談のいくつかに不快感を感じていることを露わにした。

　鈴木氏はどう対処していいのか分からなかったので，本件に関して人事部の
ラプス氏と話をするようフェルナンデスに勧めた。フェルナンデスは，鈴木氏
が彼女の悩みに関心を示してくれたことに安堵と感謝の気持ちを表した。

　ラプス氏とフェルナンデスは翌日ミーティングを持った。その中で，フェル
ナンデスは，調査のコメントを書いたのは自分であることを認めた。彼女が受
けた宗教上の教えからすると，プレゴの冗談には不快感を覚えざるを得なかっ
たという。さらに，彼が会社との間でトラブルを起こすことは望まないと述べ
た。ラプス氏はフェルナンデスが正直に打ち明けてくれたことに謝し，会社と
して社員全員にとって快適な職場を提供するという決意を述べた。

　その後，ラプス氏と鈴木氏はプレゴ氏と面談した。最初プレゴは自己弁護し
たが，彼は自分の冗談のマイナス面を理解し，将来，より注意深くすることを
約束した。

サンプル・カンバセーションに関するコメント

　本サンプル・カンバセーションでは，グローバル規模の社員満足度調
査をグローバル人事部が率先して実施し，その結果を詳細に分析するとい
う場面に直面した。どのようにして，GHQ HR が海外子会社の人事マネ
ジャーと協力し，重要な関心事項に対応したかを見た。

　本サンプル・カンバセーションのトピックは，差別とハラスメントの章
に関連している。ここで述べた行動は違法で大きなリスクを伴うハラスメ
ントを示すものではないが，認識すべき重要なポイントを示している。つ
まり，一人の従業員の行動，特に管理者の行動が，他の従業員の快適さ
や仕事に対する満足感にマイナスの影響を与える場合には，企業は，こう
した影響を最小限にする対策を講ずる責任を負う。こうした対策は，高ま

remedial action to minimize such impact. Such action is important both to prevent the escalation of legal risk and to ensure that all employees can work with comfort and satisfaction.

Key Phrases and Expressions

I would like to bring something to your attention right away.

This is a common and helpful expression for opening up a conversation when you would like to explain something of importance to another person. An alternative expression is, "I would like to explain some information to you."

Come to think of it . . .

This is a typical expression that precedes the explanation of important information which someone has suddenly come to recognize as being noteworthy during an on-going conversation.

る法的リスクの最小化と，全従業員の快適で満足感のある職場環境の保証とにとって重要である。

重要表現

I would like to bring something to your attention right away.

　これは，重要な何かを他の人に説明したいときに，話しかけたいときの一般的で有用な表現である。別の表現には，「あなたに，ある情報を説明したい」がある。

Come to think of it . . .

　これは，会話中に突然注目に値すると認識した，重要な情報の説明の前に述べる典型的な表現である。

Union Representative Visit to an Overseas Subsidiary

Background Information

Tanaka Tsuyoshi, General Manager of Global HR in the Tokyo Headquarters just finished a video conference with **Jim Barnes, HR Manager** of KSUS. He wondered to himself why Barnes reacted so strongly against his request for accommodating a visit of the union representatives from KSK in Japan to the USA. Upon the very mention of the word *union* by Tanaka, Barnes retorted, "At KSUS, we have no union activity whatsoever going on. Sending over anyone to talk about the topic of unions is not a good idea at all."

Given the cooperative and supportive relations that Tanaka and Barnes have forged ever since Barnes was hired, Tanaka was perplexed about why Barnes was so unwilling to support the request from Tokyo. Tanaka needed some advice so he contacted an American **HR consultant** named **Ryan Rogers**. Rogers, who is based in Japan and provides global HR support services to globalizing Japanese companies, drafted the following internal memorandum in order to bridge the communication between the GHQ HR in Japan and the overseas subsidiary in the United States.

• •

労働組合代表者の海外拠点への訪問

本会話の背景

　東京本社グローバル人事本部長の**田中剛氏**は，KSUS 人事マネジャーであるジム・バーンズ氏とのビデオ会議を終えたばかりである。田中部長は，日本のKSK の労働組合の代表者数名による米国訪問の受け入れ要請に対し，なぜバーンズ氏がそれほど強い拒否反応を示したのか理解できず，自問自答している。「組合」という言葉を田中氏が口にした瞬間，バーンズ氏は「KSUS では如何なる労働組合活動も皆無です。労働組合関連の話をするために誰かを送ってくることは，決して良いアイデアではありません」と反発した。

　田中氏は，バーンズ氏が KSUS で採用されて以来，両者間で協力・支援関係を培ってきたのに，バーンズ氏がなぜ東京本社からの要請にかくも非協力的であるのか，その理由が全く理解できなかった。田中氏は何らかのアドバイスを求めて，米国人**人事コンサルタントのライアン・ロジャース氏**にコンタクトを取った。ロジャース氏は日本を拠点として，グローバル化しつつある日本企業にグローバル人事支援を提供している。ロジャース氏は，日本の GHQ HRと米国子会社との間のコミュニケーションを橋渡しするために，次のような社内覚え書きの下書きを作成した。

TO: Jim Barnes, HR Manager, KSUS
CC: Kikuchi Kenta, President, KSUS
FROM: Tanaka Tsuyoshi, Global HR General Manager, KSK
SUBJECT: Request for cooperation in arranging a meeting
DATE: May 1st, 20xx

The purpose of this memorandum is to request your support and cooperation in arranging a meeting between employees of KSUS and representatives of our KSK labor union from Japan.

Firstly, please refer to the following background information to help you understand the nature of this request, as well as to select the most appropriate people from KSUS for participation.

I. Overview of labor unions in Japan

In Japan, most of the labor unions are formed as internal enterprise unions in contrast to industrial unions which are commonplace in other countries. The relationship between the Japanese union and the management of the company is generally cooperative. In this way, the labor union acts in partnership, not in conflict, with the management of the company, primarily by relaying the voice of employees up to the management. This is no different in the case of the KSK labor union.

The top executive management of KSK conducts meetings with the union representatives twice yearly in order to exchange opinions. As the HR Department, we work to support these activities by providing information when necessary to the executive management and union.

KSK employees are covered by a union shop agreement which requires employees other than management to join the union. Therefore, about 80% of

TO：　　KSUS 人事マネジャー　ジム・バーンズ殿
CC：　　KSUS 社長　菊池健太殿
FROM：KSK グローバル人事本部長　田中剛
件名：　KSK よりの会議設定の要望
日付：　20XX 年 5 月 1 日

　本覚え書きの目的は，KSUS 社員と我が KSK 労働組合代表者との面談の手配に関して貴職よりのご支援とご協力をお願いしたいというものであります。

　本依頼の性質をご理解いただき，また KSUS より最も適切な出席者を選んでいただくためのご参考として，先ず以下の背景情報をご参照下さい。

Ⅰ．日本の労働組合の概観

　日本では労働組合のほとんどは，他国では一般的な産業別組合ではなく，企業内にある企業別組合として結成されている。日本の労働組合と経営者の関係は概して協力的である。このように，労働組合は経営陣と対立した行動をとるのではなく，従業員の声を経営者に伝えることを主たる任務として，経営陣のパートナーとして活動する。これは KSK の労働組合の場合にも同様である。

　KSK の最高経営幹部は，意見交換のために年 2 回，組合の代表と面談している。人事部としては，このような活動を支援し，必要に応じて労使双方に情報を提供している。

　KSK の従業員は，ユニオン・ショップ制の下にあり，管理職以外の従業員は組合に加入しなければならない。したがって，従業員の約 8 割が組合員と

the workforce at KSK are union members.

The KSK Japan union activities are led by 10 individuals who, during their term as leaders of the union, are classified as being *on leave* from their status as regular employees of the company. During this time, they conduct activities as full-time union officials and are referred to by the title of *senju* in Japanese.

Normally, the *senju* are individuals in their late 20's to early 30's. Prior to being posted to the union they work in non-managerial positions within KSK. Selection of the *senju* is done by the union itself in consultation with the HR Department. After serving as *senju* for a period of a few years, individuals return to their status as a *regular employee* and continue to pursue a career within KSK. Within the ranks of the KSK management as well as within the HR Department, there are many individuals who had served the union in this capacity.

II. Meeting details
A. Meeting purpose

Representatives of KSK's union will travel to the United States for the purpose of meeting with employees of KSUS. The primary goal of the meeting will be as follows:

1. Considering the significant contribution KSUS makes to the performance of the KS group overall, the union representatives wish to gain first-hand knowledge of the business operations at KSUS.
2. The union representatives also wish to understand the sentiment of employees working at KSUS.

Please note: We in KSK understand that union conditions and relations between a labor union and a company are rather different in Japan and the

なっている。

　KSK Japan の組合活動は，10 人によって主導されているが，その 10 人は，組合のリーダーとしての任期中であり，会社の正社員としての地位から「休暇中」に分類されている人たちである。この間，彼らは日本語で「専従」と呼ばれる立場にあり，フルタイムの組合役員として活動する。

　通常，「専従」は，20 代後半から 30 代前半である。組合業務に従事する以前は KSK 社内で非管理職の職務を遂行している。「専従」の人選は組合自身が人事部と協議して行う。このポストに数年間付いた後，彼らは「正社員」に復帰し，KSK 社内でのキャリアを引き続き継続する。KSK の経営管理職や人事部内にも，専従としての組合業務の経験者が多い。

Ⅱ．会議の詳細

A．会議の目的

　KSK 労働組合の代表グループが訪米し，KSUS の従業員と対話を行うのが目的である。この対話の主要なゴールは以下の通り。

1．KSUS の事業が KSK グループ全体の業績に重要な貢献を行っていることに鑑み，労働組合代表は KSUS の事業運営に関する直接的な理解を得ることを希望している。
2．労働組合代表はまた，KSUS で働く従業員の気持ちを理解したい。

ご注意点：我々 KSK 側は，労働組合の状況や会社と労働組合の関係が日米でかなり異なることを理解しています。KSK 組合代表の訪問は，KSK のエン

United States; please consider the visit of KSK union representatives as an extension of the KSK employee relations function. In no way should you consider this visit of KSK union representatives to be equivalent to union activity as is typical in the United States. Please consider this to simply be an educational meeting for the benefit of expanding the knowledge and perspective of the KSK union itself.

III. Meeting details

A. Time frame:

Two consecutive weekdays during next month

B. Location:

Conference room in KSUS office

C. Participants from Japan:

KSK Labor Union Representatives (four people)

D. KSUS Participants

We would like to set up three meeting sessions of 1 to 1.5 hours in duration with the following counterparts:

Meeting 1: A manager who can speak about the KSUS business overall

Meeting 2: Approximately three to five employees who can explain the current situation in the company at the staff level

Meeting 3: Same as Meeting 2

Thank you very much in advance for your support and cooperation.

● ●

After receiving this memorandum from Tanaka, Barnes discussed the issue

プロイー・リレーションズ機能の一環であることを考慮してください。この KSK 組合代表の訪問は，合衆国で典型的な組合活動と同等であると解釈したり，公表したりしないでいただきたい。これは，KSK 組合自体の知識と視野を拡大するための教育的な会議であると考えてください。

III．会議の詳細

A．日程：

来月のウイークデイの連続2日間

B．場所：

KSUS のオフィス内の会議室

C．訪米者：

KSK 労働組合代表（4名）

D．KSUS の希望参加者：

1〜1.5 時間のミーティングを3度，次のような内容でご手配頂ければ幸甚です。

ミーティング1：管理職の方より KSUS の事業全般のご説明

ミーティング2：約3〜5名の非管理職スタッフによる会社の現在の状況を説明できる従業員

ミーティング3：ミーティング2と同様

　貴方よりのご支援ご協力を賜りますようお願い申し上げます。

● ●

　田中氏よりのこの依頼状を受け取った後，バーンズ氏は菊池社長と本件に関

with President Kikuchi. Thereafter, both President Kikuchi and Barnes worked to accommodate the request from the Tokyo Headquarters.

Commentary on sample conversation

In this sample conversation we encounter a clash of understanding regarding the significance of unions across group companies in a global group. The memorandum presented in this sample conversation is derived from a case that one of the authors of this book (Bryan Sherman) developed when advising an actual Tokyo-based GHQ HR on how to convey their perspective to the US-based subsidiary.

In the United States, HR management typically endeavors to create a company environment in which employees do not feel the need to unionize. Therefore, such a request from the GHQ HR that was made above to the overseas subsidiary would indeed be met with some resistance. However, in the actual case that Sherman advised upon, the US-based subsidiary's HR Department became less resistant upon receiving the explanation about the nature of enterprise unions. In fact, the on-line version of the Encyclopedia Britannica (www.britannica.com/topic/enterprise-unionism) explains that enterprise unions are particularly characteristic of Japan.

Key Phrases and Expressions

In this sample conversation, we encounter an exchange of ideas presented in the format of an internal memorandum. An internal memorandum is a formal business communication tool. Traditionally, an internal memorandum had been formally formatted and printed on paper to be posted within a company office. Nowadays, internal memoranda are written within the body of an email and/or are attached as a PDF to an email.

し相談した。その後，菊池社長とバーンズ氏は，東京本社からの要請を受け入れるべく協働した。

サンプル・カンバセーションに関するコメント

　本サンプル・カンバセーションでは，グローバルに広がるグループ企業間における組合の重要性に関する認識の違いを考察する。このサンプル・カンバセーションで示される社内覚え書きは，本書の著者の一人であるブライアン・シャーマンが，米国の子会社に本社の視点を伝える方法について，実際の東京を拠点とするGHQ HRに助言した際に開発した実際の事例から作成したものである。

　米国では，典型的な人事管理の目標は，従業員が組織化の必要性を感じないような企業環境の創出を目指すことにある。したがって，GHQ HRから海外子会社への上記のような要請に対しては，後者から拒否反応が示される可能性がある。しかし，シャーマンが助言した実際の事例では，米国の子会社の人事部は企業別組合の性質に関する説明を受けた後，その拒絶反応がやわらいだ。実際，オンライン版ブリタニカ百科事典（www.britannica.com/topic/enterprise-unionism）によると，企業別組合は日本の独特の特徴を有するものであると説明している。

重要表現

　このサンプル・カンバセーションでは社内の覚え書きの形式で示されたアイデアのやり取りに直面する。社内の覚え書きは正式なコミュニケーションの手段である。かつては，社内の覚え書きは正式な書式で紙面に印刷された後，社内に掲示された。今日では，社内の覚え書きは，メールの本文，またはメール添付されているPDFとして配布される。

An internal memorandum is normally written as follows:

TO: Name and position of the primary recipient
CC: Name and position of other recipient(s)
FROM: Name and position of the writer
SUBJECT: A phrase that identifies the subject of the memorandum
DATE: Date the memorandum is sent

Following the heading is the *body* of the memorandum. The body is structured according to the purpose of the memorandum.

When a memorandum is written in this format, greetings such as *Best regards* are not normally written at the bottom of the memorandum.

While it is typical to write *The End* at the bottom of a memorandum in Japanese, it is not typical to write *The End* at the end of an English memorandum.

Reference: https://www.niu.edu/wac/archives/files/memogdln.html

　社内覚え書きのヘッディングは通常，下記のように記述する。

TO：　　　主たる受け取り手の氏名と役職

CC：　　　他の受け取り手の氏名と役職

FROM：　作成者の氏名と役職

SUBJECT：覚え書きの主題を明確に示す表現

DATE：　　覚え書きが発信される日にち

　ヘッディングの後に覚え書きの「本文」が書かれる。本文の構成は覚え書きの目的に従って作成される。

　覚え書きがこのフォーマットで書かれる時，文末の「Best regards」などのあいさつ文は通常，不要である。

　また，日本語で作成される覚え書きには文末に「以上」と付すことが通常であるが，英語の覚え書きでは文末に「the End」と書くことは通常不要である。

参考：https://www.niu.edu/wac/archives/files/memogdln.html

Self-Introduction From a New Expatriate

Background Information

Abe Noriaki is a **Sales Manager** in the Sales Department of KSK in Tokyo. He was recently informed that he would be expatriated to KSC to become the successor for **Ikeda Ryuichi**, the current **Sales Director**.

To get prepared for this new assignment, Abe set up a video conference with Ikeda to learn as much as he can in advance of being dispatched to Canada. Ikeda suggested that Abe send an introductory email to **Brent Pierson, Sales Manager** in the department who is responsible for sales to non-Japanese automobile manufacturers. (Although consideration has been made for promoting Pierson to the Sales Director position, **President Inoue** requested that another expatriate be sent from Japan to fill the Sales Director position before promoting an HCN to the position.)

A few days after Ikeda and Abe spoke, Pierson approached Ikeda with a look of consternation.

新しい赴任者よりの自己紹介

本会話の背景

　阿部紀明氏は，東京の KSK 販売部部長である。彼は最近，現在（KSC の）**セールズ・ディレクター**である**池田隆一氏**の後任として KSC に赴任する辞令を受けた。

　新しい職務に備えるため，阿部氏は，カナダへの赴任前にできる限り多くの情報を得るために池田氏とビデオ会議を行った。池田氏は阿部氏に対し，非日系自動車メーカーへの販売を担当する部署の**セールズ・マネジャー**である**ブレント・ピアソン氏**に自己紹介のメールを送るようアドバイスした。（ピアソンをセールズ・ディレクターに昇進させる検討がなされたが，**井上社長**は HCN（現地国籍人材）を当該ポジションに昇進させる前に，本社からの駐在員の派遣を要請していた。）

　池田，阿部両氏が話した数日後，ピアソン氏が池田氏に心配げに話しかけてきた。

Pierson: Ikeda san, could you give me some time to talk about something of concern to me?

Ikeda: Sure. Please come in and take a seat. **What can I do for you?**

Pierson: When you told me that you were going to be sent back to Japan at the end of March, of course, I was shocked at first and, to be honest, I started to get worried. After all, you have been here for a few years and really understand our local business well.

Ikeda: Well, thanks. But as an expatriate from Japan, I have to return to Tokyo.

Pierson: And, I understand that.

Ikeda: Don't worry. I am sure that my successor Abe san will be an even better manager than I've been. I was talking to him just the other day. Indeed, he is excited to come here and work with you.

Pierson: Well, that is what I am concerned about actually. He sent me an email.

Ikeda: Good. I encouraged him to reach out to you.

(Pierson looks down and frowns.)

Ikeda: Is something wrong?

Pierson: Well, take a look at this.

ピアソン：池田さん，気になることがあるのですが，お時間頂けますか？

池田：もちろんです。どうぞ，中に入ってお座りください。**どうしましたか？**

ピアソン：3月末に日本に戻られるとのお話をお聞きし，もちろん最初はショックを受け，正直なところ，心配になり始めています。何といっても，あなたは数年間ここに滞在され，私たちの当地でのビジネスを熟知されています。

池田：いや，有難うございます。しかし，私は日本からの駐在員なので，東京に戻らざるを得ないんですよ。

ピアソン：もちろん，それは理解しております。

池田：心配しないでください。私の後継者である阿部さんは，私よりもさらに優れたマネジャーになると確信しています。先日彼と話しました。彼はここで，あなたと働くことを非常に楽しみにしています。

ピアソン：ええ，実はそれこそ，私が心配していることなのです。彼からメールを受け取りました。

池田：それは良かった。彼にあなたと連絡をとるようアドバイスしました。

（ピアソン氏は目を伏せて，困った様子である。）

池田：何か問題ありますか？

ピアソン：ちょっと，これを見てください。

(Pierson hands a tablet over to Ikeda on which the email from Abe is open. Ikeda reads the email.)

Email from Abe Noriaki

Dear Brent Pierson,

Hello. My name is Abe Noriaki. I will go to Canada soon. I joined KSK in 200x. I worked in the factory for five years. Then, I worked in the Business Planning Department at the HQ from 200x until 201x. From 201x, I went to the USA to study English as a trainee at KSUS for one year. Now I am responsible for sales again. I do not know much about the Canada market situation, so please help me. I want to improve profit for the company. Because I work in Tokyo now, I do not use English too much so I am afraid I won't speak like Ikeda san. By the way, I like golf and whisky. See you soon.

Abe

Pierson: I don't want to sound rude, but I don't understand why Japan has made the decision to call you back to Tokyo and to send this guy. He doesn't seem to know much about our business.

Ikeda: Hmm . . . well, actually Abe san is one of our best sales managers in Tokyo.

Pierson: Really? It is hard to understand that from this email. I can understand that he has some diverse work experience, but **I can't really get a sense of anything he has done well** . . . what will make him a good Sales Director like you?

Ikeda: Well, we Japanese, umm . . . what was that expression you taught me . . .

（ピアソン氏は池田氏にタブレットを渡した。タブレットでは阿部氏からのメールが開いた状態になっている。池田氏はメールを読む。）

（阿部紀明氏からのメール）

ブレント・ピアソン様,

こんにちは, 阿部紀明です。私はもうすぐカナダに行きます。私は200x年にKSKに入社しました。私は5年間工場で働きました。その後, 200x年から201x年まで本社の事業企画部で働きました。201x年から1年間, 英語を勉強し, 同時にKSUSでトレーニーになるためにアメリカに行きました。現在, 再び販売を担当しています。私はカナダの市場の状況についてあまり知りませんので助けてください。会社のために, 利益を改善したいのです。現在は東京勤務で, あまり英語を使っていないので池田さんのようには話せないと思います。ちなみに, 私はゴルフとウイスキーが好きです。近いうちにお目にかかります。

阿部

ピアソン：失礼な言い方はしたくないのですが, なぜ日本本社があなたを東京に戻してこの人を派遣することにしたのか理解できません。彼は私たちのビジネスについてほとんど理解していないように思います。

池田：うーん, 実は阿部さんは本社で最も優秀なセールズ・マネジャーの一人です。

ピアソン：本当ですか？　このメールからそれを理解するのは難しいです。彼にはある程度の多様な職務経験があることは理解できますが, **彼が何を成し遂げたのかということはあまり分かりません**…何をもって, 彼があなたのようなセールズ・ディレクターになれると言えるんですか？

池田：えーと, 私たち日本人は, あのー…あなたが私に教えてくれた表現は何

to toot . . . ?

Pierson: Ah, *to toot your own horn.*

Ikeda: Yeah, we don't like to toot our own horns. We don't brag.

Pierson: And, I can understand that. Even in Canada, we don't like people who are too haughty. But . . . if someone is going to come to Canada to take on a high-level position, I would hope that he'd explain his track record of successes and what he plans on doing here.

Ikeda: I understand what you are saying. It might have been better for Abe san to explain, not just the departments in which he has worked, but more about the contributions he has made over time. Believe me . . . over the past few years, he has made some strong contributions.

Pierson: Okay. But let me ask something else that is on my mind. He wrote that he *wants to improve profit for the company.* Doesn't he know that we have dramatically increased sales each year and that our cost reduction initiatives have resulted in record profit levels?

Ikeda: Surely, he is aware. I explained that to him. In fact, I told him that you were one of our key players here and that he should make efforts to work closely with you. So, that's why he contacted you.

Pierson: But it sounds like he thinks our profit levels are low . . . that profitability is a problem.

でしたっけ…「to toot . . .」?

ピアソン：ああ，「to toot your own horn」（ラッパを吹くように自画自賛する）です。

池田：ええ，私たちは自分のラッパを吹くように自画自賛することを好まないのです。私たちは自慢しないのです。

ピアソン：もちろん，それは理解できます。カナダでさえ，自慢し過ぎる人たちは好まれません。ですが…もし高いポジションでカナダに赴任するのであれば，私は本人から，これまでの実績と，そして当地で何をしようとしているのかを説明してほしいと思います。

池田：あなたの言いたいことは分かります。阿部さんは，これまで所属した部署だけでなく，これまでどのような貢献をしたかについても説明した方が良かったのかもしれません。私を信じてよ…過去数年間に，彼はいくつかの重要な貢献をしています。

ピアソン：わかりました。しかし，他にも気がかりなことについて質問させてください。彼は，「会社のために，利益を改善したいのです」と書いています。私たちが毎年売上高を劇的に増加させ，コスト削減施策により過去最高水準の利益を実現してきたことを認識していないのではないでしょうか。

池田：間違いなく認識しています。そのことを彼に説明しましたから。実際，あなたが当社のキー・プレーヤーの一人であり，緊密な協力関係を作るべきだと彼に伝えました。彼があなたに連絡したのはこのためです。

ピアソン：しかし，彼は私たちの利益水準が低くて…収益性が問題だと思われているようです。

Ikeda: Ah, I think this might be a misunderstanding of language. I think he is trying to say that we must continually improve . . . umm, to do *kaizen*.

Pierson: Ah, *kaizen* . . . continuous improvement. You explained that to us in a department meeting once. Even if the current situation is okay, *kaizen* refers to the efforts to continually do things better, right? But in English when someone says that we must *improve*, it sounds like they are expressing dissatisfaction with the current situation . . . that there are some problems that we must resolve.

Ikeda: I can assure you that Abe san will understand and respect the efforts we have made to develop a strong business and that he will carry out what's necessary for continuous improvement—for *kaizen*.

Pierson: Thank you. Okay. I do look forward to meeting Abe san. But indeed, we will miss you once you are gone.

After this exchange of words with Pierson, Ikeda considered the advice he should give to Abe so that Abe could begin to develop good relations with the local management and staff at KSC upon his arrival in Canada. In their next video conference, Ikeda provided the following advice: Abe should be prepared to clearly explain some of the accomplishments he has made over the years in order to illustrate how his past experience has prepared him for this assignment. Additionally, Abe should be prepared to speak clearly about his vision for continuous improvement (*kaizen*) hereafter based upon his understanding of KSC's actual current business conditions.

池田：それは言葉の誤解かもしれません。阿部さんが言わんとしているのは，私たちは継続的に向上しなければならない…「カイゼン」を実現しなければならないということだと思います。

ピアソン：ああ，「カイゼン」ですか…継続的に向上することですね。あなたが部内会議で以前，説明されましたね。「カイゼン」が意味することは現状に問題がなくとも，不断に，より良いものを目指して努力をする，ということですね？　しかし英語では，誰かに「improve」（改善）しなければならないと言われると，彼らが現状に不満を表明しているように聞こえます…私達が解決しなければならない何らかの問題があるということを意味しています。

池田：我々が盤石な事業を確立するためにこれまで行ってきた努力を阿部さんが理解し，尊重し，また，継続的な向上，いわゆる「カイゼン」のために必要なことを遂行していくことは間違いありません。

ピアソン：ありがとうございます。分かりました。阿部さんに会えることを楽しみにしています。実際，あなたが日本に帰国されるのは本当に寂しいですね。

　池田氏は，ピアソン氏との会話の後，阿部氏にどのようなアドバイスを与えれば，彼がカナダに到着後，KSC の現地管理職やスタッフとの良好な関係を築く上での有効な第一歩になるかを考えた。次のビデオ会議で，池田氏は阿部氏に次のようにアドバイスをした：阿部氏は，過去長年にわたる彼の業績の中で，今回の新たな赴任に役に立つであろう過去の経験を明確に説明できるように準備をするべきである。さらに，阿部氏は，KSC の現在の状況を踏まえて，今後の継続的な向上（「カイゼン」）に向けた自らの構想を明確に説明できるように準備すべきである。

Commentary on sample conversation

In this sample conversation, we encounter a conversation about how new expatriates may form impressions upon the Host Country Nationals (HCN) of the subsidiary where they will go work. While Abe had good intentions in writing an introductory email, we can understand from Pierson's reaction how misunderstandings may occur.

Therefore, it can be understood that the investment of time in considering how to initially communicate with the HCN will go a long way towards starting good working relations with the HCN.

Key Phrases and Expressions

What can I do for you?

This is a polite expression for a superior to use with a subordinate to open up conversation when the subordinate seems to have a concern or request for discussion.

I can't really get a sense of . . .

This is a convenient expression for expressing doubt or lack of understanding about something when there is insufficient evidence to provide support for an idea or initiative.

Distinction between *improvement* and *continuous improvement* when expressing the meaning of kaizen

It should be noted that the meaning of the word *kaizen* is more closely expressed in English as a process of *continuous improvement* rather than simply just *improvement*. To express that some condition needs *improvement* is to imply that there is currently a problem. Conversely, to speak of *continuous improvement* is not to imply that there is a problem, but rather to imply

サンプル・カンバセーションに関するコメント

　このサンプル・カンバセーションでは，新しい赴任者が赴任先の子会社の現地国籍人材（HCN）にどのような印象を与えるかについての会話に直面する。阿部氏は自己紹介のメールを書くことに前向きの意図をもっていたが，どのようにして誤解が生じるのかということがピアソン氏の反応から理解できる。

　したがって，HCN とどのように最初のコミュニケーションをとるのかを時間をかけて思案するという投資は，HCN との良好な協力関係の開始に大いに役立つことが理解できるであろう。

重要表現

What can I do for you?

　部下が話し合いをしたい懸念事項や要求があると思われる場合に，会話を開くために上司が使用する丁寧な表現である。

I can't really get a sense of . . .

　アイデアや施策をサポートするのに十分な証拠がない場合に，何かについての疑問や理解不足を表すための便利な表現である。

カイゼンという意味を表す場合，「improvement」と「continuous improvement」の用語の区別が必要

　「カイゼン」という言葉の意味は，単に「improvement」というよりも「continuous improvement」のプロセスとして英語でより厳密に表現されていることに注意すべきである。ある状態が「improvement」を必要とすることを表現することは，現在何らかの問題があることを意味する。逆に，「continuous improvement」とは，問題があることを意味するというよりは，将来，よ

that there is always the possibility of producing better results in the future. The usage of the expression *continuous improvement* can minimize a listener's defensive reaction or concern when expressed in a situation like that shown in the sample conversation above.

り良い結果を生み出す可能性が常にあることを意味している。「continuous improvement」という表現を使用すると，上記のサンプル・カンバセーションで示されるような場面で表現した場合，聞き手の防御的な反応や懸念を最小限に抑えることができる。

Planning for a Global HR Conference

Background Information

The global expansion of Kindai Systems Kabushiki Kaisha (KSK) is accelerating. With the establishment of new subsidiaries in Mexico, Germany and across Asia in Thailand, Indonesia and China, KSK is now on its way to developing a worldwide network.

However, while **Tanaka Tsuyoshi, General Manager of Global HR**, has been communicating from a distance with HR colleagues overseas, the HR professionals themselves within the KS group have not yet developed close working relationships with each other. Therefore, Tanaka has asked **Kato Atsuko, Assistant Department Manager**, to plan for the first *KS Group Global HR Conference* to be held at the global headquarters (GHQ) in Tokyo.

Tanaka has called in **Ryan Rogers**, an **HR consultant** to provide Kato with advice during the conference preparation stage.

(After greetings have been exchanged)

グローバル人事会議に備える

本会話の背景

　近代システム株式会社（KSK）のグローバル展開は加速している。メキシコ，ドイツ，並びにタイ，インドネシア，中国というアジア全域に新たな子会社を設立し，KSK は今や世界的なネットワークを拡大しつつある。

　しかし，**グローバル人事本部長**の**田中剛氏**はこれまで海外拠点の人事部同僚と遠隔コミュニケーションをとってきたが，KSK グループ内の人事担当者はお互いに十分なコミュニケーション・ネットワークを構築できていない。そこで，田中氏は，**部長代理**の**加藤敦子氏**に東京のグローバル本社（GHQ）で第 1 回目の「KS グループ・グローバル HR 会議」の開催を企画するよう指示した。

　田中氏は，準備段階で加藤氏に，助言をしてもらうために**外部の人事コンサルタント**である**ライアン・ロジャーズ氏**に来てもらった。

（挨拶を交わした後に）

Kato: (Handing over a copy of the plan for the conference) We want to hold a global HR conference. Here is the conference plan we are thinking about.

Rogers: (Looking over the documents) I see. What would you like the outcome of this conference to be?

Kato: Well, since this is our first global HR conference, we would like for everyone to get to know each other.

Rogers: Sure. In that case, I think that it is good to have an icebreaker at the beginning of the conference to get everyone relaxed and familiar with each other.

Kato: Yes, that sounds good. After that, on the first day, we will have each participant . . . from eight overseas subsidiaries . . . make a presentation. And also, on the second day, the GHQ HR should make some presentations too . . . about the corporate philosophy, about the HR system, compliance and other topics.

Rogers: Hmm. What do you want participants to take away from the presentations?

Kato: Everyone should understand the situation in each company. Then we in Tokyo can know how to support the subsidiaries.

Rogers: Well, to be honest, when there are multiple presentations in one day, and especially when participants have just arrived from overseas and may suffer from jetlag, it becomes increasingly difficult throughout the day for participants to listen attentively to presentations.

Kato: But isn't the purpose of this conference for everyone to share information?

加藤：(会議の企画書を手渡して) グローバル人事会議を開催しようと思っています。これが，今検討中の会議企画の案です。

ロジャーズ：(資料にざっと目を通して) 分かりました。この会議の結果として何を期待していますか？

加藤：はい，これが初めての会議なので，参加者全員が顔なじみになれればと思っています。

ロジャーズ：そうですね。その場合には，参加者がリラックスでき，またお互いが打ち解けられるよう，会議の初めにアイスブレークが必要ですね。

加藤：それは良さそうですね。初日のその後，それぞれの…つまり8つの海外子会社より…参加者にプレゼンをしてもらいましょう。そして，また，2日目にはGHQ HR が，当社の企業理念，当社の人事システム，コンプライアンス，その他の話題…に関するプレゼンを行う必要があります。

ロジャーズ：なるほど。参加者がそれらのプレゼンから何を引き出せばよいのでしょうか？

加藤：皆が，それぞれの会社の状況を理解すべきです。そうすれば，東京にいる我々がどのように海外子会社をサポートすべきかが分かります。

ロジャーズ：そうですね，正直に申し上げれば，一日にたくさんのプレゼンがあって，また特に参加者が海外からやってきたばかりで時差に苦しんでいるかも知れないときに，終日，彼らが集中してプレゼンを聞くことは極めて困難かと思います。

加藤：ですが，この会議の目的は全員で情報を共有することではないですか？

Rogers: Of course, information should be shared, but as we plan this conference, we need to think about how to maintain the engagement of the participants. So, let's start off by considering how the GHQ HR representatives and the participants from the overseas subsidiaries should interact with each other during the conference.

Kato: Okay.

Rogers: All right. Let's list up the topics that you want to cover in this conference. Here are some post-it notes. (Rogers provides a few yellow square-shaped post-it notes and markers.) Take a few minutes and write down one topic on each post-it note.

(Kato and her two staff begin discussions. After about ten minutes, they produced the list of topics as shown in Exhibit 1 below.)

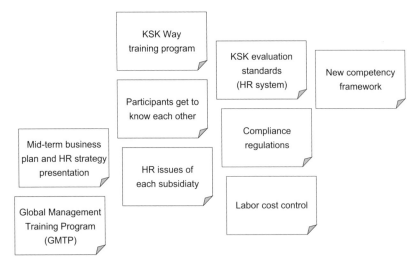

Exhibit 1   Suggested Topics

ロジャーズ：もちろん，情報は共有されなければなりません。しかし，この会議を計画している私たちは，どうすれば参加者のエンゲージメント（積極的な関与）を維持できるかを考える必要があります。ということで，先ず初めに，GHQ HR の代表者と海外子会社からの出席者とが会議中にどのように交流するのかから考えてみましょう。

加藤：了解です。

ロジャーズ：それでは，この会議でカバーしたい議題をリストアップしましょう。ここに付箋があります。（ロジャーズ氏は，黄色い四角形の付箋とマーカーを配布する。）数分かけて，付箋１枚に１つずつ議題を書いてください。

（加藤氏と二人の部下は議論を始める。約 10 分後，彼らは Exhibit 1 に示されるような一連の議題のリストを作成した。）

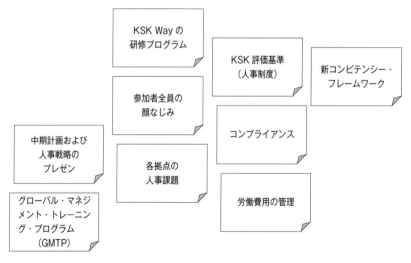

Exhibit 1　議題のリスト

Rogers: Okay. Thank you. I see that you want to cover a lot of topics. So, to develop the agenda for this conference, it is important to think about the *stance* that the GHQ HR wants to take for each of these topics.

Kato: What do you mean by *stance*?

Rogers: Ah, take a look at this material and let me explain.

(Rogers takes three copies of the supplement to Chapter 10 within Section I of this book out from his bag and passes them to Kato and her staff. After a few minutes of explaining the material, the conference planning conversation continues.)

Rogers: So, we need to look at each of the topics you've written on the post-it notes and determine the *stance* of the GHQ HR for each. Then we should consider the *interaction types* that are appropriate for the conference.

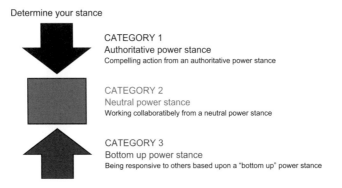

Determine your stance

CATEGORY 1
Authoritative power stance
Compelling action from an authoritative power stance

CATEGORY 2
Neutral power stance
Working collaboratibely from a neutral power stance

CATEGORY 3
Bottom up power stance
Being responsive to others based upon a "bottom up" power stance

Exhibit 2   Three "Stance" Categories

Kato: Hmm. **I think I get what you are saying. Let's get on with it.**

ロジャーズ：はい，有難うございます。かなりの数の議題をカバーしたいのですね。では，この会議のアジェンダ案を作成するために，各議題に対するGHQ HR のスタンスを考慮することが重要です。

加藤：「スタンス」とはどういう意味ですか。

ロジャーズ：それでは，この資料をご覧ください。ご説明します。

（ロジャーズ氏は，本書 Section 1 の Chapter 10 補論のコピーをカバンから取り出し，加藤さんたちに 3 部，コピーを配布する。数分間，資料の説明を行った後，会議の企画の議論が続く。）

ロジャーズ：では，皆さんが付箋に書いたそれぞれの議題を検討し，それぞれの議題に対する GHQ HR の「スタンス」を決めなければなりません。それから，会議に適切な「インタラクション型」を考える必要があります。

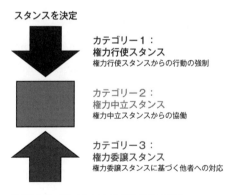

Exhibit 2 「スタンス」の 3 つのカテゴリー

加藤：ウーン。**仰っている意味が理解できたような気がします。続けましょう。**

Rogers: Okay. Well, let's first look at this topic. (Rogers picks up the post-it note that states *KSK Way training program.*) What do you want to do for this topic in the conference?

Kato: We want to discuss the KSK Way so that participants can more deeply understand its significance. Then, we want for them to plan training for all employees in their companies.

Rogers: Okay. So, I think we can divide this topic into two. (Rogers takes two new post-it notes and writes *KSK Way understanding* on one. On the other, he writes *KSK Way training program planning.*) Since the corporate philosophy originated in Japan and should be incorporated into the business operations of each subsidiary, the stance for the topic *KSK Way understanding* is *category 1: authoritative power stance, directive type*, right?

Kato: Yes. We want for the subsidiaries to understand and disseminate the KSK Way according to the HQ's vision. So, the stance we have for KSK Way understanding is clearly a category 1 directive stance. But, what about the *stance* for the planning of the KSK Way training program? We have developed a training program here in the HQ for Japanese employees. But we think the program may need to be customized in order to roll it out in each country.

Rogers: Okay, let's consider this to be a *category 2: neutral power stance, collaborative type* topic. While the participants may refer to the contents of the training program from Japan, the GHQ HR and subsidiary HR managers need to consider together how to develop a program that can be rolled out to the subsidiaries. Is this the correct understanding?

Kato: Yes. That is correct.

ロジャーズ：はい。では，この議題を先ず，検討してみましょう。（ロジャーズ氏は「KSK Way の研修プログラム」と書かれた付箋を手に取る。）今回の会議でこの議題に関して何を期待していますか？

加藤：KSK Way の重要性を参加者がより深く理解できるように議論したいと思っています。そして，彼らには，それぞれの会社で全社員を対象にした研修を企画してもらいたいのです。

ロジャーズ：分かりました。そこで，この議題を２つに分けることができると思います（付箋を２枚とりだして１枚に「KSK Way の理解」，もう１枚には「KSK Way の研修プログラム計画」と書く）。この企業理念は日本で生まれ，それぞれの子会社の事業運営に浸透させるべきであるため，この「KSK Way の理解」のスタンスは，カテゴリー１：「権力行使スタンス」の中の「指示命令型」となるでしょう？

加藤：そうですね。本社のビジョンに沿って，全ての子会社が KSK Way を理解し，浸透させてもらいたいのです。したがって，KSK Way の理解に対するスタンスは明らかにカテゴリー１の指示命令型となりますね。しかし，KSK Way の研修プログラムを計画する場合の「スタンス」はどうなりますか？日本人従業員向けの研修プログラムは本社で開発しました。しかし，当該プログラムをそれぞれの国に導入する際には，それぞれの国にカスタマイズする必要があると思います。

ロジャーズ：了解です。それではこれは，カテゴリー２：「権力中立スタンス」の中の「協働型」の議題にしましょう。参加者は，日本からの研修プログラムの内容を参考にすることができるかもしれません。他方で，GHQ HR と子会社の人事マネジャーは，子会社に導入されるプログラムをどのようにして効果的に開発するか，共に議論する必要がある。この理解で正しいですか？

加藤：はい，その通りです。

Rogers: Let's move on. How about these? (Rogers holds up two post-it notes upon which *KSK evaluation standards (HR system)* and *new competency framework* are written.)

Kato: We have clearly defined evaluation standards that need to be adopted by each subsidiary. Each subsidiary should have an evaluation standard that is based upon MBO and competencies. But we have not yet established a competency framework that can be globally rolled out . . . maybe in the future . . . we have to discuss more.

Rogers: Okay, then it is clear that you have a *category 1: authoritative power stance, managing type* regarding the *KSK evaluation standards*. You want to require each company to have an HR system that complies with the HQ's evaluation standards, but you want for the subsidiaries to evaluate competencies according to their own standards for now, right?

Kato: Yes.

Rogers: So, let's consider the development of a *new competency framework* to be a *category 2: neutral power stance* topic. During the conference, the participants can share their current competency evaluation standards. Together, everyone can determine which competency standards should be included in the global competency framework.

Kato: That seems like a good way to proceed.

(Kato and Kato's staff continue to discuss each of the topics in detail. After 45 minutes of discussion and a short break, each topic has been aligned with a particular stance as follows.)

ロジャーズ：次に進みましょう。これはどうしますか？（と言って，ロジャーズ氏は「KSK 評価基準」（人事制度）と「新コンピテンシー・フレームワーク」が書かれている 2 枚の付箋を示す。）

加藤：各子会社が採用すべき評価基準はすでに明確に規定してあります。各子会社は，目標管理制度とコンピテンシーに基づく評価基準を備えていなければなりません。しかし，当社ではグローバルに導入可能なコンピテンシー・フレームワークはまだ設けられていません…将来作られるかもしれませんが…今後の検討事項です。

ロジャーズ：分かりました。それであれば，「KSK 評価基準」はカテゴリー 1：「権力行使スタンス」の中の「管理型」であることが明確です。本社としてはそれぞれの子会社に本社の評価基準に従った人事評価制度の導入を要請したいが，現時点ではそれぞれの独自の基準でコンピテンシー評価をして欲しいということですね？

加藤：その通りです。

ロジャーズ：では，「新コンピテンシー・フレームワーク」はカテゴリー 2：「権力中立スタンス」の中の「協働型」の議題に入るということで考えてみましょう。会議の間に，参加者はそれぞれの会社の現時点におけるコンピテンシー評価基準を共有することができます。みんなで一緒に，どのコンピテンシー基準をグローバル・コンピテンシー・フレームワークに組み込むかを決定することが可能となります。

加藤：**良い進め方だと思います。**

（加藤氏は二人の部下と議題の詳細について議論を続ける。45 分間の議論と短い休憩の後，個々の議題は以下のように特定のスタンスに連動する形で整理された。）

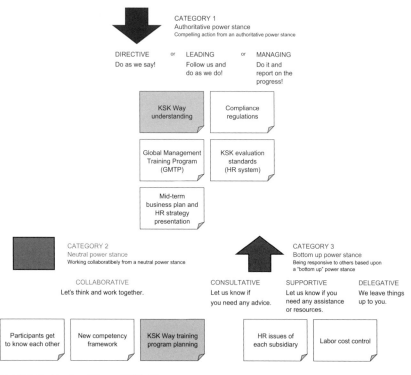

Exhibit 3   Topics Aligned With Stances

Kato: So, now that we have completed this much, how should we consider the flow of the agenda?

Rogers: This will be a two-day conference, right? After the opening icebreaker activity, I would like to suggest that we group together topics for which we have determined the same *stance*. Since participants are coming all the way to Japan, on day 1, the GHQ should convey its ideas and direction. So, we can focus on category 1 *stance* topics primarily. Then, on day 2, we can discuss category 2 issues which require collaboration and brainstorming. If time remains, category 3 issues can be fit into the day 2 schedule.

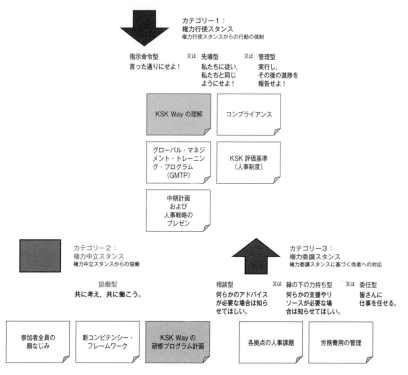

Exhibit 3　スタンスの３つのカテゴリー

加藤：さて，ここまで完成したので，会議のアジェンダの流れはどうしましょうか？

ロジャーズ：この会議は２日間ですよね？　冒頭のアイスブレーク活動の後で，我々が合意した同じ「スタンス」ごとにトピックをグルーピングすることを提案したいと思います。参加者は遠路はるばる日本に来られているので，GHQ は，最初の１日目には本社のアイデアと方向性を伝えるべきでしょう。このため，まずは主としてカテゴリー１の「スタンス」の議題に集中することができます。それから２日目は，カテゴリー２の議題について議論をすることが可能です。これらの議題は協働作業とブレーンストーミングが必要です。もし時間が許せば，カテゴリー３の議題を２日目のスケジュールに，はめ込むこ

Think of day 1 as a day to warm up . . . then on day 2, once the participants have become comfortable with each other, we focus on more collaborative discussions.

Kato: Hmm, it sounds like you have experience planning such conferences.

Rogers: Thank you for saying so. Before I became a consultant, I worked in the overseas subsidiary of a Japanese company and also in the global HQ in

Day	Stance	Topic	Detail
DAY 1	Category 1	Opening greetings	Purpose, agenda and GHQ HR staff introductions
		Icebreaker	Icebreaker activity to get to know others
		Mid-term business plan and HR strategy presentation	Lecture and Q&A with Global HR General Manager, Tanaka Tsuyoshi
		KSK Way understanding	Presentation and discussion by Training Division
		Lunch	
		KSK evaluation standards (HR system)	Explanation of the expectations of the GHQ HR for each subsidiary and confirmation of the understanding of overseas participants
		Global Management Training Program (GMTP)	Directive to select participants to send to the program that will be conducted in Tokyo
		Compliance regulations	Directive to understand and comply with legal and corporate regulations
DAY 2	Category 2	Icebreaker	Review of previous day
		KSK Way training program planning	Discussion about how to work together to develop a global KSK Way training program
		New competency framework	Discussion about what competency standards currently exist in each company and how to globally unify such standard
		Lunch	
	Category 3	HR issues of each subsidiary	Sharing of issues and identification of common issues that can be worked on together hereafter
		Action planning & wrap-up	Planning of actions

Exhibit 4   KS Group Global HR Conference Agenda

とも可能です。

　1日目はウォーミングアップの日，それから2日目はひとたび参加者がお互いに打ち解けあったところで，より協働型の議論をすると考えてください。

加藤：なるほど。このような会議の企画をされたご経験が豊富のようですね。

ロジャーズ：お言葉有難うございます。コンサルタントになる前，日本企業の海外子会社で勤務しました。また，東京のグローバル本社で仕事をした経験も

日	スタンス	議題	詳細
一日目	カテゴリー1	開会のご挨拶	会議目的，アジェンダ，GHQ HR 紹介
		アイスブレーク	顔なじみになるためのアイスブレーク
		中期計画および人事戦略のプレゼン	発表および質疑応答，田中剛グローバル人事本部長
		KSK Way の理解	発表および討議　人材開発課
		ランチ	
		KSK 評価基準（人事制度）	GHQ HR から各拠点への期待の説明および海外から来た参加者の理解の確認
		グローバル・マネジメント・研修プログラム（GMTP）	東京で開催するプログラムへの参加者の人選の要請
		コンプライアンス	法律ならびに企業規則への遵守と理解の要請
二日目	カテゴリー2	アイスブレーク	前日の振り返り
		KSK Way の研修企画	グローバルな KSK WAY 研修プログラムの開発へ協力の方法に関する議論
		新コンピテンシー・フレームワーク	各社に現在存在するコンピテンシー基準についての議論および当該基準のグローバルへの統合
		ランチ	
	カテゴリー3	各拠点の人事課題	課題の共有および今後協働できる共通課題の識別
		アクションプランおよびラップアップ	アクション・プランニング

Exhibit 4　「KS グループ・グローバル人事会議」のアジェンダ案

Tokyo of another company. I have developed a sense of how the HQ should communicate with the overseas subsidiaries in order to develop mutually respectful relations.

(Rogers connected his PC to the projector, and along with Kato and her staff started to type out the agenda.) (See exhibit 4.)

Kato: This is great. Now I see how we can create a clear and logical agenda that will engage the participants for two days.

(On the first day of the *KS Group Global HR Conference*, Kato provided the opening greetings.)

Kato: Good morning and welcome to Japan! I am so glad that we, the GHQ HR, are able to host you all here in Tokyo for the very first *KS Group Global HR Conference*!

Over the next two days, we will share information, learn from each other and develop some plans for action hereafter. The purpose of this conference is firstly for all of us to get to know each other as global KS Group HR colleagues. Also, we want to ensure that you understand the direction that the GHQ HR here in Tokyo is setting for developing a unified HR function across all of the overseas subsidiaries. Lastly, we want to create an opportunity for you all to exchange opinions about the issues which you are facing in each of your companies.

Today, day 1, we are prepared to provide you with an explanation of our expectations for all of you. Of course, we welcome your questions and

あります。お互いの立場を尊重した関係を築くためには，本社がどのようなコミュニケーションを海外子会社と取るべきかが分かるようになりました。

（ロジャーズ氏は自分のパソコンをプロジェクターに接続し，加藤氏とその部下2人とともに，アジェンダを打ち込み始めた。）

加藤：これは素晴らしいですね。2日間にわたる会議に出席する参加者の関心を引き付ける明確で論理的なアジェンダをどのように作成すればよいか理解できましたよ。

（「KSグループ・グローバルHR会議」の初日に，加藤氏が開会の挨拶をした。）

加藤：皆さま，おはようございます。ようこそ日本へいらっしゃいました。我々GHQ HRが，皆様をここ東京で開催致します第1回の「KSグループ・グローバルHR会議」にお迎えできますことを，私自身大変うれしく思っております。

　本日から2日間にわたり，参加者全員が情報を共有し，お互いから学び合い，今後のアクションプランを作り上げることになります。この会議の目的は先ず，私たち全員がグローバルKSグループ人事の同僚として深く知り合うことにあります。また，東京を拠点とするGHQ HRとして，全海外子会社を通じて統合された人事機能を作り上げるためにどのような方向性を目指しているのかを皆様にご理解いただきたいと考えております。最後に，皆様がそれぞれの会社で直面されている諸問題に関して全員で意見交換をする機会を提供できればと思っております。

　第1日目の本日は，私たちが皆様にどのような期待を持っているかについて説明したいと思います。もちろん，本日いつでも，皆様からの質問や意見を歓

comments throughout the day. Tomorrow morning on day 2, we look forward to having deeper discussions together to collaborate in planning important global-level HR initiatives. From tomorrow afternoon, you will have a chance to discuss any other issues of interest and concern so that we can identify common issues for additional work together hereafter.

And, we have a special dinner planned for this evening which we invite you all to attend.

Commentary on sample conversation

In this sample conversation, we encounter the process for planning a global HR conference with participation of HR professionals from across the group companies. The reader can understand that the process is as follows: (1) identifying the topics to be covered in the conference, (2) determining the GHQ HR's *stance* and *interaction types* for each topic, and then (3) arranging the agenda so that participants can be engaged in a variety of activities ranging from intensive listening to active discussion, brainstorming and action planning.

If the entire conference was comprised of an agenda of only category 1 issues, the participants from overseas subsidiaries might feel unempowered. However, if the conference agenda only focuses on category 3 issues, the participants may not understand the need for having gathered at the global HQ. Therefore, it is advisable to plan the conference around a combination of topics for which the GHQ HR has determined a range of *stances*.

迎します。2日目の明日午前中は，重要なグローバル人事施策の企画において全員で協力するために皆様と議論を深められることを楽しみにしています。明日の午後には，皆様が関心や懸念をお持ちのその他の案件に関して議論する機会があり，そうして，今後のさらなる協働のための共通課題を発見できるのではないでしょうか。

そして，皆様全員のご訪問を歓迎する特別な夕食会を予定していますので，ご参加ください。

サンプル・カンバセーションに関するコメント

このサンプル・カンバセーションでは，グループ会社からの人事専門家が参加するグローバル人事会議を計画するプロセスに直面する。読者はこのプロセスが，次のように進むことを理解できる：(1)当該会議で討議される議題を特定化する，(2)各議題に関するGHQ HRの「スタンス」および「インタラクション型」が決定する，そして，(3)集中的な聴取から活発な議論，ブレーンストーミング，行動計画の策定に至るまで，参加者がさまざまな活動に参加できるようにアジェンダを作る。

もし会議全体がカテゴリー1の議題だけで構成されたとすれば，海外子会社からの参加者は無力感を感じるかもしれない。しかし，もしこの会議のアジェンダがカテゴリー3の議題のみを対象にしたとすれば，参加者はなぜ全員がグローバル本社に集まる必要があったのかと疑問を持つかも知れない。したがって，GHQ HRは，「スタンス」の範囲から決めた一連の議題を中心に会議を計画することが推奨される。

Key Phrases and Expressions

I think I get what you are saying. Let's get on with it.

This is a convenient expression for indicating that you may not fully understanding what is being said, but that you would like to move the conversation forward to deepen your understanding.

That seems like a good way to proceed.

This is a convenient expression for indicating that someone's suggestion for how to move forward is acceptable.

重要表現

I think I get what you are saying. Let's get on with it.

　これは，あなたが言われていることを完全に理解していないかもしれないが，理解をより深めるために会話を前進させたいことを示すための便利な表現である。

That seems like a good way to proceed.

　これは，前に進む方法についての誰かの提案は受諾しうることを示すための便利な表現である。

About the Authors:

Shiraki Mitsuhide, Ph.D.

Shiraki Mitsuhide, Ph.D. is Professor of Labor Policy and Human Resource Management at the Faculty of Political Science and Economics, Waseda University since 1999. Previously, he served as both professor and associate professor at Kokushikan University for 9 years. He concurrently serves as President of the Institute for Transnational Human Resource Management. He earned his Ph.D. (Economics), MA (Economics) and BA (Economics) from Waseda University.

He is the author and editor of various publications including the following:

The Power of Human Resource Management, (edited by Shiraki) Bunshindo, 2018.

Development and Appraisal of Global Managers, (edited by Shiraki) Waseda University Press, 2014.

A Comparative Analysis of International Human Resource Management, (written by Shiraki) Yuhikaku, 2006.

Bryan Sherman

Bryan Sherman is the President of Gramercy Engagement Group, Inc., a professional services firm that has been providing HR consulting, training and facilitation services since 2010 to global Japanese companies. Formerly, Bryan had been an HR consultant in the United States and had worked as the Senior HR Manager within the US-subsidiary of SCSK Corporation. In 2007, he joined the global headquarters of Fast Retailing where he was involved in HR initiatives in support of the company's global expansion. Bryan is a 1997 cum laude graduate of Williams College, Williamstown, MA. He earned the Senior Professional in Human Resources (SPHR) certification in 2007. As well, he is currently a researcher of the Institute for Transnational Human Resource Management at Waseda University. Bryan currently lives in Tokyo, Japan where he gets inspiration from biking around the city and walking his dog.

著者紹介

白木三秀（しらき・みつひで）

早稲田大学政治経済学術院教授。

早稲田大学政治経済学部卒業，同大学院経済学研究科博士後期課程修了。博士（経済学）。

国士舘大学政経学部助教授・教授等を経て，1999 年より現職。専門は労働政策，国際人的資源管理。現在，早稲田大学トランスナショナル HRM 研究所所長。

最近の主な著作に『国際人的資源管理の比較分析』（単著，有斐閣，2006 年），『グローバル・マネジャーの育成と評価』（編著，早稲田大学出版部，2014 年），『人的資源管理の力』（編著，文眞堂，2018 年）等がある。

ブライアン・シャーマン

米国ニューヨーク市において日系企業を対象に人事コンサルタントとして従事後，米国 SCSK 株式会社の人事総務部長を経験。在米日系企業における人事の現場を内と外の視点で支える。2007 年来日し，株式会社ファーストリテイリングで日本本社グローバル人事業務に参画。2010 年東京にグラマシーエンゲージメントグループ株式会社を設立。代表取締役就任。グローバル展開する日本企業へコンサルティング，トレーニングおよびファシリテーションサービスを提供している。趣味の自転車での路地散歩と愛犬グラマシーから日々インスピレーションを得ている。

米国ニューヨーク市出身，米国 Williams College 卒

早稲田大学トランスナショナル HRM 研究所招聘研究員

英語 de 人事®
日英対訳による実践的人事

2020 年 4 月 30 日第 1 版第 1 刷発行　　　　　　　　　　　検印省略

著　者——白木三秀
　　　　　ブライアン・シャーマン

発行者——前野　隆
発行所——株式会社 文 眞 堂
　　　　　〒 162-0041 東京都新宿区早稲田鶴巻町 533
　　　　　TEL：03 (3202) 8480 / FAX：03 (3203) 2638
　　　　　HP：http://www.bunshin-do.co.jp/
　　　　　振替 00120-2-96437

製作……平河工業社
装丁……菊地雅志